HISTORY OF AMERICAN THOUGHT AND CULTURE

Paul S. Boyer, *General Editor*

Watch
on the
Right

CONSERVATIVE INTELLECTUALS
IN THE REAGAN ERA

J. David Hoeveler, Jr.

The University of Wisconsin Press

The University of Wisconsin Press
114 North Murray Street
Madison, Wisconsin 53715

3 Henrietta Street
London WC2E 8LU, England

Printed in the United States of America

Library of Congress Cataloging-in-Publication Data
Hoeveler, J. David, 1943–
  Watch on the right: conservative intellectuals in
the Reagan era / J. David Hoeveler, Jr.
  348 pp.   cm. – (History of American thought and culture)
  Includes index.
  1. Conservatism–United States–History–20th century.   2. United
States–Intellectual life–20th century.   I. Title. II. Series.
JA84.U5H63   1990
320.5'2'0973–dc20   90-13021
ISBN 0-299-12810-5   CIP

This book is for John

Contents

Acknowledgments

FOR VALUABLE assistance in writing this book I am greatly indebted to the Lynde and Harry Bradley Foundation of Milwaukee, whose support enabled me to travel for interviews with the principals of this study. The University of Wisconsin–Milwaukee provided me a sabbatical leave that also liberated time from other academic commitments. I also benefitted from a fellowship appointment at the Center for Twentieth Century Studies at the University of Wisconsin–Milwaukee during the last stages of work on the book. Professor Ronald Lora of the University of Toledo gave the manuscript a thorough and helpful review. Paul Boyer was all that I could ask for in an editor, demanding but always encouraging. I learned a lot about the New York intellectuals and Jewish writings when Mark Krupnick, then of the English department of the University of Wisconsin–Milwaukee, and I offered a seminar on these subjects in 1986. Of the several individuals who took an interest in this book I am especially thankful to Franklin Buchta. Kari Frederickson gave valuable assistance in helping me with reading page proofs. And I want to express thanks to several individuals associated with the University of Wisconsin Press—Barbara Hanrahan, Elizabeth Steinberg, Carol Olsen, Raphael Kadushin, Jim Sanford, and Angela Ray. I hope that my efforts have been worthy of theirs.

I wish to thank Elliott Banfield for permission to reproduce his drawing of Irving Kristol, which first appeared on the cover of the March 1979 issue of *The American Spectator,* Vint Lawrence for permission to reproduce his drawings of William F. Buckley, Jr., George Will, Hilton Kramer, and Jean Kirkpatrick, which first appeared in *The New Republic,* and Shelly Fischman, for his drawings of Robert Nisbet, R. Emmett Tyrrell, Jr., and Michael Novak.

To my wife, Professor Diane Long Hoeveler, I am again appreciative of her love and encouragement. This book is dedicated to our firstborn, John, now ten years old. He and the book contested during the last several years for his father's time. But for all the pleasure it has been to write this book, he has provided me the richer memories.

Introduction

THE "SUPERFLUOUS MEN" they were no longer. That designation seemed appropriate to Robert Crunden in 1977, when he selected it as
the title of an anthology of American conservative writings. But by the 1980s
conservative intellectuals had gained a measure of influence to which they
were unaccustomed. Their ideas had achieved an ascendancy in the parallel
movement of American politics, marked by conservative triumphs in the
presidential elections of 1980, 1984, and 1988. Around the United States,
institutions and research centers, "think tanks," were producing a conservative
literature that found application in policy-making centers of the national government. And from campus to local bookstore, one could locate an impressive
new variety of conservative journals and books.

This is a book about conservatism. It is about conservative intellectuals—
conservative intellectuals in the United States in the 1970s and 1980s, more
precisely. At the same time, this book tries to maintain a larger focus and
to consider the renaissance of these decades within the framework of a larger
intellectual outline. It suggests that there is such an entity as a generic conservatism, and it studies the American writers against the background of a literary
tradition that has given that conservatism an identity.

This effort, in fact, requires some explanation. For even though conservatism became a powerful force in American politics and even though conservative ideas proliferated, a general skepticism prevailed about the authenticity
of this collective effort as a genuinely conservative intellectual movement.
This skepticism flourished not the least among thinkers who readily embraced
the label "conservative" and who saw themselves as sustaining and contributing
members of a conservative intellectual tradition.

For these writers and others, what was passing as a new conservatism,
or "neoconservatism," in these decades was mostly a reaction, they believed,
to a radicalizing liberalism. They saw the new conservatism, in short, as

primarily a recoil from a decade of excess in the 1960s. These "traditionalist" critics were suspicious of the leftist and liberal backgrounds of certain neoconservatives and were often uncomfortable with the large Jewish representation in their ranks. Furthermore, they reproached the new conservatives for a deficiency of systematic thought. The group that I will call the Old Right believed that the new conservatism was too "ad hoc" and was insufficiently grounded in a comprehensive philosophy and view of life. The new conservatives were journalists; only a few were academics. The essay, not the treatise, was their literary weapon of choice. What the neoconservatives often lacked in systematic thought they returned in practical insight.

This book explores the variety of conservative thought in the United States in the 1970s and 1980s. It has a secondary purpose to place these decades in a larger historical context and to discern the ways in which American conservative thought in this period was continuous with the more or less permanent principles and prejudices that have marked conservative thought over two centuries. That concern, I hasten to add, has also been a principal criterion of selection in this book. I have chosen for study intellectuals who, in the range of their writings, seemed to me to afford the best opportunities for measuring continuity and change in conservative thought in the United States. I have also selected on the basis of variety. Conservatism comprises many moods and many voices, and the decades in question certainly illustrated that variety. I acknowledge, certainly, that another author undertaking this subject might have chosen other principals.

An individualist focus in intellectual history, I believe, carries certain advantages. From the outset of my work I intended to organize the book by chapter essays on prominent conservative writers. None of these is a comprehensive biographical essay, and none undertakes to review all the writings of the subjects in question. I have chosen to concentrate on those materials that appeared to me most useful in illuminating conservative thought, both its strengths and weaknesses.

A beginning chapter describes the changing intellectual and political climate in the United States as it appeared to a vocal group of conservative writers in the early 1970s. It briefly introduces and reviews a number of individuals who were succeeding in defining a conservative agenda for the 1970s and 1980s and who were making known to the American reading public a compendium of conservative prejudices against liberal culture and politics.

The concluding chapter offers some personal reflections on conservatism. However much this study confirms the pluralist nature of conservatism, some common attitudes and prejudices do, I believe, give substance to this word. I do not offer an intellectual formulation for conservatism. I have tried instead to be sensitive to a certain habit of thought and quality of imagination that joins American thinkers of the late twentieth century to partisans of an earlier time.

Having said this, I add that I have tried to let the principals of this book speak for themselves. I hope this will be a useful work for scholars in intellectual history and for another class of individuals, interested readers who might wish to learn more about some names that are already familiar. I wanted to intrude with critical commentary only as far as assessment of individuals was appropriate to the larger subject of conservatism. I resisted the temptation in other places where, readers will readily see, such judgment, of censure or approval, might be in order. Nor do I doubt that the reader will fill in the blanks. I am certain, too, that few will pick up this book having not already formed an opinion of, say, William F. Buckley, Jr. It has not been my intention to alter that opinion. I would hope only that the reader would derive from this study a wider and more useful context for understanding Buckley's place in American conservatism within the historical contours of American life.

Finally, a note on the subtitle. Historians will judge how suitable will be the use of the term "Reagan era." I am suggesting at least a rough political parallel and a closer chronological one between the writings that constitute the intellectual material of this book and the political movement that began with the election of Ronald Reagan to the California governorship in 1966 and his departure from the White House in 1989.

WATCH ON THE RIGHT

1

The Lay of the Land

IN THE LATE 1970s conservative intellectuals in the United States had a common complaint. They could cite public opinion surveys that documented a growing conservative mood in the American public since the 1960s. By the end of 1980 they could point to the electoral successes of a new generation of conservative politicians from local quarters to the United States Senate. And they could celebrate the victory of the first avowedly conservative president in the memory of most Americans.

But euphoria, never a properly conservative sentiment anyway, did not reign. These conservatives, to whom ideas and culture meant much, saw cause for disaffection. They believed that the institutions of intellectual and cultural influence in the nation had become overwhelmingly the centers of a liberal counterculture at war with the dominant values and traditions of the country. The prestigious universities, the media, the artistic and literary establishments, the movie industry—these, it was said, had become the sanctuaries of a discredited movement that had relocated from the protests in the streets to the plush corporate headquarters of the television networks, the hallowed halls of ivy, and the major philanthropic foundations. George McGovern had been routed at the polls in 1972, but the continuing cultural insurgency could not be voted out of office.

Conservative thinkers hung their hats on many different racks. But this fact of sociological change in America gave conservative efforts a common perspective. For some it was the beginning of understanding, for others it was an incidental observation in a larger worldview. But the prospect of a United States that had fallen under the cultural domination of an adversary elite must be noted as one of two common themes in the conservative literature of the 1970s and 1980s. The other common core of conservative opinion—a strenuous anticommunism—was bound directly to the first.

This common perspective has a significance for intellectual history that was generally overlooked by the conservatives themselves. By the 1980s the discourse of intellectual conservatives had taken on something of a familiar quarrel between the ancients and the moderns. Religious, metaphysical, and traditionalist conservatives displayed their discomfort, sometimes angrily, with the voices of a New Right, which included the "neoconservatives," who seemed to understand the American problem in mostly political and sociological terms. For the Old Right, the prevalent afflictions of American life were more deeply rooted in intellectual error. In looking for answers, the two groups seemed to be looking past each other, only occasionally glimpsing their mutual indebtedness. Thus, to generalize somewhat, as the neoconservatives hoped for a revived democracy to overturn the liberal elite, they exercised an axiomatic faith that the traditional, sustaining values of Western civilization reposed more safely in the broader masses of society than in the community of the learned. At the same time, the Old Right had worked for decades to demonstrate the wayward course of Western thought and to restore its safe foundations. Conservative disagreements, of course, were genuine and serious, but one concern of this book is to ask whether conservatism might find a deeper commonality amid its many variations.

By the late 1960s it was possible to speak of a vociferous New Right in the United States. The term was used to describe a large group of writers, politicians, and religious leaders who commonly decried what they believed were the misdirections of liberal leadership, the corrosive effects of the 1960s counterculture, and the disabling effects of a foreign policy inattentive to the evils of communism. This group often shared a tangential relationship with the intellectuals studied in this book. One connecting thread bears examination.

In 1973 Harvard sociologist Daniel Bell published his weighty compendium *The Coming of Post-Industrial Society,* which he subtitled *A Venture in Social Forecasting.* The book, said Bell, expressed the sense that "in Western society we are in the midst of a vast historical change." Bell drew a statistical portrait of a changing United States, describing the contours of what he and economists were beginning to call the new "service economy." The expanding sectors of health, education, research, and government, and what would become increasingly prominent as the information and communications industries were now surpassing manufacturing as the dominant forces in American economic life. But "the most startling change," said Bell, was visible in the number of jobs that required some college education. Citing the new categories of post-industrial society, Bell also noted "the new intelligentsia" that would attain unprecedented influence.[1]

As Bell elaborated on the new intelligentsia in a book that was heavy with scholarly erudition, he spoke in a manner that gave a special warning to conservatives. For the new generation of conservative thinkers, these were ominous signs. Neoconservative writers especially were profoundly suspicious of intellectual theorizing. In a century of political ideologies they saw misery and bloodshed. And in the utopian mentality they perceived one of the menaces of modern history. Bell himself also referred to his own influential book of 1960, *The End of Ideology,* which, he reiterated, warned that the exhaustion of old ideologies inevitably led to a hunger for new ones. Intellectuals would certainly find an enlarged sphere of influence, and the university, said Bell, would be "the primary institution of post-industrial society."[2]

The book had other warnings for conservatives. Post-industrial society, which Bell described as an extended communal society, invariably expands the definition of rights. Its closer social affinities elevate the needs and wishes of individuals to claims on the community. The rights of children, of students, of minorities, of the poor, become increasingly irresistible. These demands, along with the larger communal issues of clean air and water and the needs for mass transportation and more education, expand the role of government. Bell thus envisioned a new political construct in which human transactions depended less on allocation in the marketplace and more on arbitration in the public realm. That realm, in fact, would become increasingly the location of an interest politics in which coalitions advanced their demands on the state and contested for larger portions of its largess.[3]

These perspectives on a changing America began to furnish conservative writers with a major cause. They supplied the dominant themes of the emerging New Right. Thus, when Kevin Phillips wrote *Mediacracy: American Parties and Politics in the Communications Age* in 1975, he explicitly expressed his debt to Daniel Bell and used the term *post-industrial* throughout his work. Phillips, a product of Harvard Law School, had won considerable attention for his 1969 book, *The Emerging Republican Majority,* a study of politics and demographic change that forecast the conservative political gains of later years. Phillips had become an influential political strategist for Richard Nixon and increasingly a voice for a populist conservatism in the 1970s. *Mediacracy* was an important work in articulating the grievances of the new conservative populists.

Phillips reinforced Bell's statistical documentation on the new post-industrial economy, but the language was different. Phillips spoke of the "huge bureaucracies of government," the "huge communications empires," the "huge corporate giants of knowledge technology."[4] Bell had been careful to emphasize the different competing interests and factions within the knowledge industry.[5] In Phillips' descriptions, the industry assumed a monolithic character. It also exercised a precise political agenda. Wrote Phillips: "Instead of having a vested economic interest in stability, as did previous conservative business establishments, the knowledge sector has a vested interest in change—in the unmooring of convention, in socioeconomic experiments, in the ongoing consumption of new ideas. The coming of the age of the knowledge elite in the sixties was partially the result of—and then dangerous additional fuel for—a decade of social ferment."[6]

Phillips had found the keys for a political translation of sociological trends. For the first time in memory, he wrote, liberalism had become the ideology of a privileged sector of the population. He described how many of America's "chic residential districts"—Back Bay, Boston; Manhattan's East Side; Scarsdale, New York; suburban San Francisco—which were formerly the strongholds of conservative businessmen, were now strongly liberal in their political voting. The populist tones were clearly evident. Phillips referred to the "New York–Washington media axis" and its "Ivy League elitist adversary culture." He also made a passing reference to traditional elites, defenders of monarchy and church, family and traditional moral behavior. But the new elite, the liberal elite, he said, operated on an ethic of openness, of freedom, of liberation from old restraints, from oppressive conventional mores and institutional conformities. Thus Phillips could write that "post-industrialism is turning this pattern on its proverbial ear. The new knowledge elite does not preserve and protect existing institutions. On the contrary, far more than previous new classes, the knowledge elite has sought to modify or replace traditional institutions with new relationships and power centers."[7]

Phillips pulled few punches. He laid at the feet of the new Establishment the disasters of new social experiments—from busing to rent control—as well as the new political egalitarianism, tolerance of crime and criminals, and the proliferating cultural lifestyles evident in changed sexual morality and drug use. Even the war in Vietnam, in his judgment, reflected the overreaching utopianism and quest for power among the new elite. This war Phillips described as one "launched by Ivy Leaguers, university deans, and foundation executives," the first computer-programmed conflict of the Cold War.[8]

Finally, what was most important for the New Right movement in Phillips' book was his analysis of a divided America. He described a growing religious revival in the United States, cited a new ethnic self-consciousness and cultural invigoration around the country, and found meaning in the new vogue for country and western music, even in New York City. And always for Phillips the cultural pattern had its political parallel. At heart the new populist conservatism was, in his portrayal, a class war. Offering a statistical study of the

1972 presidential election, Phillips showed that the liberal Democratic candidate George McGovern tended to do best in states with the highest levels of income, education, culture, health and welfare services, and civic awareness.[9] That the conservative agenda now seemed to embrace the democratic masses of America was giving a new cast not only to the "movement" conservatives like Phillips; it furnished a surprising twist to the whole corpus of conservative intellectuals' writings in the 1970s and 1980s.

On the political front, of course, Richard Nixon had begun to exploit the apparent bifurcation in America, making his appeal directly to "middle America" and "the great silent majority." The feisty Patrick Buchanan, having joined Nixon's White House team, tried to articulate the conservative rationale of the Republican administration. In his book of 1973, *The New Majority,* Buchanan went after the media elite: "They are ranking members of the privileged class, the most prestigious, powerful, wealthy and influential journalists in all history." But Buchanan perceived too that they had made considerable political inroads, forming a new and powerful constituency in the Democratic party. The counterculture had become respectable and politically legitimate, he said. Summarizing divided American opinion on a range of issues—from the military to marijuana, school prayer to the United Nations—Buchanan wrote: "While the Nixon landslide was a victory of the man over McGovern, it was also a victory of 'the New American Majority' over the 'New Politics,' a victory of traditional American values and beliefs over the claims of the 'counter-culture,' a victory of 'Middle America' over the celebrants of Woodstock Nation."[10]

The New Right had another major voice in William Rusher, long-time friend of William F. Buckley, Jr., and publisher of the *National Review.* A Princeton and Harvard Law School graduate and practicing attorney before he joined the publication, Rusher moved increasingly in a populist and emphatically right-wing direction. His own history, *The Rise of the Right,* detailed his break from the Nixon administration, which he judged insufficiently conservative.[11] His book of 1975 added another point of emphasis to populist conservatism. Titled *The Making of the New Majority Party,* the book opened with a reference to recent Gallup poll data indicating that Americans increasingly identified themselves as conservative more than liberal. But neither of the political parties, Rusher believed, authentically reflected the changing political mood. Rusher called for a conservative takeover of the Republican party, but his book is of note to us for its supporting role in portraying an American *Kulturkampf.* Rusher described "the liberal verbalist elite" that had acquired a privileged hegemony in the nation, an elite "operating through the bureaucracy, the educational establishment, the media, and the major foundations," which, he believed, "has persistently led this nation from its moral and psychological moorings."[12]

The move from sociology to political manifesto culminated in 1983 with the publication of Richard Viguerie's book *The Establishment vs. the People*. Here was a passionate piece, a book of prejudices, written in a populist style, mostly undocumented, full of one- and two-sentence paragraphs. But the book had more than a merely emotional appeal. However acerbic the commentary, it described, page after page, the case against the American elites—their self-serving activities, their betrayal of their true leadership roles, and their isolation and remoteness from so much of ordinary life and opinion in America. Populism, like libertarianism, touches both extremes of the political spectrum. Many charges made in this book could have won endorsement on the Left. But the book also illustrated at least one major difference between leftist and rightist populism. Wholly believing in a "people's democracy," Viguerie's radicalism did not describe a sick and oppressive society that victimized the common people. The democratic masses of America were for him the trustees of the nation's wholesome religious tradition, its morality, and its patriotism. Victims they were, though, betrayed by the brightest and best.

The Establishment vs. the People incorporated familiar New Right complaints against the media, the universities, and the bureaucracies. But Viguerie's populism was more comprehensive than anything before it. Consider the chapter titles: "Big Government," "Big Business," "Big Banks," "Big Unions," "Big Education," "Big Law," "Big Media." In each of these categories Viguerie described an elite leadership at war with its constituencies. He saw business in league with government to thwart economic competition and fleece the consumer (Viguerie cited New Left historian Gabriel Kolko's *The Triumph of Conservatism,* a study of how "progressive" reforms of the late nineteenth century were urged and used by big business interests, in making his case); he castigated the privileged elite of labor union leadership (in a manner reminiscent of New Left sociologist C. Wright Mills); he described an entrenched teaching profession, symbolized by the National Education Association, at war with parents who wanted to return education to "basics"; he invoked the antibanking prejudices—real populist ones—of Jefferson, Jackson, and Bryan against the financial elites; he assaulted the arcane machinations of the legal profession and its self-serving exploitation of the law.[13] To be sure, everywhere it turned this book overshot its mark: every American ill was attributed to the elites. But if only a quarter of Viguerie's volleys hit the target, then his book would be a compelling statement, not to be summarily dismissed.

Of the political tracts of the New Right, Viguerie's polemic came closest to an embrace of the Right's other wing, the Christian conservatives, who were waging a similar cultural war against liberalism. Mostly associated with Rev. Jerry Falwell's Moral Majority but supported by an extensive cast of media preachers and their large followings, the religious Right was making its case against the new sexual morality, against abortion, against violence on television, against homosexuality, against feminism, and against communism. Viguerie's compendium of errors was similar. He earnestly defended the moral position of the Christian Right and cited the toll in social decay in America taken by the decline of traditional morality.[14] His book had a hundred specific proposals for political reform, but it was also underscored by traditional moral values, of which it could be said that only the millions of ordinary Americans were now the safe repositories.

Conservatism all the while was receiving new input from a much different source. Prominent in the membership of the conservative intellectuals were writers once allied with the Left. Many were Jewish. Most in the middle 1960s had identified themselves with the Democratic party and its New Deal heritage. Most would say that the opening of that party to the radicalism of the 1960s was the cause of their own defection from the party or of their efforts to bring it back to a more centrist position. Most would not call themselves conservatives at all. One was not always sure how to describe this group. Their case against the Left was both bitter and trenchant, but did that make them conservatives? The label "neoconservative" was certainly nondescript, but it stuck.

Neoconservatism was at once a study in the metamorphosis of the Left, a chapter in American Jewish intellectual history, and a new and important departure in conservatism. Its mode, its inner variety, and its style are represented in this book by Irving Kristol, Hilton Kramer, Michael Novak, and Jeane Kirkpatrick. This selection includes individuals of Jewish, Catholic, and Protestant backgrounds. But it was the combative editor of *Commentary* magazine who did as much as anyone to give neoconservatism its notoriety. Norman Podhoretz twice wrote his autobiography, and these apologias were major documents of the changing political culture of the United States from the 1950s onward.

Podhoretz published *Making It* in 1967. The book recounted his boyhood years in Brooklyn, the place of his birth in 1930 and the world of a bright Jewish youth growing to larger awareness of his uncertain place in a Christian America. At school, Podhoretz related, his teacher, Mrs. K., was an old-fashioned patrician who taunted him about looking like "a filthy slum child" and bought him a new suit of clothes for his Harvard interview.[15] Podhoretz was describing also, by this incident and others, his own assimilation into European and American culture. He recognized his teacher's efforts for what they were, but the larger culture proved irresistible. While at Columbia University, Podhoretz also attended the Jewish Seminary College, though, he said, "I was neither especially religious nor much of a Zionist." Very simply, traditionalist Jewish life offered little sustaining interest. At Columbia, Podhoretz enrolled in the Humanities and Contemporary Civilization course, and it captured the undergraduate's imagination. Podhoretz could sense his divided loyalties. Columbia, he said, was telling him to "become a facsimile WASP!" and the temptation could not be ignored. His old world could no longer look quite the same.[16]

Studying literature at Oxford with F. R. Leavis brought on the "second stage" in Podhoretz's "conversion to culture." He described his return to the United States and his involvement with the second generation of New York Jewish intellectuals—their quarrels, their efforts to establish their identity, and his own interactions with the membership. Still a youthful thirty, Podhoretz in 1960 became the new editor of *Commentary,* which had been launched by the American Jewish Committee in 1948 and edited by Elliot Cohen. Podhoretz resolved to make *Commentary* less Jewish, less academic, and more leftist. He opened its pages to an early voice of the New Left (Podhoretz was now calling himself "radical") and published chapters of Paul Goodman's mini-classic *Growing Up Absurd.* Podhoretz, a man who seemed to be always just a little bit ahead of the times, believed he had anticipated and shaped the course of the leftward turn of the 1960s.

Breaking Ranks is the story of his turnabout. Published in 1979, the book is a long commentary on politics and culture in the late 1960s and 1970s. A consistent thread runs through *Breaking Ranks.* While issues and events pass under review, what one sees in Podhoretz's retreat from the Left is his revulsion to its social and cultural styles—what he believed were its inauthentic sentiments, its unheroic morality, its disingenuous ideology. Podhoretz expressed his severest reservations about the peace movement: he could discern only naïveté and wishful thinking in the liberals who urged accommodation with the Soviet Union. Even in his radical mood in the early 1960s, Podhoretz saw that nation as "out to conquer the world."[17] *Commentary* under Podhoretz would be outspokenly anti-Soviet.

But his discomfort with the new counterculture was even greater. He had never taken a liking to the Beat Generation of the 1950s—the Kerouacs and Ginsbergs—nor joined the revolt against middle-class life and the "dehumanizing" routine of business America. Of course, he said, there was money to be made by trafficking in the adversary culture. And in the 1960s and 1970s, said Podhoretz, the "hustlers" of the counterculture – "rock stars, publishing tycoons, drug dealers, and other enterprising entrepreneurs" – padded their wallets by denouncing the materialism and consumerism of middle-class American life. It was not only the brazen "hypocrisy" that rankled Podhoretz. He charged that those comfortable Americans who bought into the counterculture were purchasing for themselves a smug moral superiority over others. And leftist politics swelled their conceit. Wrote Podhoretz:

Thus people (and again, not only young people) went around with straight faces saying of themselves that they were superior to most of their fellow countrymen, that they, as opposed to most others around them, cared only for higher things and nobler values. Unlike everyone else, they believed in peace and justice as the proper ends of politics; unlike everyone else they believed in love and cooperation instead of hatred and competition; and unlike everyone else, they believed in art as against commerce. In short, unlike everyone else, they were good people, decent people, people of conscience and compassion and "concern."[18]

Podhoretz had chronicled his rise from the Jewish ghetto of Brooklyn: *Making It* was a celebration of success. But he never really left the ghetto. If he were a political radical, then he had every title to be, he believed. There was something offensive to him in the chic and easy leftism of gilded upper-class white liberals – and something inauthentic. Podhoretz pointed to the liberal suburbanites who championed racial integration at no cost to themselves or their children. He denounced the "safe detractors" of the Vietnam War, intellectuals who risked nothing in sheltered academia. Thus characterizing the counterculture, Podhoretz and the neoconservatives all the more embraced the ethic that had shaped their lives, an ethic of work and its rewards of success. And the more they came to embrace it the more they made it the dividing line between their America – the real America – and the "New Class" embodiments of a counterethic. The social class factor colored neoconservatives' perceptions of themselves and their country. Podhoretz' language thus lapsed easily into populist rhetoric. He described "an aggression by a new and rapidly growing group of prosperous and well-educated people calling themselves liberals against a less prosperous and less well-educated combination of groups, mostly in the working and lower middle classes."[19] And in his book *The Bloody Crossroads,* Podhoretz reprinted his essay "The Adversary Culture and the New Class," with its familiar rightist complaints.[20]

Breaking Ranks had nearly all the markings of the emergent neoconservatism. But in what sense exactly was Podhoretz a conservative? In his virulent anticommunism, perhaps, or in his occasional defense of bourgeois morality

and middle-class culture. But when the Old Right conservatives faulted the
neoconservatives, they often seemed to have Podhoretz in mind. To be sure,
there were factors of personality involved. Many thought Podhoretz arrogant,
boastful, egotistic after the fact. Others believed that his "conservatism" never
transcended the interests of Jewish Americans or the survival needs of Israel.[21]
These concerns were prevalent in Podhoretz' works, but it would be wrong
to dismiss his writings as so narrowly motivated. What legitimately troubled
conservatives was the surface quality of Podhoretz' works. He provided no
basis—in religion, philosophy, or moral theory—for the grounding of his
opinions and judgments. His commentary attained a certain critical acuteness,
but it had no anchor. Could neoconservatism transcend the ad hoc character
of its social criticism and cultural style? Other principals in this book will
allow us to answer that question.

But one thing was certain: neoconservatism was acquiring a clearer outline
by the end of the 1960s. Another Jewish individual who gave it reinforcement
was Nathan Glazer. Born in New York City in 1923, Glazer graduated from
City College and earned higher degrees at the University of Pennsylvania
and Columbia University. His career combined journalism and academics.
He was on the editorial staff of *Commentary* from 1945 to 1953 and was
a coauthor of David Riesman's celebrated book of 1950, *The Lonely Crowd*.
Many of Glazer's essays dealt with issues of concern to American Jews, and
he wrote a thoughtful interpretive history on that subject in 1957. He taught
at the University of California at Berkeley from 1963 to 1969, and in the
sociology department at Harvard afterward. Glazer joined Irving Kristol as
coeditor of the *Public Interest* in 1973, replacing Daniel Bell. His position
joined him to the neoconservatives, however much he avoided appropriation
of that label for himself. Glazer's sociological writings added scholarly polish
to neoconservatism, and the shifts in his intellectual career provided another
key chapter in the movement's history.

In the late 1950s Nathan Glazer, like Norman Podhoretz, thought of himself
as a radical. By that term Glazer meant a person of the Left who could not
be called a liberal. The radical, said Glazer, did not share liberalism's obsession with Soviet communism. He did not have liberalism's confidence in the
ability of large bureaucracies and applied governmental intelligence to solve
the pressing problems of housing, urban renewal, and welfare. The radical,
influenced by Paul Goodman, spoke of the small, the immediate, the human
scale of things. The radical considered the whole apparatus of society, from
government to business and the complex of social institutions, to be suppres-
sive of instinct and feeling.[22] The radical was, in some ways, close to the
New Left. But Glazer would soon recognize that he was close to conservatism,
too.

In 1970 Glazer could ask this question: "How does a radical — a mild radical, it is true, but still someone who felt closer to radical than to liberal writers and politicians in the late 1950's — end up by early 1970 a conservative, a mild conservative, but still closer to those who now call themselves conservative than to those who call themselves liberal?" Glazer answered by saying that radicalism and liberalism had changed. They had taken on a large reformist agenda that was raising the specter of a leviathan government to meet its goals. What was left in radicalism was only its conservative shell — its appreciation of the small community, of individual discretion, of pluralism in the social body. But Glazer had to admit that he too had changed.[23]

There were several signposts along the way. In 1964, while Glazer was teaching at Berkeley, the free speech movement began at that campus. The event would be divisive for the liberal community. Some liberals hoped to see the student movement become a wider attack on the major institutions of society, and they endorsed the movement for its high idealism. But there were many cautious liberals, too, who perceived in this nascent radicalism the dangers of irrationalism, of a new intolerance, even of a totalitarian mentality. Glazer's voice was skeptical and critical. In his essay "What Happened at Berkeley," he looked beyond the formal issue of free speech to the more important question of authority. He would later see in this first stage of the student movement of the 1960s an explicit threat to the university itself. Increasingly Glazer was becoming sensitive to the fragile character of liberal democracy and the vulnerability, in the face of irrational and emotional forces, of the social institutions that make for order and equilibrium in a free society.[24]

The attitudes that Glazer described were reinforced during his period of service in Washington, D.C., with the Housing and Home Finance Administration. He described his work as an experience in realism. What impressed Glazer were the many legitimate claims of various social interests that confronted the Washington bureaucracy. He grew to a larger appreciation of the routine work of government in addressing and balancing these claims. However mundane and uninspiring its work, government, said Glazer, had a necessary, pragmatic role. And he added: "I learned, in quite strictly conservative fashion, to develop a certain respect for what was."[25]

Other conclusions followed and became increasingly evident in Glazer's writings. As a sociologist addressing the major social problems that the United States confronted, Glazer concluded that there were really none for which solutions lay in pursuit of an ideological formula. The hardening of ideology in the New Left became for Glazer one of its worst attributes. Its rejection of American institutions was for Glazer simply too categorical. It was also too superficial, as in its equating the United States under Lyndon Johnson with Germany under Hitler. In response, Glazer embraced pragmatic standards and methods. A true and genuine freedom, he wrote, and a true and meaningful equality would depend on strengthening the existing institutions — business, technological, governmental — of American society. In a complex society there was no alternative to bureaucracies, administrators, and experts.[26]

These judgments, one notes, were not greatly different from those of liberals who also criticized the New Left. What took Glazer in the direction of neoconservatism, however, was a change in liberalism that troubled him endlessly and which became the major focus of his writings in the late 1970s and through the 1980s. The pragmatic course of government that Glazer once praised was now, he believed, yielding to an entirely new social agenda, a utopian egalitarianism that was playing havoc with the social fabric of American society. Of all the neoconservatives, Glazer became the most outspoken in criticizing the goals of a statistical equality in the new liberalism. He took up the case against this program in his extensive writing on busing and affirmative action.

In 1975 Glazer published *Affirmative Discrimination: Ethnic Inequality and Public Policy*. It was a book written very much in the neoconservative style. While it invoked the ideal of individual merit, the standards of local choice and neighborhood priorities, and the option for pluralism, its medium was the empirical data of sociology. Thus, in a chapter titled "Affirmative Action in Employment: From Equal Opportunity to Statistical Parity," Glazer studied patterns of black employment and income levels by summarizing data based on "two sophisticated econometric analyses." Glazer wished to contrast the rationalist and ideological character of statistical parity — the fatal turn in liberalism, he believed — with the empirical realities of American life. In responding to the decline of median black income as measured against the median for whites in the late 1960s, Glazer offered statistics reflecting the causal factors of the increase of female-headed households in the black community.[27]

Its empirical weight notwithstanding, *Affirmative Discrimination* was a value-laden book. Glazer approximated government policies that considered race and sex in employment and education to the Nuremburg Laws of Nazi Germany. He resented liberal patronizing of allegedly "helpless" minorities. He charged that the new liberalism was a threat to freedom. "The tone of civil rights cases has turned from one in which the main note is the expansion of freedom into one in which the main note is the imposition of restrictions," Glazer wrote. Above all, he felt, an America defined by statistical groups betrayed an America of authentic communities. The category "white," he said, locked ethnic groups of differentiated cultures and histories into one homogeneous and indiscriminate category. Busing and affirmative action, Glazer charged, were sinister assaults on the pluralist richness of America, a rationalist obliteration of all the factors of work, community, and ethnic ways that marked that pluralism.[28]

Finally, what needs to be remarked in Glazer's works is the perspective that joins neoconservative and New Right views. In a 1985 essay in the *Public Interest,* Glazer drew upon the studies of Kevin Phillips to explain the political shifts of recent years. The key factor in these shifts, said Glazer, was the "social issue" — busing, abortion, school prayer. In following Phillips, Glazer's language took on the dichotomies used by the New Right and by the neoconservatives in their discussion of the New Class. Wrote Glazer: "Almost all of these issues involved the unelected Federal courts imposing new standards against community practices and desires. All placed the cosmopolitan sections of the country — the Northeast, the Pacific Coast, the major universities, the national media — against local forces, without the same prestige, connection with leading institutions, or access to sophisticated national media."[29] Glazer, to my knowledge, did not employ the term *New Class* himself, but his analyses utilized the cultural and class distinctions of social elite versus democratic mass that was now standard in neoconservative and New Right usage. And this was the larger point for Glazer. The pragmatic government that he had earlier celebrated had become the arena of professional reformers working to effect their special programs. The dangers to democracy were clear, Glazer believed. "The professionals," he wrote, "concentrating exclusively on their area of reform, may become more and more remote from public opinion and, indeed, from common sense."[30] For Glazer there was no other way to explain the illogic and folly of busing and affirmative action, the perversions of the new liberalism.

There remained in the United States of these years a group of conservative intellectuals who believed that they understood the sources of a faltering liberalism and all the attending social ills bequeathed by it. They were united by a conviction that the roots of decay in the West lay in the disorders of the modern mind. This Old Right provided conservatism with an edifice constructed variously on theology, metaphysics, or culture. It was by no means monolithic, for it included the Christian apologetics of Thomas Molnar and John Hallowell but also drew from the religiously sympathetic but emphatically humanist standards of Irving Babbitt and Peter Viereck.

The Old Right continued to exercise a strong influence in conservative circles, even in the heyday of the neoconservatives. In some cases, they had an active discipleship in academic circles. Furthermore, the Old Right remained strong enough to make itself a forum of dissent from neoconservatism. Its strictures against the newer voices, as described later in this study, were dividing conservatism in the 1980s and making more urgent the question of what common grounds and what principles of continuity, if any, gave unity to American conservative thought. From the expansive literature of the Old Right, it will be useful to select a few portions for review.

In 1948 Richard M. Weaver published a book titled *Ideas Have Consequences*. A native of North Carolina and a graduate of the University of Kentucky and Vanderbilt University, Weaver became a professor at the University of Chicago. The pedestrian title notwithstanding, *Ideas Have Consequences* addressed no less weighty a subject than the decay of Western civilization. It described Weaver's unyielding conviction that the degeneration of the West — the vulgarization of its society and the adulteration of its political life — were uniformly rooted in metaphysical error. Specifically, Weaver located in the triumph of nominalism over realism in the scholastic debates of the Middle Ages the roots of all modern fallacies. Said Weaver: "The defeat of logical realism in the great medieval debate was the crucial event in the history of Western culture; from this flowed those acts which issue now in modern decadence." Nominalism meant the discrediting of universals, which signified for Weaver the principle of "a truth higher than, and independent of man." With the loss of that principle, of that vision, Weaver believed, came a wholly new orientation of Western society.[31]

It would be difficult to locate, even to imagine, a book more replete with traditional conservative prejudices and convictions than Weaver's. On the metaphysical lapse of the fourteenth century Weaver hung the collapse of authority. Man had confidently proclaimed himself the new authority, said Weaver, but had fallen into drift and confusion. Turning from a transcendent reality and a transcendent truth, Western man made the earthly temple the promise of human fulfillment. Increasingly, then, said Weaver, a debilitating materialism became the norm of Western life. The defeat of realism, he believed, meant the loss of any hierarchy of values and human relationships. Indiscriminate democratic leveling and a "false egalitarianism" reigned. In social and political life, the gentlemen everywhere yielded to the politicians and the men of commerce. And Weaver, one of the later voices of the Southern Agrarians, deplored commerce and capitalism. He inveighed against capitalism's brutal and dehumanizing competitiveness. He excoriated the middle class, "loving comfort, risking little, terrified by the thought of change, its aim to establish a materialistic civilization which will banish threats to complacency." What else was bourgeois democratic government, he asked, but "a vast bureaucracy to promote economic activity"?[32]

Ideas Have Consequences was a book of prejudices underscored by a metaphysical construct. What it represented ultimately was a conservative revolt, an aesthetic revolt really, against modern life. From the daily newspaper, purveyor of cheap sentiments, and the social manners of democratic mass man, Weaver turned away in disgust. Perhaps his most poignant lament was for "the disappearance of the heroic ideal" in modern life. A social life given to science and commerce, he believed, could supply little nourishment for the human soul.[33]

It is not easy to say precisely what gave Weaver's little book its lasting appeal among conservative intellectuals of the Old Right. Of course, it was full of Burkean prejudices. Its writing, in an almost biblical style, was captivating. But these factors alone might not have sustained it over the years. Weaver provided the Old Right, however much its individual members might disagree with him in detail, their fondest hope – to ground their case against liberalism and all that it entailed on immovable philosophical rock. For as Weaver wrote, "Our conception of metaphysical reality finally governs our conception of everything else."[34]

The literature of the Old Right could be explored at length, but there were two individuals in particular who extended its influence into the 1960s and beyond. Both Eric Voegelin and Leo Strauss were émigré scholars from Germany. And both, through extensive scholarship, drew broad configurations in the history of ideas that supplied conservative schema for understanding the political directions of modern history.

Voegelin introduced *The New Science of Politics* in 1952, building on some earlier works, but he expanded on this work in his richly erudite series, *Order and History*. Voegelin was concerned with human beings' experience of "the order of being," and he traced in early civilizations and the ontological "leap" that occurred in Judaism the direct and unmediated experience of the transcendent order, or what Christianity would call "grace." This "inversion," as Voegelin described it, was also a change in the order of history itself. It confirmed a hierarchy of being in which the human soul, by its corresponding construction, itself participated.

Voegelin was preoccupied with later efforts to bridge, merge, or give a secular meaning to this order, which Voegelin called gnosticism. Gnosticism appeared onstage early, among the Greeks. Voegelin essentially meant by the term gnosticism a redivination of the world. Gnosticism placed the meaning of existence into the historical process and looked to the creation of a "terrestrial paradise" as its fulfillment. Here again metaphysical error wrought devastation. Voegelin found in the modern political ideologies – fascism and communism most blatantly – the totalitarian consequences of gnosticism. But he warned also that liberal democracy too could easily become a species of secular faith. "The true dividing line in the contemporary crisis," wrote Voegelin, "does not run between liberals and totalitarians, but between the religious and philosophical transcendentalists on the one side, and the liberal and the totalitarian immanentist sectarians on the other side."[35]

If the influence of Voegelin in conservative circles was striking but also curious, then that of Leo Strauss was extraordinary. Strauss's scholarship inspired a renewal of interest in classical political theory, and with his admiring disciples he became a minor academic phenomenon in the 1970s and 1980s. Unfamiliar even to many academics, Straussians were everywhere in American universities. They significantly extended the intellectual reach of the Old Right.

Leo Strauss's major works included *The Political Philosophy of Hobbes* (1938), *On Tyranny* (1948), *Natural Right and History* (1953), *Thoughts on Machiavelli* (1958), and *What is Political Philosophy?* (1959). The influential American conservative Willmoore Kendall said of the latter two works: "Both of these should be not required reading but scripture for everyone who likes to think of himself as a conservative."[36]

From his earliest involvement in philosophy, Strauss held the conviction that that discipline involved a quest for knowledge beyond the given data of experience and history, that it was a quest for a nonarbitrary standard by which to measure the given, and that in the success of this venture was the authentic root of human freedom.[37] Philosophy thus also had clear implications for political science. At the heart of Strauss's writings on this subject was his fundamental distinction between antiquity and modernity. Strauss located in classical political philosophy a priority of purpose and knowledge, a concern for the right or the best political order, that made it the starting and terminal point of all his succeeding judgments. Classical man, in Strauss's account, sought always to rise above his earthly existence, to overcome his base passions, and to enthrone virtue and reason. Learning for Strauss, as instructed by the Greeks, was a mode of piety, the beginning of true wisdom and the knowledge of our place in the whole hierarchy of being. Man cannot be his own end, and no greater challenge awaits him than to divine the essence of the whole of which he is part. But he must also belong to a state, a republic of virtuous citizens, that realizes these ideals. Strauss's works also honored religious revelation, as in the Judaic and Christian traditions, as the legitimate foundations of the West, the "Great Tradition." And, added Strauss, "we are impelled to [study the classics] by the crisis of our time, the crisis of the West."[38]

The crisis of our time, Strauss believed, was the legacy of modernity. The debacle that began with Machiavelli was reinforced by Hobbes and Locke and culminated in Nietzsche and Heidegger. Strauss described a succession of departures from the natural law basis of classical politics. Modernity accepted and thereby legitimated the base passions and interests dominant in human nature and aspired to found governments based on those passions and interests, in essence by channeling or controlling them. Natural right, defined by Strauss as a subjective notion, replaced the objective order supplied by natural law. What was left for Strauss was only the ethic of might and the nihilism of legislative prerogative. What resulted was moral permissiveness and the confusion of standards, all the drift of the indiscriminate open society.[39]

The Straussians—scholars like Harry V. Jaffa, Walter Berns, Martin Diamond, Charles R. Kesler, Thomas L. Pangle, and Harvey C. Mansfield— engaged in some important debates, often among themselves, about American history and above all about the meaning of the country's founding. To some, the anti-Federalists, with their ideal of the small republic, embodied the best classical notions of the virtuous state or saw the surest way to its realization. Generally, though, the Straussians recognized in the aspirations of the Founding Fathers a unique moment of antiquity in American history. Jaffa, for example, resisted the efforts of those like Irving Kristol who contrasted the pragmatism of the American revolutionists with the ideological excesses of their European counterparts. Jaffa wrote that this severing of the Founding Fathers from a natural law intellectual tradition left the nation without ideals, with nothing to guide it but positive right. Thus justice becomes the prerogative of the strongest.[40] Writing in the *National Review,* Charles R. Kesler sought to bring the American record, as well as the Whig tradition back into the intellectual context of the ancients. "Jefferson," said Kesler, "understood himself to be drawing on the agreement of such men as Aristotle, Cicero, Locke, and Sidney."[41]

Like Voegelin, the Straussians reinforced the parameters of the Old Right. Theirs was not a rigid intellectual system, but more like a cultural norm that defied any supplementary expansion by the temporal process. As conservatives, though not all considered themselves as such, they were quite removed from the Burkean standards of a classical conservatism. But the Straussians clearly did reemphasize that the right human life and the right human society required a right relation to a larger order of being. The Straussians, in short, extended the ontological foundations of the Old Right.

And its ontology could often be a political weapon. Criticizing the pragmatist philosopher Richard Rorty, Harvey C. Mansfield argued that democracy cannot be its own legitimation, and the pragmatist fails in its defense because he cannot support it by any standard outside itself. Wrote Mansfield: "The only way he [the pragmatist] can tell whether democracy works is by judging whether it is becoming more democratic." The pragmatist's democracy was therefore "a rudderless boat." The error of the pragmatists is the error of all modernists, even conservative modernists, one would have to add. Pragmatists assume, said Mansfield, that intellect cannot rise above the accidents of sex, nation, and race, "that the philosopher is incapable of transcending his historical, which means his political, situation." A philosophy based on transcendence, insisted Mansfield, alone suffices as the foundation of the right political order and of a valid judgment of it.[42]

The Straussians occupied academic enclaves generally removed from the public eye and wrote for select academic audiences. But then in 1987 there came the most unpredictable best-seller of the 1980s, Allan Bloom's *The Closing of the American Mind*. Previously the author of a study of Shakespeare and a translator of Plato and Rousseau, Bloom was a former student of Strauss and a professor of social thought at the University of Chicago. Loosely restating the obscurantism of Strauss in an often-quotable, if nonetheless usually dense treatise on the American civilization of the late twentieth century, Bloom's effort was a dramatic extension of Strauss for a wider public audience. Bloom portrayed the United States of the 1980s as a civilization bereft of its classical roots, complacent and trivial in its purposes, and indiscriminately egalitarian in its public sentiments. He described its citizenry exercising a shallow interior life and its public institutions functioning in the milieu of an official nihilism. These circumstances resulted altogether in a facile, invertebrate democracy. And yet this book was an intellectual tour as well, with discussions of Locke, Rousseau, Kant, and, most important, Nietzsche and Heidegger.

Bloom ultimately looked to the university as the only possible counterforce to a faltering American culture, but he described at the same time the institution that had failed most. To be sure, he said, the university was not entirely at fault. It received a youthful population drugged on rock music, deprived of a meaningful tradition, and expecting to learn nothing from literature, least of all what it might show about the pain and passion of romantic love. The failure of the modern university, for Bloom, was its failure to make itself a center of reason, of noninstrumental learning, of pure intellect. A Straussian purism in Bloom looked constantly back to the Greeks and to the old "Great Books" program for curricular substance. The university, in short, needed to be a counterforce to the attenuated culture of democracy. "To sum up," said Bloom, "there is one simple rule for the university's activity: it need not concern itself with providing its students with experiences that are available in democratic society. They will have them in any event. It must provide them with experiences they cannot have there."[43] This was language familiar to traditionalist conservatives, from Babbitt to Norman Foerster to Russell Kirk. It was a reformulation, too, of the conservative plea for aristocratic standards as the necessary foundations of a true democracy.

This brief topographical overview illustrates that intellectual conservatism in the 1970s was both rich and new. Other currents — libertarianism and agrarianism, for example — had their spokesmen and followers, and we shall encounter some of them in succeeding chapters. But a review of this kind is inherently sketchy and incomplete. The conservative intellectual movement of the 1970s and 1980s demands to be considered through the sharper focus and extended analysis of its major voices.

2
William F. Buckley, Jr.
Paterfamilias

WILLIAM F. BUCKLEY, JR., was always a fighter. His conservatism was always pugnacious, combative, and ready to enter the ring with any comers. The American public first took note of Buckley as a brash young man who assailed his alma mater in *God and Man at Yale,* and it wondered at his audacity. That was in 1951. His opponents on the Left soon learned to fear his wit as much as his intellect. Others marveled at his lexicon, always a Buckley trademark. Many too felt his charm—the disarming smile, the probing pensiveness that raised eyebrow and pencil, the Brahminic demeanor that gave Buckley the air of hauteur and the arrogance of èrudition (no matter how much he might disdain the savants of Harvard and Yale). But along the path of more than thirty years, Buckley evolved from enfant terrible to sage among the American conservative intellectuals. He presided over National Public Radio's longest-running program, "Firing Line." And even in the late 1980s his readership was still inquiring at the *National Review* for copies of *Quotations from Chairman Bill* and *The Best of Bill Buckley.*

Buckley was America's all-purpose conservative thinker. He was at once the champion of the free individual against the powers of the state, an exponent of a market economy, and a libertarian, albeit with grave qualifications. But he embraced a traditionalist conservatism as well, especially on matters of the Catholic faith. A conservative sense of hierarchy and deference to rank was alleged against Buckley. But on the other hand, the Connecticut aristocrat had no compunctions about speaking for the commonfolk against the higher wisdom of bureaucratic elites and zealous academics who would redesign the world by rational fiat. His occasional gestures to the demos sat unembarrassed with a mannerism that distinguished him from the rank and file. But

Buckley also won interest by being unpredictable. He defended voting for blacks simply on the basis of race. He stood against other conservatives, Ronald Reagan most noticeably, in supporting the treaties that would relinquish United States control of the Panama Canal.[1] He championed the cause of a convicted criminal.[2] He endorsed, quite seriously, a public program for free food to anyone who wanted it. (It would be "basic food materials" of powdered skim milk, bulgar wheat, soybean, and lard, and even the wealthy Hunt brothers of Texas could take it if they so desired.) And he spoke for legalizing private homosexual acts and prostitution.[3]

Some critics dismissed this unpredictability as inconsistency. They regarded Buckley as something of an ad hoc conservative who did not contribute significantly to the making of a conservative ideology or intellectual system. One of his biographers wrote, "What he has produced is more polemics than philosophy. One is apt to come away from this body of work perplexed about what conservatism is, but certain about what it is not."[4] At one point, Buckley signed a contract to write a book on conservatism, but the assignment dogged him painfully and he never pulled it off.[5]

Undeniably, though, Buckley's pluralist conservatism helped to create his leadership role in the conservative intellectual movement. His launching of the *National Review* in 1955 gave conservative writers of all kinds a forum for their views. Anti-Communists, libertarians, traditionalists, and theological and metaphysical conservatives all received a welcome in the journal that reached some 120,000 readers.[6] And it is true that when Buckley undertook to assemble an anthology of conservative opinion (which he titled *Did You Ever See a Dream Walking?)* he dismissed as trivial the concern for definition. Those who judge him on this point, however, miss an important fact. For Buckley's conservatism, I hope to show, was indeed rooted deeply in the American experience, and Buckley remained throughout his career the most articulate voice of an enduring strain in that experience. His conservatism was a matter of style as well as philosophy, of rhetoric as well as program, of cultural habit as well as ideology.

William F. Buckley, Jr., was born in 1925 to "an iron-willed oil speculator and his gentle Southern wife." William Frank Buckley, the father, was a Texan, the son of Canadian-born parents with ancestral roots in Ireland. He became a successful oil speculator, amassing an estate of some one hundred million dollars before his death in 1958. But he embroiled himself in politics and found himself on the losing side of the Mexican revolution that brought Victoriano Huerta to power in 1913. The senior Buckley joined an underground movement that assisted threatened priests and concealed church artifacts from the revolutionary armies.[7]

William F. Buckley, Jr., by Vint Lawrence

William Frank Buckley was also a proud patriarch. He was devotedly Catholic, praying every morning and attending weekly Mass. Though he never spoke about his faith, it was clear, as John B. Judis observed, that his religion revolved around a stern and demanding God, whereas his wife, Aloise, exercised a more emotional and pietistic religiosity. Buckley's father was outspoken in his social prejudices. He regarded blacks and Indians as inferiors and often railed against the interloping presence of Jews in a Christian nation. Though he had no political affiliation and indeed seldom voted, he identified mostly with southern Democrats like Mississippi senator John Sharp Williams.[8]

The Buckleys were of Irish descent, but William Frank Buckley considered himself an Irish-American in a way that nearly obliterated the Irish identity. He wanted no part of the stereotypical image of the heavy-drinking immigrant Irish. His own stern moral code derived in part from that sensitivity. On the other hand, the senior Buckley was no social climber among the Anglos. Judis reports that he once paid to have his name kept out of *Who's Who*. Catholics in a Protestant nation, southerners among northerners, the Buckleys usually felt like outsiders in their own world.[9] That perspective clearly described the intellectual style of the future conservative.

Young Bill attended Millbrook Academy in New York and then served as a second lieutenant in World War II until his discharge in 1946. He enrolled in Yale University in the fall of that year and graduated from that institution in 1950. At Yale he met L. Brent Bozell, who later married Buckley's sister Patricia. The notorious *God and Man at Yale* followed quickly after Buckley's departure from the university. Four years later he published *McCarthy and His Enemies,* coauthored with Bozell, and in 1959, *Up from Liberalism*. Buckley helped to organize Young Americans for Freedom in 1960 and shortly thereafter became a nationally syndicated, noted conservative columnist. His essays were assembled from time to time in various collections.

Buckley became practically a cult figure among many conservative readers in America, and some of his exploits were legendary. His devotees liked to remember how the brash and precocious boy of seven wrote a letter to the British government demanding repayment of its war debts to the United States.[10] Buckley himself recounted with fondness how he and his siblings responded to the erection of an unsightly billboard in downtown Sharon, Connecticut. They whitewashed the picture into obscurity.[11] At Millbrook, when the students were sent to pick apples, Buckley used the occasion to violate the school statutes by smoking cigarettes.[12] And on another occasion Buckley and his friends thought it sporting to crash-land a plane at the Ethel Walker School for girls.[13] *God and Man at Yale* surely came as no surprise to people who knew young Buckley. He had always exercised an outlaw temperament, and that trait of personality greatly colored his conservatism.[14]

Other influences also shaped that conservatism. While this son of Eli was working on the Yale undergraduate newspaper, the journal of which he would serve as editor during his senior year, the nation was taking note of some ominous affairs. It was learning of a curious man with a haunted past and a story to tell. Buckley, too, listened, and Whittaker Chambers enduringly affected the younger conservative's view of the world crisis. The two befriended each other and exchanged letters. After Chambers died in 1961, Buckley edited an anthology of Chambers' letters to him.

Chambers, of course, was the witness who pointed his finger at Alger Hiss, former employee of the State Department and president of the Carnegie Endowment for International Peace. Chambers charged that Hiss had been a member of the Communist party unit to which Chambers had belonged in the 1930s. But this issue was only nominal. As Chambers wrote in his autobiography, *Witness,* a work of dramatic influence in the conservative intellectual movement, "much more than Alger Hiss or Whittaker Chambers was on trial. . . . Two faiths were on trial."[15] Chambers confirmed for Buckley, as he did for many others, that the emerging Cold War between the United States and the Soviet Union was essentially a spiritual struggle, "a struggle of the human soul," and in the challenge of communism to freedom, the West faced "a total crisis—religious, moral, intellectual, social, political, economic." Chambers summarized his position succinctly: "I see in Communism the focus of the concentrated evil of our time."[16] The enemy was not only sinister, Chambers warned. Its zealous commitment, its fervent ideology, its transcendent purposes, and its lust to change the world had made it very formidable. However atheistic its philosophy, communism's vision was millennial, its prophecy apocalyptic.

The allure of communism to the weak of heart and the homeless of spirit was, Chambers warned, often irresistible. "Ye shall be as gods," wrote Chambers of the promise of communism. And he went on to warn that the West's greatest danger was complacency.[17] This warning from Chambers was the selection from his book *Cold Friday* that Buckley included in his own anthology of conservative writings. Communism will not be defeated, Chambers insisted, by the greater material achievement of the free world. It will be overcome only by a counterfaith, by a rival, vigilant, unrelenting spiritual brotherhood of free people.[18] Buckley would later say of *Witness:* "I was shaken by that book. I saw there a conjunction of style, analysis, romance, and historicity."[19]

Other individuals influenced Buckley—James Burnham, former Communist turned Cold War strategist, and Albert Jay Nock, impassioned libertarian and close friend of Buckley's father. But probably more important was the man whom Buckley called "my mentor," the singular Willmoore Kendall of Yale. Kendall was a native of Oklahoma, where his blind father was a preacher. He went to Oxford as a Rhodes scholar and identified himself with the Left until the time of the Spanish Civil War. That event made him bitterly anti-Stalinist, but his following of Leon Trotsky too was short-lived. Kendall returned to the United States and completed his graduate work at the University of Illinois. He was at Yale when Buckley arrived.

Chambers drew an intraversable line between communism and freedom, and Kendall similarly made hard-and-fast distinctions between liberalism and conservatism. A "battle line," he said, "stretches from the bottom of the chart of American politics all the way to the top, passing through pretty much every issue that enters our politics." Kendall warned of the "liberal revolution" that threatened America at home, and appealing to the "Great Tradition" of political theory that Kendall believed united Plato, Aristotle, Hobbes, and Rousseau, he spoke in defense of society's right to defend its cherished beliefs and values, its "orthodoxy." Rival proponents of the open society, inspired by John Stuart Mill and others, would, Kendall warned, erode this orthodoxy and betray the higher principle of democratic majoritarianism. To submit all opinion indiscriminately to the marketplace of ideas, Kendall warned, can only afflict the social will with a disabling relativism. American society is under no obligation to undergo such a trial, Kendall maintained.[20]

A militant anti-Communist, Kendall fortified his position in a manner that made him a formidable political theorist. And Kendall, who helped Buckley write *God and Man at Yale,* very likely influenced the younger man equally by force of personality.[21] Kendall was combative, abrasive, irascible. He became such a conservative thorn in the side of liberal Yale that the university opted for domestic tranquility, bought out Kendall's tenure rights, and left him to depart for a small Catholic college in Texas.[22]

Kendall's influence suggests the extent to which Buckley inherited a certain view of society that colored his perspectives on American life and politics. Kendall wrote critically of contractual views of society and excluded them from a conservative philosophy for America. Whether influenced by Kendall or others, Buckley himself was never satisfied that natural rights and self-interest could make a society, and like other conservatives Buckley considered such theoretical origins of the state to be a product of the rational liberal mind.[23] Buckley may well have accepted from Locke and Smith a kind of economic orthodoxy of free-market capitalism, but it did not thrive as a dominant ingredient of his conservatism. By the 1980s it was scarcely present in his editorial offerings. Buckley, in fact, adhered much more strongly to a conservatism of collectivity, of national community, and of cultural cohesiveness, than of Lockean rational self-interest. For him, as for Rousseau, enlightenment was never enough to establish society.

Buckley finished at Yale as the 1950s were beginning. This decade, which historians still too easily dismiss as a "conservative" era, one of dull conformity and staid tastes, would help define permanently the character of Buckley's conservatism. Actually, Buckley shared liberals' complaints that America had become complacent, its culture increasingly one-dimensional, its spirit passionless. But if that were so, then the causes were also clear to Buckley: liberalism, he believed, had become ascendant in America, and the conservative had become the outsider. Buckley reflected on his entrance into Yale University in 1946: "I brought with me a firm belief in Christianity and a profound respect for American institutions and traditions." These ideals included free enterprise and limited government. Yale believed differently and taught otherwise, Buckley later wrote. Its academic programs, as he described them in *God and Man at Yale,* promulgated a "thoroughly collectivist" economics, with redistribution of income as a "sacred goal."[24]

Nor was Yale any longer the school of the prophets. Its views toward religion, Buckley insisted, were condescending, sometimes derisive. Buckley's report was an early piece of investigative journalism. He reviewed professors' lectures and inspected the textbooks they used. What, Buckley asked, was one to make of a textbook that speculated in this manner on the sources of religious experience: "It is interesting to note that when the part of his brain thought by the phrenologists to be the center of religion is stimulated, a man twitches his leg."[25]

God and Man at Yale not only launched Buckley into prominence as a conservative writer, but it was also an early landmark of conservatism's emerging case against the New Class. Though it focused on one institution, it anticipated the divisions in the United States that became de rigueur among the later New Right and among neoconservatives too. The Yale faculty that Buckley examined seemed to be in isolated and conspiratorial revolt against the political and religious ideals of the rest of the country. Yale, after all, was assumed to be the institutional locus of American traditions, and its task was to prepare new generations that would perpetuate them. But it had become the enemy within.

Buckley himself made his extended case against the dominant culture of America in *Up from Liberalism.* Liberalism, he complained, had become "powerful but decadent." While Chambers and Kendall were outlining in their writings the great intellectual and spiritual conflicts of the age, liberals were celebrating the "end of ideology." Their spirit was pragmatic and accommodationist, Buckley believed. This spirit, he said, yielded a "dissolute disregard for principle" that eviscerated the national will. Liberalism was anemic, Buckley warned. Its spokesmen were passionate only against passion, and "they place an immoderate emphasis on moderation." Buckley recoiled from the agnostic temperament of liberalism, its disdain for permanent truths, its disrespect for the national orthodoxy that Kendall had said must be held sacred.

Reigning philosophical notions of truth, Buckley warned, were depriving truth of its partisan character, rendering it no longer something worth fighting for. In the public arena this triumphant relativism numbed the political impulses of the citizenry.[26]

Liberalism, Buckley found, presented a smiling face and a benevolent motive, but it was essentially arrogant in character, especially in its smug assumption that conservatism was no longer a live option for American life. Indeed conventional academic wisdom now taught that there was no conservatism in America at all and that there never had been in the country's history. Such a view issued from political scientist Louis Hartz in 1955, when he theorized in *The Liberal Tradition in America* that liberalism was the only tradition in the United States. Hartz recognized that liberalism had opponents, but these outsiders were only ad hoc agglomerations united temporarily by proximate interest. Liberals were also finding that one could purge America of a conservative tradition by making conservatism an aspect of abnormal psychology, a vehicle of the dark and irrational forces in certain strata of the population. From the intellectual Left that view yielded the thesis of T. W. Adorno's *The Authoritarian Personality* in 1950.[27] It served in Buckley's judgment to render conservatism prima facie an irrational idiosyncrasy.

Well into the 1960s Buckley bridled at the facile negating of conservatism in America by liberal interpreters. In a 1966 essay, "What the Professors Are Saying," Buckley took on historian and liberal Richard Hofstadter. Conservatism baffled Hofstadter. In an age marked otherwise by the enlightenment brought by rational liberalism, he could explain conservatism only as the result of certain irrational atavisms in American life. Thus, ethnic loyalties and traditions, religious attachments, sentiments of national and racial pride, and moral imperatives about freedom and liberty appeared as anomalies in the liberal understanding. When these mainstays of conservatism got in the way of the liberal program for America, said Buckley, one dared not address conservatism as a serious intellectual phenomenon. One looked instead to aberrations revealed by social psychology.[28]

And yet Buckley had to concede that the liberals had a point. For what had become of political conservatism? It had indeed been pushed aside. The liberal 1950s, Buckley believed, found its ideal leader in President Dwight D. Eisenhower. In Eisenhower, Buckley thought, Americans reared a president who dissolved the great world struggle of freedom against communism, who smiled it out of existence. Eisenhower personified to Buckley the "blandness of Modern Republicanism."[29] He was a bad influence and a "miserable President." Against the brutal and cynical powers of darkness in the world, Buckley wrote, Eisenhower opposed the benevolent goodwill of his own trusting nature and the "sentimental faith" of millions of Americans.[30]

In a historical situation fraught with peril, Buckley maintained, liberalism's armor was as lightweight as a cheesecloth. The enemy was fortified with a powerful faith that rallied the heart and the will. Its dogma provided it an eschatology that enabled its loyalists to endure defeat after defeat and still fight for the cause. No rival philosophy, Buckley was convinced, could overcome the Communist challenge if that philosophy could not rule the inner lives of people, their wills and their emotions, more dominantly than the Marxist ideology ruled the lives of its adherents. In short, Buckley wrote in 1959, "the secular ideology of liberalism, which sets the tone of contemporary Western thought, is no match for Communism because it is not a redemptive creed."[31] Four years later Buckley remarked that the United States would be losing the Cold War if there were not even a single Soviet spy in the country. Our statesmen and our foreign policy formulators, said Buckley, had drunk too much, in the colleges whence they came, of liberalism's soporific wines. "The classrooms of Harvard," Buckley wrote, "are simply no substitute for the playing fields of Eton."[32]

The needed reform, however, might begin at Harvard. What America required and what conservatism must supply, Buckley believed, was a fighting faith. On this issue, it is instructive to note, Buckley was at one with several postwar liberals such as Arthur M. Schlesinger, Jr., who were saying the same thing and warning that democracy had failed to rally the emotional enthusiasm of its people in the face of the appeal to security and belonging proffered by the world's totalitarian systems.[33] Buckley would also be in accord with later thinkers of the New Left who decried the pragmatic temperament and intellectual relativism of liberalism and who urged a recovery of ideology and absolutism in philosophy.[34] But Buckley and other conservatives nonetheless parted company with the liberals on the question of philosophical perspective. The great truths by which man lives, Buckley urged, are already known. We need only to refine and reinterpret them. Furthermore, teachers, from the grade schools to the colleges, ought not to be neutral about these verities. "Truth," Buckley wrote, "can *never* win unless it is promulgated."[35]

Nor could conservatism win unless it were rooted in some fundamental system of truth. Anxious to absolve conservatism from critics' charges that its appeal was idiosyncratic and disingenuous in character and anxious to deliver it as a power that met the emotional and spiritual needs of individuals, Buckley joined his conservatism directly to Christianity. His own commitments tied him particularly to a Roman Catholic faith that was rooted in the Church's ancient rites and commanded consent beyond what Buckley considered the fashionable and spurious innovations that were trying to merge the Church with the modern world. Buckley did not endorse the reforms of Vatican II or the discontinuance of other traditional practices, such as eating meat on Fridays. He wanted celibacy of the priesthood as a means of emphasizing Christian distinctions between the worldly and the spiritual. This dualism, furthermore, described Buckley's position on the Church and the world generally. In a 1978 *New Republic* essay titled "The Pope I Want," Buckley said that the Catholic pontiff must embrace all people, perhaps especially the poor. But Buckley felt compelled to offer an admonition: "In doing so [the Pope] must also emphasize the Church's primary mission on earth, which is to minister to the spiritual needs of man rather than to his corporal needs. Men are destined to suffer the vicissitudes of life, but the Pope is there to preside over an institution whose principal relevance is its irrelevance to terrestrial, if not mundane problems. . . . The Pope's capacity to superordinate the spiritual over the material is the highest skill his community can demand from him."[36]

But the larger importance of the religious factor is simply that by this connection Buckley's conservatism appropriated a transcendent truth, one that cannot succumb to the secular and shifting status of truth in the liberal definition. It seemed to matter little to Buckley that his argumentation was precariously axiomatic. Few will read him and be lifted into Christian theism by his claims for the faith, though to be sure Buckley never assigned himself that challenge. Furthermore, this quality of his conservatism often impaired Buckley's leadership in the conservative movement. While he welcomed anyone who brought to the movement the cause of liberty and freedom, he was quite willing, as the cases of Max Eastman, Ayn Rand, and Garry Wills demonstrated, to separate in peace from those who smarted under the heavy religious atmosphere of the *National Review*.[37]

The character of Buckley's religiosity, more dogmatic than theological in its presentation, elaborates an important point about his conservatism that we observed earlier: it was less striking for its ideology than for its style. The fact that in strict consistency it will not hold up does not negate its significance. For Buckley's pervervid rhetoric, his combative posture, and his impassioned engagement all expressed a cultural pattern deeply rooted in the American political tradition. We have to go back at least to the early nineteenth century to observe its origins.

Buckley's conservatism, through most of his career, typified the mentality of the outsider in America. In the early nineteenth century those who held this status (with the exception of Indians and slaves, who were wholly excluded from the political process) were those several populations of non-English ethnic immigrants and their first descendants. The dominant cultural strand in the United States was an Anglo-Saxon racial norm reinforced by a special

variety of New England Puritanism. That culture spread with migrating Con-
gregationalists and Presbyterians into the upper middle Atlantic, the Ohio
Valley, and the Midwest, and it established itself in both church and state.
It found political expression first in the Whig party and later in the Republican
party. The culture's leaders carried with them a precise image of themselves
and their mission. Historian Robert Kelley has written,"Whigs insisted that
they were the party of decency and respectability, the guardians of piety,
sober living, proper manners, thrift, steady habits, and book learning. . . .
Moralistic Whigs felt themselves bound by heaven itself to save such persons
[such as the dissolute folks that made up the Democratic party] from their
evil ways."[38] The rival party became in part a coalition of the outsiders – free
thinkers and the unchurched, rough, small-town commonfolk and hard-drinking
rivermen, German 48ers and other anticlericals, Lutherans and Catholics outside the pietistic boundaries of moralistic Protestantism, and, above all, Irish
Catholics.

Invariably these outsiders saw in Whig politics a kind of moral imperialism
threatening to their liberties and their folkways. The Whig political code invoked the power of the state to enhance the moral life of the nation, and
in state after state the issues of slavery, temperance, Sabbatarianism, and
other matters agitated the rival cultural groups and their political party leaders.
In their moral hegemony, in their effort to make the historical Puritan code
of New England an American national ethic, the Whig and Republican parties
often assumed a cosmopolitan cast, reinforced in turn by the tendency of
their leaders to ape English culture in fashion, manners, literature, and aristocratic
deference. The Democratic party, naming itself the party of "personal liberty,"
attracted those among the population likely to be defensive of their religion
and their folk culture. It was a party of provincials to a great extent. Democrats
defended against the moral imperialism of the Anglo-Saxon Whigs by sanctify-
ing an ethic of group loyalty, of tribal faithfulness, of clannish cohesiveness,
of ethnic differentiation. Andrew Jackson, who by deed and habit gave the
Democracy much of its character, dismissed the meritocratic standards of
office-holding in preference to a "spoils system" that rewarded personal loyalty
to the group. The Democratic party, it has been observed, became, under
the tutelage of the Irish above all, a kind of extended family, a kinship operation.[39] Proud of its folkish constituency and commonplace mannerisms, it
assumed anti-elitist prejudices that endeared it little to proper Bostonians or
others who disdained provincial habits.

This pattern in American political life is relevant not only to the early
years when it acquired form. We find it reemerging with special significance
in the Progressive Era, when Yankee reformers sought to recover lost in-

fluence in America by taking up the fight against the urban, ethnic political machines and the saloons that were their social affiliates. The personnel of these rival cultures have changed, of course, but the dialectics have not. Indeed the kind of conservatism of which Buckley is the major voice is one shaped by the mentality of the outsider, in this case by the conservative as a partisan of liberty against the moral imperialism of the liberal state. At least since the Progressive Era, when rational, impersonal standards for the moral and material improvement of the country became a dominant modus operandi of the modern state, voices in opposition have recoiled from what they persistently perceived to be the elitist and totalitarian character of the liberal state.

Moreover, in this opposition are the main wellsprings of contemporary conservatism. For what this kind of conservatism disdains in liberalism is its presumption of superior morality and higher wisdom, its propensity to remake society along the lines of its rational standards, its moralism, and its cosmopolitan pretenses, devices that convey the notion that New York and Washington speak for the nation, that federal bureaucracies, staffed by the educational elite of the eastern seaboard, can, unhelped, chart the nation on its appointed course.

What grates all the more, though, is the assumption of power by such an admixture of people who are indifferent to or disdainful of the religious and patriotic ways of the rest of the nation, the provincial Americans. Here is the same spirit that provoked the Jacksonian Democrats to recoil from what they experienced as the self-righteous superiority of their evangelical and Yankee Whig rivals.[40] And Buckley, son of a millionaire though he may have been, was also the son of a Texan and a Catholic with a provincial mistrust of the Atlantic plutocracy. Buckley also reflected in his selective defiance of authority the Jacksonian aversion to moral strictures from rulers. Buckley was no ideological libertarian, but he exercised a latitude in individual moral discretion that surpassed that of many other conservatives.

One need not make too much of this historical parallel. Buckley's conservatism derives in great part from the exceptional Buckley personality. Andrew Jackson extended his loyalty to friends to the nation at large, and he revered and valiantly fought for his country. But in another significant way the Jacksonian label fits. Let us remember that in that era the party of the provincials was also the party of a spread-eagle American patriotism, the voices of our "manifest destiny." And from the ultimate Jacksonian Democrat, Stephen Douglas, there boomed a loud nationalistic voice, championing provincial America but providential America, too.

The Democratic party ethos of the Jacksonians was heavily familial and communal. Buckley's was passionately so. In writing the introduction to the second edition of his *Overdrive,* his narrative of day-to-day life, in 1981, Buckley observed that most critics of the book had attacked it for its unabashed snobbishness (Buckley told in it, among other things, how he acquired his huge limousine). Only two critics, Buckley said, identified the book for what it was. One of them was Eliot Fremont-Smith of the *Village Voice.* This is a book about friendship, Fremont-Smith wrote. "Friends are . . . important, indeed all important. *Overdrive* is a record and celebration of connection, of how association (memories, locales, daily working intercourse, surprise, pleasure) improves the soul and perhaps the cause of civilization and bestows grace on all and sundry, by no means least of all" on the author.[41]

This author, who found liberalism too abstract, too rational, and too impersonal, always enlivened his writing with people. The conservative movement for Buckley was a family affair. It flourished with friendships within and struck forcefully at the enemy without. No reader can fail to observe this emphatic quality of Buckley's writings. From the beginning, with *God and Man at Yale,* Buckley named names. He dealt with liberalism not as a credo only but also as a power all the more real and all the more threatening because live people activated it. Liberalism became an affair of the devils and of their unwitting dupes. Then, too, personalism characterized Buckley's journalistic adventures on the conservative side. Perhaps it was because Buckley came from a family of ten children that the family style was always evident in the *National Review,* to which nine of the ten Buckley siblings at one time or another contributed. The "RIP" column of the journal regularly notes the passing of a beloved member of the extended conservative clan. From this column, the memorials penned by Buckley on the deaths of his father and mother and his sisters Maureen and Aloise have been especially moving.[42] Then in 1985, when Buckley issued yet another spy book, the dedication page listed some two dozen relatives! "We are not born for our own sake," Cicero wrote in *De Officus.* "Our country claims a share of our lives, and so do our friends."

Buckley's tribal conservatism had deep roots in American traditions. But his use of tradition differed significantly from that of other conservatives like Michael Novak, who celebrated the "new ethnicity," and Robert Nisbet, who invoked the role of those intermediate groups in American social life that deflect the direct authority of the state over the individual. The difference was that Buckley had taken the family ethic rooted in Jacksonianism and nationalized it, as indeed the early Democratic party had done. Buckley's conservatism was not "ethnic" as such: he once told a *Newsweek* interviewer, "I didn't know where Ireland was until I graduated from Yale." But his conservatism was a kind of extended tribalism. Out of it emerged the American family/nation, and it was from that vantage that Buckley judged the world. He viewed the nation as a coalition of people united by common values derived from their patriotism, their civic religion, and their general respect for a host of unarticulated norms, lifestyles, and prejudices that constitute an American way of life. These large majoritarian ideals claimed a priority, a transcendent ethic, and with them a demand for their vigilant defense against a host of assorted individuals and groups who shared no allegiance to them and who would use the courts, the media, and the citadels of learning to undermine or disparage them. From the 1950s and into the 1960s Buckley observed the progressive gains of these forces—of liberals, of vociferous radicals, of practitioners of the counterculture. In Buckley's imagination, these forces gained an ascendancy in America that, by the cruelest of ironies, made aliens in their own land all those who stood athwart the "Liberal Establishment."

The book that first dramatized this emerging state of affairs was Buckley's *McCarthy and His Enemies,* published in 1954 and coauthored with brother-in-law L. Brent Bozell. Buckley entered into the most controversial issue in American politics of the early 1950s. Wisconsin senator Joseph McCarthy had engineered a single-minded campaign to purge Communist party members and sympathizers who had made their way into positions of authority in the American government. To many, McCarthy was a tyrannical, bullying demagogue who ran roughshod over the individuals whom he so recklessly accused of disloyalty to the United States. As in all of Buckley's writings, names and personalities proliferate in *McCarthy and His Enemies,* and the book's title suggests Buckley's customary view of almost any issue.

This book's publication served as the occasion for the authors to address the charge that McCarthy was bludgeoning Americans into a yea-saying kind of anticommunism and creating an unthinking and dangerous kind of conformity in American society. The authors belittled such fears. But if McCarthyism served to solidify Americans around their traditional values, and Buckley and Bozell believed it did, then it was a healthy cause on that basis. For ultimately, the issue at stake was the right of society to defend those values. The claims for equal consideration by nonconformists and dissidents were illegitimate. "It is characteristic of society," the authors wrote, "that it uses its sanctions in support of its own folkways and mores, and that in doing so it urges conformity." Although there well may be some "thought control" in the process, it is quite reasonable and even healthy. The authors did not deny the right of new or critical ideas to be heard, but they did deny that those ideas have an equal claim to the public forum. "The Liberals," they insisted, "bewitched as they are with the value of innovation, tend to forget that a free market is one where the customers can, if they so wish, keep on trading with the same old butcher."[43]

The McCarthy issue reinforced in Buckley's mind his governing aphorism: There are those who are for us and those who are against us. Judis' biography of Buckley reports that as a boy Buckley thought of other children not merely as rivals but as "contemptible aliens."[44] And his dichotomous views highlighted Buckley's place and role in the conservative intellectual movement. The *National Review* that had welcomed all varieties of conservative opinion had molded conservatism not into an ideological movement but into a kind of spiritual brotherhood of family loyalties. In doing so the conservatives accentuated their remoteness from the rest of the intellectual community. They marked themselves as a group apart. Conservative thinkers seemed sometimes to sense a gap of communication, of language, between themselves and their leftist opponents. "There is no common vocabulary," Buckley once wrote, "between the [Irving] Howes and the [Whittaker] Chambers [sic]."[45]

In the same manner that the testimony and prophecy of Chambers helped solidify the spiritual brotherhood of conservatism in the postwar period, now in the 1970s the Russian émigré Alexander Solzhenitsyn was forging bonds anew. Solzhenitsyn had become the world's most prolific witness to the oppressiveness of Soviet communism. For Buckley, Solzhenitsyn's *One Day in the Life of Ivan Denisovich* and *The Gulag Archipelago* did more than any intellectual tracts to illuminate the great struggle against monstrous evil in which the West was engaged. "The only great eloquence in the world today," Buckley wrote in 1978, "is that of Solzhenitsyn and his fellows."[46] Buckley had said, in reference to Solzhenitsyn's books, that "by them we are annealed into a brotherhood, with a sense of mission marked by that grace which reminds us that, ultimately, we owe each other everything—even our private resources of self-destruction, of release." Solzhenitsyn was giving a new emotional élan to the conservative cause, Buckley believed, furnishing its various elements "a kind of unity that defined the struggle." Solzhenitsyn also provided the kind of personal intimacy that Buckley's family conservatism felt compelled to nourish. "I feel differently," Buckley wrote, "in the company of men who have read Solzhenitsyn." Buckley could only be appalled then when President Gerald Ford in 1975 refused to greet Solzhenitsyn at the White House. Only one explanation sufficed: "No," Buckley wrote of Ford, "he could not have read Solzhenitsyn."[47]

It is instructive to observe how Buckley carried this style of conservatism into specific issues and topical debates. Certainly one intellectual matter that tried the minds of conservatives and liberals alike was the issue of personal freedom, the just claims of the individual against the state and the priorities of individual preference against public norms. And it is at least a measure of the improving quality of debate in the last two decades that nearly all prominent conservative thinkers have moved away from frozen libertarian ideology on these matters. Buckley carried a libertarian slant into Yale, but repeatedly then and since his libertarianism was qualified by his deference to the social and cultural norms of society, by the defensive posture through which the tribal leadership protects against the incursions of the alien and against the erosion of the tribe's ancient ways. The tensions between these two persuasions—the libertarian and the majoritarian—effectively dissolved ideological consistency on Buckley's part, and they rendered his conservatism on this issue more cautious and moderate than on any other matter.

Buckley's commentary on private and public rights ranged widely over a number of specific issues. The conservative, he said, recognizes the legitimate needs of government regulations but must be vigilant nonetheless, for the liberal is simply too cavalier about the abuses of power and acquiesces too readily in the schemes of the state.[48] The conservative, even when the government oversees internal security, should, for example, blow the whistle on the use by the state of powerful listening devices against private citizens. Privacy is the key to liberty. Government ought not to legislate against smoking, however legitimately it may try to alert the public to the dangers of the habit. Ultimately the individual must choose.[49] With respect to pornography, however distasteful its artifacts, it is better, Buckley wrote, in the name of individual freedom, to be on the side of permissiveness.[50] Buckley was judicious but not ideological. Discussing the issue of no-knock rights for police investigations in private homes, Buckley warned libertarians to guard their criticism. If the drug problem in Harlem, for example, is, as Claude Brown urged, more serious to the black community than inadequate housing or poor schooling, one should not inveigh indiscriminately against practices that will wipe it out and reduce crime in the process. Privacy cannot be held so sacred that it threatens community.[51]

However much Buckley once proclaimed that mankind had learned certain fundamental truths, he had been reluctant to make them the immovable grounds of public policy. Too often, he found, abstractions and narrow ideology ran up against common sense. Such ideology can serve also to discredit prudent voices sympathetic to shared ideals. Buckley made this point in criticizing the inflexible and free-market antistatism of Murray Rothbard, whose rigid libertarianism Buckley considered injurious to the programs of more cautious proponents such as Ludwig von Mises, Friedrich von Hayek, Henry Hazlitt, and John Chamberlain.[52] Furthermore, Buckley believed, the extremist position is simply folly: it defies the national interest. "The defensive war in which we are engaged," Buckley wrote, "cannot be prosecuted by voluntary associations of soldiers and scientists and diplomats and strategists."[53]

But the liberal was no closer to the mark than the libertarian and suffered from a fallacy different in consequences. The liberal, according to Buckley, finds social prejudices, community mores, and folkways irrational. They should be made to yield to a higher reason, to an intelligent social planning, with a system of justice based on an abstract egalitarianism and formulated into as many Title X programs as needed. Buckley, paraphrasing the British conservative Michael Oakeshott, asserted that "rationalism in politics—which may be defined as trying to make politics as the crow flies—is the kind of thing that leads almost always and almost necessarily to tyranny." Let us recognize, too, Buckley added, that "many of the conventions of any society are irrational." But "a society that abandons all of its taboos abandons reverence."[54] He recalled the words of Hilaire Belloc: "We sit by and watch the Barbarian, we tolerate him; in the long stretches of peace we are not afraid. We are tickled by his irreverence, his comic inversion of our old certitudes and fixed creeds refreshes us; we laugh. But as we laugh we are watched by large and awful faces from beyond; and on these faces there is no smile." A morally neutral liberal society, Buckley believed, abandons its own self-preservation. We should have learned by now, he urged, that societies do not survive without the observances of certain common ideals and taboos. Most of these are healthy ones: they prevent chaos in the community at large and anomie among the citizenry. They deserve, Buckley believed, an *a priori* preference in law and public policy.[55]

These views of Buckley do not constitute a treatise on law and individual rights. They are far from constituting an ideology of these topics. Nonetheless, they are not peripheral to Buckley's conservatism or the traditions from which it sprang. They clearly reflect, in fact, what Andrew Greeley, in a stimulating chapter of his book *The American Catholic: A Social Portrait* called the "Catholic Social Ethic." That ethic, he found, was at odds with the modern intellectual tradition, especially in social thought. From a combination of Darwin, Marx, Weber, and Durkheim, Greeley said, "the modern" had come to mean "the rationalized, formalized, universalized, bureaucratized" restructuring of societies and the triumph of this process over "the local, the particularist, the informal, the nonrational." The Catholic Greeley spoke for the values of "the tribal, the local, the sacred, the particularistic" but found these dismissed by the modern intellect as "irrational." The Catholic social ethic brought to politics, Greeley argued, a limited role for the state to play in human affairs. "The Catholic is profoundly skeptical about remaking human nature through the manipulation of social structures," Greeley wrote. The state is more simply an agency for the facilitation of living, for effecting a measure of peace and tranquility, "in which flawed but basically good human beings can create and share common enterprises and activities by which they may stumble through life a little more easily."[56]

Buckley's views approximated this norm. Government and our laws, he believed, should have something to do with preserving the amenities of life that render it a little less strident, a little more bearable, a little less antagonistic. This prerogative can work to the well-being of minorities, too. Libertarianism should be curbed to the point that freedom for one does not mean the maligning of others. For example, is it not wrong, Buckley asked, to allow the performance of a play in which the horrors of Dachau are cast in a comic frame? Surely such a portrayal would be offensive to Jews, if not to others as well. And Buckley warned: "A people whose feelings are hurt withdraw from a sense of kinship, which is what makes societies cohere." He answered the inevitable question on censorship raised by such an issue as this: "I know all the theoretical arguments against it," he said, "but there's a tug inside me that says society perhaps has to maintain the right to declare certain kinds of aggression against the venerated beliefs of the people as taboo. This is a codification of grace, of mutual respect."[57]

Can such a codification emerge, we may ask in turn, when society divides bitterly, as it did in the United States on the question of race relations? Buckley discussed race and civil rights extensively, beginning in *Up from Liberalism,* in which he rattled his liberal critics with an extended plea for the legitimacy of the South's white majority. Liberals, he argued, had made civil rights exclusively a matter of abstract rational ideals, of racial integration, and of the extended numerical base of democracy. They had done so in defiant ignorance of historical realities, he added.[58] They had consequently missed the key to the improvement of the black race in America, the perfection of its community as a thriving ethnic culture. Buckley's pronouncements on race, naive though they often were, showed the force of his family conservatism and underscored his criticism of liberal policies.

Buckley essentially appropriated the cultural politics of the Jacksonians on this question also. Perhaps he would agree that the lesson of the experience of Irish Catholics and of other outsider groups in the American social spectrum was the necessity for them to promote their tribal ways while at the same time seeking to flourish within the larger American society. "Negroes helping Negroes," he wrote, is what the civil rights movement must come to. It is a matter of "self-consciousness," and the most astute of the black leaders recognize it, he added. "Negroes helping Negroes, relying upon themselves, educating themselves. The great psychological question," Buckley added, "is: Can Negroes achieve this solidarity, this self-consciousness, without—in pursuit of exclusiveness—encouraging the hatred of others? Can one be a proud Negro without being proudly anti-white?"[59]

Like the Cold War, the racial question also becomes a test of the inner faculties, of will and resolution. But to the question posed about blacks in

American life, Buckley answered: Of course they can be racially proud and loyally American too, as one can be proudly Christian without being anti-Semitic. Buckley wrote sympathetically about the flowering of the milder strands of African cultural nationalism that attended the black movement in the late 1960s. "They make one feel, on the whole, terribly glad for the resources of the human spirit," he commented.[60]

It must be said, though, that Buckley did not find his way easily through this problem. In 1984 Rev. Jesse Jackson became the first serious black candidate for the presidency and attempted to forge a coalition of black and ethnic groups, as well as poorer whites, into a broad reform movement. Buckley attributed Jackson's successes in some state primaries, however, to "exuberant tribalism." He warned that ethnic solidarity, on that principle alone, cannot be healthy. "We should not wish any political movement to succeed that says of a Jew or of a Protestant or of an Italian or of a Hispanic that he is primarily that, secondarily other things."[61] The Jackson phenomenon clearly appeared to Buckley as that kind of alienating tribalism that sets itself apart from the family nation.

But the white community, Buckley urged, should acknowledge and yield to the legitimate demands of blacks to be in control of their own districts and neighborhoods. The 1968 Brownsville–Ocean Hill school dispute in New York City was a case in point. This issue of local control of schools pitted a largely black residential community against mostly white, mostly Jewish schoolteachers, who insisted on the priorities of their professional discretion. Buckley argued for the higher priority of black control and against the strictly meritocratic standards that would create larger white representation in the teaching force of the schools.[62] What commanded consent, in Buckley's judgment, were those policies that enhanced a distinct group's cohesiveness. And when by the 1980s the decline of the black family had become a concern not merely to Harvard sociologists but to black leaders as well, Buckley blamed liberal welfare policies. The black family was in trouble in great part because the welfare system had deprived it of its spirit and had worked to "dissolve the bonds of loyalty" within it.[63] However one might again fault Buckley for an inward measure of a complex social problem, no one could be so smug as to dismiss as inappropriate Buckley's sensitivity to the toll on morality and morale that state paternalism was fostering in the black underclass.

Buckley's indictment of liberal leadership on this and other issues pointed to another aspect of his conservatism. For conservatism has usually been deferential to leadership and cordial to the notion that social progress is generated at the top by the rare wise and talented individuals who should be free to influence for the good of all. Historically, few conservatives have placed much trust in the wisdom of the masses or in the general opinion of mankind. That fact becomes especially interesting when raised in consideration of a person perceived by many to exude a haughty disdainfulness and aristocratic demeanor in his public role. And those polysyllabic words! What marks for erudition was Buckley trying to earn from his bewildered listeners? critics asked. Buckley, though, dismissed their aspersions as trivial. His critics, he said, do not sufficiently credit the average listener. For the average person is really "above average," he said. The charge of pretentiousness was really, he believed, a liberal feint to allege snobbishness against those who use big words. It was a ploy that masked a bogus egalitarianism. The average American was not for Buckley so banefully average as to resent the use of these words. The average American did not share the perversely democratic disdain for distinctions exercised by the learned flatterers of the people and was quite pleased to be instructed in linguistic melioration.[64] Democracy, in short, was perfectly capable of coexisting with standards and with the aristocratic spirit of improvement.

On this matter, one could easily confuse style and substance in Buckley, and probably many did. The host of "Firing Line" sounded like the Yale savant, erudite but priggish, eloquent and elitist. Buckley was often therefore described as aristocratic. But Buckley seemed not to be interested in tying his conservatism to particularly aristocratic standards. He was too much in the modern American mode. Consider that conservative writer Russell Kirk for many years wrote all his books on an old Smith-Corona typewriter bequeathed to him by his grandfather and that Kirk lived for many years in a Gothic farmhouse in rural Michigan. Buckley by contrast was featured in *Time* magazine in 1985 in an essay describing his enthusiasm for computers and word processors. That inclination of the heart should not alone deny to one an aristocratic spirit, but to an English critic like Henry Fairlie it suggested that something was missing. Fairlie also pointed to Buckley's constant mobility. His books acquired names like *Cruising Speed, Atlantic High, Overdrive, Racing through Paradise,* and *Airborne.* "Mr. Buckley is forever on the move," Fairlie wrote, "forever active, forever in flight." The true aristocrat, he added, is rooted like an oak to his estate, and he begrudges the world's intrusions.[65] Perhaps Buckley should have spent more time at his Hermitage.

Whatever the judgment on this matter, Buckley did from time to time play the role of the populist. Populism, of course, is a normal posture to assume for those who smart under Whig-liberal elitism. And to be sure, Buckley championed it cautiously and selectively. Genuine conviction rules, however, in Buckley's charge that American life rested more securely in the commonsense and traditionalist mentalities of the people in general than among the professors and literati who would presume to be their leaders in shaping the national culture. That conviction stood out in the most-quoted of the Buckley quotations: "I am obliged to confess that I should sooner live in a society governed by the first two thousand names in the Boston telephone directory than in a society governed by the two thousand faculty members of Harvard University."[66]

But Buckley was no George Bancroft, and his was not a case of the Ivy Leaguer trying to be at one with the masses. The public has its bad habits, Buckley knew, of which complacency and indifference are perhaps the most dangerous. If often cares too little for what makes for grace and beauty in public life. Regrettably, then, government must exercise some kind of higher wisdom when the short-sighted or uncaring behavior of private citizens would be harmful. From national parks to zoning laws, government must enhance the public domain and invoke, if necessary, the higher standards of civilized taste.[67] The libertarian and the traditionalist were not always at ease with each other in Buckley's thinking, but they were seldom at war.

Indifference, complacency, smugness—as Buckley observed America over three decades these characteristics of the public mind bothered him increasingly and did so especially with respect to the nation's foreign policy. Buckley's conservatism aspired to be a conservatism of the emotions and of the will. It would challenge the intellectual and moral relativism of liberalism by calling on the nation to exercise a new heroism, to take up its cross. On foreign policy, well into the 1980s Buckley believed there were still miles to go. The Bear was yet on the prowl, but American policy-makers seemed inattentive, and they had not read Solzhenitsyn. Buckley could say in 1988 what he said in 1967, when the Soviet Union celebrated the fiftieth anniversary of its revolution. Buckley, amid the toasts, made a pledge of his own: "Not to Forget."[68]

Three years later, in a 1970 interview with *Playboy* magazine, the interrogator asked Buckley to state what he thought was most important in the decade just passed. Buckley replied, "The philosophical acceptance of co-existence by the West." He added that, in a dangerous world, deference to the military might of an evil power, the Soviet Union, was understandable. But Americans, or their leaders, had convinced themselves somehow that the moral and spiritual struggle against communism no longer commanded their resolve.[69] Buckley had written as early as 1962: "Every time the sun sets, our knowledge of Communism evaporates just as little bit. Unless we work hard, day after day, to replenish our dissipating reserves, those of us who have known tend

to forget, and those who never knew — the generation coming out of childhood —
tend to grow up in ignorance of all those gruesome data about the nature
of the enemy we face." Buckley was unyielding in this concern. If the West
were not inspired by the righteousness of its cause and by dread fear of the
enemy, then, he believed, it was lost.[70]

Buckley's concern even led to some surprising judgments. As President
John F. Kennedy in 1963 sought to rally Americans to the challenge of the
moon venture, Buckley warned that a psychological peril loomed in this mission. Landing first on the moon, he warned, would be only a bogus manifestation of American national superiority. The United States did not need this
"galactic bombast" to make that point. If it had the will, then it could make
the point many times over in more tangible ways.[71] The Panama Canal was
another counterfeit issue that entrapped many conservatives, Buckley argued.
Our commitment to freedom and the defense of our sovereignty, he urged,
must not be compromised by matters of false pride. We need to emulate
the ways of the lion, not the peacock, and we would be better off spiritually
with a gesture of magnanimity and justice by assigning the canal to Panama.[72]

Let us, then, he urged, reserve our moral strength for the real fight. And
when the enemy was close at hand, Buckley could get the juices going. His
imagination scintillated, and his moral indignation rose. Two of the most
memorable pieces Buckley wrote in the early 1970s described his separate
trips to the Soviet Union and the People's Republic of China. His first tour,
in 1970, took him to the Soviet Union. Buckley immersed himself in the
splendor of old Russia, the imperial kingdom of the czars. He marveled at
the Winter Palace in Leningrad, a sterling blend of the "ridiculous and the
sublime," as he called it. There was nothing like it in all the West, he wrote.
Buckley explored imperial Russia with an expansiveness of emotions and
imagination. The czars' material collections, he related, "outmatch in vulgarity
and in beauty anything of the sort anywhere" and help us to understand why
Bolshevik culture is by contrast so drab.[73]

Then followed a visit to the Tsarskoe Selo, the summer palace of the czars,
and here too past blended poignantly with present in Buckley's reflections.
In this place, he recalled, the czar and his family once rested in captivity
in the aftermath of the revolution. Here Soviet guards taunted the fallen leader
by poking sticks into the wheels of the bicycle that he used for exercise.
The pathetic titan persistently picked up body and machine and renewed his
efforts. Sixteen months later, Buckley added, the czar and his family would
be shot dead in the cellar at Ekaterinburg.

What do these events tell us? Buckley asked. They show the new leadership
of Russia "already beginning to practice the trade in which it would become

proficient: ordering the execution of royal families, dissident ideologues, small landowners, prisoners of war, hundreds, thousands, millions." Buckley disavowed any wild leap of the imagination in these reflections, and added: "I thought, as I walked through the grass, towards the gutted palace, that it is all no more difficult than understanding the men who tumbled the czar's bicycle, an act, under those circumstances, as exhausting of the resources of human cruelty as would be the signing of the order to eliminate a million kulaks in order to prove a large institutional point."[74]

More momentous for history was the sojourn of President Richard Nixon in China in 1972. Buckley was invited as part of the entourage of reporters who accompanied the president, but he would have preferred that the trip not have taken place at all. Nixon described the venture as an opportunity to break decades of coldness between the two nations and to enhance the opportunities for peaceful relations. For Buckley, the whole thing was a sellout. This unwarranted gesture, he averred, was merely a measure of our indifference to the moral character of international affairs and of America's loss of faith in its own superior values. But something more about the trip bothered Buckley. Nixon was raising what should have been at best a mundane affair, perhaps a needed concession to world realities, into high moral drama. Only by reason of our "rare combination of satiety and self-abuse," Buckley wrote, could this sordid event take on so rosy a hue. There stood the president, "his glass raised high to Mao Tse-tung, toasting to a long march together, he and we, likening our two revolutions to each other." Such cordiality, said Buckley, bestowed on "the most merciless chief of state in the world," makes the great moral choices that modern history forces on us seem as incidental as a casual preference for gingham over calico.[75]

Very likely Buckley's judgments here reflected his recoil from the bitter experience of America's involvement in the Vietnam War. Buckley supported that involvement in principle but deplored its execution. Indeed the whole character of that war showed to him how much the United States had succumbed to an anemic will, how much it had lost an accurate sense of the struggle against communism, and how much it was betrayed from within. We need not review all Buckley's commentary on the war. It mostly illustrates the continuity of his Cold War perspectives. America's worst mistake, he said, was to see the war only in terms of military and political strategies. The character of the enemy, however, had not changed, and the world Communist movement still aimed ultimately at the defeat of the United States. Behind the North Vietnamese, he warned, stood the Soviet Union, "the greatest assault ever mounted on the human spirit." For Buckley, the world remained as Whittaker Chambers had described it. Buckley could write of the war,

"What is happening in Indochina is a contest of wills," but America was not up to the sacrifices needed to prevail.[76]

Precisely here Buckley's conservatism became precarious. However much, to its credit, it attained a degree of righteousness in its moral measure of communism, to that extent it risked not seeing things whole. If Vietnam was "a contest of wills," then it was a matter of the internal strength of the rival parties, a spiritual engagement in the manner of Chambers' formulation. But this turning inward of the conservative focus produces a narrow and abstract morality, one that fails to comprehend the inclusive situation in which statecraft takes place. As Hendrik Hertzberg wrote: "This argument implicitly recognized that the fate of Vietnam was, by itself, peripheral to the national security of the United States; it shifted the ground of discussion from the geopolitics of the map to the geopolitics of the soul."[77]

Buckley's family-style conservatism often had healthy effects, but when applied to the realm of foreign affairs, there were certain perils. For the Cold War in Buckley's rhetoric had all the markings of Highland clan warfare or timeworn family feuds in Appalachia. There was something reminiscent in it of the Hatfields and the McCoys. Not to Forget. Insult and injury neither die nor fade away. Past deeds are contemporary truths. To be sure, some things should not be forgotten, least of all the death toll of Soviet communism, among its own people most conspicuously. But the Cold War had long been a struggle for allies, the effort of the rivals to win the rest of the world over. In those quarters, family quarrels do not speak to realities. The United States has seldom been successful in causing the Third World to see modern history as the great drama it feels it so intimately to be. Other nations have their own family matters to confront.

The aftermath of the Vietnam War, however, can hardly be a source of comfort to those who criticized Buckley for his hard stance on it. Buckley's indignation continued to rise as, in the wake of the war, neighboring Cambodia collapsed into a sickening course of genocide at the hands of the Khmer Rouge. Indifference, acquiescence, and mere moral protest never seemed so callous in its consequences, and Buckley fumed. Congress, he argued, should have authorized funds for an international military force to save the Cambodians from their cruel murderers. "Our inactivity in respect of Cambodia is a sin," he wrote, "as heinous as our inactivity to save the Jews from the holocaust." And he asked, "Is there no practical idealism left in the world?"[78]

Just how far was Buckley ready to go in attributing to spiritual degeneration the horrors of contemporary history? In one instance, the Vietnam War brought out the worst in Buckley. As Americans learned with incredulity of what became known as the My Lai massacre, in which a young American commander, Lieutenant William Calley, ordered the indiscriminate shooting of Vietnamese villagers, women and children included, all of whom were presumably innocent of any action against the Americans or their allies, Buckley pondered how such an atrocity could have happened. The spiritual torpor of contemporary America emerged once again as the root cause. It was not the war itself that had destroyed the moral equilibrium of our soldiers, Buckley offered. The Lieutenant Calleys had already been unbalanced by their home culture. "Unbalanced by a society . . . deprived of the strength of religious sanctions [had Buckley forgotten the vandalism and desecrations of the Crusades?], a society hugely devoted to hedonism, to permissive egalitarianism, to irresponsibility, to an indifference to authority and the law."[79] But does not such a judgment deprive conservatism of one of its virtues, one often celebrated by Buckley himself—its stress on personal choice and moral responsibility for our individual actions? Is there nothing left then of individual guilt, either in the urban rioter who seizes the occasion to loot his neighbor's store or in the American soldier who makes the grim logic of war an excuse for barbarism?

Ultimately, nationalistic tribalism emerged as the dominant quality in Buckley's works. Once, when Buckley was a television guest on the popular "Johnny Carson Show," the host suggested that in our pursuit of armaments we were just as reprehensible as the Soviets. What! Buckley was enraged to see in Carson's comment a presumption of moral neutrality between the two superpowers. Had moral relativism become that pervasive?[80] It had, Buckley believed, and hence there was all the more reason to speak out bluntly. Referring to the United States and the Soviet Union, Buckley asserted: "The difference between us isn't that we are saints, and they are sinners. It is that we seek to be saints, and they seek to be sinners."[81]

It was, of course, just that point of view that gave a moral arrogance to Buckley himself. Provincial culture and patriotic love yield qualities of pride, mutual trust, and respect for ordinary people, and Buckley in his career displayed these qualities many times. But at another level this culture becomes defensive and vicious. It fosters smugness and self-satisfaction. How, Buckley asked, can anyone compare American "imperialism" with that of the Soviet Union? "I can't think of any country that we've 'dominated,' or 'imperialized,' Buckley wrote, " . . . that is worse off as a result of its experience with America than it would have been had we not entered into a temporary relationship with it."[82] American economic ventures in Latin America, Buckley boasted, provide for 20 percent of the jobs there.[83] And he rested his case on statistics. Overall, as Buckley presented it, the American cause was so right that any means to fulfill it became excusable. If our government "dissimulates," as

the "Pentagon Papers," revealing a secret war in Vietnam in 1971 demonstrated, why worry? "We feel, in our pores," Buckley wrote, "the ethical
difference" between this lying and the mendacious declarations of a Soviet
government that proclaims, for example, its desire for democracy in Eastern
Europe.[84] In 1984 when the United States secretly mined the harbors of Nicaragua, Buckley decried the stupidity of the act. We should, he said, simply
have declared war on this totalitarian regime and dispensed with the legalities
of our "peacetime" action. For if we are not prepared to bring down this
noxious government, even by dirty means, then, he said, we should repeal
"The Star Spangled Banner."[85] *La lutte continue.*

By the middle of the 1970s Buckley the outsider was becoming an insider.
A conservative mood was settling on the American people as Vietnam faded
from the headlines and as the Watergate drama exhausted its toll of national
self-abuse. By 1981 the country had in Ronald Reagan a president who publicly
called himself a follower of Buckley and a reader of the *National Review.*
Patriotism was in vogue and in 1984 the national media made much of its
rejuvenation. But as the insider, Buckley had a role to which he was not
accustomed and not adept (like most intellectuals in similar situations). His
critical commentary lost some of its edge, though it still reflected Buckley's
erudition. And it was troubled by the fact that, for all the fury of the antinuclear
protests, the Cold War seemed to have lost its chill. As presidents Ford and
Carter pursued accommodation with the Soviet Union, Buckley endured the
interminable talk about "détente" with a growing feeling of vexation. The
apparent rapprochement with the Soviets indicated to him how blunt the moral
edges of history had become. For mostly what came of détente, Buckley
found, were exchanges of toasts with Communist tyrants. So he could write
in 1975, with a seriousness that one is at risk in doubting, "I for one, yearn
for the days of the Cold War."[86]

   But the Cold War remained for Buckley every bit a reality, and he waged
it into the 1980s. He referred to the Soviet Union in 1983 as a "vast and
aggressive slave empire." He responded especially to events that would seem
to reinvoke the Cold War dramatically, especially events that gave him the
occasion again to sharpen his rhetoric and appeal to the imagination. Thus
in that year when the Soviet Union shot down over its territory a wayward
Korean passenger plane, Buckley made the lesson of it clear: "The awful
death of 269 people in a single airplane reminds us, more starkly than an
old-fashioned purge of a million of so faceless men and women whose lives
we never share, what it is like to be at the mercy of the new barbarians,

who have hold of the electricity Lenin coveted."[87] In the era of Mikhail Gorbachev, when the Soviet Union and the United States under President Reagan moved forward with major peace efforts, Buckley was there to sound familiar warnings. In his hand was a list of continuing Soviet abuses—in Nicaragua, Cuba, Ethiopia, North Vietnam, and around the globe. And yet, Buckley was ready to move perhaps one inch. He wrote: "Mr. Reagan does well to encourage changes in the Soviet system. Something wildly exciting is indeed going on in the Soviet Union. But to greet it as if it were no longer evil is on the order of changing our entire attitude toward Hitler on receiving the news that he had abolished one concentration camp."[88]

For foreign policy remained for Buckley a matter of loyalties, and he did not look lightly on flirtations with members of the rival clan. When Communist leaders like Nicolae Ceauşescu of Rumania or Tito of Yugoslavia visited the Carter White House and were toasted with proclamations of each country's interest in economic and social justice, Buckley delivered a sharp censure.[89] When Queen Elizabeth of England received Hua Guofeng of China, Buckley was roused to cite the litany of abuses associated with that country's forty-year experience with communism.[90]

In the late 1970s Buckley turned to a kind of vicarious living of the Cold War, for at that time he took up the mystery and spy novel genre. There now issued from his word processor such cloak-and-dagger adventures as *Saving the Queen, Stained Glass,* and *Who's On First?* Why this new literary departure? "To demonstrate that we are in a historical situation where we are the good guys and they are the bad guys," Buckley said.[91] So Buckley now contrived Blackford Oakes—Ivy Leaguer, adventurer, lover. There was every reason to think that Buckley might flourish at this literary trade. He had always enlivened his prose with people and their peculiarities; his commentary always had the keen moral tone and emotional élan that gave it verve and animation. But perhaps for these reasons, the Buckley spy novels were disappointing. Their characters were flat, their plots simplistic, their dialogue, with some notable exceptions, ordinary. They received a lot of good press, perhaps because their author was himself a striking media figure and an extraordinarily engaging personality. But what made Buckley compelling were his encounters with real people, especially with flesh and blood enemies, with nefarious powers and sinister movements. Buckley fought these opponents better and with greater inspiration than Blackford Oakes battled his fictional enemies.

Some would wish that Buckley might have vented his combative spirit in these imaginary realms and by these means buried it in the past. For it is a dangerous world, and Buckley's fighting words, to friend and foe alike, could be intimidating. But few had done better than he in seeing totalitarianism for what it is. Americans are a sentimental people and desperately wish that the world were a nice place. Buckley was a force for the good in telling them that it is not. And at a time when national self-hatred and a feverish hypochondria were infecting academy and press, there was even something healthy in Buckley's chauvinism, his tribal nationalism.

But these qualities of his conservatism were also its problems. They left Buckley vulnerable on two counts. Conservatives in the 1970s and 1980s often insisted that liberalism had fallen victim to naiveté and sentimentalism in shaping America's approach to the world and especially to its enemies among the totalitarian Left. They urged in turn a realist mentality and a franker assessment of America's enemies. Geopolitical considerations were urged as America's measure of a terrestrial conflict in which the struggle for power was constant and in which its response must be pragmatic. But family politics is not pragmatic. Its emotions, its memories, its dualism of friend and enemy, cannot always pause to take account of geography or the implications of politics beyond the immediate arena of conflict, the interlacing network of people and parties touched by national rivalries.

Second, conservatives like Buckley had the past on their side—leftist totalitarianism is the greatest political killer of people in the twentieth century—but they could offer less for the future. When every prospect of peace or every gesture of change appeared from the rival camp, conservatives could only warn of history's bleak record. But they could not indicate under what conditions some accommodation, some reduction of arms, even some mutual trust between the Soviets and the United States, might be possible. In this century, also marked by unrelenting and surprising change, conservatives of Buckley's disposition gave no openings. What they needed was a Jamesian sense of possibility, of contingency, of the unexpected. Who, after all, anticipated the annus mirabilis of 1989? Memory had taught conservatives much, but it had quieted confidence and hope. In a world in which the United States Constitution seemed the only document impervious to change, conservatives should have had the boldness to believe that continuing change in human affairs proffers possibilities. Too often they displayed a temperament at one with their political opposites, the prophets and doomsayers of the nuclear freeze movement, who saw only a one-track course of history. Conservatives needed to envision different roads to the future.

William Buckley liked to tell this story: "There are two strangers taking wine at a city in the French provinces. After a while one addresses the other, and asks, 'Do you like Americans?' 'No' is the curt answer. 'Well, then, do you like Frenchmen?' Again, 'No.' 'Well, do you like Jews?' 'No.' 'Catholics?' 'No.' Finally, with some exasperation. 'Well, whom do you like?' Without looking up from his newspaper. 'I like my friends.' "[92] Buckley fought for his friends.

3

George Will
American Whig

ONE HAD THE impression that George Will was born conservative. No radical ghosts lurked in his closet awaiting an exorcising in their keeper's maturer years. Will liked to boast that he was a member of only two organizations—the Victorian Society in America and the National Trust for Historic Preservation, both guardians of the republic's ages of splendor. He defined "old" as the loveliest word in the English language and asserted that "a lot of things I frown upon would, I know, be an inventory of the modern age."[1] Even the way he wrote suggested to others Will's elegant antiquarianism. Said one commentator: "Mr. Will writes prose as polished as a silver candelabrum, by the light of which he would like to be read." But the reviewer also added that a Will essay reads just as well on a New York City subway.[2]

The immediate intellectual influences on Will were familiar ones. His grandfather was a Lutheran minister who served parishes in Pennsylvania and Maryland. A household that wrestled with such conundrums as free will and salvation by faith seems to have inspired the philosophical mind of Frederick Will, George's father, who taught for many years at the University of Illinois. And however much such weighty matters also gave intellectual sobriety to the Will home in Champaign, where George was born in 1941, they did not chill the enthusiasms owed to youth, and Will remembered happy midwestern beginnings in this citadel of academia and agriculture, where the Illinois Central Railroad pursued its journeys between Chicago and New Orleans, visible for miles in an awesomely flat and majestic terrain. Something in these roots, one might speculate, preserved Will from the trendy styles of New York or San Francisco and the fashionable modernities of suburbia. This resistance prevailed despite Will's eastern education at Trinity College in Hartford, Connecticut, and, after a period in England, graduate work at Princeton University. But the choice of the latter institution, Will avowed, was dictated by its location between two National League baseball cities, New York and Philadelphia, that afforded Will access to his beloved Chicago Cubs.

For a time Will aspired to an academic career. He had earned a doctorate in political science at Princeton and held brief teaching positions at Michigan State University and the University of Toronto. But Will felt isolated from the American scene in Toronto, and when the invitation came from Colorado senator Gordon Allott to join his Washington staff, Will responded eagerly. Politics suited his literary inclinations. Will became Washington editor for the *Washington Post* and *Newsweek*, then contributor to the *National Review* and the *American Spectator.* In 1977 he received the Pulitzer Prize for distinguished commentary. By this time he had garnered esteem and recognition. His Sunday appearances with David Brinkley on ABC television, his widely syndicated editorializing, and his own professional embroilments were making Will a subject of the news itself. When Phil Donahue described guest George Will as the most influential journalist in America in 1987 he was not simply exercising the courtesies of a host.[3]

There was, in fact, one liberal skeleton in the Will closet. Will had entered the 1960s enthusiastic for a reinvigorated America as promised by John F. Kennedy. This young Democrat's calls for a United States renewed by its commitments to freedom around the world, by its resolve to close the missile gap between the United States and the Soviet Union, and by its evocation of a youthful patriotism found Will lending his applause. But this kind of liberalism was in its last years of nationalistic idealism. Will, like other conservatives and neoconservatives alike, would watch it grow tepid, compromising, and waning in its conviction of America's moral superiority to its rivals.[4]

Will loved to call himself a "Tory" conservative. For his American readership, unaccustomed to such language, Will gained a measure of notoriety and luster. There seemed to be something quaint and curious in this self-labeling, and Americans who otherwise depended on "Masterpiece Theatre" and other embellishments of English finery for the veneer of high culture were quite possibly among those readers who found Will at the very least a beguiling eccentric.

We shall have to confront the Tory designation, for indeed it had its deceptions. But Will pressed it forcefully, and no less so than on writers and solons who called themselves conservatives. As much as any writer of his time, with the possible exception of Russell Kirk, Will tried to define the real meaning of conservatism. Too few "conservatives" in America, he believed, had any notion of it. "The conservativism for which I argue," wrote Will, "is

George Will by Vint Lawrence

a 'European' conservatism." He traced his philosophical pedigree to Edmund Burke, John Henry Newman, and Benjamin Disraeli, but that lineage should not obscure an American conservative tradition that includes Irving Babbitt, Paul Elmer More, Peter Viereck, and Russell Kirk.[5] It is a traditionalist conservatism rooted in respect for antiquity and in a profound skepticism toward human nature and in turn toward all claims for the easy perfection of human

life. For Will and his intellectual progenitors adhered to a conservatism especially sensitive to the forces of disorder and social disintegration. This conservatism has sought to locate the stabilizing influences of time and place as
correctives to the heady impulses of the day. It has attempted to link the
past with the present. Burke celebrated these objectives in the eighteenth century, and so did G. K. Chesterton in the twentieth. "Tradition," said Chesterton, "means giving votes to the most obscure of all classes, our ancestors.
It is democracy of the dead."[6] No true conservatism can flourish without
that spirit, Will insisted. A mere defense of liberty will not suffice. Mere
free-market economics will not suffice. And the loyalty to such contrivances
among some "neoconservatives" rendered them, in Will's judgment, conservatives manqués. The neoconservatives, Will wrote, "do not have stained-glass
minds."[7]

In fact, however, Will's conservatism was quite willing to step outside cathedral doors and walk among the people in the streets. Will used the Tory
label too much for his own good, and to critics and friends alike it fostered
the deception, to those who knew not the conservative tradition of a Burke
or a Disraeli, that Will was obstinately aristocratic, even an American snob.
But at the heart of Will's conservatism was a certain democratic enthusiasm
and a respect for the decent civilization wrought by ordinary Americans.
In his historical reflections Will's writings showed more appreciation for the
diurnal achievements of plainspeople in sod houses on the prairie than for
the bewigged authors of the American Constitution. American civilization
grew from "the routine mud of common experience," Will wrote, and its
accomplishments were more than a little heroic. "In the United States," Will
urged, " . . . the achievements that stun the imagination were not performed
by politicians, or generals with shiny boots, but by plain people with mud
on their boots—the sort of people who walked to Oregon behind creaking
wagons."[8]

It would be difficult, in fact, to affix an aristocratic label to a columnist
who could editorially praise the charms of such maligned cities as Cleveland.
But Will did so with ease.[9] And what shall we make of a "Tory" conservative
who could warm to the mass hysteria of a Bruce Springsteen rock concert?
(Will's misguided attempt to read Springsteen into the conservative camp betrayed
conservatism's own rule that enthusiasm should not overrule reason.)[10] What
was one to make of a Victorian apologist who could thrill to the enthusiasm
of Nebraskans for their beloved college football team?[11] But Will's conservatism was in fact quite expansive. Travel a little way outside of cloistered
Washington, D.C., and follow Will to La Plata, Maryland, where Little Leaguers
and their fans have gathered for the annual all-star game at the American

Legion field. The occasion offers the reader a glimpse of George Will's America, and it offers the columnist the opportunity to make some invidious distinctions. Will observes the phenomenon at La Plata of "tailgating." "But La Plata tailgating," he points out, "is not what is done with Volvo station wagons at the Yale-Harvard game, where the Perrier flows like water, washing down pâté." La Platans prefer RC Cola and hot dogs.[12]

Such discoveries also represented for Will another profound point, that conservatism is a celebration of place, of regional variety and local color. Russell Kirk once called it "an affection for variety and complexity." For the traditionalist mind, Will believed, such enthusiasms are crucial. They distinguish love of democratic norms and the ways of common people from heady, indiscriminating populism, and they defend against the mechanical uniformity and standardization that inspire the rationalist and utopian reformers who would so readily change the world by ideology and blueprint.[13]

What there was of a conservatism in these references is a prejudice for the tried and habitual against the new and fashionable. At least by the end of the 1970s Will was finding that middle-class America had succumbed to all kinds of trendiness, and by 1984 journalists were referring to the visible votaries of these ways as "Yuppies." Will found the landmarks of this life curiously but not innocently superficial—the butcher-block kitchens, the pasta-makers, the Nautilus exercise machines, the stress-management courses, the cordless phones. Will feared that America had become, as historian Daniel Boorstin described it, a series of "consumption communities," where the thin and random associations of the marketplace had replaced communities of memory and continuity. Only a few years before Will had witnessed the social transformation firsthand, in his years with the Colorado senator. Will described Allott as a product of the old Colorado, that of the mining camps and the wheat fields of the West. But he became the political victim of an inrushing new constituency in the state—educated, affluent, mobile, young, modern, and indifferent to the old ways. They made Colorado an enclave of New England–style ski resorts and chic boutiques. But fashionable America, Will warned, was making a science of snobbery and forging for itself a desolate and soulless inner life. Listening to Alexander Solzhenitsyn use a Harvard commencement address to decry America's obsession with materialism, Will applauded.[14] And Will, who himself lived in comfortable Maryland suburbia, apparently believed that one can be in the world but not of it.

Another characteristic of Will seemed also to be little noticed. While commentators said much about his polished prose, they said little about his wit. But humor too is a conservative trait, and in Will it came in many varieties. He once wrote of columnist Jimmy Breslin that "he unfailingly indicates where

wisdom lies by taking positions diametrically opposed to it."[15] He dismissed
the pretensions of philosopher Jean-Paul Sartre by defining existentialism
as "the belief that because life is absurd, philosophy should be, too."[16] Will
wrote in 1984 that "Phil Donahue has moved his show from Chicago to New
York, improving the cultural life of both cities."[17] But Will's humor was
also playful. When he once referred to America's "newspaper of record,"
he added parenthetically for the uninformed that of course he was referring
to the *Sporting News*.[18] On learning that some scientists had studied the brain
of Albert Einstein and located the part of it responsible for the deepest thinking,
Will suggested that we might now better understand baseball's infield fly
rule.[19] And on another occasion, Will wrote: "Thirteen months ago I bought
my first Elmore Leonard novel, in Cleveland, his kind of place. . . . Recently,
a newspaper story announced his new novel, *Glitz*. I put down my sandwich
and drove to a bookstore. It was a peanut butter and pickle sandwich, so
you know that Leonard is good."[20]

To many, and to conservatives especially, Will seemed something of a
maverick conservative. For Will, being antimodern did not mean being an-
tiprogressive. Conservatism, he believed, should not equate with an opposition
to those social programs that have become staples of the modern industrial
state and the prime responsibilities of government. For not only did
conservatives—Disraeli and Bismarck—inspire and engineer state welfare,
they did so, Will believed, for reasons intrinsically conservative and not merely
utilitarian. The Social Security system born of the New Deal years was one
such program that Will staunchly defended. It reflected, he insisted, an essential conservative notion of citizenship, the bonding of generations and the
ideal of the collective well-being of a people who constitute themselves a
nation. But he found American conservatives fighting a "reactionary" war
against the philosophy that legitimates this and similar programs. The effect
was to make conservatism, and the Republican party in which such sentiments
were often housed, not only unpopular but irrelevant to some of the nation's
most important purposes.[21]

Will's attempt at reconciliation with the New Deal legacy was not a new
mode in the literature of American intellectual conservatism, however much
Will felt compelled to invoke Disraeli and Bismarck as his models. Will's
point here in fact reflects the spirit of Peter Viereck's important contribution
of 1949, his book *Conservatism Revisited*. Restating a Burkean idea that every
nation must be guided in its policies by the ideals, institutions, and traditions
that have shaped it, Viereck reminded his readers that in the United States
the only authentic political tradition was liberalism. It was time, he believed,
for conservatives to accept the New Deal as expressive of the humane values

Americans revered.[22] The problem of democracy for Viereck, and for Will, was the protection of democracy from its worst tendencies, an indiscriminate leveling and the culture of mass society. In essence, both Viereck and Will would champion a conservatism that incorporated empathic aristocratic principles, carefully defined and described.

Will insisted that conservatism always has something to do with the collective higher values of a people. But these values do not spring intuitively or spontaneously from the national life. Their existence is a product of nurturing, their survival a process of education. Such was the role of the trustees of the culture. But the matter did not end there. Will insisted that citizenship is also economic, that it builds on material security and a sense of belonging that derive from the fulfillment of basic human needs.[23]

Will appealed to Lord Shaftesbury, the late-seventeenth-century reformer/aristocrat: "His life reminds us," Will wrote, "that a determined assault on poverty is not only compatible with conservatism, but should be one of its imperatives in an urban, industrialized society."[24] Furthermore, Will said, conservatives should be leading the fight for welfare programs that prevent disintegration of families. For the toll that social disintegration takes in crime, unemployment, and ignorance is a deduction from the cohesive bonds that preserve the social organism.[25] Will wanted to extend a protective paternalism to all helpless members of society. Without the minimum conditions of material security, Will warned, society is fractured by alienated, uprooted, and angry elements. The order that society needs may then find its source only in a brutal totalitarianism that absorbs all freedoms. Germany in the 1930s teaches us this lesson, Will believed, as does Iran in the 1980s. Apprehensively, Will asked the question, "Can there be conservatism with a kindly face?"[26]

Will's political philosophy bears further examination within the literature of American conservatism, and one fruitful comparison is with Irving Babbitt. To be sure, Will never formulated a conservative philosophy in quite so sharp and supple an outline as did the influential Harvard literary scholar, author of such works as *Rousseau and Romanticism* (1919) and *Democracy and Leadership* (1924). But Will cited Babbitt as an important figure in his own canon and furthermore provided a late-twentieth-century illustration of a traditionalist mode of conservation, of which Babbitt was the most profound voice. Will, with a journalist's sensitivity to the events and trends of the day, also gave substance to Babbitt's idealistic conservatism.

Both Babbitt and Will believed that human nature and human society were fragile entities. Babbitt and his colleague Paul Elmer More based their New Humanism on a philosophy of human duality. They emphasized a principle of discipline and control in the human personality, set against a countervailing principle of expansiveness and resistance to all restraints. In his writings Babbitt judged the French romantic Jean-Jacques Rousseau the major corrupting influence on Western culture and always associated romanticism with the celebration of the specific individual at the expense of a universal human nature as best depicted in classical and neoclassical literature.

But for Babbitt this dualism had long been under siege in the West. Its enemies were Rousseau and his heirs, but the attack came also from a later tradition of philosophical naturalism which as readily dissolved the inner tensions of the human soul by describing all of human behavior as product of the dominant external forces that shaped personality. It is perhaps useful to note how much George Will's writings placed themselves into that kind of perspective and what additional uses he made of Babbitt's philosophy. For when Babbitt measured the impact of the antidualistic traditions of romanticism and naturalism on American life, he felt compelled to label the country at once the most sentimental and the most mechanical of civilizations. Will's essays over nearly two decades reflected that judgment year after year.

Will's writings amounted to a long chronicle of the triumph of the individual over the priorities of the larger community. We shall return to Will's sustained critique of individualism and the libertarian ideology, but we note at this point that Will shared with Burke, Babbitt, and other conservative thinkers an acute sense of the fragility of the social order and the imperative need to devise protections for it. In appealing to the "moral imagination" of Burke against the "idyllic imagination" of Rousseau, Babbitt insisted that the problem for society was the same as the problem for the individual—how to supply for it the contents of a higher self that will be the stabilizing, disciplining, and controlling influences against the dominant, emotional appeal of the hour. Americans, Will urged, should not be smug about the fate of Germany in the 1930s. A great nation fell with surprising ease to the centrifugal forces in modern social life, providing a lesson in how rebarbarization can occur even in a nation of illustrious cultural achievement.[27]

In the United States, Will believed, a history of immigrant diversity and democratic hostility to form have enfeebled the sense of higher national life and the symbols that express national unity. Will observed that in 1977 at the same time that Queen Elizabeth II in England was celebrating her Silver Jubilee amid regal splendor and public rejoicing, President Jimmy Carter in this country was going before national television sporting a sweater.[28] One is reminded of Babbitt's regretful comment that in the romantic culture of democracy "we descend to meet."[29] Democracy cannot automatically be the source of its own better life. Will and Babbitt confronted an authentic conservative problem in trying to locate those appeals to the imagination that were both unifying and ennobling.

Conservatism, Will believed, begins with a sense of collectivity, with the fact of belonging among all members of a nation. But conservatism is not democratic deference and is not at home in a society that is indiscriminately commonplace. Nor can it trust to nature or history to produce the standards of decency and decorum that make life sufferable. "A society can no more subsist without gentlemen," Will quoted John Adams, "than an army without officers."[30] But ladies and gentlemen are social artifacts. They represent adherence to a high human ideal that requires social training for its realization. Will denied any society the right arbitrarily to change its historical norms and models. In an age of changing sexual habits and ideologies, that kind of traditionalism made Will a controversial voice of dissent. The American Psychiatric Association, Will believed, was simply wrong in its decision to remove homosexuality from its list of "mental disorders." However uncertain the causes of homosexuality, Will wrote, we know that it is abnormal. And it is not incumbent on states to favor by statute the demands of every group that prefers nonconformity.[31]

In the United States of the later twentieth century, Will believed, a transcendent public spirit was losing out to omnipresent dissenting factors. Such a condition was a wholesale conspiracy against the flourishing of any authentic conservatism. For "politics," Will wrote, "should be citizens expressing themselves as *a people,* a community of shared values."[32] But our politics, he added, has become "an anarchy of self-interestedness" that reflects a social disease, an inability to think of the public interest, the common good. The cynical and self-serving conspiracy known as Watergate dramatized this problem as much as any other in the 1970s. But Will saw no lesser sins in the earlier lawlessness of southern white supremacists, in self-righteous and militant civil rights activists, and in the antiwar obstructionists in the Vietnam War years. All had in common a contempt for institutions and the laws that sustain them. Will urged that the fabric of authority in American society had a "transcendent value" more commanding of loyalty than any passing or narrow interest.[33]

Could contemporary America foster the kind of unity of spirit for which Will pleaded? Could a nation of 230 million people, as one commentator asked, create such a sense of community? After all, the observer said, we are no longer in John Winthrop's little Puritan colony.[34] Will maintained that a nation does not need uniformity (the ways of a totalitarian state) and only some unity. But he did believe that modern liberalism had become excessively tolerant of some things that are clearly defiant of that minimal unity. A case

in point was the controversy over bilingual education. Will considered bilingual education an affront to the common culture of America, and he cited
the unfortunate experiments with it in Belgium and Canada. The partisans
of this education, he warned, were functioning under a degraded concept
of citizenship. "This age," Will warned, "defines self-fulfillment apart from,
even against, the community. The idea of citizenship has become attenuated
and is now defined almost exclusively in terms of entitlements."[35]

Will, however, did not lay the weakening cohesiveness of language at the
feet of poor immigrants and their myopic sympathizers. Other forces were
at work. Advertisers sold gas-guzzling automobiles that they labeled "personal
size Buicks." Language becomes corrupted, Will said, when the official terminology of law and public policy changes the word "prison" to "correctional
institution" and neuters the moral content of crime in the process. Our language, Will wrote, is being reduced to a "shapeless, tasteless pulp." And
the consequences are not trivial. For as our language weakens, as it obscures
fact and distorts meaning, so does its usefulness as a bond of unity and trust
among members of society diminish. People consequently develop a general
and unhealthy skepticism about communication, in the marketplace and in
the political arena.[36]

The decay of public spirit in American life became a recurring theme in
Will's journalism. It was a matter about which conservatives especially, he
felt, were insufficiently concerned. They were so, he believed, because conservatism in the United States had too long embraced a libertarian ethos that
had celebrated the rights of individuals over the prerogatives of the state
and the judgments of the community. Will, to be sure, was no enemy of
freedom, and his critique of liberalism faulted it for neglect of liberty in
favor of equality. For Will, however, there were simply too many freedoms
in contemporary America—freedom for abortion, for pornography, for businesses trading with the Soviet Union, for exemption from the military draft.[37]
Thus, the live-in partner of actor Lee Marvin, flaunting social norms in the
name of personal choice, sues for Marvin's wealth and appeals to society's
laws for recompense. Few, said Will, note the contradiction.[38]

Will seemed to feel that the effective way to get something was not to
describe a personal or public benefit from one's action but to demand that
something as a right. Sadly, said Will, we have reached the point at which
Congress, in the Pregnancy Discrimination Act, requires employers to pay
for leaves of absences for female employers to obtain abortions, even discretionary ones.[39] Meanwhile, fifty million abortions are performed annually
around the world. But cant prevails over moral sensitivity. We chant "a woman's
right to control her body" and let the matter rest.[40]

The philosophy of rights, pushed to extremes as Will believed it had become in the United States, was strong on ideology and short on common sense. Will opposed such proposals as legalization of marijuana by appealing to a basic principle: the state has an interest in preventing people from losing those habits that are essential to self-control and those traits of character that society needs for order, sobriety, and survival.[41] Will, in fact, seemed virtually prepared to apply a social measurement to every right claimed by individuals and was insisting, as were other conservatives like James Q. Wilson, that the notion of purely individual rights and private choice had become almost meaningless in the contexts of modern society.

These convictions often made Will seem harsh and negative. One Will editorial, for example, decried what he called "porn rock," popular music with sexual references and suggestiveness. "The concern," Will wrote, "is less that children will emulate the frenzied behavior described in porn rock than that they will succumb to the lassitude of the de-moralized" or lapse by overindulgence into a state of emotional and moral torpor. He registered similar fears about the movies and especially the genre, very popular in the 1970s and 1980s, of "slash films"—*Prom Night, Halloween, Friday the Thirteenth*—and their seemingly endless serializations. American youth, Will feared, were undergoing a process of desensitization by exposure to a heavy assault of graphic, visually powerful violence and calculated emotional manipulation. A consciousness so distorted would became increasingly unable to recognize or respond to subtlety and nuance, in the arts or in life, and the consequences for social stability could hardly be positive. Will's larger point was that public entertainments are not matters of indifference to government and cannot be brought automatically under the dangerously expanded rubric of personal liberties. The English parliamentarians who outlawed bullbaiting in the nineteenth century understood that principle.[42]

And in the long run, Will said, the libertarian dogma will be its own undoing. For a society that has become so brutalized by an inhumane public culture, so desensitized, will care little for the values and the sense of human worth on which First Amendment rights rest.[43] Here indeed were the cultural contradictions of libertarianism.

There were other compelling reasons, Will believed, why conservatism should break its antiquated partnership with libertarianism. Will believed that libertarianism renounces a government of laws but yields to a government of the inner appetites, one that threatens public authority and all notions of the public good.[44] There was an erroneous notion of freedom at work here, he believed, not so troubling save for the fact that it seemed to describe the simplistic ideas of too many Americans. Freedom, Will warned, "is not only the absence of external restraints. It is also the absence of irresistible internal compulsions, unmanageable passion and uncensorable appetites."[45] Liberty for Will thrived within its own internal paradox. It could function only when it incorporated principles of restraint, even on itself. That restraint must come from a basis of decency and toleration and a deference for the sustaining values of a community, which in fact even restrain the full exercise of liberty. But it is just these "rare and fragile traditions of civility," the norms to which individuals subordinate impulse and caprice, that secure liberty and supply the social order necessary to it. This was a Burkean principle, and Will's own formulation of it was virtually a paraphrase of the great conservative. "The restraining strength of individual habits and social conventions," Will wrote, "must be inversely proportional to the strength of restraints enforced by law. In the best of times, there is a high ratio of the former to the latter."[46] In this way conservatism is consistent with traditionalism. It is an alliance always under assault from the partisans of individualism. Will regretted that that impulse seemed peculiarly irresistible to Americans. For an echo from Emerson whispers to each of us: "I am an endless seeker with no past at my back." Defined apart from our society, our personal truth becomes our unyielding personal need, and our personal need becomes a legal right unassailable. For Will, the consequences were clear and dangerous. "It is time," he wrote, "to come up from individualism."[47]

It has been the lament of conservatives from Babbitt through Viereck and Will that America has become a culture of subjectivism. Babbitt had complained early in the century that American life had become drugged by sensations, the pursuit of thrills, and the self-indulgence of feeling.[48] Will saw these consequences at their worst in the radical culture of the 1960s, a culture that, he said, "celebrated senses over mind" and gave us "sensitivity training" and "consciousness raising" in abundance.[49] Emotionalism became narcissism. In college classrooms students were asked to state their personal feelings about *Hamlet* as literary analysis shifted to affective impression. The educational system at all levels modified Descartes: *Sentio ergo sum.*[50]

For Babbitt and for Will the consequences of sentimentalism were sometimes harmlessly frivolous, even therapeutic in their own way. But Will could not disguise his distaste for some of the maudlin trappings of American life. John Lennon, rock star, is killed in New York, and we lapse into an orgy of bathos, public vigils, weeping and gnashing of teeth. America endures a national humiliation as Iranian fanatics hold its officials hostage, but when the ordeal ends without retaliation, our mood is festive. "America 50, Iran 0," a banner proclaims. A nation built by muscle and blood, Will wrote, is now awash in indiscriminate sentimentality.[51] It would seem that for Will the American problem was the problem of excess. The country had become, as Babbitt had warned, at once the most sentimental and the most mechanical of civilizations. But even more than Babbitt before him, Will carried that judgment into an extended analysis of American political life, and what resulted was a sustained critique of liberalism.

Liberalism, Will believed, is a genuine expression of the American psyche. It rests on the assumption that there is plenty in nature to fulfill all human wishes. It operates on a *Weltanschauung* of abundance that is a given of nature and a right of the population.[52] Liberalism, Will wrote, is "the politics of the pleasure principle," and it has made the American political arena a forum of aggressive private and group interests.[53] Will, as we shall see, attributed these effects to the Founding Fathers themselves, but he also described a more recent liberalism that derived from the New Deal. Liberalism at that juncture of American history turned directly to the state as the means by which it would fulfill the right of happiness. From this point, the state would exist not merely to assure the conditions by which individuals might secure material well-being, but it would supply the goods as well.[54]

Actually, Will did not undertake an extended quarrel with the New Deal reforms themselves and, as we have observed, considered many of them essential and legitimate. But Will was at one with the neoconservatives in seeing the New Deal as the beginning of a liberalism run amuck. He shared their complaint that liberalism had moved from an ideal of equality of opportunity to an ideal of equality of results. Government, Will believed, had arrived at a condition in the United States in which it must be all things to all people. Besieged by the petitions of special interests and factional social groups, it had metamorphosized into G. K. Chesterson's fearful "servile state." But "every government benefit," Will warned, "creates a constituency for the expansion of the benefit, so the servile state inflames more appetites than it slakes." Rare in this country, he added, is the political leader who dares pronounce the virtues of material moderation and deferred gratifications. When Will found one, as he did in the unlikely place of the California governorship, he gave Jerry Brown his due credit. Conservatives, Will wrote, believe that government is too strong. In fact, he answered, government is too weak. It is incapable of saying no to whom it should. It yields to the most vociferous plaintiffs.[55]

The course of American politics compelled Will to ponder the larger foundational weaknesses of the American political tradition. If contemporary politics seemed increasingly to recognize only races, sexes, and interest groups, Will said, then there was perhaps some larger defect in the American system as organized at its beginnings. Will explored this notion in his book of 1983, *Statecraft as Soulcraft*, a book that many Will admirers did not like.

Will argued that the Founding Fathers of America established democracy on a basis that betrayed the great classical tradition of political theory, one that had flourished from Aristotle to Burke and that concerned itself with the means by which, in the matter of government, the virtuous citizen might emerge and prevail. The Founders, Will believed, took note, in their views of the social organism, only of interests, of "factions" in Madison's famous terminology, and they made statecraft the art and science of managing and balancing those interests. This assignment gave to the state an essentially negative function. It could act when matters of public order and social stability were at stake, but it incorporated and exercised no transcendent moral or symbolic function and conveyed no such meaning through its existence — nothing, in short, that made the state the embodiment of the nation's higher self.[56] Will believed that the Fathers breathed too much the spirit of Adam Smith. For the dangerous legacy in Smith, he felt, was the tradition of minimal government. Classical liberals like Smith, and those in his tradition since the late eighteenth century, imagined only a passive role for government, assuring it an essentially prosaic life in the modern age. In a United States born of this tradition, we should not be surprised, said Will, that the public has always held government in low esteem. But an American political system so regarded is also one easily victimized, rendered defenseless against society's most aggressive interests and factions.[57]

Eighteenth-century liberal ideas misled American political notions in another way, Will believed. They gave credence to the faith that by some invisible hand the frenetic pursuit of self-interest would enhance the public good. Today, however, said Will, we see the results of this "Cusinart" theory of justice. San Francisco police go on strike in defiance of the law, and it proves expedient to settle the affair by forgetting the law. That affair, one of many like it, documented for Will the erosion of citizenship and respect for law in American public life. Everywhere the rhetoric of entitlements fills the air, and the interests behind it rend the state.[58]

Will did not consider himself a detractor of the American political system in any wholesale way, but his judgments certainly provided a clear clue to the "European conservative" label he appended to himself. Was Will too harsh in judging the first generation of American political leaders? To be sure, there is a substantial scholarship that argues that the makers of the Constitution moved away from the notions of virtue that were so widely trumpeted in the literature of the American Revolution, that is, among the generation that led the fight for independence from Great Britain and who justified it by extensive use of a classical tradition of republican virtue.[59] But even among the authors of the Constitution, Will might have located voices sympathetic to his own concerns. Madison's famous Federalist Paper Number 10, for example, should be read as a quest for an elite leadership for the new country, one liberated from the factional politics of the local democracies and recommending itself to the nation as a whole by its broad and visionary sense of the national good. Secondly, would it not have served Will usefully to recognize the Founders as the cool and reasonable judges of human nature that they were? Will, like some of the Straussians, claimed that the framers of the Constitution were too skeptical. They could see only self-interest in human affairs, and they gave us a government in kind.[60] But his judgment seemed odd coming from one who cautioned repeatedly against romantic and flattering views of human nature and who advised that nothing better secures us from the folly or tragedy of radical schemes for social betterment than a sense of human limitations, of human nature's capacity for evil. A generally pessimistic view of man, Will would have conceded, is the beginning of political wisdom.

Will's strictures on the legacy of the Founding Fathers raised serious questions for American history and were crucial in their implications for American conservatism, and they would seem to have put Will at cross-purposes to himself. For if Will were correct in *Statecraft as Soulcraft,* how then would a conservative in the Burkean mold search the American past for the content it could supply as a heritage for the present, as an enrichment of the national life, as a source of common culture and social unity? Will looked at the record and found only factionalism and self-interest, and he lamented their legitimation in the governing law of the land over two centuries. But Will, in the 1970s and 1980s, was not alone in asking these questions about the dawning of American political life. The subject had become one of intense and provocative historiographic debate. It bears looking at for some insights on Will's conservatism.

In the 1960s some American historians began to modify certain assumptions about American culture and ideology. Scholars in the Progressive tradition of historiography, such as Louis Hartz, had argued that the only political tradition in American history was liberalism, meaning a postmedieval social and political structure and a Lockean economic ethic of individualism and private property. Some modifications to that interpretation occurred in the works of Bernard Bailyn and Gordon Wood, who connected the cultural heritage and political ideology of the American Revolution to classical sources as revised and extended by the Whig school of political theory in Great Britain. The significance of this incorporation was the expansion of the American political heritage to include a republican literature, often located in Renaissance humanism, that stressed the ideal of virtue and its notions of civic pride and activity for the public good as the essentials of citizenship. In an important book of 1975, J. G. A. Pocock extended the classical influence through a longer record to the American colonies. His *The Machiavellian Moment: Florentine Political Thought and the Atlantic Republican Tradition* gave two concluding chapters to discussions of the classical content in revolutionary American thought and the writings of the constitutionalists.

These scholarly ventures began to take on an evident polemical tone when Garry Wills in 1978 published *Inventing America: Jefferson's Declaration of Independence.* Wills intended to take Jefferson out of the Lockean context in which he had been placed earlier by the renowned historian Carl Becker, and he did so by making Jefferson into an apostle of the Scottish Enlightenment. It was an ambitious effort, but Wills stuck to two essential points. He argued that Jefferson found a wealth of meaning in the moral sense philosophy of Francis Hutcheson and extracted from it the essentials of Hutcheson's social ethic, one that stressed the ideals of benevolence and disinterested virtue in the larger interest of the common good. And from the Common Sense philosophy of Thomas Reid, another major figure of the Scottish Enlightenment, Will traced Jefferson's idea of the democratic intellect and the intuited good sense of the common people. The effect, in Wills's reconstructed Jefferson, was the transformation of this influential American from a Lockean individualist into a communitarian and egalitarian democrat. The implications for the beginnings of American political ideology were important indeed.[61]

Wills's book invited controversy. Kenneth S. Lynn, a scholar at Johns Hopkins University and a conservative critic, reviewed the book for *Commentary.* He charged that Wills was anxious to dislocate Jefferson from the Lockean tradition because that tradition, with its philosophy of a contractual government that secures individual liberties, cut against the "collectivist" ideals of Wills's leftist inclinations. Jefferson, in short, needed to be redefined so as to appropriate him for the modern liberal agenda, argued Lynn. He disdained the insidious effort and accused Wills of attempting to change the Declaration of Independence into a "communitarian manifesto" and to supply the American republic "with as pink a dawn as possible."[62]

One year after George Will's *Statecraft as Soulcraft,* historian John Diggins published *The Lost Soul of American Politics: Virtue, Self-Interest, and the Foundations of Liberalism.* Surveying all the historical literature that had sought to read Locke out of American political origins and to relocate those origins in classical traditions, Diggins brought the record, from the Founders to Lincoln, under close scrutiny. The result was a ringing rebuke to the revisionists. Reading their scholarship as an effort to locate the sources of virtue in public citizenship and service to the state, Diggins demonstrated that the American constitutionalists entertained no such possibilities and no such hopes. If anything, Diggins' Founders reflected what Pocock, Caroline Robbins, and others had described as a "Court" (as opposed to "Country") philosophy that saw pride, passion, and self-interest in human motivations and that sought to contrive a form of government whose mechanics would at most neutralize these unyielding drives. The modern state would in fact have no reliance on the man of virtue. The "new science of politics," as elaborated by John Adams, one of Diggins' major examples, would be based on the passions of men.[63]

What Diggins wished to add to the content of American liberalism was religion, the neglected factor in both the Lockean and classical schools of American politics. In some superb essays on de Tocqueville, Emerson, Melville, and Lincoln, Diggins recovered the legacy of Calvinism in American thought and derived from it the only redeeming elements in its Lockean and Humean strains, the ideal of a "virtuous materialism." What these added to the American liberal ethos were the insights of Christianity, and Diggins even called his book "a Niebuhrean corrective to the pretensions of American virtue."[64] It was through its Christian content, said Diggins, that liberalism acquired its moral corrective to Lockean self-interest and made possible the dissolution of the ancient tension between "virtue" and "commerce." But as it turned out, Calvinism was the true "lost soul" of American politics. When Calvinism lost its cultural force in the American social ethic, Lockean liberalism was loosened from its ethical moorings. Virtuous materialism succumbed to the vulgar pursuit of wealth and the unbridled exercise of narrow self-interest. Diggins could locate no foundations of classical virtue in the American liberal tradition, but he took no comfort when he surveyed the ultimate results — "a liberal society dedicated to nothing more than the pursuit of self-interest and the pleasures of consumption."[65]

It may strike us as strange that *virtue,* a term dear to the hearts of conservatives (note Will's book, *The Pursuit of Virtue and Other Tory Notions),* should have been appropriated by the anti-Lockeans and made the apparent basis of a liberal critique of the individualist and capitalist foundations of American history. Will seemed to reinforce the point by castigating the framers of the Constitution for their abrupt departure from classical ideals of service and citizenship. His interpretation must be disturbing to conservatives who have had difficulty enough in locating any kind of usable past in the American

experience. If the great early statesmen of the republic can furnish no inspiration of a moral history worthy of veneration, then how is a traditionalist
American conservatism possible at all?

Diggins provided one partial answer, of course, when he reintroduced the
religious influence in American political culture and extracted from it a fragile
compound, virtue and materialism. But another possibility is to bridge the
chasm that intellectual historians have placed between the classical and Lockean traditions. James T. Kloppenberg made that effort in 1987 in an essay
for the *Journal of American History,* seeking, as he said, to "suggest a way
out of our historiographical inferno" through "a rediscovery of the virtues
of liberalism." Kloppenberg built on the studies of Joyce Appleby and Donald
McCoy, whose conclusions he summarized: "The [American] Revolutionists
did not intend to provide men with property so that they might flee from
public responsibility into a selfish privatism; property was rather the necessary
basis for a committed republican citizenry." Kloppenberg examined Madison's
and Jefferson's views, but undertook also to place Locke, and Adam Smith
as well, in a larger tradition of Christianity, natural law, and moral philosophy.
In doing so, he concluded that "just as Locke's enterprise is misunderstood
when his liberalism serves as the midwife of possessive individualism, so
Smith's purpose is distorted when the market mechanism he envisioned as
a means to a moral end is presented as itself the goal of political economy."
Kloppenberg thus moved the idea of a virtuous materialism back into American
political beginnings, but he conceded its demise in the nineteenth century
under the forces of industrial capitalism, evangelicalism, and southern slavery.[66] Kloppenberg thus suggested a reading different from Will's, but his
conclusion will require that we later ask the question whether the nineteenth-
century American experience affords any historical connection to Will's particular conservative ethic.

Will found the principle of self-interest so woven into the fabric of American
life and thought that it had tainted liberalism and conservatism too. Our conservatism, he asserted, is too much a by-product of eighteenth- and nineteenth-
century liberalism. He found it still dominated by the ideals of free-market
capitalism. The self-interestedness of capitalism thrives within the medium
of a restless, nervous acquisitiveness that engenders desire and celebrates
instant gratification. Marx was right, Will wrote: "Capitalism undermines
traditional social structures and values; it is a relentless engine of change,
a revolutionary inflamer of appetites, enlarger of expectations, diminisher
of patience."[67] And it doth traditional ways unking. American capitalism,
generating the forces of a dynamic commercial economy, Will said, has taken

its toll most heavily on those values and institutions that conservatives should most revere — family farms, local governments, traditional craftsmanship, historic homes and buildings. When conservatives ask what they should conserve and can answer only with "free enterprise," they will ever be untrue to their own best values.[68]

There is, to be sure, a kind of traditionalist conservatism that thoroughly disparages capitalism, mostly on moral and aesthetic grounds. G. K. Chesterton and Hilaire Belloc articulated it in England, and their followers among the Southern Agrarians in the United States did also. Will believed that capitalism should receive its due but no more. Capitalism, he said, is a superb device for allocating economic resources and commodities efficiently and with general fairness. And our sense of the harmful effects of capitalism should not propel us into a foolish embrace of socialist alternatives. But let us not, on the other hand, be too lavish in praise. "The market has a remarkable ability to satisfy the desires of the day," Will wrote, but "government has other, graver purposes."[69] For capitalism is short-sighted. It does not think of future generations and their needs. Government must consider the future. And Will thought it wholly right, as a case in point, for the state to force automobile manufacturers to design and sell smaller and more fuel-efficient cars.[70]

True conservatism binds the present to the future as it binds the past to the present. This effort, Will believed, required a certain quality of imagination, as Burke and Babbitt had repeatedly stressed. But capitalism, he wrote, has always tried to dazzle us with the new. It fosters a mentality of contemporaneity. In a suggestive essay, Will commented on how difficult it is for us today to have a sense of the remarkable achievement of our forebears in this country, a feeling for the heroic accomplishments of ordinary people. Consider, said Will, that in our "fatted nation, where football telecasts are interrupted by commercials inciting suburban home owners to buy power saws for trimming the family elm, few can have the faintest idea of what it meant to settle in the middle of a Minnesota forest because the wagon axle had splintered. Or to face the task of clearing a farm, one axe stroke and one stump at a time." The spiritual life of a society diminishes when its sense of awe is confined to the technological splendor of the latest computers.[71]

But if our spiritual life suffers, it is because both conservatism and liberalism have allowed it to, Will believed. A key aspect of Will's conservatism was his turn to government to supply the want. Government should be the expression of our collectivity. The marketplace, said Will, may serve the ends of individuals, but government must take note of common interests. If we do not have government that is concerned with morality, then we will have government that is indifferent to morality. It is an arresting thought, Will believed, that in modern times this concern has ceased to be axiomatic in the conduct of public life. For as government has expanded its role, its office has diminished in prestige and importance. It has alienated itself from a concern with high ideals and moral life. Will was left to ask: "Have they all been mistaken, all the philosophers and statesmen from Plato to the present, who have argued that particular forms of government have social and cultural prerequisites, including shared ideas, values, and character traits in the citizenry?" A society that proclaims moral ends, Will insisted, had better incorporate moral means.[72]

Will looked to America's recent past to note how far the country had moved from this prime consideration. It is a paradox of the modern liberal state, Will said, that it has taken to itself an expanding role in influencing the allocation of wealth and opportunity, while it has withdrawn in proportion from any role in influencing society's moral life. Witness, he wrote, the courts' restrictions on obscenity laws, liberalization of abortion, decriminalization of sexual activity among consenting adults, prohibition of any compulsory religious or patriotic practices (school prayers and flag salutes).[73]

Conservatives have not always done much better, however. Will saw in the presidential administration of Gerald Ford a singular preoccupation with enhancing what the president liked to call Americans' "disposable income." Will commented: "What is missing [in this administration] is political leadership that summons individuals to citizenship, to the pursuit of something in addition to the expanded personal freedom that disposable income conveys." It was the Democratic president Jimmy Carter, said Will, who at least aspired to better uses of government, who invoked piety, family, community, and restraints in the pursuit of material abundance, and who believed that government should be at the service of these values.[74]

American politics, Will conceded, did include issues creditable to its record, however, and he referred to the Civil Rights Act of 1964 as an example. Congress here correctly decided, he said, that the rights of property and ownership in hotels and restaurants, when exercised in an invidious way, must yield to higher priorities. The Civil Rights Act, though it did indeed seek to improve the material conditions of certain people, was also intended to enhance the moral sensitivity of all Americans.[75]

Those individuals and groups that deprived government of its moral influence headed Will's list of the enemies of the republic. And this issue raised for him a related problem of conservatism in America. The United States, he wrote, has never equaled European nations in providing people with the symbols, the pageantry, and the historical emblems that furnish a common imagination for a nation. The relative brevity of our history was indeed a factor in this loss, but our ideology was as much to blame. The idea of public space simply does not command a claim on our attention or our priorities, he argued, and consequently the public domain has been ravaged by commercial interests or neutered by special claimants. In an age in which the media is a powerful influence on the public airways, we have allowed our homes to be invaded by commercials promoting everything from toilet paper to cures for hemorrhoids.[76] We do indeed "descend to meet." Or we have allowed our lives to be drained of meaningful expressions of traditional rites, in an unnecessary yielding to minority vetoes. Thus today, Will commented, pornographers enjoy more rights under the law than do school children who wish to perform a Nativity play. The vigilantes of the American Civil Liberties Union, Will believed, were seeking out for litigation all state-supported or even state-sanctioned expressions of our religious and patriotic heritage. It was a sad and dangerous fact, he warned, that public life in America was becoming bland and sterile, stripped of its colorful and historical vestments and rendered symbolically naked.[77]

It was a sadder fact still, Will avowed, when government itself denigrated its higher public functions. Too often it reflects and appeals cynically to the dominant materialism of our national life. Will was not at all amused, for example, that half of the states not only legalized gambling in casinos or at horse and dog races but also sponsored state-run lotteries. It mattered more to the lawmakers, apparently, that the states gained revenues from these operations than that the beguiling advertising used to promote them made losers of 99 percent of the participants, many of whom had no means by which to cushion their losses. "Gambling is debased speculation," wrote Will, "a lust for sudden wealth that is not connected with the process of making society more productive of goods and services. Government support of gambling gives a legitimate imprimatur to the pursuit of wealth without work."[78]

Into the 1980s this conservative writer who was defending the uses of government was also drafting a litany of its abuses, especially abuses by its leaders. Above all, government, Will believed, can betray its function by making itself trivial. Our democratic culture, he insisted, has made irresistible the tendency for public officials, even the highest in the land, to make themselves appear as ordinary citizens. It was not, for Will, a harmless flattery of the masses in which they indulged. Leaders are trustees of their offices, and these offices must embody the highest aspirations and the most meaningful symbols of our common heritage. Government, Will warned, must not be merely mundane. Nonetheless, our leveling tendencies give us President Ford buttering his own English muffins in the White House kitchen before a national television audience or President Carter in his sweater as he presumes to lecture the nation on the energy crisis as "the moral equivalent of war." We also have the Department of Transportation making a study of car pooling and finding, to its horror, that mostly males do the driving. It ponders what to do about this impending crisis, and, as guardian of the public safety, declares that "in the end, the issue is equality." Elsewhere, the Department of Health, Education, and Welfare looks at the public schools in Oak Ridge, Tennessee, and commands the high school cheerleaders there to cheer equally for the girls' and the boys' athletic teams. Though laughable, the matter is serious, Will insists. He admonishes: "Government cannot make a fool of itself, day after day, without diminishing its ability to deal with matters that are not trivial." Sooner or later its lack of serious purpose will deprive it of public suasion. True conservatives, Will added, must exercise the faith that there exists in the public a passion for ennobling qualities in public life. Disraeli, Bismarck, and Churchill knew this fact and acted on it.[79]

These leaders knew something else, too. They knew that sound democracy did not spring automatically from the exercise of some "divine average" latent in the citizenry. George Will belonged to a group of American conservative thinkers that maintained that democracy works best when it incorporates and reflects aristocratic values—a deference to superiority in superior persons, a measured respect for elitism, a striving for improvement by conscious self-discipline. Babbitt defined America's highest political values as an aristocratic and selective democracy.[80] Peter Viereck wrote that "democracy is the best government on earth when it tries to make all its citizens aristocrats."[81]

Will's sentiments concurred entirely. Democracy, he suggested, needs a precious combination of the common and the superior. It needs leadership that carries not just power but also eminence, influence, and moral example. Leadership is unworthy of the title if it does not stand out in character from mass tastes and even mass opinion. We do well to note, Will said, that in the "century of the common man" its greatest leader was born in a palace and remained attached throughout his life to a romantic and aristocratic ideal of government. Wrote Will, "the virtues of a Churchill—independence, imagination, spiritedness, character, eloquence—are not distributed with democratic evenness across the population, one allotment, one voter." The sentimental notion that one man is as good as another is, he believed, the surest sign of a decayed democracy.[82]

George Will's conservatism sought to impose on the expansive and individualist forces of American life the cultural discipline of a self-styled Toryism. The effort gave a special stamp to Will's conservatism and made of it a kind of intriguing curiosity, for the Tory label would seem not to fit easily into American standards. But in an important sense, Will had forced himself into this device. He had recourse to a "European" conservatism because he could not, in confronting the political origins of the United States, locate any affinities that might be the building blocks of an effective American conservative tradition. He saw only Lockean individualism and Madisonian factionalism. But Will was little motivated to look beyond the Founding Fathers and in despair resigned the American political tradition to a legacy of liberalism destructive of the organic state. From the Founders of the 1780s to the interest group politics of the 1980s, Will could see in American history only the amoral and depressing chronicle of partisan assaults on government and the resulting erosion of the public weal.

For a commentator who could read the American scene with such insight and acuteness, Will did his conservative philosophy a disservice in drawing the outline of American political culture so narrowly. Will in fact belonged to a viable political tradition in the United States, one that ran directly counter to the one he described as singularly dominant. This tradition had its roots in Puritanism and in the republican ideology of the American revolution, but it flourished most expressively in the Whig political culture of the nineteenth century. The various expressions of this tradition were never wholly consistent with one another, and often they thrived mostly as a countercultural dissent against the unruly and too intensely individualist strains in Jacksonian America. But they are persistent enough to suggest that Will's conservatism expressed a native tradition. It was not as "European" as he imagined.

From their inceptions, American political ideas have expressed themes of community priority and the ideals of the organic state that anticipate Will's brand of conservatism, set off as it was from the individualism that he believed had impaired both conservativism and liberalism in our history. John Winthrop aboard the ship *Arbella* gave an eloquent rendering of the communal priorities that inspired the "Holy Commonwealth" of the first Puritans. Later the "Whig" political ideology of the American Revolution years borrowed from English and classical sources to embrace ideals of republican virtue and the political system that could spring from it. What ties these pieces of American political thought to the kind of conservatism espoused by Will is their invocation of a moral republic, with the state at its center. Government, it is insisted, has something to do with the moral habits, even the inner moral constitutions, of its citizens. Forrest McDonald, in describing the intellectual origins of the Constitution, showed how the revolutionary generation's concern for virtue carried over into the first state constitutions of the late 1770s. In his book *Novus Ordo Seclorum,* McDonald cites the Massachusetts Bill of Rights. "Constant adherence," it said, to principles of "piety, justice, moderation, temperance, industry and frugality, are absolutely necessary to preserve the advantages of liberty." Pennsylvania's constitution said that "laws for the encouragement of virtue, and prevention of vice and immorality, shall be made and constantly kept in force." Under these principles the states passed laws, in the pattern of English sumptuary laws, that proscribed a host of vices, from those with brutalizing tendencies to even the wearing of anything that smacked of elegance and finery. Republican virtue was a prerogative of government's protective functions.[83]

The disturbing events of the 1780s, which some historians refer to as the "critical period" of American history and which to the emerging group of Federalists was a period of democratic and egalitarian excesses, did not, however, quiet the champions of a republic characterized by order and internal self-discipline. Robert Kelley has described how, particularly among New Englanders, fears grew about new threats to American society. Settlement of the West and the violence of slavery in the South suggested a recourse to barbarism and social regression, or a lapse into primitivism. These prejudices informed the political culture of the Federalists, but the Whigs of the middle nineteenth century gave them an even more pronounced moral rendering, especially in their willingness to make the state a caretaker of the public's moral health. Kelley's descriptive list of Whig social ideals — decency, respectability, thrift, and sobriety — could provide Will with usable historical models.[84]

Furthermore, in his excellent study, *The Political Culture of the American Whigs,* Daniel Walker Howe described three preoccupations evident in the writings of the politicians, academics, journalists, and others who expounded the values of the Whig party. They were concerned first with "providing conscious direction to the forces of change" in their society. They had little faith in automatic progress, either in society as a whole or in its individual members. Nurture and cultivation were their chosen devices for improvement. Second, Whig rhetoric emphasized "duty" rather than "rights." "Whig morality," wrote Howe, "was corporate as well as individual; the community, like its members, was expected to set an example of virtue and to enforce it when possible." And both these Whig norms coincided with a third, the organic unity of society. Whereas Jacksonians saw individuals, groups, and rival economic factions in America, the Whigs blurred these distinctions and emphasized the interrelating interests of the corporate society.[85]

Finally and equally suggestive, Howe stressed in his study the biographies of major Whig leaders and spokesmen. Personality, he found, tells as much about Whig political culture as do ideology and political prejudice. So Howe offered chapter essays on John Quincy Adams, Henry Clay, Alexander Stephens, and Abraham Lincoln, with further glimpses of Daniel Webster, Rufus Choate, and Horace Greeley. Here too he saw a recurring theme. The Whig

personality was a controlled one, and it idealized restraint. Whig leaders typi-
cally engaged themselves in lifelong struggles of self-mastery and often had
a horror of the passionate and unruly forces within themselves. They also
carried their fears of the darker side of human nature into their social outlooks.
They became obsessed with locating the stabilizing values of their country
and the institutions that would foster them. Abraham Lincoln, seeing spreading
violence in America, could thus hope that respect for the law would become
a new "religion of democracy" in a land where human passions were dangerous
centrifugal forces.[86]

Will's essays might have been measured many times over in the context
of American Whiggery. They reflected recurrently a concern for inner discipline and for stabilizing social institutions, and they emphasized an anti-
individualism and social organicism reminiscent of Whig sympathies. Will's
Whig style was tempered, to be sure, by a lesser enthusiasm for economic
modernization than the Whigs displayed. Will's conservatism, born of a
twentieth-century perspective, judged the economic modernization of industrial capitalism productive more of vulgarity than of virtue and placed him
and other conservatives we will examine in an uncertain relation to the American past. But Will's connections to one part of that past were more than
superficial, and the Whig culture of the American nineteenth century suggests
that Will's Toryism need not have been a European surrogate for a missing
American tradition.[87]

Commentators on Will's conservatism often described it as unorthodox. Liberals
often found themselves rendering Will a fair measure of appreciation, especially those older liberals who traced their political ideology to the New Deal
reforms and to the tough-minded anti-communism of the Roosevelt and Truman years. Will himself showed his affinity with this group in an editorial
essay on Washington senator Henry "Scoop" Jackson titled "The Finest Public
Servant I Have Known." Jackson had a liberal domestic record and maintained
a strong anti-Communist position in his foreign policy views. Will wrote
of him: "He never wavered from his party's traditional belief that there is
no incompatibility between government with a caring face at home and government with a stern face toward adversaries."[88]

Historian William Manchester reviewed Will's book *The Pursuit of Happiness* and wrote: "Like most members of my trade, I considered myself a
liberal—or did until I read this collection of essays by a writer at the other
end of the spectrum, with whom I find myself in agreement 90 percent of
the time."[89] But Ronald Dworkin would not grant liberals any visa into Will's
domain. Dworkin insisted that liberalism, alone among the modern political

philosophies, does not look to the state for a model of ideal life or cultural norm. Fascism on the Right and Marxism on the Left do. Will's conservatism represented to Dworkin a familiar and dangerous form of rightist elitism. He also found unconvincing Will's claims for a progressive conservatism in the tradition of Shaftesbury. Will, like Shaftesbury, cared for the poor, Dworkin believed, not out of sympathy for their suffering but for the threat they posed to civilization. In short, said Dworkin, Will's heart wasn't in it. The conservative prefers statecraft, Dworkin added. The liberal prefers justice.[90]

Nor was Will a thinker easy for conservatives to assess. James Nuechterlein, writing in *Commentary*, found that Will's "progressive conservatism" made him too sanguine about the modern welfare state. Conservatives may embrace the ideal of social organicism, but, Nuechterlein asked, does a benevolent state truly enhance the moral quality of its beneficiaries? Does it make them more virtuous? Was not Will, Nuechterlein asked, at cross-purposes with himself in allowing a protective state to erode those qualities of self-reliance and initiative that conservatism reveres? Nuechterlein concurred with Will that the modern state will necessarily be a large state. But for this reason especially the true conservative has a vital role to play. He must be vigilant against the leviathan state, for it will otherwise devour him.[91]

Joseph Sobran, a *National Review* columnist and admirer of Will, nonetheless faulted Will in a similar way. He asked if Will really understood Burke, whose pithy quotations invigorated *Statecraft as Soulcraft*. Sobran believed that Burke had become for Will too much a kind of persona. Sobran reminded readers that Burke was an eighteenth-century Whig, a staunch defender of the rights of property and one who characterized the role of government in social programs as a violation of the order of nature. Sobran appreciated Will's contribution to the conservative cause, but he admired the real Will more than the Burkean mask.[92] Sobran's point illustrated again the precariousness of Will's headstrong recourse to European models for an American conservatism.

But the most sustained assault on Will came from Henry Fairlie. Fairlie, who traded heavily on his own English background and loved to describe himself as a Tory, was an occasional, almost always interesting contributor to the *New Republic*. Fairlie smarted when Will used the same label that he did. He judged Will's conservatism superficial and Will himself a quoting gadfly, a rummager of the past who fashions from it a pastiche of wisdom by which to accent his recoil from the crudities of modernity. What Fairlie missed in Will was a sense of conservatism's inner life, its spiritual struggles, of the combat of idea against idea in the chronicles of civilization. Fairlie found Will's conservatism lacking in substance. "Will makes culture evaporate,"

Fairlie wrote. "In his hands it becomes a thing of no gravity. This columnist who so manfully shoulders the burden of upholding our culture is an Atlas bowed under a balloon."[93]

Fairlie clearly matched Will in wit and sarcasm. But his lengthy essay, itself a pastiche of Will quotations, duplicated the error of which he accused his rival. He threw together a potpourri of scattered reflections by Will but disdained to see any thematic core in them. Will, to be sure, could have done more to give his conservatism an American context, and this essay has tried to suggest how that context might be located. But Fairlie missed even the barest outline of the conservative philosophy that forces itself on any casual reader of Will's essays.

Let us end this discussion of Will with a lament that he cited from Burke: "The age of chivalry is gone. That of sophists, economists, and calculators has succeeded, and the glory of Europe is extinguished forever."[94] Will himself at least was never quite so despairing. But the quotation insists, as Irving Babbitt never ceased to remind us, that conservatism is, fundamentally, a quality of imagination more than a program or a philosophy. Some of the best of Will's essays dealt with the failure of imagination in our jaded modern world. And Will's imagination was more than the moral imagination of Burke, of whom we have seen plenty already. It included the capacity to locate mystery and wonder in life, even in the most modern contexts. Gothic spires or Roman temples could give inspiration to some conservative minds. Space exploration in the late twentieth century could provide it for Will's. But our age, Will believed, has little capacity to sustain genuine awe and wonder. The space program that once thrilled soon bored us. The modern imagination can anchor in little that is solid. The danger is that when so little in the world of common experience can inspire us, the imagination is loosed to wander in what Babbitt called its own "empire of chimeras." It projects before us the dreams of new world orders and this-worldly utopias, or it atrophies altogether.[95]

What is left, then, for the true conservative, is to thrill to small victories for humanity wrung from a too-often unlovely world. In New York City, Will urged, he might rejoice to see that a venerable Episcopalian church, now set on valuable real estate, fights the designs and offers of millions of dollars from those who would build yet another skyscraper. Against these allures, some valiant souls avow no sale at any price.[96] And in Washington, D. C., there stands the National Cathedral, prominent above the city's skyline. It is a gray Gothic eminence, and it urges, said Will, a pause for reflection. "In the great cities of the West, the noblest buildings served religion. They are stone memories of a premodern age when cities were supposed to be something other than mere arenas for acquisition, when civil society was supposed to serve ends other than the pursuit of self-interest, when civil law was supposed to be patterned after a higher law." In a city that more than any other in America represents the pursuit of self-interest and partisan ends, the National Cathedral, Will wrote, invokes a transcendent ideal. In a city where billions of dollars are disbursed daily by government, the National Cathedral awaits the mere fifteen million dollars that will complete it. Whatever the odds, Will found the effort heroic.[97]

Ultimately, like the other American conservative intellectuals of the 1970s and 1980s, Will founded his ideas on the reality principle. The conservative expects no great victories from life but manages to thrill to small gains for the human spirit. The conservative shuns the utopian outreach of the imagination because he knows that it is doomed to futility. Two kinds of people, Will said, should be conservatives. One kind is those who study history. "The best use of history," he wrote, "is as an inoculation against radical expectations, and hence against embittering disappointments."[98] The other kind is the Chicago Cubs fan. This person knows, usually by June, that the world is "a dark and forbidding place," where yesterday's promises of bright new beginnings and of a new order in the National League have become like the left field ivy in winter.[99] "All things preach to us," Emerson once wrote. "What is a farm but a mute gospel?" Will would have agreed. All things preach to us—the transactions of athletes on Wrigley Field's natural turf and the Gothic splendor of an uncompleted church. Will took both the low road and the high road to conservatism.

4

Irving Kristol
Bourgeois Gentilhomme

IRVING KRISTOL WON the nickname Godfather of Neoconservatism and seemed to revel in it. To many he seemed the quintessential biographical model of the neoconservative. He was born in Brooklyn in 1920. His family were Eastern European Jews of orthodox identity. Kristol remembered his paternal grandfather as very learned, a "melamid," a student of Jewish culture without an interest in the rabbinic life. His mother and father were immigrants to the United States in the 1890s. The father, from the age of twelve, spent his life in the garment industry. He was never particularly religious and only marginally tied to the synagogue, but the family did faithfully observe the high religious holidays, had candles for Sabbath evening, and observed kosher practices. Irving attended the public schools and the local heder (Hebrew school) as well. He remembered, though, that Jewish organizations were "peripheral to my life." Irving's mother died when he was sixteen. Economically, it was not an easy path for the Kristol family. But the mean circumstances did not foster any loyalty to radical politics in the family. The elder Kristol considered himself a Social Democrat, not a socialist.[1]

Kristol entered the City College of New York in 1936 and propelled himself into the raging political warfare of a largely Jewish group of young intellectuals and their professors. Here began Kristol's long involvement with the "New York intellectuals" and their intriguing history. The four-decade journey that this group took from radicalism to conservatism was, of course, never smooth and never uniform. Along the way Trotskyists fought Stalinists, interventionists in World War II fought others on the Left who would have no part in a war of capitalists. In the 1950s a new spirit of accommodation with American life, with liberal democracy and even capitalism, cast some of these

New Yorkers in a conservative position, one that elicited warnings of their complicity in a new "age of conformity," as Irving Howe defined it. Then later the rich history of the New York intellectuals gained in interest, and in renewed intramural quarreling, with the publication in the 1980s of the memoirs of Howe, William Barrett, Lionel Abel, William Phillips, and Sidney Hook.[2]

Personal memories, in fact, greatly colored the thinking of this group. When neoconservatives warned in the 1960s against the treacherous consequences of hardened ideologies, against the deceptive allure of utopian thought, against the passionate and consuming commitments of the zealous reformer, they could claim that they had been through all this before and had seen the dire consequences firsthand. The City College politics that engaged Kristol's interest was but one focus of the Jewish radicalism in New York and one phase in the generational transformation in the American Jewish community.

Kristol himself represented the Jewish youths who were twice alienated— first from the norms of white middle-class life in America, with its dominant Protestant values, and, second, from the religious life of their Jewish parents. The younger generation had its own passions—a lust for ideas and a craving to make a mark in the world of thought. The circumstances of the Depression made socialism the answer to these drives. For many, it was the resolution of all their inner dilemmas about their place in American society. For socialism, as Alexander Bloom has noted, forged a new community, one with openings to the contemporary world and to a future world in which Jewish identity would not make any difference. These Jews, the cosmopolitan intellectuals who began to write for the *Menorah Journal* and *Partisan Review,* these modernists and Marxists, would solve the problem of being Jewish by putting the problem all behind them.[3] As Irving Howe remembered of his own early years: "The [socialist] movement eased my loneliness, gave me a feeling of place, indulged me in the belief that I had scaled peaks of comprehension."[4]

Irving Howe claimed that he recruited Kristol into the City College's Trotskyist youth group in 1938, though not until after graduating did Kristol join the Young People's Socialist League of Trotskyists.[5] What was the appeal to one like Kristol of the Trotskyist faction in the larger spectrum of collegiate radicalism? For one thing, it suited the almost otherworldly character that described the commitments of many of these young partisans. Theory was everything to them; they were strikingly indifferent to the vulgar real world. At City College, Howe recalled, politics was a "function of pure mind," an "autotelic" activity. The Trotskyists, he said, "brought with them an aura of certainty, a quickness in referring to Marxist texts." They made the best claim for "revolutionary purity."[6] At the college's famous Alcove 1, "dark-

Irving Kristol by Elliott Banfield

stained, murky, shaped like a squat horseshoe," there gathered the dissenters and schismatics of the Left, radicals outside the Communist party authority. At Alcove 2 were the more numerous and powerful Stalinists who gave the Young Communist League a membership of four hundred and who drew support from a large faculty contingent.[7] An interest in art and politics animated the denizens of Alcove 1, in contrast with the more pedestrian minds of the Stalinists. Their group found new inspirations in *Partisan Review,* the journal of the anti-Stalinist Left, which was indeed the freshest and most intellectually scintillating magazine of its time. Kristol was one who gourmandized on *PR.* "I would read each article at least twice," he wrote, "in a state of awe and exasperation—excited to see such elegance of style and profundity of mind."[8]

Kristol met his future wife Gertrude Himmelfarb when both were involved with the Young People's Socialist League. But Kristol, working as an apprentice in the Brooklyn Navy Yard, was too poor to marry. The Second World War followed closely on Kristol's graduation from City College. He fought with the Twelfth Armored Division in Europe and saw action as the Allies moved through Germany at the war's end. After their marriage, the couple remained in England for two years while Gertrude began a distinguished career as historian of English culture. Indeed she became a revisionist, as Kristol was in his own way, of the much maligned Victorian era.[9] Kristol did not join his wife in pursuit of an advanced degree and a career in academic life. He wanted to do serious journalistic writing on literary and political subjects. His essays appeared in the *New Leader, Politics, Reporter,* and *Commentary* (for which Kristol was an editor after its founding in 1948). All these journals were liberal anti-Communist publications and outlets for those in the American Left who carried the anti-Stalinist position into the Cold War era.[10] But Kristol was already moving toward conservatism, more quickly and farther than any in the New York group. Back in London in 1953 he became cofounder, with poet Stephen Spender, of *Encounter* magazine, with which he worked for five years. Under the sponsorship of the Congress for Cultural Freedom, a liberal anti-Communist organization headquartered in Paris, *Encounter* directly involved Kristol in the American government's Cold War stratagems.[11]

Going into the 1960s Kristol could judge himself a good liberal Democrat. He shared the party's dominant anticommunism and its commitment to preserving and extending the moderate New Deal programs of reform. But meanwhile a growing conservative movement was rallying many segments of discontent and finding focus in the effort that won Senator Barry Goldwater the Republican presidential nomination in 1964. Kristol could not echo the sentiments of liberals who at the time dismissed conservatism as an irrational and atavistic current in American political life. Goldwater voiced too much the politics of nostalgia, Kristol said, but he represented a genuine malaise in the country, a serious discontent.[12]

What was even more troublesome for Kristol was the erosion he saw in the Democratic party later in the 1960s. In the campaign efforts of both Eugene McCarthy and Robert Kennedy in 1968, Kristol saw excessive sectarian appeal to the militant segments of the party's constituency. He believed that neither McCarthy nor Kennedy genuinely represented the majority views of students, blacks, or academics, and he urged that the party could only alienate itself from the electorate by yielding its platform to the fringes. But the Democrats did just that in 1972, and when George McGovern became the party's presidential candidate, Kristol became a Republican. McGovern, Kristol said, signified the leftward turn of liberalism, and he added that "in order to become a neoconservative all you had to do was stand in place."[13]

Kristol's career was now moving in important new directions, into conservative journalism and corporate fund-raising. With Daniel Bell, the Harvard sociologist and sometime affiliate of the emerging neoconservative group, Kristol began publication of the *Public Interest* in 1965. At this time he was also editor of Basic Books in New York, and for a few years he issued the new journal from his office there. The *Public Interest* attained only a moderate subscription list (it numbered about fifteen thousand in the middle 1980s), but it did become a giant influence in the conservative intellectual advancement. The magazine was intended to deliver to the Great Society and the ambitious liberal reform agenda of the 1960s a heavy dose of "reality therapy," as Kristol called it.[14] Cool-headed skepticism that would emanate from empirical scholarship would demonstrate the limitations of reform. The *Public Interest* was academic sociology for conservatives. Contributors presented their analyses in statistics-laden studies—on education, urban renewal, housing, taxation, and other worldly matters. They attempted article by article to deflate both the utopian visions and the doomsday forecasts that reverberated through the years of political upheaval.

Kristol made his own contributions to conservatism after 1969 as Henry Luce Professor of Urban Values at New York University and later as John M. Olin Professor of Social Thought in the graduate school. In 1978 he established with William Simon, a former Republican secretary of the treasury, the Institute for Educational Affairs. It raised money for the American Enterprise Institute, one of the most powerful of the conservative "think-tanks" and a major source of advisers to the Reagan administrations. The new institute also spent money to nurture conservative student publications at Harvard, Yale, the University of Chicago, and other campuses, and in 1982 it assisted in the launching of Hilton Kramer's the *New Criterion*.[15] And of this man who so often decried the bad influence of intellectuals in politics, it was reported that his book *On the Democratic Idea in America* was purchased in bulk by the White House and read by President Reagan and his speechwriting and domestic policy staffs.[16]

Kristol had become a study in power and ideas. In 1972 he became a member of the *Wall Street Journal's* board of contributors and provided monthly editorials for that publication. One could hear Kristol quoted from the corporate boardroom to the university seminar, for his writings provided verbal coinage that traveled far. After Kristol defined a neoconservative as "a liberal who has been mugged by reality," that handy aphorism was likely to surface in any meeting place for political conversation. Or another definition: a liberal is one who says that it's all right for an eighteen-year-old girl to perform in a pornographic movie as long as she is paid the minimum wage.[17] But wit mixed with anger and harshness in Kristol. He said in a 1974 interview: "Look, I do not think that the United States today is an altogether admirable place. I am not particularly happy with it. I think this society is vulgar, debased, and crassly materialistic. I think the United States has lost its sense of moral purpose and is fast losing its authentic religious values."[18] Acquaintances, though, described Kristol as a mild-mannered, mellow individual, indisposed to seek the public limelight through television or other media. What lay behind the passion of Kristol's judgment of America, the discontent of a man who liked to say of himself, in a way that is meaningful for this chapter, "I live a civilized bourgeois life"?[19]

The answer to this question takes us back to the 1950s and the altered mood of the New York intellectuals. The decades of the 1930s and 1960s, it has been argued, were the critical ones for the making of the neoconservative movement. It is not a momentous issue, but a better case can be made for the 1950s.[20] First, that decade, when the conservative liberals made their final emphatic departure from the Communist Left, required them to define the terms on which one could claim to be an authentic intellectual. By this means the group began to acquire its own identity. Second, in this decade, the conservative liberals adopted a style of intellectual advocacy, even a new methodology, that neoconservatives virtually made their stock-in-trade as they took up their struggle against the counterculture in the 1960s and thereafter. And third, the 1950s, as we have seen, produced a significant accommodation to bourgeois culture among the New Yorkers. All these turns have a special significance for understanding Irving Kristol.

In a famous essay, "The New York Intellectuals," Irving Howe wrote that the group in question had provided the United States with its only true intelligentsia. They furnished this exemplary model, said Howe, because of their stress on critical thinking. The role of the thinker, said Howe, is to dissent, to criticize, to judge. The New York intellectuals, he wrote, like the Russian intelligentsia in the previous century, had persisted in their stance of active opposition, their alienation from the provincial smugness of ordinary citizens, and they had struggled to create both a culture of modernism and a new cosmopolitanism.[21] When Howe wrote the essay in 1968, he was really trying to hold up to the American Left a mirror image of its own best profile, one, he believed, that had become sadly marked by the fatigue of age. Howe saw in the radical New Yorkers of the 1930s a true cast of intellectuals, unrelenting critics, who by the 1950s had compromised their calling by their accomodationist stance, by their acquiescence in American norms.

One who challenged Howe directly in his views was Irving Kristol. Howe's basic assumption, he charged, was flawed. "Behind Mr. Howe's perspective," Kristol wrote, "there lies an unexamined premise: that there is something unnatural in an intellectual being anything but politically radical, a man of the Left."[22] Kristol by this time had, like other New Yorkers, welcomed the decline of partisanship among the group, especially as denoted by the waning appeal of abstract political thinking and idealism of any kind. These qualities had made radical dissent a victim of leftist totalitarianism, he said, and had made it anything but critical. The view that now prevailed in Kristol and others found virtuous qualities in American life—its pragmatic style of politics, its social pluralism, the centrist characteristics of its nondogmatic political parties, and its tolerance, if not its encouragement, of experimentalism in the arts. The new mood signified that these intellectuals were not about to go hunting elsewhere for new models of social perfection. Diana Trilling wrote that "the idealist finds virtue only where he is not—in the country which is not his country, in the class which is not his class."[23] Needed now, some were saying, was greater specificity in the focus of intellectuals, attention to the immediate arena of the nation's problems, and piecemeal adjustments to change.[24]

This emphasis on a pragmatic American tradition served both to orient the once-alienated New York intellectuals toward the mainstream of American life and culture and to guard intellectuals generally, the pragmatists hoped, from the snares of ideology and utopianism. If pragmatism signaled judgment based on experience, a general skeptical posture toward human pretensions, and level-headedness rather than emotionalism, then that standard could be used also for intellectual life itself. The conservative intellectuals cast out their Communist rivals by dismissing them as either too sentimentalist, too abstract, or too idealistic on the one hand, or too slavishly loyal to an orthodoxy of Marxism on the other, an orthodoxy refashioned for expediency by the Communist party. The Communists, it was now charged, betrayed the intellectuals' standards of independence of mind, the suspension of belief, and the openness to truth. Howe himself, speaking as an anti-Communist socialist, argued that Communists were not free intellectual agents and neither, therefore, were they legitimate intellectuals.[25]

The issue of Joseph McCarthy brought these matters into high relief. There was every reason, one might have assumed, why these New Yorkers should have counted themselves among McCarthy's opponents. McCarthy seemed to speak for an irrational populist strain in the country and to garner his support from native Protestants in provincial America and from Catholic ethnic groups in the working classes. Indeed the New Yorkers did not like McCarthy. But what has struck many as curious and others as condemnable was the silence or the co-option of liberals in the years of the Wisconsin senator's anti-Communist campaign. The situation was especially complex concerning the Jewish intellectuals, but two concerns are significant and must be approached if we are looking for origins of neoconservatism.

First, many anti-Communist liberals were painfully purging themselves of their own pasts, their earlier zealous radicalism, of which it was discomforting to be reminded. Some, like Harold Rosenberg, denied that past to themselves, proclaiming that there were no radical skeletons in the closet.[26] Nevertheless, to take up the cause against the Communist remnant was a means of exorcising those memories that haunted, of eradicating the demons within. In short, the nightmare of the 1930s, it was urged, must never be repeated, not in the 1950s nor in the next decade. And when the specter of Marxism did reappear then, these liberals warned against the designs of a "New Left" and won for themselves the label neoconservatives.

Second, the Jewish anti-Communists among the New Yorkers recognized that they had an opportunity, in the postwar decade, to create a leadership role. Throughout the McCarthy era, the New Yorkers defended a reasoned anticommunism. Theirs did not make its appeal to the nativist strains in American life; it was not consumed by a blind and boastful national chauvinism; it did not define the Cold War struggle as one of American religion versus Soviet atheism.[27] The New York intellectuals believed that they had won the right to define a "higher anticommunism." The whole issue, which we will examine later, had something of an ethnic and class dimension about it. Nothing more enraged the sons and daughters of the city proletariat than to look into the camps of the fellow travelers and find among them the "respectable" upper-class intelligentsia of familiar Waspish credentials. It was time to reclaim anticommunism from nativist demagogues and liberalism from the foolish and sentimental elites.[28]

The New York intellectuals made that effort through their journalistic outlets, *Partisan Review* and *Commentary*. Philip Rahv and William Phillips, the editors of *PR*, had led the leftist break in America from the party loyalists, and now in the postwar period they had put together the famous symposium the magazine presented in 1952, "Our Country and Our Culture." The editorial preface defined the issue succinctly: "The purpose of this symposium is to examine the apparent fact that Americans intellectuals now regard America and its institutions in a new way." A formidable list of intellectual notables, Jewish and non-Jewish, addressed the matter, most of them focusing on the place of art and culture in the United States and most affirming that, despite the country's detractions and shortcomings, America was happily bereft of the totalitarian movements that had suffocated art and culture elsewhere. The genuine pluralism of American society, the contributors believed, left critical breathing room for the artist and intellectual. Alienation and ideological dissent were judged no longer to be mandatory, and the choice between an oppressive Communist state and a strong democracy was assumed to be obvious.[29] At *Commentary*, meanwhile, the recently established journal of the American Jewish Committee drew attention to subjects of more specifically Jewish concerns, political questions as well as others. In editor Elliot Cohen *Commentary* had a man described as "nearly hysterical" in his anticommunism.[30] In Sidney Hook, Nathan Glazer, and Irving Kristol the magazine reflected a milder if nonetheless empathic anti-Communist liberalism.

When anticommunism became a domestic political issue, one individual among others from the New Yorkers who entered the fray was Irving Kristol. Kristol had joined the American Committee for Cultural Freedom in 1951 and helped to organize anti-Communist intellectuals. His major contribution came in articles that addressed the constitutional questions surrounding anticommunism, especially questions of personal liberties—freedom of speech and the rights of intellectual dissent. Writing in *Commentary* and *Partisan Review*, Kristol sought to circumvent these questions. To approach the issue of communism as merely a constitutional matter, he said, was wrong. It was wrong because that response failed to take account of "the nature of the communist movement." Communism, he urged, was not simply an opinion that one held regarding history or politics, such that that opinion contributed to meaningful intellectual discourse. "It is obvious to almost everyone by now," Kristol wrote, "that Communism . . . is a fanatical conspiracy, whose basic ideas are a set of paranoid illusions, and whose 'opinions' are stratagems." Kristol said that he did not wish to encourage a wave of public hysteria about, nor a vindictive reaction against, those who might at one time have been members of or sympathizers with the movement.[31] But Kristol did make one statement of which people in his circle took notice and which has been a scourge against him since its utterance. Kristol was speaking about Joseph McCarthy and about the liberals who denounced him: "There is one thing that the American people know about Senator McCarthy," Kristol said. "He, like them, is unequivocally anti-Communist. About the spokesmen for American liberalism, they feel they know no such thing."[32]

Polemics like this were heating up the political debates of the early 1950s. But in this decade also a quieter but equally important transformation occurred among many of the Jewish intellectuals. Lionel Trilling, one of the most influential literary critics of the middle twentieth century in the United States, signified most emphatically the intellectual reorientation that took place. By no means is it suggested that Trilling carried the day, but what he said about

the liberal imagination and about the American literary tradition clearly affected the views of Irving Kristol. Trilling was a graduate of Columbia University and the first Jewish professor to be tenured at that institution. His own
career reflected the transition in his generation of Jewish intellectuals from
the sectarian radicalism of the "downtown" Jews of working-class origins
to the cosmopolitan standards of gentility, polite letters, and English tastes
of the "uptown" Columbia academics. Indeed the subject of Trilling's first
book was Matthew Arnold, the humanist and man of letters.[33]

Trilling became important for many reasons, but his literary references
to bourgeois culture especially made him an early influence in neoconservatism.[34] Trilling contributed to his 1955 collection of essays, *The Opposing
Self*, a remarkable and highly suggestive essay on the American novelist William Dean Howells. The subject itself was surprising, for as Trilling conceded,
few critics had any more use for Howells. He was too "mild," too "genteel,"
for this age of passion, modernist boldness, and even literary contempt for
the ordinary aspects of life. Today, said Trilling, "we are lovers of what
James called the rare and strange, and in our literature we are not responsive
to the common, the immediate, the familiar, and the vulgar elements of life."
Trilling was echoing a concern of Hannah Arendt about the glamour of evil
and the demonic in the modern imagination. This obsession, she said, dangerously obscured from us the possibilities of goodness in the quotidian dimensions of our lives. "The extreme," Trilling added, "has become the commonplace
of our day."[35]

What, then, about Howells? With a glance, surely, to his radical friends,
Trilling reminded the reader that this novelist of American middle-class life
was also one of the major social critics of capitalism and its injustices. But
Trilling at the same time warmed to Howells' account of the small Ohio towns
in which he had grown up. Howells had written of the citizens' lively interest
in English politics, their knowledge of the important literature of the day,
their enthusiasm for Shakespeare. Trilling commented on Howells' own passion for learning and his early mastery of four languages. In all these efforts
the aspiring writer had the proud nurturing of his community. Howells' own
literary efforts, furthermore, conveyed to Trilling the author's appreciative
depiction of the norms of middle-class American life. "At the heart of Howells,"
wrote Trilling, "there is a loving wonder at the fact that persons of the most
mediocre sort somehow manage to make a society."[36] As Mark Krupnick
wrote in his study of Trilling, "Howells exemplifies for Trilling the decent
republican culture of the American nineteenth century." Trilling appreciated
in Howells his sense of "the charm of the mysterious, precarious little flame
that lies at the heart of the commonplace."[37] Perhaps with Trilling most in

mind Philip Rahv declared that "we are witnessing . . . the embourgeoisement of the American intelligentsia."[38]

For Trilling, the problem in recovering appreciation of middle-class culture was the middle class itself. Trilling had become aware by the 1960s that something had occurred in the United States that none of the radical generation of the 1930s had ever expected. For it was now all too clear that the commitment to modernism, which began and which one had assumed would remain forever the commitment only of an elite corps of critics, writers, and artists, had expanded far beyond this charmed circle. Modernism, which carried so much of the aesthetic revolt against bourgeois life, now had made itself a fashionable infection of the bourgeoisie itself, a contemporary counterpart of the gout. One of Trilling's important essays, published in *Beyond Culture*, referred to a special feature of the modern era, to wit, "the bitter line of hostility to civilization which runs through modern literature," which Trilling described as "the disenchantment of culture with culture itself" – or with bourgeois culture, to be precise. The old ideals of Matthew Arnold, Trilling wrote, the ideals of order, convenience, decorum, and rationality, seemed only to point, in the eyes of the moderns, "to the small advantages and excessive limitation of the middle-class life of a few prosperous nations of the nineteenth century."[39]

The heart of Trilling's lament was his charge that a hostile modernism born of the generation of 1914 had become the wider "adversary culture" of the 1960s. But the bearers of that culture were no longer an alienated fraction of literary and artistic aesthetes. The adversary culture had become ascendant in the universities and the media and in the popular culture itself. The norms of American life, Trilling indicated, now reflected "the socialization of the anti-social . . . the acculturation of the anti-cultural . . . the legitimation of the subversive."[40] The problem of the decay of the middle-class culture, in short, was the middle class itself. Probably it was Trilling, too, who coined the expression "modernism in the streets" to convey the pervasiveness of the adversary culture and its pedestrian qualities. At any rate, Diana Trilling could plausibly ask the question: "Why does the idealist middle-class think so little of itself and everything that pertains to it?"[41]

But is it not correct to assert that any conservative philosophy in the United States must address itself positively to middle-class values and to the economic and cultural norms that the admittedly elusive term *bourgeois* entails? For even the traditionalist conservative, who has not always esteemed those values, must concede that an authentic conservatism genuinely expresses the enduring life of a people (we use a Burkean standard here). This being so, an American conservatism must find some accommodation with capitalism, with our traditional, dominant bourgeois values, and with liberal democracy. Conservative thought in the United States has long drawn inspiration from a European and aristocratic critique of these historical forces and has added eloquence, to say nothing of an enduring wisdom and a religious insight, to its dissent in doing so. But that conservatism has also paid a price in appearing to many to be irrelevant to the American condition or appearing to be quarrelsome, petty, and elitist. Conservatives of this kind have often congratulated themselves on the alienation their judgments have created and have even made it a badge of their superiority. Many among the Old Right who defended this conservatism into the 1980s faulted the neoconservatives for their secularism and modernism and wished to cast them out of the conservative circle. Bearing these tensions in mind, we turn to an extended examination of one who, as much as any other individual considered in this book, addressed the whole weighted question of capitalism and the culture it has wrought.

Irving Kristol in the 1960s was responding to the shifts in liberalism that, he said, made neoconservatives of those who did not follow them. In fact, though, Kristol's account of himself is misleading. This chapter will argue that Kristol became a conservative in a traditional sense and should have been designated one even if the journalistic label had not intervened to suggest that something new was taking place in the American Right. It was really not until the 1970s that Kristol's accelerating antiliberalism took on a substantial intellectual outline. Until then, there was perhaps an ad hoc quality about his neoconservatism, an unsystematic series of responses to the unsettling crises of a turbulent decade. We have already seen some of the beginnings of Kristol's conservatism. In the 1970s he was giving it a larger historical framework, and the result would be a more comprehensive and integrated expression of an American conservatism for the later twentieth century.

Kristol came to believe that the American experience was in many ways exceptional and that it owed its special character to the influence of certain cultural habits. These habits have their beginnings in the Western religious experience. In one of his most important essays, Kristol argued that Judaism and Christianity have always contained identifiable dialectical tensions, which he described as rabbinic, or "orthodox," on the one hand, and prophetic on the other. Kristol asserted that the prophetic tradition was gnostic in character. It finds the world sinful, imperfect, and unyielding, but it considers these limitations factitious and confronts the world by seeking to reshape it according to a metaphysical order of reality or by a schema of the imagination. The gnostic temper becomes millenarian. Its political expression is utopianism, and in its quest to create a worldly perfection, it generates in itself a hostility toward the present imperfect state of things. "These gnostic movements," Kristol wrote, "tend to be antinomian—that is, they tend to be hostile to all existing laws and to all existing institutions." The prophetic imagination envisions an ideal order, and it strains against everything in its path to make that order a reality. It differs to that extent from the "orthodox" character of religion. Orthodoxy, Kristol wrote, seeks the betterment of human life through moderate improvements in the routine of daily life and within existing institutions. The orthodox temper, in the face of the world's evils, is stoic. Its faith teaches that somehow these evils can be made the vehicle of good, but it warns that in this life things may not ultimately be fair or just.[42]

What most crucially divides the prophetic from the orthodox, Kristol believed, are their fundamentally different views of human nature. The prophetic vision, he wrote, turned much of Judaism and Christianity increasingly away from original sin. Attention shifted from the inner self and its spiritual torment to the outer area of public life and made that the locus of moral redemption. For Kristol, the new doctrine of original innocence signified a whole new political orientation. It meant, he said, "that the potential for human transformation here on this earth was infinite, which is, of course, the basic gnostic hope." This hope was illusory. Wrote Kristol: "Human nature and human reality are never transformed."[43]

Western culture, Kristol was saying, has long felt these dialectical strains. He observed that Christianity was born at a time when Jewish gnosticism was very active and that Christianity inherited a large measure of gnostic spirit. The different mentalities continued to be influential even in the more secularized culture of the eighteenth century, and Kristol moved his attention to aspects of the Enlightenment that had important implications for American history. He compared the Anglo-Scottish Enlightenment with the Continental Enlightenment. The latter, which had its culmination in the French Revolution, reflected, Kristol said, a gnostic mentality that it bequeathed to the revolution itself. Giving a secular statement to the prophetic religious roots from which it sprang, the French Enlightenment, Kristol believed, had imposed on the world a political eschatology that the revolution tried to fulfill. By contrast, the Anglo-Scottish Enlightenment envisioned no immanent new order. Its spirit, Kristol said, was meliorative rather than revolutionary. Whereas one Enlightenment yielded a Robespierre and a Saint-Simon, the other yielded a James Madison and an Adam Smith, men of practical temperament and chastened views of human nature. The Anglo-Scottish Enlightenment accepted an imperfect human nature and tried to channel intractable self-interest safely into a competitive marketplace economy. And it relied on existing social institutions and traditional moral values to make free society safe and civilized.[44]

Kristol believed it a matter of great significance and good fortune that the American Revolution was born of the more sober influences of the Anglo-Scottish Enlightenment. While the French philosophers thrived in the fashionable salons of Paris, remote from the rest of society and "alienated" as an intellectual class, the Anglo-Scottish thinkers were respected community participants and members of improvement societies everywhere. At home in the world, they were content to find practical means of improving it, Kristol said. America's early leaders, Kristol wrote, "understood that republican self-government could not exist if humanity did not possess . . . the traditional 'republican virtues' of self-control, self-reliance, and a disinterested concern for the public good." James Madison's acute sensitivity to the "degree of depravity in mankind" fortified democratic theory against unrealistic hopes that might ultimately bring the harshest judgments against it. The realistic temperament also explained why the American Revolution was, according to Kristol, a "successful" revolution.[45]

Kristol's intellectual outline was too dialectical and too generalized to serve as much more than a framework for his analysis of contemporary politics, but it did provide him some useful insights on that subject. Kristol was anxious to apply his outline against a background of economic change, the cultural incidence of capitalism particularly. He stood in the tradition of Karl Marx, Max Weber, and Joseph Schumpeter, and, in his own time, of Daniel Bell, in his account of the cultural contradictions of capitalism. What he added to them was the larger intellectual outline we have reviewed. The crucial matter for all these thinkers was the failure of capitalism to secure its own legitimacy in the intellectual and cultural life that it created. The modern Western world, Kristol believed, had been for more than a century a civilization at war with itself, fighting hopelessly against its own degeneration into nihilism and undermining its traditional moral and political ideals. For Kristol, this history was summarized by the decline of bourgeois values. Nearly every situation that constitutes the crisis of legitimacy in our times, he believed, owes its origins to the lamentable erosion of those values.[46]

Capitalism, Kristol explained, orients individuals to the marketplace: it is a system for the enhancement of material ownership. The bourgeois ethic orients individuals toward themselves: it is a means for regulating the innate drives of individuals toward pleasure, toward the enjoyment of those material acquisitions that capitalism furnishes abundantly. The capitalist ethic is an ethic of freedom; the bourgeois ethic is an ethic of control, of self-discipline, above all of delayed gratifications. The bourgeois code of life, the familiar "Protestant ethic," gave capitalism its moral legitimacy, Kristol believed, and made it something other than a mere principle of hedonism. It also moderated the capitalist endorsement of personal liberty in the economic realm by invoking the authority of social and religious institutions and trusting these to inspire in individuals an inner check on their appetites and expansive lusts. And for a while, Kristol believed, this alliance worked well. Wealth and material gain roughly approximated the personal virtues of those who amassed them. Capitalism, Kristol wrote, "had a genuine relation to the individual as a moral person. One acquired riches by being honest, diligent, prudent, pious, and fortunate." Economic success thus had a tolerable moral legitimacy that gave business enterprise at best some esteem and at least a tolerance among the middle-class public.[47]

Economists of all persuasions have chronicled the fate of capitalism and the bourgeois ethic since the late industrial revolution. Kristol's own account is but one version of how one devoured the other. The estrangement of capitalism from the moral system that legitimized it became for him the central cultural problem of America in the twentieth century. For capitalism in its economic success created a climate in which the demands for immediate enjoyment of its fruits proved irresistible. The inner self-discipline that marked the bourgeois personality yielded year by year to a culture, a capitalist culture, that rendered no account of inner restraints and gave itself over to an imagination of indefinite material gratification. Not only immediate but also unlimited fulfillment became the social norm of capitalist life, and both private enterprise and government granted that norm a moral legitimacy.

But the main conspiring culprit in this moral transformation, Kristol said, was business itself. Advertising spawned a pervasive consumer ethic and created a system to make it flourish. Kristol soured on this outcome. If you hear a banker decrying the decline of the work ethic, Kristol wrote, ask him if he believes in people buying on the installment plan. There often appeared in Kristol's writing a nostalgic sigh for the lost world of a responsible bourgeois citizenry. Probably there was something acutely personal in this regret. Kristol, for example, recalled the working-class circumstances of his youth and its rigorous economic code. Buying anything on credit, he said, was then judged to be the way of wastrels, people of weak character, individuals lax in the control of their appetites. "To buy now and pay later," Kristol remembered, "was the sign of moral corruption."[48] The disintegration of this taboo, he genuinely believed, had occurred throughout society. He accepted from David Riesman's study *The Lonely Crowd* a general theory of the change, the decline of the inner-directed personality of the nineteenth century. Kristol added: "The kind of personality I am describing may be called the bourgeois citizen.

He used to exist in large numbers, but now is on the verge of becoming an extinct species. He has been killed off by bourgeois prosperity, which has corrupted his character from that of a *citizen* to that of a *consumer*."[49]

The late nineteenth century, Kristol wrote, also began to make another change that impaired the legitimacy of capitalism. After the Civil War, he argued, business enterprise and its defenders succumbed to Social Darwinism, a code of the jungle, that effected a critical break from the alliance of wealth and personal morality in capitalist society. The untrammeled reign of business over the rest of society and its indifference to the public interest produced, Kristol judged, "one of the most bizarre and sordid episodes in American intellectual history."[50] Kristol again simplified a bit, both in assuming that Social Darwinism more than an old-fashioned version of Ben Franklin's secular puritanism inspired businessmen in their apologetics and in failing to note how much such a spokesman for capitalism as William Graham Sumner utilized religious moral standards in a secular Calvanist vocabulary. Capitalists were those who won out because of their inner discipline and willingness to accept delayed gratifications, Sumner asserted, and they deserved what they reaped. Capitalists alone save the rest of an indulgent species from its own moral failings.

Nonetheless, Kristol did make a point. The capitalist ethic was being voided of moral content, taken over increasingly by a libertarian ethic, that is, an ideological allegiance to personal liberty as its moral rationale. It is an issue, Kristol believed, that went back to Mandeville and Hume in the eighteenth century and extended to Friedrich von Hayek and Milton Friedman in the twentieth. They all made the fatal assumption, Kristol argued, that private "vice," the individual's pursuit of his own economic gain, would yield public virtue. These assumptions registered a romantic notion that the external freedoms these theorists honored would not spawn inner corruptions, the unrelieved hedonism that a free society could not indefinitely tolerate. The basic problem, Kristol believed, was that the capitalist ethic had assumed a dangerous libertarianism, a defense of freedom for its own sake. Referring to Nobel Prize winner Friedman, Kristol summarized the ethical debasement of the capitalist rationale: "The idea of bourgeois virtue has been eliminated from Friedman's conception of bourgeois society, and has been replaced by the ideal of individual liberty."[51]

These disparagements notwithstanding, Kristol rejected an anticapitalist ideology that had moved from a conservative, aristocratic elite to a leftist intellectual elite. From the small coteries of café savants to the New Class of today, these intellectuals incorporate essentially elitist values and resent what Kristol insists is the veritable democratic character of the free market. For the free market means one dollar, one vote. A system that operates on this principle invariably reflects the common preferences of ordinary people, for better or worse. But the registration of these preferences in the society and culture, Kristol argued, offended the tastes of intellectuals and aesthetes, who pronounced them "vulgar." They recoiled from the norms of a society they judged to be jaded and unheroic, given over to selfishness. Those thus alienated, Kristol explained, took recourse to politics and to some form of benevolent despotism by which they would impose their own superior ideals on the rest of society.[52]

Perhaps it was a mark of Krisol's own radical past that he was somewhat sympathetic to the moral stance of the anticapitalists. The results of their pursuit of alternative societies were invariably destructive, but the effort to fill the moral vacuum that capitalism was opening was, he allowed, not without its own legitimacy. Furthermore, Kristol wrote, bourgeois civilization is "the most prosaic of all possible societies." He illustrated that point in a reference to literary history, specifically to the literary changes that accompanied the capitalist revolution. Concurrent with the advance of capitalism, Kristol wrote, was the triumphant emergence of the novel as a major literary device. The novel marked the transition away from the epic and heroic poem, the religious hymn, and the lyric — forms befitting an aristocratic era. Novels became increasingly chronicles of ordinary people in their more mundane and commonplace activities. Furthermore, Kristol argued, the earlier literature suited a society that lived with a transcendent vision of a higher and nobler life than bourgeois society could render, a vision that never credited our earthly life with anything more than a finite and provisional value or meaning. But bourgeois society, Kristol believed, "is uninterested in any such transcendence, which at best it tolerates as a private affair, a matter for individual taste and individual consumption."[53]

The intellectual inroads of capitalism followed another course, and Kristol placed himself in the tradition of Weber and Schumpeter in describing them. Capitalism, they had argued, thrived on a spirit of worldly rationalism that discredited all authority derived from tradition, dogma, or supernatural sanction. Capitalism inevitably placed a premium on the new, and that category of things came to seem inherently superior to the old and established. Rationalist capitalism thus created its own cultural biases. It deprived society of inherited authority while its pervasive skepticism, Kristol believed, promoted "an anarchic, antinomian, 'expressionist' impulse in matters cultural and spiritual."[54] This attendant defect in the culture of capitalism was a problem for Kristol and for many of the conservative thinkers examined in this book, who sought to repair the damage by shoring up traditional morality or religious authority. But there was another problem, too. For at the same time that the rationalist temperament eroded traditional authority, the disaffection with capitalism itself generated a new gnosticism, a quest for new and radical alternatives.

But for Kristol these contradictions of capitalism reached the height of their absurdity when business institutions themselves confirmed the logic of the adversary culture. Kristol wrote in 1978 that the business corporation in America had become "a nice, big, fat, juicy target for every ambitious politician and a most convenient scapegoat for every variety of organized discontent."[55] A capitalism that had made a virtue of the liberty to pursue indiscriminate gain could not be expected to be free from that indulgence itself, even to the point of profiting from the very adversary culture that would annihilate it. Reflecting on the decade of the 1960s and its aftermath, Kristol charged that American business enterprise, from books to records and movies, traded in the commodities that were disseminating the antibusiness, anti-middle-class culture of the Left. But that fact merely confirmed for Kristol that liberal capitalism had arrived at the point at which it could muster no ideological or moral resistance to the libertarian ethos of the profit motive. Why should a nihilistic capitalism, having lost its own ethic of restraint, not refrain from harvesting the dollars to be made off its own enemies? Kristol asked. Sadly, he said, none of the heirs of Adam Smith—not von Hayek, not Freidman— could offer any reasons why business should not prosper in this way.[56]

These observations so far reveal a pessimistic and despairing conservative, one who saw America disintegrating from within though smugly complacent to its circumstances. At other times, Kristol seemed more hopeful, finding among the population a residue of the bourgeois values of an earlier period. But Kristol felt compelled to ask how long a people in whom these virtues persisted would tolerate a "real world" in which dishonesty, corruption, and self-interest severed the crucial nexus of business success and personal moral integrity. For here was another way in which American life was at war with itself. "The 'outside' of our social life," Kristol wrote, "has ceased being harmonious with the 'inside'—the mode of distribution of power, privilege, and property, and hence the very principle of authority, no longer 'make sense' to the bewildered citizen." When personal virtue is no longer related to wealth by "some morally meaningful criteria," Kristol wrote, "people will no longer accept a society in which such disparities abound."[57]

Enter Irving Kristol, the Wall Street editorialist. Here was a unique but wholly suitable role for Kristol to play. Into the boardrooms themselves Kristol marched, to lecture, to admonish, to tell the corporate leaders to get their moral houses in order. This scourge of the Left, of the socialist utopians, of the liberal intellectuals, of the romantic humanitarians, came now to talk turkey to the elite of American capitalism. If they would save their economic system, then they must first save themselves. It was not, to be sure, a new assignment for a conservative. Traditionalists and antireformers like Irving Babbitt fully knew the ethical abuses of business and had warned about them. But the answer lay not in destroying the system itself. "Our real hope for safety," Irving Babbitt had prescribed in 1908, "lies in our being able to induce our future Harrimans and Rockefellers to liberalize their own souls, in other words to get themselves rightly educated."[58] So we find Kristol in his Wall Street columns excoriating business for paying exorbitant salaries, for practicing sleazy accounting methods that deceive their stockholders, for failing to police the corrupt companies in their midst, for simply failing to draft and enforce a code of ethics. Even if they were motivated wholly out of self-interest, if they were simply to "think politically," as Kristol urged them to do, then the gestures, Kristol said, would be legitimate. Business leaders needed to show a skeptical public that some place yet exists for moral responsibility in the domain of free enterprise.[59]

One might perceive some desperation in Kristol's efforts to save capitalism from its worse sins. But Kristol saw no alternative to his stance. Capitalism was the only system that coexisted with human freedom, he insisted, and the only one that promised the measure of material well-being that was indispensable to human aspirations for liberty. Kristol urged individuals of liberal sentiments, people enamored of freedom and human rights, to acknowledge the contributions of free-market capitalism to their ideals. Of one thing, at least, Kristol was certain: "Never in human history has one seen a society of political liberty that was not based on a free economic system—i.e. a system based on private property, where normal economic activity consisted of commercial transactions between consenting adults. Never, never, never. No exceptions."[60]

Echoes of the intellectual warfare of the 1930s and 1950s sounded through Kristol's vigorous warnings on this lesson of history. The warnings addressed themselves mostly to those on the Left who still romanced the socialist dream, who saw it still as the alternative to capitalism and totalitarianism. But the dream was just that, Kristol urged. In one of his most widely printed essays, Kristol described the lost soul of the political Left. "Socialism: An Obituary for an Idea" first appeared in 1975 in a collection of essays edited by R. Emmett Tyrrell, Jr., *The Future That Doesn't Work: Social Democracy's Fail-*

ure in Great Britain. "The most important political event of the twentieth century," Kristol stated, "is not the crisis of capitalism but the death of socialism." For the socialist ideal was the one authentic traditional dissent from bourgeois liberalism that was itself rooted in the Judaeo-Christian tradition, if in its gnostic strain. The loss of that alternative as a realistic choice left anticapitalism to the barbaric totalitarians, the makers of the Marxist and fascist dictatorships. Kristol was taking no comfort in this fact. "It is nothing short of a tragedy," he wrote, "that anticapitalist dissent should now be liberated from a socialist tradition which—one sees it clearly in perspective—had the function of civilizing dissent, a function it was able to perform because it implicitly shared so many crucial values with the liberal capitalism it opposed."[61]

For Kristol the socialist ideal had been written off by history. Whenever he discussed the subject, then, it was usually in reference to those bearers of the gnostic imagination who still clung to a vision of a world remade. But in the later 1970s and through the 1980s Kristol was giving extended attention to economic thought and looking for some new rationale, indeed a new program, for the conservative movement. With surprising vigor and amid new controversy, there emerged "supply-side" economics, and it moved right into the White House.

Supply-side economics became the conservatives' alternative to the Keynesian form of liberal economic theory. The supply-siders looked back to classical economic thought as expressed in Say's Law, the formulation of the early nineteenth-century French theorist Jean-Baptiste Say. He had asserted that supply creates its own demand and in doing so ensures an equilibrium in the marketplace that obviates the need for interference from outside. Say held considerable authority in economic thought until the 1930s, when John Maynard Keynes published his influential work *The General Theory of Employment, Interest, and Money.* Keynes maintained that the kinds of equilibrium that Say promised did not emerge automatically, and he advocated government spending to increase the demand for goods.[62] The economic program of the New Deal showed how Keynesian economics worked in the United States, and it established an economic role for the federal government that went unchallenged through succeeding Democratic and Republican administrations. President Nixon had said that "we are all Keynesians now." Well, not everyone. Free-market theorists, monetarists, and strong-minded conservatives continued to dissent. Other conservatives looked for a new model. By the end of the 1970s they had found one, one that was in fact very old.

We need not relate here the history of the supply-side story, curious and interesting though it is. It will suffice to take account of Kristol's role in it and his defense of the idea. As described, albeit with an accent of liberal sarcasm, by Sidney Blumenthal, supply-side economics became the missionary effort of a young economist fresh from Yale University, Arthur Laffer. Laffer, who considered himself a political liberal, assumed a position at the University of Chicago. When he later made the acquaintance of Jude Wanniski of the *Wall Street Journal*, he won over an individual who was also in a crusading mood. Wanniski had been a youthful enthusiast of President Kennedy and of the optimistic and confident spirit he conveyed. Furthermore, Laffer, in explaining the soon-to-be-famous Laffer Curve, had based his formula for national economic growth on the Kennedy tax cuts of the early 1960s. The cuts, Laffer explained, generated new spending and investment that in turn actually increased the income of the federal treasury.

The ideas soon gained ground in the conservative institutes, and here the role of Kristol was nearly decisive. Kristol had become a close friend of Wanniski, who told Blumenthal how he won Kristol over to the supply-side cause. Kristol had also, around 1973, made the acquaintance of Randolph Richardson, who that year gained control of the family Smith-Richardson Foundation. On Richardson's request for a nominee to dispense the foundation's money, Kristol suggested Leslie Lenkowsky, who took the position with the foundation in 1975. Lenkowsky wanted to promote free-market ideology ambitiously, and he approached William Baroody, Jr., of the American Enterprise Institute to elicit his interest in a new resident journalist program at AEI to be funded by Smith-Richardson. Kristol, by now AEI's leading neoconservative, recommended Wanniski as the first appointee. In 1977 Wanniski went to AEI to spend a year and to produce the first monograph for supply-side economics, a book with the immodest title *The Way the World Works*. Richardson decided to commit even more funds to the supply-side cause, and there resulted George Gilder's book *Wealth and Poverty* and then Michael Novak's *The Spirit of Democratic Capitalism* to complete what Lenkowsky called the supply-side "trilogy."[63]

What was in all this for Kristol? Lenkowsky had said of supply-side economics that "it is less an economic theory than a philosophy, an ideology . . . We're in the world of ideas."[64] Kristol saw the matter pretty much the same way, though his ideological case for supply-side economics involved different motivations. His discussion of the theory seldom involved references to taxation, investment, federal revenues, or employment. What he abstracted from supply-side theory was a renewed case for the bourgeois virtues that he could in turn use against the academic orthodoxy of the Keynesian liberals. Indeed, as Kristol noted, the supply-side cause was an "outsiders" movement. It had few supporters among the professoriat, and Kristol regarded it as a maverick thrust against an entrenched liberal elite whom he labeled "an oppressive nuisance," a group "too clever by half" to advance economic theory on a realistic or morally correct basis.[65]

Liberal economic theory, Kristol said, employed in its Keynesian construct a mechanistic model for the economy. This updated Newtonian arrangement caused economics to look like a complex machine that needed the fine tuning of technical experts to maintain its proper functioning. A vast and sophisticated data base of computerized extracts provided the occult wisdom by which the "economic engineers," as Kristol called them, calculated and prescribed economic policy. This process, Kristol countered, showed more faith than realism. The economy, he said, is less like a machine than an organism and will not conform to the "static behaviorism" assumed in the Keynesian model. Kristol even described supply-side economics as a humanist revolt against behaviorist theory. By stressing the productive side of economic activity, he explained, supply-side theory recovered the essential fact, as he put it, that capitalism is about "economic growth as the consequence of entrepreneurship." Supply-side thinking thus shifts the whole economic question back to the critical matter of character and the system of work, reward, and incentive that motivates the talents and ambitions of creative individuals. The supply-side focus, Kristol exhorted, is on productivity, the creation of wealth, and economic growth, in contrast with the liberal preoccupation about the distribution of wealth.[66]

In striking at what he believed to be one of the main components of liberal thought, Kristol was actually carrying further a disenchantment that had been evident in his writing since the early 1960s. For some of the major national magazines, he had been writing articles on federal welfare programs, giving them such titles as "Is the Welfare State Obsolete?" and "Welfare: The Best of Intentions, the Worst of Results."[67] This growing disaffection should be noted, because it indicates that Kristol's neoconservatism grew as a response not only to the emergence of a New Left movement in the 1960s but also to the effects of liberalism itself. He also pointed out the differences in the two entities but saw in both of them one common fact—the near exhaustion of America's redemptive bourgeois values.

Considering liberalism first, we note that Kristol was becoming increasingly convinced in the 1960s and 1970s that a dangerous shift was occurring. Kristol and others began to use the term *old liberalism* to describe a political tradition that they believed had a legitimate relation to American moral values. The old liberalism defended the use of government to help individuals lead the kinds of lives they could usefully pursue.[68] Kristol was imprecise in this outline, but he meant presumably that government legislation regarding minimum wages, Social Security, and education provided citizens with a modicum of material well-being and intellectual resources to be both productive and materially secure. But this was not enough for many people, Kristol said. The liberal impulse had always been animated by a vision of perfectionism, he added, a legacy of the Puritans, that pushed it toward more ambitious and idealistic ends. This perfectionist streak made Americans impatient with any shortcomings in their national life and rendered too many of them overzealous in seeking the immediate eradication of flaws. In Kristol's analysis, the Populist and Progressive movements of the late nineteenth and early twentieth centuries breathed new life into this strain and gave a permanent secular and materialist character to what had been the religious and moral inspiration of the Puritans. Political discourse took on more and more of the "vernacular utopian-prophetic rhetoric," Kristol said, and eventually embroiled the nation in its drive to realize a this-worldly Great Society in the twentieth century. Kristol did not deny that democracy and capitalism needed the ballasts of a moral idealism as correctives to their materialism. But we move too easily, he feared, from the moral to the moralistic, from a concern for what is right to a passionate self-righteousness. We become too quickly intolerant of human faults and social deficiencies and relentlessly assault a stubborn world to gratify the inner demands of our perfectionist fervor. Liberalism, Kristol asserted, had become infected by this unyielding moralism.[69]

The result, he believed, was a "new liberalism." The earlier concern for helping people lead the kind of lives they wished had yielded, in Kristol's estimate, to a desire to prescribe the kinds of lives they should lead. The environmentalist movement illustrated for Kristol the nature of this change. Environmentalism, a cause that arose with surprising rapidity in the 1960s and afterward became for Kristol a showpiece of an ideal that was made uncompromising and shortsighted in its application. For this movement, Kristol believed, quickly ran up against economic common sense and began to proliferate restrictions everywhere. Especially on a national priority like energy development, he wrote, the movement lost its reasonableness. Is it really wise, Kristol asked, to be so concerned about the mortality rate of fish in the Atlantic Ocean that off-shore drilling be prohibited as a result? Kristol also cited restrictions on the strip-mining of coal. But he wondered too why other nations facing similar choices, Britain and Norway for example, showed fewer compunctions than the United States. He offered a reason: Our country, he surmised, unlike those others, is agitated by the historical influence of an "evangelical reformism" that seems to accent discussion of every national priority. This particular movement, Kristol lamented, "has become an exercise in ideological fanaticism."[70]

Kristol wished to distinguish between morality and moralism in his effort to recover a bourgeois ethic. He spoke specifically about the decay of family authority. Parents ignored their responsibilities and turned over their prerogatives to the schools, which in turn abandoned them altogether. Schools, in fact, seemed no longer interested in developing what was once assumed in their objectives, "moral character." And parents today, Kristol observed, simply cannot answer their children's question, Why not? The same children react against their parents and against every social institution that treats them permissively with understandable disdain. Kristol went directly to Edmund Burke to locate what was wrong. We need to recognize, Kristol wrote, that it is part of people's rights to have responsibilities. Not to have obligations is a diminution of humanity. It holds one in a state of permanent immaturity. But our social institutions were moving, Kristol feared, in this direction, caught in a fetish of "responsiveness" and a politics of concessions. As examples Kristol cited Congress' lowering of the voting age to eighteen, an action taken apart from any national movement for the change. New York City replies to the cries of black parents that the public schools do not teach their children to read by declaring open admissions for them into the university system. The result, Kristol said, was clear: people do not have respect for institutions that do not have respect for them, and they will not have a prideful sense of belonging to a society so characterized.[71]

The challenge to Kristol's bourgeois America came not only from a debased liberalism but also from a more radical and vociferous movement of the 1960s, the New Left. Kristol had complained of the counterculture that it was fostering a pervasive, smug, disdainful demeanor toward capitalism and bourgeois values. But he was also chastising business, with its singular standard of the bottom line, for exploiting the adversary culture to its own advantage. The New Left considered this phenomenon differently and explained it as a form of co-option. It considered the whole economic-cultural complex of capitalism to be hegemonic, to work by a comprehensive and subtle methodology of absorbing into itself every element of opposition to the system. Thus an impassioned, ideologically motivated rebellion of youth against an oppressive technological society translates in the advertising rhetoric of the corporations into the "Pepsi generation." Long hair and dirty blue jeans, symbols of the movement, become devices for the selling of those commodities that sustain the "euphoria in unhappiness" (to use the expression of Herbert Marcuse) that describes our oppression. Kristol took seriously the New Left critique, but he counted co-option as no gain for bourgeois values or for "the system." At times Kristol seemed even more certain than Marx that liberal bourgeois democracy would not survive.

Kristol, to be sure, had no ready explanation for the unexpected developments of the 1960s, the militant student movements and the rise of a powerful intellectual challenge to liberalism, the New Left. What is striking about the explanations Kristol did offer is that they reveal a critique, often a sympathetic one, that, one is tempted to say, could derive only from an intellectual with Kristol's own leftist background. But the critique was informed as well by a perspective that was becoming more and more appreciative of traditional moral and religious values and that valued these perishables as the only antidotes to America's nihilistic culture.

In its heady revolt against bourgeois civilization, the New Left, Kristol observed, partly resembled the Old Right of Europe and its moral and aesthetic distaste for the society wrought by industrial capitalism.[72] In the United States, Kristol could have added, the New Left critique even perpetuated arguments made by the Southern Agrarians in the 1920s and 1930s, by traditionalist thinkers, that is, who denounced industrial America as a civilization bent on the endless and valueless production and consumption of goods, an open universe of acquisitions. Significant here is the fact that Kristol considered the judgments of both the Old Right and the New Left to be at least superficially legitimate. Young people, Kristol believed, were decrying the ineffectiveness of moral authority bequeathed by a permissive and relativistic liberalism. We should not have been surprised, he added, that dissenting students cast admiring eyes on Cuba and China and saw in those countries a generation and a leadership motivated by an uplifting idealism. This contagion captured the imagination of the New Left. However misleading and deceptive this notion may have been, Kristol could nonetheless write that "today the New Left is rushing to fill the spiritual vacuum at the center of our free and capitalist society."[73]

Kristol identified a spiritual vacuum that cut across the whole public culture of the United States. He was a writer who could cry out for censorship of pornography and who could praise Victorian culture for its deference to womanhood.[74] What Kristol sorely lamented was the loss of republican virtue in Western life, and behind that loss, he believed, was the decline of religion. The decline did not constitute for Kristol a merely curious cultural shift. It lay at the base of every issue that liberal and conservative political ideologies confronted. The loss of faith, Kristol wrote, was the "most important *political* fact of the last hundred years." In fact, he said, the death of God "haunts bourgeois society."[75] The decay of religious values, he believed, had left the moral and spiritual stock of Western democracies depleted.

Kristol's response to this problem, more than any other aspect of his neoconservatism, joined him to the traditionalist and religious thinkers in the Old Right. Some of them, like Paul Elmer More, T. S. Eliot, John Hallowell,

Thomas Molnar, and Russell Kirk defended a specific Christian church tradition (overwhelmingly Roman Catholic or Anglo-Catholic). Others, like Irving Babbitt and Peter Viereck, wanted religion to enhance the humanist standards they ultimately defended.[76] But all these thinkers issued a common warning, that Western society could not thrive under the culture of materialism and secularism and the pragmatic and relativistic moral framework they had fostered. Kristol voiced the convictions and the fears of this group. He wrote: "For well over a hundred and fifty years now, social critics have been warning us that bourgeois society was living off the accumulated moral capital of traditional religion and traditional moral philosophy, and that once this capital was depleted, bourgeois society would find its legitimacy ever more questionable."[77] This lament occurred throughout Kristol's writings. It was not the sigh of a momentary despair. And he summarized the sad results of this devolution. We have today, Kristol wrote, "a social order that is sick because it has lost its soul."[78]

Kristol's own interest in religion seems to date back to the postwar period. His occasional autobiographical recollections do not mention a religious interest in his early years. To this extent, Kristol rather typified the perfervid secularism of the New York intellectuals, among whom surrogates for religious faith abounded. Lionel Abel remembered of his early years that "Jews in the left-wing movement were supposed to give up, or at least forget about, their Jewishness for the sake of the universalist . . . principles they were supposed to serve."[79] The cosmopolitanism that broke them out of parochial ways became a self-conscious identity among the New Yorkers. "We thought of literature and our literary profession," William Phillips wrote, "not as Jews, but as heirs to the Western tradition. Certainly, this was the feeling of all of us who considered ourselves to be socialists."[80]

But the Holocaust and the painful awakening it created among Jews everywhere aroused them to interest in their religious past. Irving Howe, who also remembered the loss of Jewish consciousness among his generation of New Yorkers, wrote that later some felt shame at having cast off all sense of Jewish distinctiveness. The Holocaust did not make his group religious necessarily. Rather it simply confirmed in their minds a fact: "Jews we were," Howe wrote, "like it or not, and liked or not."[81] Kristol himself certainly changed his orientation toward Judaism, and in 1949 he involved himself in a study group, with Daniel Bell, Nathan Glazer, and Milton Himmelfarb, that convened to discuss the *Misneh Torah* of Maimonides, the twelfth-century Jewish scholar. The writings of Leo Strauss were also a special focus of this group, and Kristol ranked Strauss along with Lionel Trilling as the greatest intellectual influence on his own development. As for Judaism, Kristol said that he and other like-minded Jews were "groping to establish rapport with the Jewish tradition, standing at the synagogue door, 'heart in, head out.' "[82]

Religious conservatives might have perceived in Kristol's piety a mere gesture, a confession of loss of faith in the world and a turn to any stabilizing influence amid the ruins of war, genocide, and the secular ideologies that caused them. Kristol himself never became a partisan of Jewish causes, religious or political, and his theological interests were broad enough to embrace, for their positive influences, Christian thinkers like Reinhold Niebuhr. Kristol called himself "a believer" but did not participate in Jewish religious life "as much as I should." Furthermore, he generally valued religion for its social effects, for the public discipline and stability it promoted, more than for the cleansing of the individual soul. "People need religion," he said. "It's a vehicle for a moral tradition. A crucial role. Nothing can take its place." But Kristol wrote also about religion's indispensable compensation and consolation to the despairing soul.[83] By the 1980s, furthermore, Kristol doubted that any way out of the resulting malaise could be effected apart from an authentic religious recovery.

Irving Howe wrote in his autobiography, "God died in the nineteenth century, utopia in the twentieth."[84] Kristol was not as certain about the death of utopia. His essays, in fact, bristle with judgments against this unexorcised demon of modern history. And for Kristol the subject of utopia raised the related question of intellectuals. For the persistence of the utopian vision was largely the doing of an intellectual community that found itself hopelessly at odds with capitalism and bourgeois culture. Kristol confronted all those aversions, from the millennial Left to the New Class.

Paul Hollander had referred in his book of 1981, *Political Pilgrims,* to the emergence in the United States of a "massive culture of alienation," an "establishment of estrangement."[85] Kristol, too, believed that this culture had become pervasive. "It is hardly to be denied," he wrote, "that the culture that educates us — the patterns of perception and thought our children absorb in their schools, at every level — is unfriendly (at the least) to the commercial civilization, the bourgeois civilization, within which most of us live and work." Graduates of our colleges and universities invariably emerge from them with a lower opinion of our social and economic life, he added.[86] On this subject, Kristol's pronouncements over the years became increasingly bitter and angry. Think of it, he said. The country in the 1980s was becoming more conservative. A popular conservative president won a landslide reelection in 1984. But our major universities, Kristol observed, "seem to be living in some kind of time warp, still casting their votes for George McGovern." And in 1986, despite the gains of neoconservatives on American campuses, indeed despite a whole new generation of conservative scholarship that Kristol himself had done much to sponsor, he rendered this summary judgment on higher learning in America: "Never in American history have major universities been so dominated by an entire spectrum of radical ideologies as today. Never in American history have these universities so militantly divorced themselves from the sentiments and opinions of the overwhelming majority of the people."[87]

Kristol, despite the hyperbole, did touch an unfortunate prejudice in American institutional life. But the legitimate criticism that he raised against intellectuals began to deepen into a hardened rancor against intellectual life altogether, which led Kristol into dangerous generalizations about intellectuals. Kristol feared that America, with its expansive university systems, was producing what he called "a mass society of Intellectuals."[88] Given the intellectual-political climates of these universities, that fact augured ill for the nation. Alienation, nonconformity, and nihilism could only intensify. The damage would be compounded, furthermore, Kristol believed, as more areas of American life were submitted to the theorizing of sociologists, psychologists, political scientists, and the like.

Kristol delivered some of his most categorical statements in his judgments on these matters. On the inability of public authorities to deal effectively with crime, he wrote: "This is what results when one permits 'sophisticated' theories – elaborate ideologies really – to prevail over common sense and traditional wisdom." On the matter of child rearing, "experts," Kristol wrote, have taken over a process whose success comes from knowledge "intuitively available to us."[89] The whole enterprise of academic sociology Kristol virtually condemned. "In sociology," he wrote, ". . . after almost two centuries, there simply does not exist a body of knowledge that permits sociologists to talk with more authority about society than someone who may never have received sociological training."[90] Nor did Kristol restrict his derogation to sociologists. "There is no reason to think," he said, "–there is not the slightest shred of evidence–that the organized, collective intelligence of professors has anything whatsoever to contribute to our social, economic, political, or moral problems."[91] William F. Buckley, Jr., thought it frightful to be ruled by the Harvard professors; Kristol thought it folly.

Kristol's writings illustrate a curious modern phenomenon – intellectual anti-intellectualism. Assembled under the common heading of the betrayal of the intellectuals, they could make a small book, and indeed they could form a large one if Kristol were joined by other American conservatives. Intellectual anti-intellectualism was a visible theme in the conservatism of the post-modern age, and it focused on a new ruling elite that American conservative intellectuals liked to call the New Class. In Kristol's case it brought together many of the points against liberalism and modern culture.

What we see in Kristol's depiction of the New Class, that is, his contempt for it, reveals the tendency of conservatives too often to lapse into conspiratorial accounts of what is taking place around them. On such questions as the disintegration of authority in American life, the decline of morality, or the erosion of patriotic affection, it was tempting to identify cynical forces at work. Kristol's New Class appeared hegemonic, sharing a common blueprint for a reconstructed America. Perhaps his case was overstated without being entirely wrong. It might be more accurate to say that the New Class was as opportunist about its own advantages as was the business class when it marketed the counterculture for its own profits. Kristol and the neoconservatives were pointing to a situation in American life that was curious in itself. Let us remember what Karl Marx and Friedrich Engels had written in *The German Ideology,* that "the ideas of the ruling class are in every epoch the ruling ideas, i.e. the class which is the ruling material force of society, is at the same time its ruling intellectual force."[92] In an ironic sense that aggrieved him, Kristol was saying that Marx was right. Capitalists and intellectuals did not as a rule celebrate a bourgeois ethic. They were the elite who ruled a culture whose essence was itself countercultural, for the bourgeois ethic was no longer the underpinning of capitalist America. But this turn in the position of the "ruling class," Kristol knew, was not at all what Marx had foreseen. Marx was right only in a cruelly ironic sense.

Finally, on this topic one speculation is irresistible. Kristol usually displayed in his writings a cold, logical demeanor, often caustic to be sure, but seldom impassioned. Almost exclusively on the subject of intellectuals did he arm for heavy rhetorical combat. Perhaps some reflections on the careers of the New York Jewish intellectuals may cast some light on Kristol's obsessions with this subject.

The literary critic Alfred Kazin was only one paragraph into his memoir *Starting Out in the Thirties* when, in describing his turn to socialism, he fired this blast: "I had the deepest contempt for those middle-class and doctrinaire radicals who, after graduating from Harvard or Yale in the Twenties, had made it a matter of personal honor to become Marxists, and who now worried in the *New Masses* whether Proust should be read after the Revolution and why there should be no simple proletarians in the novels of André Malraux."[93] Irving Howe offered a similar reminiscence of this period. His youthful socialist activities in New York brought him and his colleagues into the company of some Vassar College radicals who were "patrician prim, yet somehow always following the Stalinist line." His own group, Howe recalled, was "hopelessly plebeian, New Yorkers caustic in speech and often uncouth in manner." They detected in the Vassar attitude toward them an "air of patrician condescension." Howe added: "The combination of upper class coolness and Stalinist politics was too much."[94]

Later in the 1950s these mutual suspicions resurfaced, and they gave to the anticommunism of the Jewish liberals a particular accent. The Alger Hiss case illustrated it best. Many of the eastern intellectual elite defended Hiss (though several, like Arthur M. Schlesinger, Jr., Bruce Bliven, and Murray Kempton, doubted his innocence). As Richard Pells observed, Hiss exuded the appearance of the radical turned organization man. His connections to the State Department and the Carnegie Foundation suggested one who had replaced the radical in overalls for the corporate leftist of pin-striped respectability. Harold Rosenberg, for one, had only contempt for his like, "the middle class careerists" who aspired to ascend the social ladder into government and the universities.[95] Diana Trilling observed of the Hiss case that the accused's defenders were the well-healed, well-educated, and well-bred people of social distinction. "The roster of Hiss supporters," said William Phillips, "reads like a page out of the social register."[96]

Did this kind of prejudice, this perception of something "radical chic" in the leftism of the elite, linger yet in Kristol's hostility toward the New Class? Though many of them were Jewish, the New Class seemed to convey to neoconservatives a disingenuous radicalism. Their liberalism seemed contrived and inauthentic, trendy and fashionable. The New Yorkers had reclaimed radicalism as their birthright, and even after they forsook it, they were not prepared to yield it to the impostors, their social betters. Revealingly, Kristol once described the people who helped launch the *Public Interest* with him. Practically all of them, he went out of his way to say, "had themselves risen from the ranks of the urban poor." They had relied on work and education as their only effective delivery from poverty. But those who were authoring the Great Society programs were, Kristol continued, "upper-middle class graduates of elite universities who had been dazzled by trendy sociological theories."[97] Here the New Class designs of the elite ran smack against the bourgeois ethic of poverty's children.

By the middle of the 1980s the conservative intellectual advancement was threatened by internal strains. In fact, Kristol and the neoconservatives were coming under attack both from the Old Right group of religions and metaphysical conservatives and from other conservative writers who were breathing new life into capitalism by making an appealing intellectual case for it. Let us recall Kristol's comment that bourgeois society is irredeemably "prosaic."

"It is prosaic," Kristol added, "not only in form but in essence. It is a society organized for the convenience and comfort of common men and common women, not for the production of heroic, memorable figures. It is a society interested in making the best of this world, not in any kind of transfiguration, whether through tragedy or piety."[98] Even the most liberal dissenter must ask whether the United States is so low and uninviting a civilization, as Kristol here describes. Did Kristol dream of chivalrous knights in armor or saintly ascetics to expunge the material dross from our sated society? Was there no boon to the human spirit in the discovery of a cure for polio or in the exploration of the heavens or even in finding a way to bake potatoes in ten minutes?

The historian Robert Crunden reviewed Kristol's *Two Cheers for Capitalism* and titled his review "Cheering Is Not Enough." Describing himself as one who had "never felt the allure of American liberalism," Crunden laid down the challenge to defenders of capitalism. The challenge, he said, "is to relate capitalism to the human personality, to demonstrate the connection between a rational system of rewards and punishments to the development of motivated children, artistic creativity, an ordered environment and other categories by which we measure 'a meaningful life.' "[99] Paul Hollander, in turn, reflected on the negativism of the intellectual class and the toll he believed it took in society's loss of self-esteem, lack of will, and general malaise. But he had to conclude that the neoconservative intellectuals in the United States had failed to counteract the kind of estrangement from their own society that had become normal for other intellectuals.[100]

Along came George Gilder. When *Wealth and Poverty* appeared in 1981 it became a surprising best-seller, the intellectual manifesto of the Reagan years. What Gilder added to the long list of capitalist apologetics was a lively and vigorous book, but above all one that presented capitalism as a spiritual and moral adventure of inspiring dimensions. Gilder's opening statement could have been extracted directly from Kristol. "The most important event in the recent history of ideas," Gilder wrote, "is the demise of the socialist dream." The first sentence of his next paragraph might have come from Kristol or Daniel Bell. "The second most important event of the recent era is the failure of capitalism to win a corresponding triumph." And no thanks to the neoconservatives, Gilder added. Gilder found it "a curious fact" that a celebrated group of conservative thinkers, often heralded as the saviors of business from its detractors on the Left, forecast the same unhappy future for capitalism as Marx, Veblen, and Schumpeter. Gilder traced the flaws in the capitalist defense back to Adam Smith, who, he said, was more intrigued by the marvelous mechanical contrivance that was capitalism than he was by the heroic and creative processes taking place within it, the adventurous creation of wealth. "The market," Gilder wrote, "provides only the routine climax, the perfunctory denouement of a tempestuous drama, dominated by the incredible creativity of entrepreneurs, making purposeful gifts without predetermined returns, launching enterprise into the always unknown future."[101]

Gilder's book generated commentary everywhere. Among conservatives, a meeting of the Intercollegiate Studies Institute held at the Mayflower Hotel in Washington, D.C., featured a session in the Star Ballroom that included Kristol and Gilder. In his remarks, Kristol called *Wealth and Poverty* "three-fourths a great book." And clearly, in the pleas of Gilder and Kristol for supply-side economics, in their measure of the moral toll of the welfare state, and in their mutual attitudes on many other issues, Kristol and Gilder were kindered spirits. But in his commentary Kristol went on to say that it is nonsense to glorify capitalism. No poet ever wrote a paean to the businessman, for the very good reason that the profit motive is neither noble nor magnanimous. Capitalism promotes some admirable moral qualities, Kristol said, but they are insufficient for a complete and worthy life. They do not by themselves inspire patriotism, physical courage, or charity.[102] But Kristol's most revealing judgment against Gilder, rendered in his review of the book, concerned religion. Gilder's morality, Kristol charged, lacked "a religious sense." The bourgeois values, Kristol said, can provide us a degree of decency and material comfort, but they do not answer life's most important questions. Life confronts us with too many moral questions, and no worldly philosophy can answer them. "Only a morality embedded in a transcendental religion," Kristol insisted, "can cope" with the inescapable fact of life's basic unfairness. "Benjamin Franklin," he wrote, "is neither Moses nor Jesus Christ, nor even John Calvin."[103] Such animadversions have a particular relevance when considered against the charge of the Old Right that neoconservatism thrived only in the worldly milieu of sociology and political economy.

The problem with Kristol's conservatism, the contradiction, perhaps, was of a different nature. In fact it could be said of Kristol that his weakness as a conservative thinker was also his great strength. His essays offered brilliant commentary on specific subjects to which he brought his critical mind. Collectively, however, they failed to make a satisfactory whole. They were astute in perceiving the utopian overreach of the modern mind, and none can discount the toll in social turmoil that it has taken. But Kristol leaves us with few guidelines in marking off the utopian hope from the innate human aspiration for a better world. It would have been easy, for example, to dismiss the quest for racial justice in America, inspired by much lofty rhetoric in the 1950s and 1960s, as another exercise in utopian folly. And the effect would have been a discredit to the moral record of American history. The price of ideals is their invariable excesses. But the challenge to conservatism was to preserve its skeptical sense of human nature, its appreciation of the darker side, while yet pointing to inspirations that can rule our higher nature. That quest led Kristol back to religion, however incomplete for many was his outline of its spiritual content. Among all the conservative intellectuals of his day, Kristol did the most to join the modernism, the practical spirit, and the sociological temper of the neoconservatives to the enduring ideals — traditional, religious, metaphysical — of classical conservatism. He had officiated at the marriage of a new conservatism with the Old Right, although the union yet awaited consummation.

5

Hilton Kramer
On the Battlefield
of Modernism

LIONEL TRILLING called it "the bloody crossroads," where literature and politics meet. Norman Podhoretz used these words as the title of his book of 1986. I use the expression "the battlefield of modernism" as the subtitle for this chapter to describe a war of minds that has centered, for a half-century at least in this country, on the direction of culture in the modern world and the relation of that culture to the changing political scene. What, we will ask, did literature and art—and mostly painting in this case—indicate about the evolving conditions of American society? What did the aesthetic life, and particularly the modernist idiom, signify for the changing norms, the altered states of consciousness, and the habits of the heart in bourgeois America? The subject moves quickly from private to public realms, not because artists themselves intended specific social consequences for their works but because the cultural movements of a half-century have been chronicled with keen interest, and with many a political axe to grind, by critics, scribes, and polemicists of all kinds. And when in the 1960s these observers began to describe a new "post-modern" episode in the cultural arena, a new battlefield was prepared. The antagonists, however, were familiar foes.

A conservative literary renaissance whose literature included essays on baseball and Rodeo Drive, fountain pens and computers, summer camps and peanut butter, could be expected to embrace the subject of artists and their paintings. Hilton Kramer filled that category abundantly. His first collection of essays, published in 1973 as *The Age of Avant-Garde: An Art Chronicle of 1956–1972*, contained some one hundred fifty essays, on a host of subjects from Monet and Degas to the contemporaries Robert Motherwell, Willem de Kooning, and Ad Reinhardt. Eighty-four more essays found their way into *The Revenge of the Philistines: Art and Culture, 1972–1984,* which concluded with a section called "Art for the Eighties." The essay format, in the manner of the neoconservative literary style, was Kramer's forte. He employed it heavily against those who pirated art to press it into the service of political and ideological causes. He used it more often, though, as a means of describing aesthetic experience in its manifold variety. The collected essays, originally published in newspapers and art journals, highlighted what was enduring, vital, fresh, or new at any moment and in turn exposed the imitative, the fashionable, and the pretentious. Kramer was resolved to uphold high aesthetic standards, and the job kept him busy for many years amid shifts in fashion and taste and amid unceasing proclamations of new and revolutionary movements in American painting.

To the ancient Chinese a picture was worth a thousand words. In Kramer's best essays, five hundred fit the equation. With Buckley, Tyrrell, and Will, Kramer gave rhetorical polish and flair to intellectual conservatism. He displayed a masterly sensitivity, a penchant for the mot juste, as he guided the reader through a kind of museum tour of one artist's renderings. His essays, to be sure, were sometimes technical, falling back into the in-house language of critics, but Kramer could map, for even the most prosaic of minds, an artist's place in the great tradition. He could delineate with precision the nuances and effects that gave artists their special signatures. When Kramer located good painting, his enthusiasm for it was graphic and contagious. Consider, for example, his commentary on the American portraitist Philip Pearlstein, whose paintings of the early and mid-1970s Kramer reviewed in 1976:

His aim is objectivity, and to achieve it he places his subjects in the "objective" light of the studio. This harsh studio light—the bright, cold, even, artificial light that is an essential coefficient of the painter's studied neutrality—creates an atmosphere of unrelieved interrogation. It is a light that renders his subjects defenseless; it neutralizes their charm and even their beauty and underscores their vulnerability. No one, not even a babe in arms unmarked by the ravages of time, could possibly emerge from close and prolonged observation in this light as anything but a casualty of experience, and no one does.[1]

In 1980 Kramer judged the works of social realist Jack Beal. Kramer was somewhat critical of social realism, but he considered Beal a compelling artist and singled out for praise one painting in particular: "The setting is Mr. Beal's farm at Oneonta in upstate New York. The time is summer, the foliage is verdant, and the sky almost as unclouded as the sky in a picture postcard.

Hilton Kramer by Vint Lawrence

The whole scene is, indeed, an environmentalist's dream—this is surely the cleanest air anyone has painted since Winslow Homer quit the coast of Maine."[2]

But what does an extended series of art essays amount to? What makes Kramer an appropriate subject for a study of American conservatism? For one, Kramer repeatedly insisted that there is a realm of life and experience that is properly labeled the aesthetic and that great art, furthermore, the art that commands and deserves our study, takes place within an ongoing art tradition. That emphasis led Kramer to mark out carefully his own points of agreement with and dissent from such critics as Harold Rosenberg and Clement Greenberg. In fact, Kramer wished to steer between the heavy social and political context of the one and the formalist/purist emphasis of the other, however much he sided with Greenberg generally. That effort provided much of the special character of Kramer's essays. They became literary exercises, cultural discussions that searched for those points of contact between the individual creator and the immediate social milieu but preserved the more important context of a higher universalism, an ongoing dialogue of the artist with a kind of autotelic, separate, sustaining tradition of art.

Consider, for example, Kramer's suggestive essay on the American painter Charles Sheeler. Born in 1883, Sheeler became an American exponent of cubism and painted stylistic, architectonic renderings of the American industrial landscape. What Kramer found instructive in Sheeler, though, was his translation of a European-style modernism into the controlled and immaculate exteriors of his subjects in a way that suggested American "Puritan" influences. "There is a history to be written," Kramer said, "of the influence of the Protestant mind on Cubist aesthetics — on what happened when Cubism was removed from Paris to the colder climates — and Sheeler would have a place in that history." Kramer elaborated:

For Sheeler, the city is as innocent as the countryside. Skyscrapers, too, are a version of pastoral. The machine is assimilated to the folkloric sensibility. Not even the massive impedimenta of modern industry can break the precious thread of continuity with the emotions of the past. . . . The barn and the factory, the hearth rug and the skyscraper, the still life and the smokestack — they are all fragments of the same dream. They are all immaculate and innocent. They are all acquitted of having any difficult or complex relation to experience. In fact, they are depicted as existing outside the realm of experience — untouched and inviolable.[3]

"I've never attached myself to any particular movement," Kramer once told an interviewer, "because I could see what was good and bad . . . in all kinds of art."[4] This was true enough, to a point, but Kramer never shied from judgment, and his criticism was not disinterested. His prejudices were never obscure. He asserted forcefully that the great tradition of modern art is that which connects Cézanne, Picasso, Miró, Mondrian, and Matisse. It was the tradition of "high purposes and moral grandeur" that gave modernism its distinction. It was the tradition that seemed to have culminated in the powerful New York school of artists, who revitalized a fading and nearly moribund modernism by giving it new vigor, complexity, and graphic expressiveness.

This identification of Kramer with modernist genre, though it was never un-qualified and though Kramer railed against the facile extensions of modernism, marks Kramer's place in the modernist wing of American conservative opinion. To be sure, it defied the imaginations of some conservative thinkers to concede that the modernist movement in art, attended as it always was by pronouncements of new and revolutionary sensibilities, the systematic demolition of tradition in the political or aesthetic realms, the priorities of originality and the liberation of art from interfering moral norms, could ever be accommodated to a properly conservative view of life. Nor should it be said that accommodation was Kramer's intention. But the course of art in the twentieth century and its apparently inevitable political affiliations in the hands of its interpreters conspired to make Kramer's writings on art decidedly a part of the conservative literature of his time. It is a curious and interesting story. And it could not have been effected by anyone before the 1960s.

Kramer accepted for himself the neoconservative label. That affiliation joined him to a group of neoconservatives, Irving Kristol and Peter Berger among them, who sought a reconciliation with modernism and who, in doing so, set themselves apart from Old Right antimodernism. Berger at one point had even divided the conservatives into two distinct groups: the neoconservatives, who basically accepted "the modern consciousness" in matters of culture and intellect, and the Old Right, who were fundamentally at war with modernism.[5] Cultural conservatives, from the New Humanists to Daniel Bell, had espied in the modernist movement the erosion of traditional values, moral and religious, the signs of the disintegrating social bond, the dissolution of bourgeois discipline in favor of an indiscriminate expansionism, individual self-indulgence, and hedonism. Sometimes it was fear of the radically new, sometimes personal taste, that sparked these animadversions. But compare Kramer's commentary on the sculptor Mark di Suvero with that of another conservative intellectual. Kramer wrote: "Among the sculptors of the younger generation who may be said not only to be practicing their art with some distinction but to be transforming it in quite far-reaching ways, the single most interesting figure is Mark di Suvero. He seems to me the most significant new American sculptor to have emerged since the generation of Alexander Calder, David Smith, and Isamu Noguchi and . . . to be producing work that will have the greatest consequences for the future of this art."[6] When George Will, on the other hand, wrote an essay on di Suvero in 1976, he titled it "Junk."[7] (I remember the public row touched off in my city in the middle 1970s when the Common Council of Milwaukee accepted an anonymous gift to purchase a di Suvero sculpture and to place it near Lake Michigan, where it would imitate, supposedly, the eastern view of the lake at sunrise. Angry letters to the local newspapers showed what many Milwaukeeans thought of modernism.)

Hilton Kramer was born in Gloucester, Massachusetts, in 1928. He was descended from generations of Russian Jews that included paternal grandparents who came to the United States in their teens. His other grandparents did not emigrate. Of his parents' religion, Kramer said that they were "observing without being orthodox." Politically the family was solidly in the Democratic camp, as Kramer's father and older brothers were strong admirers of Franklin D. Roosevelt. A brother of the father, who lived in Revere, Massachusetts, and had Communist party loyalties, was considered "an embarrassment" to the rest of the family. Loyalty to the American cause in the Second World War seemed axiomatic among the Kramers, and when one of the clan cast its first Republican vote in 1952, there seemed to be nothing sensational about it.[8]

Kramer's early academic interests were literary. He remembered a high school teacher in Boston who excited these interests and who helped him improve his writing skills. Through his college work at Syracuse University and graduate work at Columbia University, Kramer concentrated on literature, with a secondary interest in philosophy. In fact, Kramer had no academic training in the study of art or art history. That focus emerged when he decided not to pursue an academic career (a brief teaching stint at Indiana University made him hungry for the cultural heights of New York City). He had met Philip Rahv, and Rahv in turn published Kramer's first art criticism in *Partisan Review*. Back in New York City, Kramer maintained friendships with a circle of local artists and increasingly undertook reviews of exhibitions. An avocation soon became a career.[9]

In 1954 Kramer began work at *Art Digest,* and then a year later he undertook the managing editorship of *Arts Magazine.* For three years, until 1961, Kramer was art critic for the *Nation.* His essays and reviews were now appearing in *Commentary,* the *New Republic,* and *Commonweal.* He was becoming familiar as an articulate voice of modernism, though by no means an uncritical one. Then in 1965 Kramer became the art news editor of the *New York Times,* writing reviews on exhibitions and longer pieces on trends in culture. The latter often appeared in the Sunday *New York Times Magazine.* The *Times* affiliation made Kramer a critic of substantial influence, and he became increasingly controversial. In the 1960s and 1970s Kramer's opinioned essays became more and more steeped in political skirmishing. He watched the rising revolutionary fervor of the Left and the gains of neo-Marxist scholarship on art and other subjects in the universities, the efforts to turn museums into institutions of ideological expression and art itself into politics. The *New York Times* gave Kramer complete editorial freedom in addressing these issues, but in 1982 an opportunity for a new kind of work appeared, and Kramer embarked on a new path.[10]

The *New Criterion* was born of one hundred thousand dollars of start-up money from the John M. Olin Foundation and of the determination of Kramer to raise the critical standards of judgment for contemporary art. The journal appeared monthly beginning in September 1982, with ten issues annually plus a usual special summer number. In appearance, the *New Criterion* reflected the judicious combination of traditionalism and modernism that it aspired to realize as the right and delicate balance of expression in the realm of art. It used a Galliard typeface, a modest contemporary variation of the traditional Granjon lettering of French Renaissance origin. Contemporary nonbasic colors and pastels were assigned to each month of a volume's ten numbers, and the color was repeated for that month in successive volumes. Only October, which was yellow, and the special summer issues came wrapped in conservative, traditional hues.

Kramer had become convinced that the art world had lost its sense of direction and art criticism had lost its standards. His essays portrayed collectively this scene: the demise of modernism had prepared the way for a rash of experimental ventures (that much was owed to modernism itself), many of them falling under the general rubric "post-modernism" and most of them flourishing only because modernism's standards and its critical literature had badly slackened. The art world had become an open highway with many a vagabond traveler and peddler roaming its way. Populist ideology, with its anti-elitist disdain for modernism, added its own corrupting effects. Museums were denounced as sanctuaries, snobbish enclaves, ivory towers of privilege, wealth, and reclusive isolation. And the museums themselves too easily succumbed to the new norms, opening their halls to every maverick artist and self-proclaimed new "movement" that a democratic and indiscriminate taste would tolerate. Thus, at New York's Metropolitan Museum of Art "Harlem on My Mind" and other "scandals" of the museum's patronizing administration indicated to Kramer the betrayal of standards. At the Museum of Modern Art the new director in 1970 pontificated officially that "I happen to believe that everybody is an artist." Such vacuous pronunciations piqued Kramer's editorial ire.[11]

The opening statement in the *New Criterion* also included an editorial aside that is worth noting. It spoke of the political corruption of art and criticism by the political Left. "Not since the 1930s," said the editors, "have so many orthodox leftist pieties so casually insinuated themselves into both the creation and criticism of literature, and remained so immune to resistance or exposure." There remained from the 1930s, the editors believed, a persistent animosity toward bourgeois and capitalist society, despite all the apparent changes of a half-century of American life, including, most important, a long period of political reform and cultural vitality expressive of the norms of the civilization. Most writers on the Left, the *New Criterion* said, had not forgiven American history for failing to live up to their expectations of it. They clung still to a radical alternative vision of the country. The religious dogma of socialism or Marxism would not loosen its grip. Capitalism remained the intellectuals' blind spot. But the *New Criterion* spokesmen would insist on one point—that "capitalism, for all its many flaws, has proved to be the greatest safeguard of intellectual and artistic freedom . . . that the modern world has given us."[12]

What lay behind this special point of emphasis? For in truth, the discussion of capitalism and bourgeois life proved hardly to be a recurring subject for the *New Criterion,* however much it took on the subject of Marxism. Behind the statement there lurked a half-century of dogmatic warfare about art and politics and their relation to capitalism and bourgeois society. The issue must take us back briefly to the fateful decade of the 1930s. For like Irving Kristol, Hilton Kramer wrote an extended chapter in the history of the New York intellectuals.

Partisan Review formulated its famous program of radicalism in politics and modernism in culture in 1934. We have seen how the first part of the program waned in succeeding years and even, in neoconservatives like Irving Kristol, lost out altogether among some of the New York intellectuals. But what of modernism? What became of the commitment to a high and serious culture and all that it implied about the possibilities of a new consciousness that would extend to the social and political realms as well? Among the Left, there were, of course, many dogmatic voices who were calling in the 1930s for a radical literature that expressed the heart and mind of the proletariat. Mike Gold and the writers for the *New Masses* spewed a reductionist aesthetics that measured the value of literature by the singular standard of its usefulness for revolution-making. But what made the leftism of the *Partisan Review* so much more engaging was its maturer attitudes toward culture, the far greater sensitivity toward art and literature that its editors and contributors displayed. Very soon, that sensitivity made the *PR* formula inoperative.

Aesthetic modernism and revolutionary politics proved to be an unstable compound in the *Partisan Review* format. When Stalinist Popular Front politics brought democratic writers from Whitman to Sherwood Anderson into an acceptable antifascist alliance, *PR* recoiled from this appropriation of bourgeois culture. Harold Rosenberg and Philip Rahv decried the sell-out, and *PR* writers retreated increasingly into a formalist defense of letters. Rahv stood with T. S. Eliot, his "fascist" politics notwithstanding, against his detractors on the Left, and Clement Greenberg drew sharp discriminations between "Avant-Garde and Kitsch."[13]

The New Yorkers saw more hope than prophecy in their call for a new culture in the United States. To theirs and many others' surprise, however, the nation only a few years later witnessed an avant-garde movement in painting that had domestic and international influence. The emergence of the New York school of painting, from obscure and impoverished quarters in Lower Manhattan to prestige and fashion in middle-class America, is one of the surprising twists in our cultural history. Many of the artists were sons of immigrants—Arshile Gorky, Willem de Kooning, Hans Hofmann, Mark Rothko, and Barnett Newman, among others. Some were native sons, including the most renowned of them, Jackson Pollock. In the early 1940s, of course, New York was home to many artists exiled from Europe, whose presence directly influenced the course of the New York school. Piet Mondrian, Marc Chagall, Marcel Duchamp, Max Ernst, and André Breton helped move the European tradition in abstract art in the American direction of abstract expressionism. These factors have caused art historians to point out that a combination of familiar styles joined with a bold and determined experimentalism among the Americans to create the new idiom. Kramer for one always stressed that the New York school extended European modernism but revitalized it at a time when its freshness and vigor were nearly spent.

Abstract expressionism must be considered as a particular form of modernism. But defining modernism and its relation to modern society became a fertile ground of controversy for Kramer and other interpreters. When Irving Howe, an important voice of the New York intellectuals, took up the subject of modernism, he outlined several features of a movement that began in the late nineteenth century and crystallized in the early twentieth with new directions in literature, painting, architecture, and music. The aesthetic mood of modernism, Howe said, was subjective, a mood born of its profound skepticism toward inherited intellectual and ethical norms and its determination to experiment with new sensations and to find new truths, however private they remained. Modernism brought to its world a sense of historical impasse, Howe added. The modernist spirit was awed by the uniqueness of its own age, especially the world's unprecedented catastrophic condition. Modernism saw a traditional culture in ruins and despaired of any restorative effort to recover the broken continuity of Western civilization. Modernism did not aspire to provide permanent answers and was content merely to ask questions, to ask them over and over again in new ways. Modernism, according to Howe, reflected a culture at war with itself, one weary of its own rationalism and its own decorative refinements. Modernism's pioneers believed that something vital had been lost, eroded from our human powers, and that sense gave modernist art its malaise. Modernism thus conveyed a mood of alienation.[14] Howe's socialist preferences led him to position modernism against bourgeois norms. And this classic enmity of modernism and bourgeois civilization, which conservatives also acknowledged, would be the key challenge for Kramer's aesthetics.

The New York painters enjoyed an unforeseen success. They gained stature and recognition in the art museums of New York City, but their works, in the years after World War II, became the cherished possessions of the buying public as well. The rival Regionalist school faded into obscurity as slick art journals, suitable for coffee tables in suburban living rooms, made familiar the expressive icons of the American modernists. This confounding development left critics to ponder what might become of art when the avant-garde itself became the art establishment in the culture that it sought to assail. It was on understanding this turn of events that much of the critical warfare of the period, from the late 1950s and into the 1980s, centered. And how one made sense of the fate of modernism in capitalist America very much determined how one would decode the mysteries of the "post-modern" culture that followed. It is one of the most unusual twists of American intellectual life that the defense of the modernist achievement in art would make of Hilton Kramer an embattled neoconservative.

The discussion of modernist painting was most lively and informative among the New York intellectuals, who prepared the way for its acceptance in the United States. Kramer's own art criticism found its context within the literature produced by this group and especially its two major protagonists, Clement Greenberg and Harold Rosenberg. Greenberg upheld an essentially formalist aesthetics. Kramer called him "the finest art critic of his day," though he faulted Greenberg for an essentially impersonal sense of art history that Kramer traced to Greenberg's Marxist background.[15] But that deficiency, in Kramer's judgment, paled before the egregious polemics of Harold Rosenberg. Rosenberg, with his celebration of New York "action painting," linked abstract expressionism to a revolutionary moment. In the New York painters Rosenberg saw a contempt for bourgeois norms equal to his own disdain, and he conjoined radical political sentiments with modernist styles in painting. Kramer, though, found Rosenberg's essays, affixed to *New Yorker* magazines destined for suburban living room coffee tables, utterly misdirected.[16]

It was imperative, Kramer believed, to place the modernist tradition correctly. Perhaps the most important of all Kramer's essays was "The Age of Avant-Garde," which served as an introductory piece for his book of that title. In many ways the essay formed the basis of the extended critical warfare in which Kramer engaged the Left during the 1970s and 1980s, and in its own right it provided a suggestive and intriguing interpretation.

Kramer's essay reviewed a situation familiar to neoconservatives and Marxists alike—the process by which an avant-garde movement motivated by its sense of suffocation and moral constraints under bourgeois society was in turn taken up by that society and even flaunted by its ancient enemy. The avant-garde thus became a cultural norm of bourgeois life and also forged a profitable alliance with the official institutions of culture that had once been its traditional antagonists—the media, the universities, and the marketplace. The strategic advantages thus gained transformed the host culture into an "official" adversary culture in a state of tension with the society that claimed it.[17]

But Kramer refused to dismiss the relation either as one of co-option, the effective neutering of oppositional forces within capitalism as often described by the Left, or as a cynical takeover of the bourgeois moral ethos and its despoliation by the forces of a debilitating nihilism. For Kramer, the avant-garde was a vital coefficient of bourgeois culture. It represented no war of the aesthete and the philistine, however much the avant-garde artists did bear a certain hostility to bourgeois norms. The relation was actually a symbiotic one. For bourgeois society, Kramer insisted, was itself the first expression of modernism. With its apparatus of industrial machinery and technology, it made a revolutionary impact, more than any movement of culture that corresponded to it or fought against it. Politically, also, the advancement of the bourgeoisie meant the establishment of liberal democratic governments equally revolutionary in their consequences for an older political order. In its own way, therefore, the bourgeois movement produced an ethos of liberation, a progressive ideology of openness, newness, antitraditionalism, and expansiveness, that was as important as its moral, reactionary side, however much some avant-garde artists chose to see themselves immersed in and seeking liberation from that side exclusively.[18]

The implications of this progressive ethos for art were profound, Kramer believed. The bourgeois spirit created a tradition that was both classical and dynamic, explosive, and innovative. The modernism born of bourgeois life was not only nihilistic, almost indiscriminately antagonistic to its entire environment, but extremely self-conscious also, preoccupied with and carefully extending a tradition of its own. And it was precisely this kind of circumspection, Kramer insisted, that gave the avant-garde its vitality but withal, also, its conservative character. In speaking of Matisse, Picasso, Eliot, Yeats, Schönberg, and Stravinsky, that is, in looking at the modernist movement across its several frontiers, Kramer wrote:

The point not to be mistaken is that these historical innovations, from which nearly everything we most value in the art of the twentieth century has derived, represented in [the artists'] own eyes no essential rupture with the classic works that had nourished them. Their most radical efforts were, indeed, the only way these new masters could keep faith with their classic inheritance. The past had to be absorbed before it could be seriously extended and added to. It had to be *felt* if any really new emotion were to be distinguished from it and given a new form.[19]

Kramer here deradicalized modernism, separating it from the sporadic, factional, polemical avant-garde elements that launched their "guerilla raids" against the culture. Modernism, by contrast, derived meaning and attained enduring significance only as a part of a formal artistic tradition. But this tradition, Kramer explained, had always been scorned by a cultural establishment that tried to discredit it. Modernism, in effect, was a tradition at war with the philistine, pedestrian conservatism wielded by the official guardians of taste, the cultural establishment. Here the progressive and the reactionary clashed forcefully in an ongoing warfare, which illustrated the cultural schizophrenia that sprang from the dynamic of bourgeois history. As Kramer wrote, "A constant reconsideration and revaluation of the past is precisely what the master artists of the avant-garde were forcing upon the official guardians of taste, and doing so not out of any conscious determination to 'subvert' tradition, but on the contrary, to rescue it from moribund conventions and redefine it in the most vital terms — terms that spoke directly to the sensibility of the age."[20]

The "classic view" of the avant-garde's true position respecting tradition, Kramer wrote, could be found in T. S. Eliot's essay "Tradition and the Individual Talent," published in 1919. One of the most influential statements about art penned by the giant of modernism, this essay forwarded the author's claims to sever art from a romantic, individualist, antitraditionalist standard. Kramer reviewed for his readers Eliot's salient points, his efforts to turn judgment of art away from the unique factors of the artist's personality and genius and toward his connections with a larger literary or artistic history, a formalist tradition. Eliot had written that "we shall find that not only the best, but the most individual parts of [the artist's] work may be those in which the dead poets, his ancestors, assert their immortality most vigorously."[21]

Here ultimately was the avant-garde's relation to that bourgeois culture. Modernism gave visual expression to the dynamism, power, and innovative spirit bequeathed to it by the explosive historical movement of capitalism and its sundry movers and shakers. Inevitably that spirit came to express itself against certain aspects of bourgeois culture. Kramer wrote in *The Revenge of the Philistines* that "much — if not quite everything — that we continue to esteem in the creative achievements of the last two centuries owes its existence to this curious compact between the bourgeoisie and its licensed opposition." In turn, to be sure, the bourgeoisie, in a manner without historical precedent, accommodated itself to every challenge the avant-garde could mount, to the point that the negating impulses of the avant-garde assumed dominant status within the mainstream itself. Increasingly, capitalist society selectively created institutions – art museums, exhibition societies, schools, publications, and foundations – that actually served as agencies of a legitimized dissent in its own domain. To this extent, bourgeois society remained true to its own liberal ethos, its openness, its ideology of freedom. And in all political situations in which that liberal ethos eroded and gave way to totalitarian alternatives in the middle and late twentieth century, so too did the avant-garde undergo a brutal eradication.[22]

The reaction against modernism took a new direction at the end of the 1950s, and the following decade saw a variety of new expressions that gave currency to the label "post-modernism." Champions of the modernist movement, including the not uncritical Kramer, believed they were seeing its hard-won gains fading before the assaults of a multifaceted movement that displayed a mocking attitude toward its predecessor. The hegemony of modernism slowly crumbled, and the movement dissolved into fragments, which frequently became unoriginal pantomimes of the movement itself. Such was the modernist lament.

However elusive and various the post-modernist phenomenon appeared to be, observers nonetheless were finding some distinctive traits, above all a new mood, among its practitioners. Post-modernism evidenced a new kind of realism. Art turned away from the inner anguish of the spirit, from the strenuous quest for a new mode of self-realization in its retreat from an objective reality that could supply no permanent truths. Pop art, op art, and minimalism – the post-modernist forms – deflated the angst-ridden and expressive power of modernism and located itself among the common objects (Andy Warhol's Campbell's Soup cans) and geometric forms of a visible reality, often the meretricious world of everyday things that facilitated emotional disengagement. Observers often noticed the parallel shifts in literature and cited the French writer Alain Robbe-Grillet's stylistic innovations, his abandonment of emotional content, and the substitution of things for events. "Now the world is neither meaningful nor absurd," he wrote. "It simply is."[23] So it could be said of the new artists, however distinct the content and techniques of Frank Stella, Jasper Johns, or Kenneth Noland, that they "conceived of their art less as a mode of revelation or self-discovery, as had the Action Painters, than as a set of specific facts, or a carefully controlled and legible system to be patiently elaborated."[24] Even in 1986 one could continue to speak of a persistent post-modernist mood. "The decisive mark of postmodernism," wrote Denis Donoghue, "is its cool acceptance of the belatedness of

experience. There is no longing, as in modernism, to wipe the slate clean
or to keep it safe for the inscription of one's chosen few images. . . . No
artist's desire reaches out for spontaneity or an original relation to the world."[25]

Were there political implications in post-modernism? The speculation proved
irresistible. By the middle 1980s it seemed plausible to Donoghue that post-
modernism reflected the larger conservative mood of the country, its apparent
contentment with middle-class values, and the material signs of its civilization.
It reflected, apparently, a loss of negation and dissent, of inner rebellion
seeking expression in art and corresponding to a political atmosphere similarly
described.[26] Sam Hunter and John Jacobus, in their survey of American art,
however, looked at the junk materials that Robert Rauschenberg and Allan
Kaprow utilized in their paintings and drew a different conclusion about post-
modernism. These works, they wrote, "could be read as a symbol of alienation
from the dominant folkways of an aggressive consumer's society which ex-
travagantly valued a gleaming, ersatz newness in its possessions. By forcing
a confrontation with derelict and despicable object fragments, these artists
effectively countered a culture maniacally geared to the creation of an artificial
demand for new products."[27]

For Kramer, post-modernism reflected the ambiguity, ambivalence, and
irony that seemed always to explain the workings of art and the larger social
contexts of art movements. He did not believe that post-modernism could
be understood as merely an adversarial stance against modernism. Like a
child's rebellion against its parents, this dissent was never that simple. Post-
modernism's disassociation of itself from the high seriousness of modernism,
though indeed that was a fateful turn in the 1960s, marked a rueful and deceptive pose that betrayed for Kramer the subtle continuity the movement bore
to modernism. The clue lay in the meaning of *camp,* which Susan Sontag
had offered in her famous *Partisan Review* essay of 1964. It marked a major
aesthetic defense of pop art and the post-modernist projects. For "camp,"
Kramer believed, legitimated a kind of "comic intimacy" with the objects
it pretended to mock, the crude or even vulgar products of our fulsome commodity society. "It endorses them in an atmosphere of flirtation and familiarity," he wrote. Camp created an "in" culture, whose appeal was through parody,
as it conveyed a message, delivered through a kind of knowing wink to its
select clientele of aesthetes. What Kramer was suggesting seemed to recall
the ways of the eighteenth-century philosophers and their references to what
they habitually called the "vulgar," the unlearned masses. Kramer put it this
way: "Camp, in short, confirms legitimacy on what it pretends to ridicule.
But the kind of legitimacy it confers is distinctly double-edged. For what
it offers to the cognoscenti—a 'forbidden' pleasure in objects that are corny,

exaggerated, 'stupid,' or otherwise acknowledged to have failed by the respectable standards of the day—is not at all the same as what it bequeaths to the 'straight' public that believes itself to be abiding by those very standards." In this way, Kramer believed, post-modernism, at least in its camp aesthetic, effectively preserved for its charmed audience the distinction it fancied had also existed in modernism between the avant-garde and the philistines—between "us" and "them"—at the same time that it revived the philistine art, that is, the crude representational art that modernism was supposed to have given a proper burial.[28] Post-modernism to this extent was a harbinger of a newer kind of radicalism—though Kramer himself did not explicitly point to it—that would press its special traits forcefully in the years ahead, traits that combined a populist rhetoric that masked elitist pretensions.

But for Kramer this continuity with modernism did not suffice to redeem post-modernism from its worst effects. The new playful, self-deprecating forms clearly indicated to him a loss of standards, seriousness, depth, and complexity. But to understand why this shift had transpired, Kramer felt compelled to look again at the ambivalent and uneasy accommodation of art to its bourgeois environment. Post-modernism was writing another chapter in a continuing saga, he believed. The post-modernist movement followed the triumph of modernism in the marketplace, the galleries, the schools, and the museums. But the triumph, he said, appeared to be hollow, for by another curious twist, modernism was subverted from within. The avant-garde had succeeded, so much so that the bourgeois spirit that gave modernism its expressive élan was now in utter remission, "supine and demoralized," Kramer wrote, the outcome of the avant-garde's successful assault on it. Deprived of its traditional enemy, the bourgeois culture it loved to hate, the avant-garde was the only tradition left, and it itself became a kind of academy.[29]

Kramer made this observation in 1972. In 1985 he noted a further irony. With the demise of the bourgeois opposition, he observed, the art world seemed actually to have developed a nostalgia for the old bourgeois world, its own mother's milk. Now the latter-day art institutions were roaming amid the ruins of a lost civilization and sponsoring exhibition revivals of every kind. Kramer reviewed these with exasperation in the 1970s and 1980s and judged them a major theme of these decades, one that annoyed him to no end. Kramer witnessed in the art world not only a confusion of standards, but also an utter confusion of direction.[30]

The museums and galleries, he lamented, were betraying their essential purposes. Museums, he believed, were properly trustees of the higher culture and should play an educating role for a public that wanted to be instructed in an enduring tradition. But now, Kramer believed, they functioned more like the old curiosity shop than as agencies of selection and arbiters of taste for the interested art public. They ravaged the discredited artifacts of the past as the antiquarian interest in post-modernism became increasingly indiscriminate. Amid the relaxed and cool mood of post-modernism, architect Philip Johnson pioneered stylistic change with the AT&T building in New York City, decked out in a pastiche of historical ornamentation. Kramer recoiled in horror. The mad search through the rummage of history became a progressively frivolous venture, he believed. "In our museums," Kramer wrote, "everything from Salon painting to the inanities of kitsch has been dusted off, freshly labeled, and solemnly placed on exhibition, almost as if the modern movement had never altered our view of them." This was not conservatism, Kramer said. It was reactionism. Under the benign and winsome exterior of post-modernism lurked a debilitating nihilism.[31]

The philistines were taking their revenge. Undemanding audiences, Kramer wrote, were thankful to be relieved of modernism's heavy intellectual weight. Everything in the new art was easily accessible, a situation that recalled Greenberg's earlier distinction between avant-garde and kitsch.[32] Pop art, furthermore, had the effect of making all art appear as a put-on, a gag. The high seriousness of modernism seemed to stand exposed for its pretense. Kramer was unsparing in his attack on the revivals, from the Beaux Arts to the Salonists to the Victorians (e.g., Edwin Landseer, "the quintessential embodiment of Victorian philistinism").[33] His list of rejects included artists who might appeal to people of safe conservative tastes, in art or politics. Kramer spared none, and when Grant Wood, 1930s American regionalist, was given a return performance in New York, Chicago, and other places in the early 1980s, Kramer gave him a very unroyal welcome.

From the 1960s on, Kramer's defense of the high standards of modernism made him a controversial critic, all the more so because that defense was now situated within the great ideological agitation and the cultural and political warfare of those decades. The discussion of art was embroiled in these polemics, and the direction of art and criticism left Kramer alienated and angered at what he considered the effort of the Left to make art a component of its political program. Kramer's role in this *Kulturkampf* rendered him in the eyes of his critics a reactionary Cold Warrior, and they accused him of plotting a wholesale derogation of the 1960s and all its progressive activities. The *New Criterion* came to symbolize the neoconservative retreat from the 1960s and the mood of reaction that marked the next two decades.

What should be observed first of Kramer's criticism of art and politics in these years is his perspective. Kramer, like the neoconservatives in general, understood what was happening from the viewpoint of the long half-century life of the New York intellectuals. It could hardly have been otherwise. The critical history of modernism in American culture was tied directly to *Partisan Review,* to Rahv and Phillips, and then to Greenberg and Rosenberg. The divisiveness of the Cold War and the drama of the anti-Communist movement at home dominated the concerns of the New Yorkers in the 1950s and 1960s. In the latter decade especially it became clear to many that this whole ideological struggle was being renewed and that the issues of the 1930s had to be fought again. Kramer, however reluctantly, threw himself into the conflict.

Though the radical commitments of *Partisan Review* were somewhat muted during the war years and seemed to have been wholly obliterated in the 1950s, Kramer believed that a residual nostalgia for the revolutionary cause persisted. Even in the 1950s, he argued, an afterglow of the 1930s lingered; the heart was still warm even after a failed romance. What clinched the case for this view, he believed, was the position taken by *PR's* two editors in the 1960s, when the heated atmosphere of that decade rekindled old radical passions. Philip Rahv put his anti-communism aside, accused Irving Howe of being too much an anti-Communist, and defended the Soviet Union against the United States – according to Kramer.[34] Also, William Phillips, however much at odds he and Rahv were becoming, bought into the radical direction of the 1960s. The new sensibility of the counterculture led Phillips' interests into camp, pornography, and popular culture, into a cultural position, Kramer said, that in spirit and substance "represented the exact opposite of everything *PR* had stood for in the past." In the new post-modernist period and amid the new political radicalism, Kramer charged, the venerable journal seemed embarrassed about its past, its defense of the highest standards in art and of art's independence of political ideology.[35]

Worse for Kramer than the Left's political revival was its attempt to manufacture a comprehensive cultural agenda for the United States. As Kramer addressed at length the complexities of the art world and art criticism in the 1960s and afterward, his discussions centered increasingly on political motifs. He stood now at a new bloody crossroads.

Incidents abounded. Art exhibitions, Kramer complained, often took on a blatant ideological emphasis and offered themes such as "Women and Politics," "Art and Social Conscience," and "Dreams and Nightmares: Utopian Visions in Modern Art."[36] At *Artforum,* Kramer reported, the new editor Max Kozloff heralded a new departure for the journal, renouncing all claims for the aesthetic autonomy of art and focusing on art in its socio-political situation.[37] Robert Morris, pioneer artist of minimalism, closed his exhibition at the Whitney Museum to protest the American bombing of Cambodia in 1971. Art critic Barbara Rose proclaimed that the art of the past few decades must be scrapped because it did not speak to the masses. This came from a critic, Kramer accused, who had welcomed every new stylistic wave to come down the pike.[38] The National Endowment for the Arts legitimated a political criterion for art and slanted its fellowship program toward the leftist art community. (Wrote Kramer: "My own impression, after studying the list of fellowships from 1972 onward, is that a great many of them went as a matter of course to people who were publicly opposed to just about every policy of the United States government except the one that put money in their own pockets."[39] Of course, one wonders how many artists could be found who were not so politically inclined.)

Another issue in the art and politics couplet of the years in question was art by blacks. Demands that the museums open their display halls to black artists, and subsequent demands to do the same for women artists, reflected an intention to make American public life more responsive to a wider element of the population. The demands also carried their own more weighted political baggage. They often reflected a deep animosity toward the whole "oppressive" and "elitist" character of American society and culture and a resolve to dismantle it. But Kramer rejected any concessions to what he considered a political intrusion into the museum's proper function. He spoke directly on the matter: "However painful the truth may be and no matter how profound our political indignation may be over the historical conditions that have produced this unfortunate truth, the fact is," Kramer wrote, "that black artists in this country have not yet produced a body of work which has earned, by virtue either of its quality or its special, identifiable artistic characteristics, a separate museological status."[40] It took guts to write that in 1970. But Kramer was at least consistent, for his pronouncement echoed his cardinal tenet that museums must serve the public by sifting the historical and contemporary movements of art and by displaying their products in a manner that illuminates the ongoing life of a high tradition.

Few conservatives would object to this kind of defense, to its apparent effort to preserve standards against democracy's more indiscriminate tastes. As an art critic, Kramer served that function well. But a certain kind of conservative, one increasingly visible in the 1970s and 1980s, might aver that Kramer was being unduly selective and restrictive. Conservatism in the decades mentioned was stressing more and more the qualities of difference and variety in American life and in its cultural house. Many conservatives were pleading for the rich and varied texture of the human fabric of the United States against a rationalist and uniformitarian liberalism that they charged with insensitivity to these concerns. (The chapters on Michael Novak and

Robert Nisbet especially elaborate this theme.) The art museum might have a legitimate, traditional role in the manner Kramer assigned to it, but might it not also have a different educational function, one by which it served as an institution of communication between the many components of the American public? The high and rigorous standards of aestheticism might usefully bend a little to enrich the public's awareness of the compelling breadth of human experience in American life and history and the often heroic elements in it that art helped to convey.

Nonetheless, Kramer's stance offered some useful reflections on art and politics in the 1960s. In his introduction to *The Age of Avant-Garde* Kramer measured the prevailing motivations of the Left. The politicizing of art by the Left, he believed, had been mandated by the historical fact that all previous proclamations that attended the avant-garde movements in art had looked to the forging of a new sensibility, one with revolutionary implications for the course of politics. But the new sensibilities created by art had clearly failed to vault the domain of the aesthetic into the realm of the political, and politics had pretty much gone about its business in the familiar manner. This disillusionment with the utopian hope of art led the political champions of the avant-garde, Kramer said, to join the populist chorus of the New Left and to welcome every form of art, no matter how pedestrian, that could be enlisted for political soldiering. Now art for the masses assumed a high priority, and to modernism was ascribed an elitist, privileged, undemocratic character. Kramer deplored this sentencing. "What is most interesting—and most alarming—" about the situation, he wrote, "is the unacknowledged contempt for art itself which is so clearly implied in this campaign to impose political criteria on every decision affecting the creation and exhibition and judgment of works of art. For in this new political scenario, art is assumed to have no defensible social functions apart from its alliance with specific political objectives."[41]

The art question took on political content even at the level of the Cold War. Serge Guilbaut's book of 1983, *How New York Stole the Idea of Modern Art: Abstract Expressionism, Freedom, and the Cold War* fueled the controversy. The author described the cultural ascendancy of New York over Paris after the French city's fall in 1940 and could not resist the temptation to conjoin American supremacy in the art world with America's emerging political and economic domination at the international level. Guilbaut advanced the thesis that abstract expressionism, with its visual and emotional power, its sense of adventure, its openness to the world, and the qualities of universalism it aspired to convey, coincided with an America that was forsaking its isolationist past and preparing itself for its adventurous new role in the "American Century."[42]

It seemed especially appropriate to Guilbaut that the New York intellectuals should have anticipated this situation. Greenberg's championing of Jackson Pollock, for example, represented to him more than a critic's encouraging of a new pioneer in art. It represented also a judgment about recent history. The New Yorkers, who had for years denounced Stalin and had witnessed with everyone else the fate of the modernist movements under all the totalitarian regimes, now advanced the plausible thesis that the expressive vigor of the new painting reflected appropriately the conditions of individual freedom in the artists' own country. The lessons were not lost on the United States government, Guilbaut believed, when in 1946 it sponsored the Advancing American Art Exhibition. The event would show how the American artists provided a genuine mirror-image of a vital and free American society, one in which individual liberty in all its problematic dimensions spoke through an energetic, dynamic art. The lesson demonstrated for Guilbaut was art's unwary complicity in the propagandist designs of the United States at the outset of the Cold War.[43]

Avant-garde artists, now politically "neutral" individualists, articulated in their works values that were subsequently assimilated, utilized, and coopted by politicians, with the result that artistic rebellion was transformed into aggressive liberal ideology. The new painting was made in the image of the new America, powerful and internationalist but anxious about the Communist threat. By the end of 1948 this new America was able to recognize itself in avant-garde painting because it had been intricately responsible for the elaboration of the new style.[44]

Hilton Kramer found Guilbaut's study disturbing and unacceptable. All along the New York school of artists had been subjected to interpretations that Kramer believed detracted from its singular achievements in painting. Guilbaut's study added to that literature. For Kramer it was another matter of modernism's guilt by association with political and social aspects of worldly history. Meyer Schapiro had once denounced modern painting for the heavy presence he detected in it of the "pleasure principle," its aesthetic hedonism, one that Schapiro's Marxist leanings inclined him to associate with the baseness of capitalist individualism and that led him to assert that the modern artist's aestheticism predisposed him to support the interests and attitudes of the leisure class.[45] Now modernism was being implicated in another unsavory aspect of capitalist-bourgeois society, its aggressive imperialism. Kramer had to wonder where it would all end, how far the alleged political references of painting would detract from or obscure its intrinsic aesthetic qualities. "What has happened, in short," Kramer wrote, "is that the New York School has been hauled into 'court' . . . and made to stand trial on charges of aiding and abetting the influence of the American political system." Guilbaut's history, Kramer charged, took place in ideological scenarios wholly removed from the real life of art, and it denied to art any role in determining its own life. This judgment was not quite fair to Guilbaut, in whom Kramer perceived "only the old Marxist methodology given a new vocabulary," by which he dismissed the Cold War involvement of American painting as "the sheerest rubbish."[46] Kramer's forceful rebuke showed how important the mostly formalist position had become for him by 1985, one that should be seen against the background of an aggressive neo-Marxist scholarship that had gained in authority by this time. At any rate, Kramer chose not to stress the suggestive relation of modernism to capitalist freedom but to retreat instead to the standard of art's autonomy.

The fate of modernism presented a disturbing challenge to the intellectual Left in Europe and in the United States and gave rise to a substantial literature on this subject and on the meaning of the post-modernist phenomenon that followed. What hopes for a renewal of revolutionary consciousness, once so bright a promise of modernism, could one expect from the post-modernist challenge? Scholars and critics who took up this question usually appreciated the highly elusive character of the matters with which they were dealing. And there was no issue, in the polemical literature of the Left and the Right in the United States, that yielded more divided opinion, not so much between the polar antagonists but within each side's own ranks. Hilton Kramer stood prominently as a factional conservative champion of modernism against cultural conservatives. And on the Left neo-Marxists measured the post-modernist expressions and mined them for political usage. But they failed to unearth any unalloyed substance.

The attack on modernism from the Left was well under way by the 1960s, with the focus of the attack on modernism's allegedly elitist, intellectual, and undemocratic character. Critics such as Susan Sontag and Leslie Fiedler attracted fascinated audiences in their recoil from modernism's pretensions. Pop art and other pairings of post-modernist expressions—op, kinetic, minimalist, and concept art—won appreciative welcomes. The mass culture and kitsch so disparaged by modernism and its critical defenders now seemed to have important secrets to disclose about advanced technological and consumer society. So thought Robert Venturi, author of *Learning from Las Vegas*, and Charles Jencks, who wrote *Modern Movements in Architecture*. And in the American universities, where Marxism enjoyed an academic vogue, the shifts came under close scrutiny.

The neo-Marxist literature on this subject was prodigious, and we shall be able to sample only a portion of it. But a brief survey is necessary for understanding Kramer's place in the debates and for assessing an important aspect of conservative opinion in the 1970s and 1980s. Andreas Huyssen, an editor of the neo-Marxist journal *New German Critique,* wrote extensively on the modernist and post-modernist experiences and gave some suggestive and sensitive readings of the cultural shifts among them. Huyssen understood clearly why post-modernism had become necessary, at least politically. He cited the spectacle of Robert Frost, Pablo Casals, André Malraux, and Igor Stravinsky in the White House of the Kennedy years and concluded that modernism had taken on a domesticated political status. The irony was apparent: a modernist movement in art, born in revolt against institutionalization and official art, art that exercised a "hegemonic" role, was now itself institutionalized. Post-modernism, in its more explosive dimensions at least—street theater, acid rock, pop vernacular—was groping, Huyssen said, "to recapture the adversary ethos which had nourished modern art in its early stages, but which it seemed no longer able to sustain." Huyssen wrote, "The modernism against which artists rebelled was no longer felt to be an adversary culture. It no longer opposed a dominant class and its world view, nor had it maintained its programmatic purity from contamination by the culture industry." Modernism, in short, had been absorbed into the affirmative culture.[47]

Huyssen was never sanguine about post-modernism's capacity to carry through on modernism's failed promise to energize a culture of dissent. But he was emphatically sympathetic to the new populist expressions of the 1960s and the new creative relationship they formed with different elements of society, especially as they conveyed the self-assertion of excluded groups. Breaking modernism's rigid dichotomy between high and low culture, kitsch even seemed to be a prerequisite for this new advantage. Adventurous explorations into mass culture, according to Huyssen, were uncovering buried dimensions of human experience that might successfully help to dismantle an oppressive system. For Huyssen, post-modernism, which he felt bore a close relation to modernism, must in its turn resist the unrelenting pressures of a conservative revival if it were to make itself an effective resistance. Among the several obstacles to that possibility, he believed, were the efforts of Kramer and others to uphold the standards of a domesticated modernism as an aesthetic orthodoxy. Kramer's strategy, Huyssen said, was to bury the 1960s and cast into oblivion its manifold legacy of dissent.[48]

Others on the Left still hoped that art, specifically the post-modernist phenomenon, would yet bring about the altered state of consciousness that had long informed the radical agenda. But the leftist generation of the 1970s and 1980s was more chastened than its 1930s predecessors. One simply cannot locate any consensus in the Marxist literature of the later period on the possibility that art can register a negation powerful enough to resist the dominant culture. Certainly there was no consensus in these quarters on the meaning and likely consequences of the post-modernist situation. Hal Foster, for example, in introducing a collection of essays under the title *The Anti-Aesthetic: Essays on Postmodern Culture,* acknowledged that post-modernism exhibited qualities of both resistance and reaction. This indecisive character of post-modernism suggested that contemporary culture was an open field that might yet be directed toward liberation. The essays in the book, he said, undertook to explore how that hope might be realized. "A postmodernism of resistance," wrote Foster, "arises as a counter-practice not only to the official culture of modernism but also to the 'false normativity' of a reactionary postmodernism."[49]

Many neo-Marxist scholars cautioned against the reactionary character of post-modernism. Fredric Jameson, for example, speculated that the post-modernist culture corresponded to "the newly emergent social order of late capitalism." Classical modernism, he wrote, reflected a concurrence with a powerful individualist force in capitalism and a correspondingly powerful subjectivist content in its artistic mode. But Jameson also pointed out that the direction of scholarship in a variety of fields—sociology, linguistics, psychoanalysis—had been raising the theme of the "death of the subject." This phenomenon paralleled capitalism's emergence into a corporate structure of bureaucracy and organization that negated the alleged individualism of its earlier stage. The later capitalism, particularly through its control of the media, engineered in the consciousness of the consumer a bewildering rhythm of fashion and style changes, creating a kind of perpetual present of perpetual change. This fragmentation of time and of personal identity, which Jameson in his essays related mostly to cinematic themes, dissolved all connotations of tradition, rending the perceptual milieu in a manner that obliterated distinctions. This post-modernist assault thus carried no oppositional weight. The earlier modernism, Jameson argued, did at least function in ways that could be described as negating, critical, adversary, even subversive. "Can anything of the sort," he asked, "be affirmed about postmodernism and its social moment?" It would be more accurate, he believed, to say that post-modernism "replicates or reproduces—reinforces—the logic of consumer capitalism."[50]

The implications of post-modernism and the uncertain conclusions drawn from it promised to expand a critical literature already very large in the late 1980s. Neo-Marxists and conservatives like Bell divided sharply between and among themselves—that much was clear. But for Kramer, the critical literature was seriously flawed. The individuals in question, he said, evidenced a common fallacy, a misjudging of art by its alleged political and social references. The distortion was mostly a habit of the Left, but Kramer censored Daniel Bell too for judging modernism by the influence in moral decay that he attributed to it in his book *The Cultural Contradictions of Capitalism.*[51]

This context for Kramer demonstrates especially how neoconservatism became linked to modernism in culture, for Kramer did stand in the tradition of Greenberg. He did understand how culture, even modernist culture, was vulnerable to many corruptions, many of which were the consequences of its location in bourgeois society itself. However much modernism, in Kramer's account, might express a genuine inflection of bourgeois dynamism, its interaction with the bourgeois milieu threatened to assimilate it to entertainment, therapy, commercialism, academicism, or kitsch. In fact, this was precisely the lesson of post-modernism. But only a commitment to the highest standards of the great tradition could effectively counteract these powerful tendencies. Bourgeois civilization, Kramer insisted, could flourish only by a continuing dialectical relationship between its uneasy cultural siblings.[52]

For our purposes, what needs to be identified in this critical warfare is the double-edged assault on traditional humanism. It came in part from the French sector, where radical forms of post-structuralism were especially effective in discrediting the notion of a meaningful reality that is disclosed by intellectual interactions of subject and object. This Descartian model, though long under assault, lost more suasion as deconstructionists invalidated all logocentric formulations of reality. Reinforced by Lacanian theories of the self, for example, they rendered subjectivity itself a problematic entity. Authorial foundations of literary truth lost credibility as indeed literary texts turned in on themselves. There was "nothing outside the text," one learned, and within lay only the acute problematics of word meanings. Nothing remained of representation, truth, or higher reality in the traditional humanist understanding of the world.[53] Deconstruction was in fact a severe kind of formalism, but it could attach art to no sustaining tradition in the manner that Kramer had done to rescue modernism from a meaningless solipsism.

The Marxist assault was probably even more destructive. Marxism was reducing all cultural expression to ideological purpose and that in turn to the intractable class conditions of capitalist society. Humanist ideals, therefore, in the writings of British Marxists like Raymond Williams and Terry Eagleton and American theorists like Fredric Jameson, became codifications in a hegemonic culture of control. They were denuded of any "timeless" expressions of truth and conscripted for a Marxist program that embroiled literature and art in the whole complicated nexus of production and commodity exchange. This does not deny that much of the Marxist scholarship was highly suggestive and creative. But though it had liberated Marxist theories from simplistic formulations of "base" and "superstructure," it had not freed itself from dogmatic assertions about the economic grounding of all cultural experience. In the Marxist canon, all formalist ideas of art were suspect, themselves the inventions of "bourgeois" ideology. One heard little about the creative subject or the autonomous artist, but much more about the historical, social, and economic milieu of cultural "production." The Marxists could cite several reasons to be at odds with post-structuralist aesthetics, but in discrediting the postulations of traditional academic humanism they formed a powerful common cause with their rival.[54]

It was just this question, what the new critical methodologies meant for the humanities, that truly gave the *New Criterion* a cohesive purpose. In article after article its contributors mapped an assault on the insurgents and sought to recover a humanist tradition of learning that they saw as now discredited by a new hermeneutic elite. A distinguished scholar who spoke out forcefully in the pages of the *New Criterion* was René Wellek, a Yale University professor who had written several volumes on the history of literary criticism, among other works. He described the new challenges as "an attempt to destroy literary studies from the inside" and foresaw in them "the breakdown or even the abolition of all traditional literary scholarship and teaching." Like most of the *New Criterion* writers, Wellek lamented what he judged to be the antihumanist character of the new scholarship. He believed that the new criticism imprisoned man in a house of language that severed him from reality. "In its extreme formulation, which looks for the abolition of man, denies the self, and sees language as a free-floating system of signs," wrote Wellek, "the theory leads to total skepticism and ultimately to nihilism." Wellek mentioned the Yale scholars J. Hillis Miller, Paul de Man, and Jacques Derrida (the immensely influential French writer who sojourned frequently at Yale) among the miscreants.[55] And Norman Cantor of New York University attacked the new directions collectively: "Marxism, structuralism, and deconstruction may each define this order somewhat differently," Cantor wrote, "but in each case a system external to and dominating the individual is envisioned. The self-sustaining, objective codes of this order will eliminate the legitimacy, creativity, and efficiency that 'decadent' liberalism has accorded to the individual."[56] Here again was the conservative complaint that the defeated radical politics of the 1960s had gone underground to resurface in the universities, where it sought to undermine the cultural assumptions of bourgeois capitalism.

What was so particularly conservative about the sustained efforts of the *New Criterion* intellectuals to uphold a traditional humanism, one actually under longer assault than the leftist thrust of the 1960s, deserves mention. For it was not only their partiality for the "classics," for education as our link with history and the continuity between generations, or for the allegedly elitist character of the literature and art that elicits the conservative designation. Were these considerations alone important, the place of Hilton Kramer and the *New Criterion* in the conservative movement would have been questionable, if only because a loyalty to a modernist ethos, as in Kramer's defense of the New York school of painters, was at odds with much in American conservative thought. What was also significant was the manner of Kramer's and the *New Criterion's* defense of humanist principles, the intellectual points that differentiated them from the newer "humanists" they opposed. It is worthwhile to recall that Irving Babbitt's book of 1919, *Rousseau and Romanticism,* engaged in a two-sided war—against what Babbitt considered to be the individualist and solipsistic quality of romanticism on the one hand, and on the other hand against the naturalist impulses of a modern culture that dissolved the self altogether into its determining biological and physical environment. What was lost, Babbitt believed, and what he tried valiantly to restore in his humanism, was a genuine dualism, one that posited a struggle between warring factions within the individual soul but that also posited the soul as an empirical reality, an autonomous entity, that, to borrow from William James, felt the push and presence of the cosmos at every turn. The *New Criterion* writers, surely, were fighting the same double battle. Their humanism was both antiromantic, in its opposition to the nihilistic aestheticism of the post-structuralists, and antinaturalistic, in its opposition to the social determinism in much of structuralism and Marxism. But such a middle way between extremes, expressed in the name of an autonomous feeling and thinking individual, had, in the face of ideologies that battled to control the university, apparently become a species of reactionism now thoroughly suspect.

What we have discussed of Kramer to this point has situated him squarely in the formalist school of criticism. His essays on painting detailed graphically and powerfully the fine points of color, technique, and expression that gave an artist's paintings their location within the aesthetic movements and traditions that illuminated their meaning. These considerations were sources of understanding more useful to Kramer than their specific social and political contexts, though Kramer never discounted historical factors that could be helpful in illuminating the significance or character of an artist. Art does, of course, carry on its own dialogue with the world, and Kramer's essays continually brought to his readers' attention artists whose works show us new and extraordinary relations to the world, the world transformed by the artist's imagination, but a world of substance nonetheless. Perhaps, then, the most lively and engaging of Kramer's essays were those about artists who creatively elaborate the artistic tradition while keeping good company with ordinary experience. Art for Kramer was never an aspect of the mystical or transcendental. Even abstract expressionism belonged to the tradition of empirical humanism.

That appreciation appeared clearly in Kramer's assessments of two American realists—Thomas Eakins, whose partiality for science, said Kramer, also conveyed a weighty moral earnestness, and Edward Hopper, who moved beyond the French manner of his early training in the direction of a successful nativism.[57] And Kramer's feeling for the worldly quality of art sometimes came in fresh and revealing ways. In an essay on the Swiss sculptor Alberto Giacometti, who died in 1966, Kramer drew attention to the preponderant large feet of the artist's figures. The feet seemed to join the figures as if by massive weight to the base of the statue. Kramer did not read into this stylistic quirk any facile surrealist device. Instead he first emphasized in the feet a point about the artist. "The place where the figure meets the earth was, for Giacometti," Kramer wrote, "the only still point in a turning world; and it was at that point that sculpture—as he understood it—was required to begin again and again and again." But the stylistic technique also had wider aesthetic meaning for Kramer. "To build upon that isolated point of fixity," he continued, "was what Giacometti was 'trying to do,' and it was this self-assigned task, so distant in spirit and in result from the freewheeling belief in the autonomy of art that mesmerized his contemporaries, that made him a 'conservative' in the art of his time. For Giacometti, art enjoyed no such autonomy but was, on the contrary, doomed to be tethered to the life of the earth."[58] Kramer strained to make a point. One can read in his account here a quest to locate a principle of stability and permanence within the flux of a dynamic modernist tradition. But the effort could be only partially satisfactory at best, a selective accomplishment. How a Rothko or a Motherwell could be similarly situated we are not informed.

But Kramer did achieve something of a reconciliation in a different respect. He analyzed a movement, modernism, whose every nuance in the realm of culture was suspect, if not anathema, to Old Right conservatives, and he upheld in it high aesthetic principles of art. His critical language was joined in this way to a traditional conservative apology for elitist standards amid the countervailing tendencies of democratic society. In this important way Kramer also forged another significant link between the newer, conservative modes of the 1970s and 1980s and the traditionalist conservatives and their defense of high cultural standards. For those standards above all, Kramer seems to have preserved from the early New York intellectuals a serious, uncompromising, even elitist deference toward serious creative culture. Deprogrammed from its radical political alliance of those earlier years, this kind of aestheticism opened itself liberally to the more unalloyed defense of modernism rendered by Kramer. And in drawing the whole workshop of modernism out of the dynamics of bourgeois society, Kramer helped temper one of the more conspicuous aspects of neoconservatism, such as that voiced by Irving Kristol – the recalcitrant alienation that it felt toward the staid and prosaic character of modern bourgeois life. Indeed that accomplishment would most likely be Kramer's singular contribution to the literature of American conservatism in the later twentieth century.

Nonetheless, the question of Kramer's place in the conservative renaissance would likely devolve also on the character of modernism itself. In the later 1980s many expressions of dissent from neoconservativism arose from partisans of the Old Right, who brought to their judgments a traditional conservatism's adherence to moral and metaphysical truths and an appreciation for expressions of continuity and tradition that gave imaginative force to the presence of history in any contemporary setting. Kramer's standards were emphatically neoconservative in character. He did not uphold in art any didactic role, he did not look to art to sustain traditional morality, and he was not disappointed that art had failed to serve as a cultural surrogate for religion, preserving the authority of the timeless and sacred against the corrosive inroads of a profane contemporaneity. But at a time in American history when both neoconservatives and Old Right conservatives, and indeed many others of different intellectual persuasions, were asking important questions about the need to preserve a sustaining core of values and to forge a usable public philosophy for the United States, surely it was not an impertinence to ask what role artists and writers were to play in such a program. In 1975 Kramer attended at the Detroit Institute an exhibition called "French Painting, 1774–1830: The Age of Revolution." The works on display inspired Kramer to write appreciatively of the exhibition: "It recalls to us a time when painters had important public duties to perform, and it reminds us that these were by no means inimical to achievements of the greatest splendor."[59] Kramer's comment leaves us to wonder whether he, or another critic or historian of the twenty-first century, could ever conclude similarly about the great masters of modernism in our time.

6

Jeane Kirkpatrick
America and the World

"FOREIGN POLICY," wrote Arthur M. Schlesinger, Jr., "is the face a nation wears to the world." But Schlesinger also found that Americans were quite literally two-faced. Their double countenance, expressive of attitudes and moods that went deep into their history, created confusions when they had to decide what roles to play in world affairs. On the one hand, said Schlesinger, Americans are famous for being a practical people, for favoring fact over theory, trial and error over deductive logic. On the other hand, a strain of idealism has always motivated Americans. A recurrent vulnerability to cosmic generalities or to large and benevolent causes has claimed American purposes at various times in the nation's history. Schlesinger saw this moral idealism at work from the Puritan beginnings in the seventeenth century through Woodrow Wilson's gospel of world order and John Foster Dulles' invocation of a holy war against communism in the twentieth century.[1]

Conservatives and liberals alike have had to wrestle with this dual heritage. For like liberals, conservatives believed that America's position in the world related directly to the character and purpose of her nationhood. But for conservative intellectuals the subject of foreign policy was a particularly vexing one, and their discussions produced a troublesome irony. On the one hand, foreign policy, in at least one aspect, gave the conservatives a bedrock of consensus: they were of one voice in decrying the evils of communism and in citing the threat to American interests and to world peace posed by the Soviet Union. They all believed liberalism had failed, for reasons of ideology, naïvete, or willful perverseness, to assess correctly the threat of communism.

But on the other hand, the subject of foreign policy landed conservatives in a confusion of cross-purposes. Bonded by a kind of emotional élan that

energized their anticommunism, conservative intellectuals could not secure
that unity on a consistent ideological foundation. For what constituted a conservative foreign policy? How did conservatism's priorities—its respect for human liberties and freedom, its concerns for continuity and tradition, and its
quest for authority—find application in an international setting? Some conservatives could, consistent with their values, celebrate the pragmatic tradition
of the United States, its happy disengagement from ideological politics and
utopian formats for the reconstruction of society. Should that pragmatism
then recommend for the country a realpolitik that prudently invoked only
the standard of national self-interest in its dealings with the rest of the world?
Or should a conservative foreign policy embody America's exceptional liberal
past, its democratic tradition, its evolving progress in extending human freedoms? Would not a foreign policy that made these freedoms the standard
of its conduct, as well as its measure of other nations, reflect an authentic
conservatism that honors history and tradition and makes of foreign policy
an organic extension of the nation's domestic life? Or might these considerations lead one to conclude that the American experience, as exceptional, is
not translatable to other nations, that history and tradition have operated differently in other places and have made other nations immune to those ideals
that seem axiomatic to American understanding of human justice and legitimate government?

    None of these questions was new in the 1970s and 1980s. But all were
acquiring a special urgency. They assumed a greater explicitness among American political leaders, especially in the presidency of Jimmy Carter. They
became clearly more visible and more hotly debated in the political literature
of these years. And one individual in particular became a primary focus of
these discussions. Jeane Kirkpatrick was a pioneer of the neoconservatism
of the 1970s. She had the distinction of an influential scholarly career that
made her writings a center of attention for virtually every foreign policy
discussant and the prominence of a major diplomatic assignment that significantly shaped the face that America presented to the world during the first
Ronald Reagan administration. In the surprising career of Jeane Kirkpatrick,
American conservatism found a direction. Her influence did not induce una-
nimity of conservative opinion, but she did more than anyone else to provide
a focus for it. She made possible some distinctions and applications that extri-
cated conservatism from some of its inherent dilemmas.

    In the years under consideration, intellectuals acquired an ascendancy in
foreign policy discussion and formulation that made theoretical issues prominent. Henry Kissinger, Zbigniew Brzezinski, and Jeane Kirkpatrick all had
impressive academic careers, and together they served in four different presiden-

Jeane Kirkpatrick by Vint Lawrence

tial administrations. Indeed nearly all of the large questions around which foreign policy discussions took place could be related directly to the pronounce-ments of these three scholar/diplomats and the policy formulations they in-fluenced. At least they establish the essential background for a review of conservative opinion on American foreign policy.

Zbigniew Brzezinski had not yet entered the inner circle of the Carter administration when he published his book of 1970, *Between Two Ages: America's Role in the Technetronic Era*. He had already forged a distinguished and productive scholarly career, writing books such as *The Soviet Bloc: Unity and Conflict* (1960) and *Ideology and Power in Soviet Politics* (1962) that had made him a leading authority on the politics of Communist nations. He had been most recently associated with Columbia University. In his new work, expounding one of several "modernization" theories about foreign policy current in the early 1970s, Brzezinski sought to formulate American priorities for a foreign policy in the post-industrial age.

Brzezinski stated at the outset of his book that "a new pattern of international politics is emerging. The world is ceasing to be an arena in which relatively self-contained, 'sovereign,' and homogeneous nations interact, collaborate, clash, or make war." Brzezinski offered a clear and by now familiar description of the "post-industrial" era, pointing to the social, cultural, and even psychological influence of the revolution in technology—electronics, communications, and the computer. The impact in these facets of human life outpaces that of the industrial process, he wrote, and affects the interactions of nations as well. Brzezinski described the resultant "global city," one characterized by "a nervous, agitated, tense, and fragmented web of interdependent relations." The new global city, he believed, lacked the intimacy and shared experience that once described the nation-states. Nor did it have the self-correcting mechanisms that nation-states in the nineteenth century could apply to diplomatic conflicts. That older familiar world was dissolving, Brzezinski argued. Racial and ethnic ideologies were losing force, as were political ones. Brzezinski felt generally positive about the changes. A commonality of shared concerns among the nations of the world became more widely perceived, he believed. Matters of human justice were more commonly pursued in the international arena. Old social and bureaucratic elites (especially in the Communist countries) were on the defensive and doomed to lose influence. And the Cold War itself was becoming more rhetorical than substantive.[2]

But Brzezinski would have warnings for Americans, and he outlined them in a *Foreign Policy* essay published just before his entrance into the Carter administration as national security adviser. The emerging world order, Brzezinski believed, will challenge American ideals of individualism, free enterprise, and the work ethic, for the new order advances statism. This fiat of change would not be an easy adjustment for Americans, who have always hoped that their national example would be a model for nations aspiring to material improvement. So Brzezinski issued this admonition: the United States should not inject into its foreign relations "the ideological claim that the contemporary world struggle is between liberal democracy and various forms of despotic statism." Such an ideological assertion could be only counterproductive, enhancing America's global isolation. In addition, said Brzezinski, America also needed to overcome an outmoded nineteenth-century view of foreign policy that saw balance of power and spheres of influence as the primary diplomatic concerns. The new world order, he argued, was dissolving national demarcations and conspiring to make any "static" view of power relations ineffective.[3]

Brzezinski's visionary view of foreign policy rose to challenge a more traditional school of thought that had gained from the writings of some respected and influential thinkers. Realist thought, as advanced by Reinhold Niebuhr, Hans Morgenthau, Walter Lippmann, and George F. Kennan, was to receive heavy reinforcement from its most prominent spokesman and practitioner in the late 1960s and afterward, Henry Kissinger. However diverse these writers often were in their analyses of particular issues, each sought to dissuade Americans form certain aspects of liberalism that he believed had distracted them from a proper assessment of America's world role.

Theoreticians like Hans Morgenthau insisted repeatedly that the pursuit of power is the strongest motivator of individuals and nations, so that the world political scene is an unending theater of struggle. These unhappy assumptions, however, became, paradoxically in Morgenthau's understanding, the essential foundations of order and world peace. His system was never amoral. Morgenthau simply denied that any transcendent universal morality can function as an effective restraint on the behavior of nations. It was almost always for Morgenthau the intrusion of moral crusades and religious fanaticism that proved to be the destabilizing and ultimately destructive forces that caused great international conflicts. Wrote Morgenthau: "A foreign policy derived from the national interest is in fact morally superior to a foreign policy inspired by universal moral principles."[4]

In works such as *Politics among Nations* (1948) and *In Defense of the National Interest: A Critical Examination of American Foreign Policy* (1951), Morgenthau had criticized the United States for wavering from these primary considerations. America had been the victim too often, he believed, of four faults: utopianism, legalism, sentimentalism, and isolationism. These deterred the nation's policy-makers from their singular responsibilities, "the balance of power and policies aiming at its preservation," which alone defined for Morgenthau his ideal of national self-interest as "interest defined by power." Both Morgenthau and Kennan, who also warned of the moralistic mismeasure of American national interests, faulted American statesmen of the early Cold War period for raising American political competition with the Soviet Union to the level of a universal moral struggle. Kennan, who had been most influential in warning in 1947 of the threat posed by the Soviet Union, was discouraged to see an issue of strategic state rivalry become so soon an indiscriminate moral war waged by the United States against an alleged international communism.[5]

Realism defined its opposite as liberal internationalism. Its vision was that of an activist, interventionist America that pursued both freedom and world order. Liberal internationalism upheld the two standards of universalism and moralism, the bane of realist proponents then and in the 1980s. But realism, it has been argued, also had its softer side. It harbored a nostalgia for the diplomacy of the predemocratic era of statehood, for the personal diplomacy of the eighteenth and nineteenth centuries, and for the hierarchical ordering of states. It was uncomfortable with the prerequisites of mass democracy.[6]

Henry Kissinger believed that the United States must recover the main tenets of realism in its foreign policy. This scholar, counsel, diplomat, and general bon vivant exercised a remarkable influence and power during his two terms of office, as national security adviser and secretary of state for Presidents Nixon and Ford in the eight-year period from 1969 to 1977. During this time Kissinger virtually dominated foreign policy news and shaped the dialogue of politicians and intellectuals on matters practical and theoretical.

Kissinger's A.B. thesis at Harvard University, "The Meaning of History: Reflections on Spengler, Toynbee, and Kant" (1951), and his first book, *A World Restored: Metternich, Castlereagh, and the Problem of Peace, 1812–1822* (1957), introduced themes that Kissinger stressed in all his ensuing scholarship and that gave a theoretical framework to his remarkable memoirs of his White House years.

Kissinger feared that American history had ill prepared Americans for the contemporary realities of world politics. The Founding Fathers had exercised a judicious realism, said Kissinger in his memoirs, understanding the European balance of power and manipulating it skillfully. But in the years after Waterloo the nation was shielded by geographic remoteness and British sea power. Those conditions gave the United States a sense of immunity from the necessities that impelled other nations. American citizens came to view diplomacy with suspicion, as not in line with their idealistic and moralistic views. When in 1917 events propelled the country into European conflicts, a legitimate national interest became a matter of high legal and moral idealism. The inevitable disillusionment, Kissinger wrote, loosed the tide of isolationism. But American isolationism was, in Kissinger's judgment, but another aspect of idealism, a "moral conviction." It prepared the way for the tragedies of the 1930s. America spurned the notion that the security of the postwar world might depend on an equilibrium of power and might demand American presence to secure it.[7]

But in the World War II years and afterward realism seemed finally to dawn on Americans' understanding of their world situation. Wrote Kissinger: "After two world wars in this century, the responsibilities and the burdens of world leadership proved inescapable. The United States had despite itself become the guardian of the new equilibrium. It is to the lasting credit of that generation of Americans that they assumed these responsibilities with energy, imagination, and skill."[8]

A critical aspect of Kissinger's realism was his understanding of the Soviet Union. An idealistic nation like the United States, Kissinger said, is likely to ask another country to define its ultimate ends and purposes and the ideals it seeks to realize. A country like the Soviet Union, seemingly armed with a governing ideology, is especially likely to be so interrogated. Kissinger admitted that the Soviet Union exercised a special combination of ideology and historical nationalism, but it was not a nation with a daily, functioning ideology, he believed. It was far more a traditional state, confident in the flow of history but merely "ruthlessly opportunistic" in practice, playing a familiar game of power politics. It was a nation immune to Western notions of goodwill, as when it sacrificed its reserves of sympathy after World War II to obtain a locus of control in Eastern Europe. The Soviets, Kissinger elaborated, have acted similarly ever since, and he cited examples. Kissinger also believed that those Western leaders most bent on showing "understanding" toward the Soviet Union had been least successful in dealing with it. Kissinger sounded much like Kennan had in the late 1940s: "In every policy choice the Soviet leaders have identified their interests not with the goodwill of countries that Soviet doctrine defines as organically hostile but with strategic opportunity as they saw it. To expect the Soviet leaders to restrain themselves from exploiting circumstances they conceive to be favorable is to misread history. To foreclose Soviet opportunities is thus the essence of the West's responsibility. It is up to *us* to define the limits of Soviet aims."[9]

The modernization theory of Brzezinski and the several expressions of realism, however different in emphasis, had one important common denominator. They both, whether historically or *a fortiori,* ascribed the behavior of nations to similar influences. They insisted that at heart international relations are the playing out of omnipresent forces that affect all states and that the competition among nations is ultimately the seeking for strategic advantages within these strictures.

In the 1970s and 1980s a large body of conservative literature emerged to refute these assumptions. For conservatives maintained that the rivalry that had dominated world politics at least since 1945 — the conflict between the

United States and the Soviet Union—was a unique and dangerous situation, one essentially without historical precedent. Furthermore, that rivalry could not be understood, or successfully pursued by the United States, through either modernization or realist understandings of world politics. Only the briefest sampling of conservative opinion is necessary to measure how deeply rooted were these convictions and how clear were the implications that conservatives drew from them when they sought to influence American foreign policy.

For example, Norman Podhoretz, writing in *Commentary* in 1981, sought to refute the argument that Soviet foreign policy was merely historical expansionism, similar, for instance, to Germany under the kaiser, and thus continuous with power rivalries that have always prevailed in Western politics. Asked Podhoretz: "But what if the Soviet Union is not a normal nation-state? What if in this case ideology overrides interest in the traditional sense? In short . . . what if the Soviet Union bears a closer relationship to the Germany of Hitler than to the Germany of Kaiser Wilhelm?" The Soviet Union, Podhoretz urged, was not a traditional state. It represented, he wrote, "a radically different idea about how to organize social, political, and economic life on this earth from the one that prevails in the world of its adversaries." The difference, he insisted, was the role of ideology, which propelled the Soviet Union into an expansionism that defied the usual constraints of national interest.[10] Sidney Hook thought similarly: "No Russian statesman in his wildest hegemonic dream ever conceived of a day when Russian forces in various political guises would make an appearance in Africa and Central America. Czarist Russia even let Alaska go for a song."[11]

Conservatives in these years were not, of course, merely responding to foreign policy theoreticians. They were responding also to events and trends. In his essay in which he differentiated between old Russia and the Soviet Union, Podhoretz mentioned Soviet gains in Africa, the Middle East, and the Far East and, of recent memory, the Soviet invasion of Afghanistan. Calling the Soviet Union "the last great empire on earth," Podhoretz cited a trend that had become ominous since 1962: "In every category of military power, conventional and nuclear, strategic and tactical, on land, on the sea, and in the air, the Soviets moved relentlessly forward."[12]

But the discussion would revolve around theoretical issues nonetheless. For when the radical differences between the Soviet Union and the Western democracies became axiomatic, then so did the nature of the Cold War. It assumed the character of an inviolate ideological struggle, a war between incompatible moral and even ontological principles. Traditional concepts of balance of power and national interest could have only secondary impact, because different historical forces affected the combatants and more ultimate objectives were at stake, at least for the Soviet Union, than traditional statecraft dictated.

Conservatives, therefore, habitually employed the language of bipolarity in describing the continuing Cold War. Almost everything reduced to opposites. Midge Decter could write summarily in describing the Soviet Union as "a revolutionary force," because communism was a "revolutionary principle." The leaders of the Soviet Union were prisoners of an ideology that drove them toward world power, she believed. Soviet survival, Decter insisted, depended on the progressive establishment of subservient satellite states. "Communism must grow or die," she wrote, so that "in the long run, either Communism in some variant or Western-style democracy in some variant must prevail. It is a case of 'them or us.' "[13] Decter's husband Podhoretz raised the rhetorical ante even higher. "In sum," he wrote, "the conflict between the United States and the Soviet Union is a clash between two civilizations. More accurately, it is a clash between civilization and barbarism."[14]

Much of the vigorous anticommunism of these decades came from neoconservative members of the old New York Left. Outspoken in this group was Irving Kristol. As late as 1968 Kristol had argued that the Cold War was not an ideological issue; it was simply a conflict of great powers. The czars could return to power tomorrow, Kristol wrote, and the world would be little changed.[15] But Kristol wrote in 1985: "We have an ideological conflict, a conflict of world views, a conflict over the future shape of civilization." He compared the rivalry of the United States and the Soviet Union to the medieval enmity of Christianity and Islam. He added, in reference to the United States and the Soviet Union: "This is not a typical 19th century conflict of great powers fighting over resources and raw materials. To the degree that it is a conflict over strategic positions, that is only because of the underlying ideological conflict."[16]

Kristol spoke out as forcefully as any of the conservatives in denouncing the realist concept of foreign policy. The United States, he said, had unfortunately inherited the nineteenth-century view in which, as he described it, nations jockey for position and influence within a stabilizing equilibrium measured and balanced by the activities of professional diplomats. But this view, Kristol warned, did not accurately describe American rivalry with the Soviet Union, and it did not help us understand the major trouble spots of the world — the Middle East and Iran under the mullahs, for examples. Realpolitik is short-sighted because it is a too-secular and too-pragmatic measure of world conditions, Kristol believed. It misses the ideological/religious quality and substance of prevailing world politics.[17]

But whereas some conservatives warned that realpolitik was simply not effective, Kristol condemned it in principle. Realpolitik, he said, is "the vulgar substitution of expedience for principle" in American foreign policy. A nation content merely to pursue objectives of power and interest has sacrificed its moral foundations for cynicism and has "cast a pall of illegitimacy" over its national ideals. Kristol thus conjoined his complaint about the erosion of American bourgeois culture with the defects of its foreign policy. The moral and religious content that evaporated from those bourgeois ideals was similarly absent from Americans' sense of their place in the world. Needed was a foreign policy that expressed the legitimate public philosophy of the nation. That policy, Kristol asserted, would be frankly aggressive, indeed heroic. It would acknowledge the moral superiority of the United States over the Soviet Union and aim to defeat the rival power. Insisting that "pure amoral *Realpolitik* is no part of the American political tradition," Kristol hoped that a renewed moral quality in American foreign policy would both express and invigorate the high moral and religious qualities that once sustained and legitimated bourgeois civilization.[18]

Should American foreign policy then assume a large moral dimension? How dangerously close to the idealism and, as conservatives themselves often called it, the utopianism, of Woodrow Wilson would American foreign policy come if it were to take on such attributes? Should the United States seek to impose the standards of its democratic ideals and its bourgeois norms of public life on other nations? To answer these questions would compel conservatives to reconcile their traditional suspicions of high moral ideals invoked to refashion the world with their conviction that communism is a continuing threat to democracy and to world peace. In short, conservatives needed distinctions. As much as any individual, Jeane Kirkpatrick helped to provide them.

She was born Jeane Jordan, in Duncan, Oklahoma, in 1927. Her father, an oilman, embodied traditional moral views, especially about the roles of women in American society. Jeane was more actively involved with her mother, who influenced, through reading to her daughter, the precocious young intellect that Jeane became. At the age of twelve, having saved three dollars, Jeane Jordan purchased a thesaurus.[19] But if there was intellectual life in her Oklahoma home, then there was political activity in even greater abundance. "My family was always in politics," Kirkpatrick recalled. And they were all Democrats—grandparents, parents, aunts, and uncles.[20]

Kirkpatrick's Anglo-Saxon genealogy had deep roots in America. She had three great-grandfathers who fought with divided loyalties in the Civil War. Her own kin were Southern Baptists, and she was reared in that denomination of Protestantism. But outweighing any of these influences was a more general regional culture that one can cite as an enduring influence on Kirkpatrick's career. The Oklahoma of her youth was barely postfrontier America, and Kirkpatrick remembered a buoyant, positive spirit and an ethos of self-confidence, a "can-do spirit," and an ethic of personal responsibility among the people she knew. It was not an individualism, however, that translated into any kind of antistatist Social Darwinism. Kirkpatrick asserted that at no time in her life did she have antigovernment feelings, and in fact she had "an inherited belief in the welfare state." Certainly her family had no difficulty in translating the Jacksonian social culture of their Oklahoma setting into an embrace of the New Deal in the 1930s and a continuing loyalty to the Democratic party. Kirkpatrick even remembered a father who had no reservations about her dating a Catholic but admonished her, "Don't you dare bring home a Republican."[21]

The rough democratic spirit of Oklahoma and of southern Illinois, to which her family removed when Jeane was twelve, became the source of another Kirkpatrick trait that would have clear political consequences for her later career. For Kirkpatrick always resented the claims of superior wisdom alleged to reside in special groups. She felt inherently more comfortable with the intelligence and sentiments of ordinary people than with the special credentials of the better educated or more powerful. Her extended case against the New Class elite in America would be the most forceful expression of these prejudices.[22]

Kirkpatrick completed a two-year program at Stephens College in Missouri, earning an A.A. degree in 1946. Then she moved on to Barnard College in New York City, where she acquired an A.B. degree two years later. She pursued graduate study in political science at Columbia University, earning a master's degree in 1950. But along the way to a doctorate seventeen years later, other opportunities beckoned. She studied at the Institut de Science Politique at the University of Paris, where she met Evron "Kirk" Kirkpatrick, who served many years as executive director of the American Political Science Association. They were married in 1955, and the three boys born to the couple kept their mother busy in what to the casual observer might appear to be a traditional role of motherhood.

But Kirkpatrick possessed an indomitable spirit. She could not forego her academic interest and her concern for world politics. For a while she worked at the State Department, where she analyzed interviews with Eastern European refugees and conducted interviews with Chinese who had surrendered to MacArthur in Korea and had refused repatriation. These firsthand experiences influenced the making of a very anti-Communist Democrat. "They were terrible stories," she remembered, "like the Ancient Mariner's."[23]

By the time Kirkpatrick had earned her doctoral degree, she had edited a book of essays titled *The Strategy of Deception: A Study in World-Wide Communist Tactics,* published in 1963 with her own vigorous introduction.

But her special academic interest was comparative politics, with a focus on Latin America. Her doctoral thesis became her first book, *Leader and Vanguard in Mass Society: A Study of Peronist Argentina,* published in 1971. There followed *Political Women* (1974) and *The New Presidential Elite: Men and Women in National Politics* (1978).

Meanwhile, Kirkpatrick pursued two careers. "A woman who voluntarily deals herself out of motherhood is making a terrible mistake," she once said. This, however, was no concession to the cult of True Womanhood. Kirkpatrick had interrupted her career at the State Department in 1957 to care for a growing family. But she had the same judgment of mistaken options toward women who gave all to domestic life at the expense of their intellectual or professional skills. However difficult it might be to decide between career and motherhood, Kirkpatrick upheld for women the motto "Refuse to choose."[24] She refused to choose and embarked on a distinguished academic career at Georgetown University.

The appointment by President Reagan of the first woman United States ambassador to the United Nations was major news in 1981. And the controversial career of Jeane Kirkpatrick that followed kept her constantly in the public eye. Her visibility even gained for her writings on foreign policy and comparative politics an attention that reached beyond the scholarly community. Journals of opinion and even popular magazines addressed the academic career that was now shaping American policy in the world. But her scholarship needs to be seen as part of a whole. Until the end of the 1970s Kirkpatrick wrote mostly about domestic politics. She was, in fact, a pioneer of neoconservatism. Her writings on American political parties especially demonstrate the points of continuity in her academic and public career. In Kirkpatrick we have a nearly composite picture of the neoconservative mentality. How that neoconservatism applied to foreign policy marks Kirkpatrick's significance in American intellectual conservatism.

Kirkpatrick was at Barnard College in 1948 and was following the presidential politics of that year. It was the year of her "first, serious, independent political judgment," however much it confirmed the strong Democratic party loyalties of her family. The college had its several partisan factions – not only the Thomas Dewey Republicans and the Truman Democrats but the Henry Wallace "progressives" among the Democrats also. For Kirkpatrick that group was her first exposure to "radical chic," and she was ill at ease with the fashionable leftist reformism of the Wallacites. Truman, she remembered, was an unfashionable candidate on an Ivy League campus. Recalling the Hollywood coterie of aesthetes and prima donnas that flocked to the Wallace movement, Kirkpatrick wrote that "Harry Truman's effective liberalism was to

Henry Wallace's Progressive Party what diamonds are to rhinestones—it was the real thing." Years later she would register dissent against another Democratic schism in the takeover of the party by George McGovern. But this time she would find the results damaging and permanent.[25]

The riotous Democratic party convention of 1968, marked by protests and police arrests in the city of Chicago, led to a reform program intended to break the hold of traditional power factions in that party—the coalition of big city mayors, local ward healers, labor leaders, and other individuals and groups that made up the long-standing "organization." The party elite would now be dismantled. The caucuses would be open, and racial and sexual quotas would be imposed for delegate selection to the nominating convention. In the goals of the reformers, the party would begin to reflect the larger constituency of the American public. The reforms were advanced in the name of a more authentic and representative democratic politics. But to Kirkpatrick, the Democratic party, a party of grass-roots organizations, a collection of tribal loyalists bound by a hierarchy of leaders and an organization, had with one act been transformed into a party of narrow and partisan factions. With the dissolution of the traditional party structure and leadership, she wrote, the Democratic party had become "ad hoc assemblages of candidate and issue enthusiasts." The new open party, she believed, became a sitting target of narrow adversarial interests and single-minded reformists. Kirkpatrick was pained by the change.[26]

Another transition that Kirkpatrick saw in the reforms was the transferred influence from ward healer to media consultant. Both individuals had a similar function, of course. They were paid to mobilize and deliver the vote. One received "walk-around" money, the other consultant fees. One rang doorbells, the other used direct mail literature. There was consequently a difference in substance, Kirkpatrick said. The new media people were sophisticated, educated professionals, products of business school methods of market research and communications technology. They were essentially independent of party, contracted to it by a cash nexus. They were, in short, the post-industrial representatives of the New Class. Kirkpatrick traced not only their influence in politics but also their greatly increasing representation at Democratic conventions. By 1976, in their various forms they numbered, by her account, about half the delegation. Party reform and New Class interest, in Kirkpatrick's judgment, went hand in hand. "There can be little reasonable doubt," she wrote, "that the reform rules of the Democratic party, which stress persuasive skills, self-presentation, ideological motivation, and such nonpolitical characteristics as sex, race, and age, have greatly aided the rise to political influence of the new class and at the same time dramatically decreased the political value of such assets as local ties, organizational skills, and team loyalty."[27] The Democratic party, in short, lost its Jacksonian political culture.

One could argue that the Democratic party changes registered the irrepressible alterations of post-industrial America, that in fact the new constituency reflected the sociology of the late twentieth century, and that the changes were to that extent actually "democratic." There was certainly then a note of neoconservative nostalgia in Kirkpatrick when she recounted the effects of the reforms.

Her consideration of party reform raised a theme that Kirkpatrick addressed many times in her writing. The New Class ascendancy and the reform objectives associated with it represented to her the dangers of rationalism. She described this process as the effort to effect social change in accordance with abstract ideals of justice and fairness, or some higher notion of what an ideal society entails. Kirkpatrick's essay "Politics and the 'New Class,' " first published in *Society* in 1979, was her most forceful effort to link New Class influence with rationalist politics. She described the goal of the New Class reformer, whether liberal or conservative, as an effort to shape policy by abstract norms and ideals. New Class politics, she acknowledged, was as old as Plato, and the critique of it was as old as Aristotle. Kirkpatrick accepted the Aristotelian judgment. Rationalist politics was "utopian." It overestimated the world's plasticity, ignoring the distinction between the possible and the probable. Concentration on the manipulation of words and symbols induces an exaggerated notion of malleable reality. Limits are defined only by intellectual speculation and artistic imagination. In turn, the inevitable disillusionment born of the hopes engendered by rationalism brings cynicism and despair, as well as a generally negative perception of the everyday world. Kirkpatrick wrote: "It seems almost certain that the rationalist orientation creates disenchantment with concrete people, places, and practices. When today's housing, health care, or income levels are compared with those of the last decade or those of other societies, the society may look progressive and reasonably successful. But when society is measured against an abstract conception of a just order, it will be seen to have failed."[28]

For Kirkpatrick the 1972 presidential election, and particularly the turns taken by the Democratic party, were landmark events. She was not alone in describing that year in broad and summary terms. The success of George McGovern in capturing the party was the culmination, in Kirkpatrick's analysis, of "anti-bourgeois attitudes" that had become increasingly widespread over more than a decade. What had been an avant-garde culture in the 1950s spread with the growth of the college population and found currency in the electronic media and mass-circulation magazines. Its agenda was a systematic overhaul of everything that could be labeled "establishment" — family, schools, trade unions, business, and, above all, government. The 1972 election, Kirkpatrick wrote, overrode traditional bread-and-butter issues to become a referendum on the legitimacy of American society, a *Kulturkampf* that polarized the nation. She summarized the new situation as "a cultural class struggle." The Republican Richard Nixon, said Kirkpatrick, was now the leader of the masses of American society against "an embattled revolutionary elite" that had united under the McGovern banner. Liberalism, she argued, had become "the ideology of the privileged" and conservatism "the position of the less privileged."[29]

This election was making neoconservatives out of old Democrats, and foreign policy questions were at the heart of the changes. George McGovern had campaigned on a commitment to bring American forces home from Vietnam unconditionally, and he made unambiguous his moral denunciation of American involvement in the war. McGovern's harangues provoked many members of his party who saw in them a betrayal of the party's honorable record of anticommunism and internationalism. The divisiveness that McGovern engendered can be appreciated only against the perspectives that the emerging neoconservatives held of their party's history, its record of liberal anticommunism. Irving Kristol thus could write about what seemed almost to be a golden age of American liberalism, the early years of the Cold War. "It was the liberalism that sanctioned the Truman Doctrine, constructed NATO, fought the Korean War, and originally sponsored our intervention in Vietnam," he wrote. Its best and clearest expression in the early years, said Kristol, was Arthur M. Schlesinger, Jr.'s, book *The Vital Center.* Now Kristol found the Democratic party falling into a "new isolationism."[30]

The year 1972, finally, saw the decisive formation by dissatisfied Democrats of the Committee for a Democratic Majority. Its organization was a dramatic illustration of the divisions that had become pronounced in American liberalism. With Podhoretz, Midge Decter, Daniel Patrick Moynihan, Ben Wattenberg, and others, Kirkpatrick formed this dissenting wing of what were now often called "old Democrats." Kirkpatrick was as active as any of the CDM members in spelling out the group's differences with the new Democratic program.

Two events of the 1970s figured largely in the academic and diplomatic career of Jeane Kirkpatrick. Under the presidential administrations of Nixon and Ford, Henry Kissinger worked to achieve with the Soviet Union a policy of détente. In explaining détente, Kissinger appealed to realism. American world economic hegemony, he indicated, had ended in the late 1960s.

The United States' percentage of the world's Gross National Product was decreasing by 10 percent each decade. Kissinger wanted American foreign policy to express correspondingly fewer universalist goals and to employ less universalist language. He wanted the American rivalry with the Soviet Union to be more narrowly focused, more playable by rules, more manageable. Détente with the Soviet Union, marked by agreements on strategic arms limitations (SALT II) and on national boundaries in Europe, was always for Kissinger a realist course for the United States, one that would be characterized by vigilance and pressure on its part and supported by a program of nuclear deterrence, with the national interest of the country always foremost.[31]

Détente prepared the way for the second controversial policy of the decade, the human rights initiative announced by President Carter. Liberals who had called for greater American accommodation with the Soviet Union and Communist China had seen their clothes stolen by Republicans, who initiated détente and Nixon's opening to China. Some now accused Kissinger of "amoral callousness" in his program, especially in regard to the Soviet Union, with whom the oppression of Jewish citizens now became an issue.[32] Realpolitik was again attacked for its amorality, for the narrow conception it held of national interest. In liberal ranks there was a demand for a foreign policy expressive of American ideals, of a universalist morality that sought the amelioration of all people. Even before the Carter administration took up the issue, Congress established human rights criteria and required periodic review of them for all nations with whom the United States did business.[33]

In the new agenda, Carter had the collaboration of his national security adviser, Zbigniew Brzezinski. Brzezinski, consistent with his theme in *Between Two Ages,* identified human rights as an emerging world force and linked American strategic advantages to its support. The United States, he feared, was becoming "lonely" in the world, and its standing among Third World nations especially was deteriorating. The human rights cause, he believed, would demonstrate the contrast between the American democratic system and the practices of rivals. "The best way to answer the Soviets' ideological challenge," wrote Brzezinski, "would be to commit the United States to a concept which most reflected America's very essence."[34] Likewise the president also rejected the notion that human rights was a choice of idealism over realism, of morality over power. American idealism would win America friends and respect. It would encourage authoritarian allies of the United States to liberalize their regimes, thus helping remove the revolutions that put leftist totalitarian governments in their stead.

As we shall see, many conservatives endorsed a version of this formula too. But the new emphasis nonetheless stood out as qualitatively different from Kissinger's approach. Carter could summarize the pragmatic advantages of human rights and still insist, in a Southern Baptist kind of way, "It was the right thing to do."[35] Foreign policy scholar Robert Tucker summarized the Kissinger and the Carter-Brzezinski differences: "The world of Henry Kissinger was one dominated by the 'old politics' with its parochial interests, its hierarchical ordering and marked inequalities, its obsession with equilibrium and the careful balancing of power, and its reliance on forcible methods. By contrast, the world of the Carter Administration was characterized by truly global interests, by growing mutual dependencies, by far less hierarchy, by less concern with equilibrium, and by the recognition that much less reliance could be placed on the forcible methods of the past." The Carter administration, in short, said Tucker, was impressed by the amount of change it saw in the world and wished to place a constructive role on that change, to get on the right side of history.[36]

Jeane Kirkpatrick was not trying to address human rights when she published her essay "Dictatorships and Double Standards" in *Commentary* magazine in 1979. Nor were the distinctions she was making between authoritarian and totalitarian governments original with her, for they built on previous work by Hannah Arendt and Carl Friedrich. Nonetheless, this essay became the most influential contribution to foreign policy discussion in the conservative literature of two decades. Though it may have been nonpartisan in intention and though it never employed the term "human rights," conservatives seized its themes and made them canonical in the guidelines they tried to shape for the conduct of American foreign policy.

Kirkpatrick was speaking to traditional American concerns in "Dictatorships and Double Standards." Americans, she said, have always been interested in how their democratic example might influence others, and they have judged others by their proximity to American democratic standards. Authoritarian regimes on the Right and totalitarian regimes on either side appear as countermodels to American ways of government. But Kirkpatrick wished to demonstrate that this view was too rigid. She wanted to show that any foreign policy was misguided if it simply equated all the nondemocratic states. Her essay therefore made two points: Authoritarian rightist governments are capable of evolving or collapsing into approximate democratic states, whereas leftist totalitarian regimes are not. And authoritarian states are milder in their effects and do less violence to the history and social structure of their nations than do totalitarians ones.

It was almost self-evident why Kirkpatrick's distinctions appealed to conservatives. "Although there is no instance of a revolutionary 'socialist' or Communist society being democratized," she wrote, "right-wing autocracies do sometimes evolve into democracies."[37] The United States should clearly be more sympathetic, it followed, to the authoritarian states, many of which were key American allies anyway, than to the leftist totalitarian states. This policy would be consistent with American ideals.

But at another, less evident, level, "Dictatorships and Double Standards" expressed conservative and neoconservative themes. Kirkpatrick described the tribal and familial nature of the political life of authoritarian regimes, the habits that reflect the traditional social ways of their countries. These traits, of course, may flourish amid clear inequalities of wealth and power in a manner offensive to American liberal standards. But authoritarian rulers, Kirkpatrick wrote, "worship traditional gods and observe traditional taboos. They do not disturb the habitual rhythms of work and leisure, habitual places of residence, habitual patterns of family and personal relations." Here Kirkpatrick invoked the organic rhetoric of the Burkean conservative and the tribal rhetoric of the neoconservative. She provided authoritarian states a safety valve of tradition, history, and continuity by which one could measure them against the violence and rending of the social fabric wrought by leftist revolutions and the claims by Communist states for total control over all aspects of national life and culture. And lest these seem to be merely academic differentiations, one need only consult, she said, the contrasting record of refugees from the two kinds of states.[38]

Kirkpatrick's essay addressed another question. She believed that American attitudes, as expressed by the Carter administration, were prejudiced against authoritarian states. She suggested that those governments, based on kinship and other personal relations, did not set well with an American universalist ethic of justice and American rational standards of efficiency and modernization. The contrasts of wealth and poverty are likewise offensive to American egalitarian norms, she added. On the other hand, said Kirkpatrick, "socialist" nations and revolutionary movements in the name of socialism convey a quality of modernity and "progress" that compares favorably with the hardened traditionalism of authoritarian states. Reform movements, with their invocation of science and reason, their secular quality, and their bureaucratic rationalism, appeal to us, said Kirkpatrick, as extensions of the liberal Enlightenment. They gain a great symbolic advantage with us, invoking the symbols and values of democracy. And they have a special appeal to progressive Christians, she believed, who see in the liberating forces of history a redemptive process congenial to their special hopes for human betterment. Here Kirkpatrick pointed directly to Jimmy Carter. "Carter was," she wrote, *par excellence,* the kind of liberal most likely to confound revolution with idealism, change with progress, optimism with virtue."[39]

One reader impressed by Kirkpatrick's *Commentary* essay was Ronald Reagan. He wrote her a long letter and asked for a meeting.[40] When Reagan became president of the United States, Kirkpatrick became the American ambassador to the United Nations. It was a choice worthy of an administration that intended to set American foreign policy on a course of more vigorous opposition to Communist expansion and to unseat the mood of self-chastisement that beset foreign policy in the post-Vietnam era. Reagan was calling for a renewal of American pride and confidence, and he never hesitated to assert the moral superiority of democratic over Communist systems of government. In Kirkpatrick he also had a team player determined to mince no words in exposing the true character of Soviet designs. And in Kirkpatrick the United States also had a worthy successor to Adlai Stevenson, Henry Cabot Lodge, and Daniel Patrick Moynihan, other forceful representatives to the international forum.

Kirkpatrick's adjustment to her new post was not easy. She never felt that she fit into the routine and protocol of UN life. She brought to her new work the habits of the academy and the perspectives of a professor. She saw herself as a questioner, as a skeptic in "the French intellectual tradition."[41] She placed herself outside the various "subcultures" of the UN and did not become a mingler at the social events and lounge gatherings that supplemented the formal political agenda.[42] But although low-key she was not by any means uninvolved. "My first approach," she wrote, "was to learn everything about a subject and do everything. Read everything, write everything, decide everything."[43] And call everybody, as she was roused to do especially when "friends" voted against the United States. Here, no doubt, was a source of the "confrontational" label that was pinned on Kirkpatrick. Some charged that she was not a good listener, too forceful in asserting her opinions and trying to win others to them. Her offsetting practices prompted a charge that "she practices diplomacy by insult."[44] It was, at least, a dour visage that she projected. Kirkpatrick was not known for humor and seemed to find cause for it only in the grimmer realities of UN business. Once, after she reported to an American audience that the United States had lost 135–1 on a UN vote, she injected better news: "I am happy to tell you," she said, "that we were able to double our influence the following vote and it was only 123 to 2."[45]

It was really world politics, ultimately, that made the UN so inhospitable a place for Kirkpatrick. Any notion that this international forum was a place of dispassionate discourse that might function as a reasoning adjudicator of opposing national interests had long since died. Likewise the hope that the UN might somehow express some transcendent world interest to which individual nations would subordinate their narrower pursuits had passed beyond credibility. Kirkpatrick expected no such realizations for her ambassadorial function, but neither was she quite prepared for all the stubborn realities of UN politics. The most hardened realist, she found, could hardly have foreseen the hypocrisy and cynicism prevalent in that body. After about six months at the UN, Kirkpatrick later wrote, "I stopped rubbing my eyes" and confronted UN politics as its necessities dictated.[46]

Actually, as she reported, UN politics worked like any democracy. Its vehicle was bloc interests. The UN had several blocs, and even the Third World nations might be divided into blocs. But the preponderance of numbers and an overriding ideology made the Third World the ascendant force at the UN. It meant too that a kind of universalism prevailed in the organization, though one much in contrast with the universalism of liberal democracy that the United States once hoped the UN would embody. Since the early 1960s, as Daniel Patrick Moynihan pointed out, most of the more than six dozen nations that had joined the UN had passed from some form of constitutional democracy into dictatorships.[47] This new ingredient boded ill for Western values at the UN, but matters were made worse, Kirkpatrick believed, by what she now found to be a paramount "Third World Ideology" there. This ideology replaced narrow national interests and national symbols. It thrived on the rhetoric of "globalism," spoke of the "world community," and demanded for all an equitable share of the "world's wealth." Fortified by supporting ideologies of Marxism and socialism, the Third World ideology colored all aspects of UN politics. An anti-Western and especially anti-American fever, said Kirkpatrick, flourished in UN deliberations in a manner that raised regional and national conflicts into large global issues. Kirkpatrick commented on several occasions that UN issues—those of Israel and the Middle East, for example—could not be addressed in traditional realist fashion. Geopolitics became global, ideological politics when moved to the UN forum.[48]

We will give most of the rest of this discussion to the subject of conservatism and foreign policy and Kirkpatrick's contribution to it. The challenge for her and others was, in part, to use the realist position against liberal advocates of other approaches, even against those liberals who embraced a new version of realism in the aftermath of Vietnam. But realism was never sufficient for Kirkpatrick or any conservative advocate considered in this study. Somehow a place for a higher moral appeal, wholly consistent, by most conservative judgments, with American traditions, needed expression and application. Conservative ideologies here were not inherently different from certain liberal ones. It would require some careful distinctions, then, to discern what form a conservative outline of American policy should assume. Kirkpatrick was central to that effort.

Kirkpatrick wished very much to preserve distinctions — distinctions about the historical nature of the Soviet Union and the United States, about the ends of each rival in world diplomacy, and ultimately about the moral character of each. Her essay "Dictatorships and Double Standards" reviewed Brzezinski's book *Between Two Ages* and the associated modernization theories of world politics. What she found objectionable in these theories was their strain of determinism. She believed they encouraged the view that events are manifestations of persistent historical forces that have their own logic of development and that the most any nation can expect is to be a "midwife" to these processes in a way that might gain some advantages for itself. But for Kirkpatrick, this view was an unduly optimistic product of an Enlightenment sense of a rational and progressive history. It was deterministic and moralistic, even locating a moral teleology in the historical process. It was also cosmopolitan, obscuring American purposes within a worldly, cosmic scheme that became the legitimating basis of decision and action. "It identifies modernization with both revolution and morality," Kirkpatrick wrote, "and U.S. policy with all three."[49]

In advancing her views on the nature of the Cold War, Kirkpatrick shared much in common with the influential realist interpreters. Morgenthau had argued that the main influence in Soviet behavior was historical Russian imperialism, of which Marxist ideology was only a recent vehicle of expression.[50] Kirkpatrick agreed that there was an ideological dimension to Soviet action, but the Cold War was not in her view "primarily a contest of ideas." The character of the Soviet Union, she maintained, "derives from a tradition of oriental despotism, from a czarist synthesis of economic, social, and bureaucratic state power." The United States was therefore in conflict with the Soviet Union because it was "an expansionist power, with imperialistic aspirations and imperialistic habits."[51] Here, then, Kirkpatrick stood at odds with Kristol and others who stressed the inescapable influence of Communist ideology in shaping Soviet behavior.

Kirkpatrick concurred with the realist analysis in another way. "Communism," Kennan had written, "is like a malignant parasite which feeds only on diseased tissue."[52] Kennan had warned in the early years of the Cold War of the opportunist character of the Soviets and stressed Russian history over Marxist ideology in understanding Soviet conduct. Kirkpatrick pronounced similarly. As early as 1963 she wrote that Marxist ideology played an inconsistent role in Soviet history and had little to do with how the Soviets pursued their expansionist goals in different parts of the world. Soviet methodology, she maintained, was singularly consistent: the Soviets intended to exploit any areas of weakness in any society and to play on and manipulate the situations of any social element in which disaffection and alienation existed. Those segments varied considerably. Factors of tribal membership or ethnicity and religion might be at work. Sometimes racial discrimination or regional discontents produced disaffection, and in the Western democracies often intellectual alienation or middle-class estrangement resulted in discontent. Communist efforts, wrote Kirkpatrick, "are concentrated on whichever group is most alienated from existing authority, or least integrated into the existing structure of authority."[53]

Soviet gains, then, did not derive from application of a Marxist understanding of history. This perspective critically affected Kirkpatrick's judgments on world events. Communists seldom came to power through mass movements of indigenous oppressed peoples, she believed. Her neoconservatism led her to see the poorest and least privileged classes in undeveloped nations as "profoundly traditionalist," their life expectations shaped by centuries of history and centered around traditional loyalties and traditional rivalries. Only manipulative agencies could transform these stabilizing influences into mass revolutionary movements. In Latin America especially, Kirkpatrick believed, insurgents, agents of the Soviet Union or its client state Cuba, had learned to manufacture alienation from the institutional structures of the society and government by incapacitating them. "Such groups," she wrote, "rely on terrorism to destroy public order, to disrupt the economy and make normal life impossible, to demoralize the police, and to mortally wound the government by demonstrating its inability to protect personal security and maintain public authority." This reasoning forced on Kirkpatrick the conclusion that the relation of indigenous Communists to native masses is "manipulative and exploitative." Kirkpatrick denied that she and the Reagan administration overlooked the genuine social roots of disorder in revolutionary situations, but her emphasis seemed to obscure deep historical forces that spawn revolutionary movements.[54]

Kirkpatrick's measure of the opportunist character of communism may have gained her some useful insight on world politics, but it created problems too. She had faulted modernization theories for their historical determinism. But it was also a kind of historical determinism, in which tradition and culture weighed heavily, that underscored her conservative appreciation of authoritarian states. It supplied for Kirkpatrick and others a point of distinction between the stabilizing forces in these societies and the disruptive effects of the ahistorical utopianism and revolutionary zeal that motivate leftist totalitarian governments. But the gains of these perspectives, and they should be appreciated, were offset somewhat by another problem. However acute they were in describing Communist tactics and in deflating the pretentious moral ideology that obscured the real functions and effects of these methods, conservatives were not so quick to recognize the alienating conditions that Communists did exploit. Kirkpatrick herself, for example, drew from her understanding of Communist methodology the lesson that the United States should fortify authoritarian regimes against Communist movements, as in Latin America. The United States will only delude itself, she warned, if it succumbs to "affirmative pressures for change," if it takes the "progressive" side, in short. Such a policy will impair the morale and confidence of weakened traditional regimes, she said, and prepare the way for violent and unfriendly successors.[55]

Kirkpatrick's position, though realist in its description of the Soviet Union, did not endorse a traditional realist foreign policy. Nor did conservatives generally. Norman Podhoretz, to cite one case, strongly criticized Kissinger's détente initiative not merely because of its results – an acceleration of the Soviet military program and more adventurous Soviet inroads in Africa and elsewhere – but he faulted the whole basis of realpolitik. The realist preoccupation with geopolitics and balance of power considerations, said Podhoretz, "robbed the Soviet-American conflict of the moral and political dimensions" that might rally idealistic Americans to make the necessary sacrifices to pursue the Cold War effectively. Americans, he warned, would never accept so prosaic a foreign policy as realism offered, and the new isolationism that would follow would leave the field open for further Soviet expansion.[56] In this view, it should also be pointed out, conservatives who stressed the moral factor in American foreign policy often shared similar ground with anti-Communist liberals. Theodore Draper, for example, advanced an extended moral critique of Kissinger's diplomacy.[57] But neither, in the end, could Kirkpatrick herself validate a singular standard of realism.

A realist who reflected on the Kirkpatrick thesis in "Dictatorships and Double Standards" might conclude, in the manner of Senator William Fulbright of Arkansas in the 1960s, that the United States simply had no quarrel with any nation that did not try to export its revolution or its system of government. Kirkpatrick did not like this kind of realism. It moved in the right direction but was not a "prudent guide," and it was essentially amoral. Kirkpatrick wished to restore the moral factor to American world politics without making moral ends a singular criterion. She believed that in the 1960s and 1970s there had been a dislocation of moral values from American policy. "The most deadly thing that happened," she said in an interview, "was the decoupling of morality and the national interest. The pursuit and defense of the American national interest *is* a moral goal fitting for a free people." And she had some clear ideas about what American moral values entailed.[58]

In May 1981 the new American ambassador to the United Nations was in Rome, where she gave a talk titled "The Reagan Phenomenon and the

Liberal Tradition." This student of comparative politics, who slighted the role of ideology in Soviet behavior, was urging that the United States had an ideology that it ought to make the burden of its foreign policy. She spoke of the liberal tradition of democratic freedoms and restrained state power and announced that the new presidential administration in the United States augured the recovery of those values in American life and in the American approach to world events. And in Washington the following December Kirkpatrick delivered another talk, "The Reagan Reassertion of Western Values," which also helped to reaffirm the ideological contours of the Cold War.

Many Americans in the early years of the Cold War described the rivalry between the United States and the Soviet Union as one between freedom and totalitarianism, or some variation. Later some critics recoiled from these "simplicities" and ideological rigidities and looked for a brighter season in American-Soviet relations. But Kirkpatrick did not remember the early "dark years" of the Cold War in quite this way. They were for her relatively auspicious times when the West was united and confidant and when democratic values enjoyed a world-wide ascendancy, even if not a universal practice. What had transpired since could only be considered tragic, Kirkpatrick believed. The West, and the United States not least of all, had become skeptical, if not cynical, about its historical values. A cultural relativism had called all social institutions, all agencies of acculturation, into question and had rendered patriotism a demeaning expression of chauvinism or ethnocentrism. A "reflexive anti-Americanism" was triumphant in many quarters of the country, said Kirkpatrick, and its promulgators regarded as progressive those violent movements everywhere that scorned American liberal values.[59]

To a Democratic party member like Kirkpatrick, this erosion of American ideals was especially acute, for that party harbored much of the counterculture that sought political incorporation. Kirkpatrick, we have seen, had spoken out against the countercultural inroad in the party but concluded that a losing battle loomed. After three years of service in a Democratic administration, she joined the Republican party and addressed its national convention in Dallas in 1984. But still she spoke with the heart of a Democrat. She quoted President Truman on the economic and spiritual strength of America. She cited the achievements of Democratic party leaders in building NATO, launching the Marshall Plan, and advancing the Alliance for Progress. "They were not ashamed to be resolute nor to speak of America as a great nation," Kirkpatrick said. "They did not doubt that we must be strong enough to protect ourselves and to help others. . . . . They happily assumed the responsibilities of freedom."[60] But Kirkpatrick now looked to the Republican party to lift the fallen banner and to revive a weakened spirit. She could speak of the "sea-change" of 1980

that the Reagan ascendancy signified, and she affirmed that the new administration was "moved by a certain idea of the United States" and committed
to "a reaffirmation of the basic principles of the liberal democratic tradition."[61]

With Kirkpatrick's own aiding and abetting, the American-Soviet rivalry
was renewing its ideological outline. Her two speeches of 1981 were efforts
to delineate systematically the differences in philosophy and practice between
Marxism and liberal democracy, the essentially irreconcilable differences in
their views of individual freedoms and the legitimate powers of the state.
Kirkpatrick wished to read Marxism completely out of the Western tradition,
and she felt constrained to make this point because of the progressive image
that Marxism had assumed in many Western cultural circles. Marxism, she
wrote in an address titled "We and They," may have had some roots in the
European liberal socialist tradition, but it was otherwise wholly antithetical
to Western values.[62]

Kirkpatrick considered Marxism a utopian worldview and in neoconservative fashion cited its deadly effects. She applied her assessment specifically
to foreign policy considerations and used it to enhance her distinctions between
authoritarian and totalitarian states. Authoritarian regimes are much truer
reflectors of human nature, she believed. All totalitarian regimes, Kirkpatrick
said, underestimate the power of habit in human society. They neglect the
wisdom of Burke, Hume, and others in doing so. "The role of habit in human
affairs," Kirkpatrick wrote, "carries with it a pervasive pessimism about the
practicability of blueprints for broad reform. It breeds sensitivity to the possibility that revolution may increase the total of human misery without increasing
man's moral, intellectual, or spiritual perfection." Totalitarian ideologues,
said Kirkpatrick, must invariably become ruthless in their efforts to attain
their ends. They have no patience, least of all sympathy, for the petty corruptions in social affairs or the quotidian materialism of ordinary life. Their
raison d'être is the inspiration to fill the gap between actual people and an
image of what they might become.[63]

Ambassador Kirkpatrick's UN papers illustrated by many examples the concrete meanings of these different political styles. For instance, she compared
Marxist Cuba with authoritarian Chile. The comparison was particularly appropriate, for Chile had come under UN censure for human rights violations,
whereas Cuba's record never attracted such scrutiny. Kirkpatrick offered nar-
ratives and statistics regarding political imprisonment, judicial independence
of state control, freedom of assembly, trade union rights, state censorship
of book publishing, and freedom of the press. The record was clear. "By
almost any objective standard," she said, "Cuba is a far more repressive country than Chile."[64]

These and other comparisons, offered in formal speeches and public addresses, were Kirkpatrick's effort to accentuate the moral factors in foreign
policy considerations. What offended her especially was the charge that whatever the descriptive differences between the Marxist Soviet Union and the
democratic United States, each of the superpowers was oppressive or immoral
in its exercise of power over other nations and peoples. Speaking before
the Security Council of the UN in 1983, Kirkpatrick took up the complaint
of a Soviet representative who argued that United States' intervention in the
Dominican Republic in 1965 disqualified American censures of Soviet hegemony in other nations. Kirkpatrick edified the Soviet delegate and the UN audience. "That difference," she said, "is that, like the Dominican Republic,
the states which were the objects of U.S. intervention are today independent
states, mostly democratic states, who enjoy self-government and self-
determination." In comparison, states like the former Baltic republics and
the Ukraine had never reestablished their autonomy.[65]

In the face of the American embroilment in Vietnam in the 1960s, some
American liberals embraced a new form of realism, one that deflated moralistic anticommunism. This turn may explain why conservatives, however
much they criticized the "idealistic" human rights policies of Jimmy Carter,
could nonetheless not quite dismiss these policies altogether. They continued
to insist, that is, on the relevant moral distinctions in the Soviet and American rivalry. This fact in turn may explain the discomfort of some liberals
like Schlesinger with the Carter program. In discussing human rights and
morality in foreign policy, Schlesinger quoted George F. Kennan on the arrogance of Americans who profess to know with certainty the needs of other
peoples and who would impose their own values on them indiscriminately.
Schlesinger thought it also appropriate to invoke Reinhold Niebuhr's explanation of why nation-states cannot be moral agents in the way that individual
people can be. What Schlesinger perceived in the human rights campaign
was a rekindled American messianism that could only distort the United States'
real national interest and further agitate the turbulent waters of world politics.
Like conservatives, liberals could be both moralists and realists in foreign
policy dogmatics.[66]

    For conservatives, the human rights question in foreign policy was an even
more devilish one, and it proved to be almost utterly confounding. Let us
consider Irving Kristol again as an example. None was quicker than he to
sniff out "utopianism" in politics, which he had come to see as the substance
of the leftist movement of the 1960s and afterward. Kirstol could not then
be expected to endorse universalist American notions of rights and liberties
and their application against what conservatives always saw as the brutal

facts of political reality in other parts of the world. To this end, Kristol could sound ultrarealist in writing about foreign policy questions. The United States should never have been in Vietnam, he said, if it merely intended to set up an American-style democracy. Its only real interest in that part of the world, he added, was to help stabilize the region and prevent further gains for communism. The character of the political regime in South Vietnam was not an issue for Kristol. "If such a regime prefers corrupt elections to the kind of overt military dictatorship that usually prevails in that part of the world, this is its own affair."[67] Kristol changed his views of 1971 somewhat, but in 1980 he was still making clear his vexation with the moral quotient in American foreign policy. He wrote in 1980 that "it is the fundamental fallacy of American foreign policy to believe, in the face of the evidence, that all peoples everywhere, are immediately 'entitled' to a liberal constitutional government." American foreign policy discussion seemed to Kristol to be "tormented" by moral factors.[68] Kristol linked human rights morality to a liberal program that, he believed, sought to universalize entitlement programs and the welfare state.[69]

But Kristol did not himself hold to this antimoralism. We observed earlier his changing posture on the Cold War. In the later 1970s Kristol was stressing the serious ideological conflict between the Soviet Union and the United States, a conflict that now appeared increasingly to him as a moral drama or, as he described it, "a profound moral conflict." He was now concluding, moreover, that "Realpolitik a la Disraeli is unthinkable in America."[70]

It was implementation that troubled conservatives about using human rights as a foreign policy objective. They could seldom slight any discussion that emphasized values and morality, whose demise in the culture of relativism they had long lamented. Neoconservatives, though, were less likely to invoke moral standards that were embraced by traditional conservatives. William Barrett agreed that human rights had a legitimate place in American foreign policy, but argued that a separate human rights policy would not yield much good.[71] Likewise Nathan Glazer agreed that "human rights will, and should, affect American foreign policy," but he did not like the "self-righteous arrogance" by which the United States made itself the perpetual judge of every other nation's behavior. "We cannot and should not go around the world pinning medals on some countries, recording debits for others," Glazer wrote. "It is truly not our business."[72] And Sidney Hook pointed out that if the United States in the 1940s had designed a human rights component for its foreign policy similar to that of the Carter administration in the 1970s, it would have never been in a position to aid the Soviet Union against Hitler.[73]

Generally neoconservatives resolved the problem of moral idealism and realism in a more direct way: they simply conjoined the two values. The extension of American influence in the world was a human rights program, they argued. The United States, said Peter Berger, has from its beginnings been attached to a certain political creed, one that has had enemies on the Right and the Left. But the main threat to liberal democracy since World War II, Berger believed, had been "the expansive Soviet superpower." The struggle for human rights, said Berger, lay in resistance to Soviet expansion and hence was linked to the American national interest. "Even a *Realpolitik* worthy of that name," said Berger, "will have to take this aspect of social reality into account."[74] Seymour Martin Lipset also made the link directly. "What is needed," he wrote, "is a practical moralism, a commitment to democracy and human rights which is tied to national interest. The two elements, of course, are reinforcing, for the more widespread democracy, the stronger America, but equally, the stronger the United States, the greater the chances to expand democracy and human rights elsewhere."[75] Midge Decter concurred. "Insuring the strength and success of the United States of America," she wrote, "*is* a human-rights policy."[76] Norman Podhoretz agreed: "To oppose Communism in the world of ideas and ideologies is therefore in itself a necessary condition of fighting for human rights; anyone who fails to oppose Communism forfeits the intellectual and moral right to speak in the name of human rights." For Podhoretz, foreign policy could never be merely realism. It was not in the nature of the American people, he believed, to pursue the mundane ends of balance of power or simple strategic position and advantage. Looking at the record of European diplomacy and the toll of two world wars, Podhoretz discredited the claims of realism as the safer and more prudent course of international relations.[77]

Jeane Kirkpatrick addressed the question of human rights very cautiously. Her approach was born of her innate neoconservative skepticism toward rationalist abstractions, and human rights, she believed, was just such an idea that could be easily rendered in this fashion. She described her skepticism as a Burkean suspicion of grand ideals and high moral principles and demanded with Burke to know how these would be located in specific institutions and how they would affect the habits of a people. Applying Burke to foreign policy, Kirkpatrick urged against "the globalist approach which denies the realities of culture, character, geography, economics, and history in favor of vague abstract universalism."[78]

Kirkpatrick also had much to say about the application of human rights to American foreign policy, and she became one of the most outspoken critics of the Carter administration and of the UN on this issue. Neither was acting with any consistency, she believed, and she echoed recognizable conservative opinion in this critique. Of the Carter program she simply posed the question

"Why were South American military regimes judged so much more harshly than African ones?"[79] She refused to credit the argument that Carter human rights policy had induced liberalization in South America, and she attributed changes that did occur there to familiar historical patterns of cyclic politics in those countries. It was as foolish of the United States, she said, to be the moral strongman with authoritarian countries as it would be, out of a foolish consistency, to break relations with the more brutal African states.[80]

But the alternative for Kirkpatrick was never an amoral realism, and neither her Burkean historicism nor her antirationalism led her wholly in that direction. Governments, she wrote, must act from a vision of the public good characteristic of their societies, or from an ideal of their societies. This need is especially strong in democracies, she added, where moral legitimacy is a persistent question in politics. In the United States above all, the moral question was inescapable. Kirkpatrick maintained that the very fact of America's social and cultural pluralism demanded some overriding unity, some transcendent ideals that forged a national purpose out of a mixture of peoples. Human rights — liberty, property, security — supplied a common moral base. And, Kirkpatrick wrote, "defending these rights or extending them to other peoples is the only legitimate purpose of American foreign policy."[81] She specifically chided the realists — Kennan, Morgenthau, and Niebuhr — who admired American pragmatic politics at home and in turn lamented the nation's lapse into moral idealism in its foreign policy. But this expression, Kirkpatrick believed, was inescapable. Granted, she said, it had both its overzealous forms and its contradictory expressions, producing the democratic outreach of Wilsonian idealism and the purist withdrawal into isolationism. But the moral imperative of American foreign policy was ingrained in the national character. Realism was inconceivable. "The notion that foreign policy should be oriented toward balance of power politics, or realpolitik, is totally foreign to the American tradition," said Kirkpatrick, "and, in fact, foreign to the American scene today."[82]

The challenge, clearly, was to incorporate human rights into American foreign policy without succumbing to moral "purism" or rationalism. And national interest must be the mediating consideration. It shared primacy in Kirkpatrick's writings with American moral commitments, and if there was nothing formulaic in her priorities, then there was not consistency either. Kirkpatrick wanted flexibility and pragmatism, especially in dealing with non-democratic countries, authoritarian regimes who sided with the United States in its anticommunism. Human rights policies, which, she believed, were often derived from modernization theories that dissolved political differences among nations, ignored strategic questions important to the national interest. Therefore, Americans ought not to apply human rights policies in the abstract, said Kirkpatrick, but should consider in each case the severity of the violations, the accessibility of American influence by other channels, and the potential for democratic evolution in a given nation. "The central goal of our foreign policy," wrote Kirkpatrick, "should not be the moral elevation of other nations, but the preservation of a civilized conception of our own national interest."[83]

In the end, Kirkpatrick, like other neoconservatives, created an uneasy compatibility of these rival foreign policy principles. Human rights were legitimate ends, she said, but they needed precise means for their fulfillment. Ultimately, Kirkpatrick argued, only democracies do an adequate job of protecting human rights, so that the strengthening of democracies should be the first priority of those committed to advancing and protecting human rights. It also followed that this cause required a strong American presence in the world. Kirkpatrick wanted to make that fact an axiom of American public philosophy. It was the only way that the moral idealism, the coefficient of American liberal democracy, could be effectively joined to a realist conception of the national interest. It would be a selective application, to be sure, a strategic weapon of anticommunism and not a universal ideal to be applied against friendly authoritarian nations. Thus did Kirkpatrick redefine the moral character of the Cold War in the Reagan years.[84]

But however useful Kirkpatrick's categories for conservatives were, they could often, of course, be at cross-purposes with certain conservative perspectives on politics. For example, Kirkpatrick had described the Shah of Iran as a prototypical authoritarian ruler and warned against the application of high-sounding human rights policies against his regime.[85] A conservative historian like Paul Johnson could reach conclusions about Iran profoundly different from those of Kirkpatrick. Johnson's book *Modern Times: The World from the Twenties to the Eighties* won considerable favor in conservative circles. But what Johnson wrote about the Shah's program illustrated the intrinsic difficulty of determining, to say nothing of applying, conservative standards to American foreign policy. Johnson reviewed the Shah's historical modernization policies for Iran and concluded: "The programme as a whole was a deliberate assault on tribal diversity, local patriarchs, family cohesion, provincial accents and tongues, regional dress, customs and interest groups, anything in fact which offered alternative centres of influence to the all-powerful central state." Here indeed was a traditionalist and neoconservative judgment against an authoritarian ruler. In fact, Johnson labeled the Shah's program "radical totalitarianism."[86]

Finally, Kirkpatrick's efforts as scholar and ambassador would seem to reflect certain qualities of conservatism and elude others. Conservatism thrives with a sense of the richness of history and tradition. It wants to join the past to the present, because it is the conservative answer, more even in the era of democracy and mass society than in that of Burke and Rousseau, to questions of stability and continuity and legitimacy and authority. Kirkpatrick, as we have seen, wrote and served with the sense that America had fallen into a state of unwarranted self-deprecation, of cynicism about its own past and the legitimacy of its own values. She believed too that the West in general had succumbed to what she called the "will to disbelieve." It had forgotten the meaning of its own values and had come to view as progressive the vicious and destructive forces of the Left that undermined every humanist value of Western civilization. In a 1984 address Kirkpatrick cited passages from Alexander Solzhenitsyn, Saul Bellow, Jean-Francois Revel, and Paul Johnson on the hollowness of the West's self-confidence and its deceptions about its rivals. She herself wrote: "Almost as strong as the will to disbelieve the shackling of freedom imposed on society after society by our only major contemporary adversary is the will to disbelieve our own worthiness. The will to disbelieve that we value freedom and intend to expand and preserve it has been translated into an expectation that we are almost always wrong."[87]

Even as she commented, though, Kirkpatrick's lament had relevance for a smaller segment of the American population than it had a dozen years before. American public sentiment, many in the 1980s believed, had been captured by a wave of patriotism. Businesses, always with a sharp sense of the prevailing popular mood, exploited these feelings lavishly, and American themes flourished in commercials. There was a question, however, of how much the new patriotism reflected a sober assessment of history and a serious examination of American values. Many rightly saw in it a facile sentimentalism and an indiscriminate chauvinism.

This was a special problem for traditional conservatism. Writers in the Burkean tradition, Irving Babbitt and Peter Viereck, for example, looked to history and tradition for their disciplining effects, as curbs against the expansive tendencies of human nature, against the overheated emotions of the present, and against the reflexive conventional wisdom of the day. Traditionalism, in the judgment of these conservatives, served most usefully to counteract the effects of romantic culture as it functioned not only to inflate the imperial egos of individuals but to encourage the self-worship of nations as well. Babbitt, it should be remembered, vigorously denounced the nationalism of his time and decried the attending imperialism that had made international politics a scene of warring national egos.[88] And Viereck located the destructive international wars of the twentieth century in the romantic ennoblement of the *Volk* and the reckless nationalism that it fostered in the nineteenth.[89] Both Babbitt and Viereck sought to override these tendencies by appealing to a higher Western culture. They did not always make it clear, however, how the appeal to tradition, evoked for its stabilizing influences, might not in turn feed the expansive lusts of nations.

Conservative interest in national traditions, which is at its best an effort to select and refine what is most useful in a national heritage, will always lead conservatives to link national ideals to foreign policy. The conservatives we examine in this book all wanted to make that connection, but they seemed torn between two tendencies. In opposing the narrow view of Cold War politics that they attributed to the realists, they raised American-Soviet rivalry to a high moral plane. In doing so, however, they often came close to the rationalist politics that they so criticized in their opponents, that is, the application of universal norms without respect to the truly pluralist character of world politics. And as with the Left, rationalism easily became idealism. Kirkpatrick thus invoked a kind of conservative rationalism in her speech on Reagan and Western values. "A new foreign policy," she said, "must begin from the irreducible fact that the United States has nonnegotiable goals and nonnegotiable moral commitments."[90] This was the language of Jimmy Carter, but neoconservatives were prone at times to employ it. President Reagan invoked American moral ideals in comparing the Contras in Nicaragua to the patriots of the American Revolution and by calling them "freedom fighters." This kind of conservative idealism could be as blind to the brutalities of the anti-Communists as the liberalism that ignored the atrocities of Marxist revolutionaries. Furthermore, it confused conservative objectives. Conservatives who denigrated human rights campaigns as utopian often defined, for example, as an American foreign policy objective in Nicaragua the creation of a democratic government with free elections. Idealism opened such conservatives to charges of inconsistency: they pressed for democratic reforms in Marxist Nicaragua but not in authoritarian Chile.[91]

Hans Morgenthau had spoken of the "tragic antinomies of political life," those felt by statesmen who confront situations armed only with their understanding of what is effective and necessary on the one hand and their judgment about what constitutes the least of evil alternatives on the other.[92] Conservatives had won an important intellectual and moral victory in their campaign, documented with fact and pressed with passion, against the human rights record of the totalitarian Left. And they carried their victory into the 1970s. As Kirkpatrick wrote and as Paul Johnson confirmed, communism's legacy still took a heavy toll in human misery.[93]

But conservatives could also be entrapped by their own fundamentals. Their worldview, as noted earlier, made little room for change, for historical contingency, for the unpredictable. The argument that totalitarian states could not convert themselves into open systems became an axiom of conservative understanding of the Soviet Union in the 1970s and 1980s. But the arresting events of the Gorbachev era in Soviet history forced suspension of all such assumptions and compelled rethinking of American-Soviet relations. In 1977 Jean-Francois Revel began his book *The Totalitarian Temptation* with the sentence "The world today is evolving toward socialism."[94] In 1986 *Time* magazine carried a special section essay titled "A New Age of Capitalism" and described a trend, in many places around the world, of turning away from socialism.[95] The future answers to no one's prophecies, as conservatives on many occasions have stated.

Conservatives would necessarily have to find their way between the claims of moral principles and national interest, American ideals and geopolitics. But in considering America's world role they might do well again to remember the admonition of Irving Babbitt that true and effective leaders lead ultimately by example.[96] President Theodore Roosevelt, no shy violet when it came to foreign policy, wrote in 1904:

Ordinarily it is very much wiser and more useful for us to concern ourselves with striving for our own moral and material betterment here at home than to concern ourselves with trying to better the conditions of things in other nations. We have plenty of sins of our own to war against, and under ordinary circumstances we can do more for the general uplifting of humanity by striving with heart and soul to put a stop to civic corruption, to brutal lawlessness and violent race prejudices here at home than by passing resolutions about wrongdoing elsewhere.[97]

The world had changed since 1904, but not so much that Roosevelt's conviction did not have relevance. Taken to excess, however, this exhortation could activate another kind of conservative sentiment. In 1821 John Quincy Adams, then secretary of state, wrote: "Wherever the standard of freedom and independence has been or shall be unfurled, there will be America's heart, her benedictions and her prayers. [But] she does not go abroad in search of monsters to destroy. She is the well-wisher to the freedom and independence of all. She is the champion and vindicator only of her own."[98] But surely there is as much of naïvete and innocence in such an expression as there is in that tedious inquiry, What has war ever accomplished? Leadership by example must sometimes be leadership by action. It requires conduct that will not permit an amoral geopolitical course to dominate United States behavior in the world and will insist that ultimately the nation cannot be in league with ungodly despots. But neither can America's own imperfections be an indefinite restraint and rationale against intervention on behalf of greater liberty and democracy. The United States must also face the question of when action on behalf of certain principles combines with a judicious respect for national self-interest and a realist expectation that such principles might be transplanted into fertile soil.

7

Robert Nisbet
Resisting Leviathan

IN 1986 ROBERT NISBET published a book with the title *Conservatism: Dream and Reality*. It was a short work that attempted to trace conservative thought from its origins in the late eighteenth century, and like other works of similar subject it acknowledged conservatism's debt to British statesman Edmund Burke. Indeed quotations from the great conservative appeared throughout Nisbet's text. But Nisbet did more than pay homage to Burke. He paused to consider Burke's era and the special conditions of Western Europe in his day. He made this observation:

In addition to the church, there were the historic towns and guilds throughout Western Europe which turned increasingly, as the cosmopolitanism of the Enlightenment spread, to their own native histories, traditions, saints, heroes, governments and crafts. There were poets, composers, performers, artists, artisans, annalists and chroniclers quite content to work with the materials of their own communities instead of going off to Europe's capitals for possible fortune and fame. Search for native dialects, folk literature, long-ignored creators in the arts, military heroes of the distant past, and others comparable to these, was in full swing in many parts of Germany by the middle of the eighteenth century. The fascination with the Middle Ages that would grip so many minds by the middle of the nineteenth century was greatly evident in Germany and Eastern Europe throughout the eighteenth century.[1]

This statement tells us almost everything that underscored the conservatism of Robert Nisbet. The book itself brought into focus and effective summary the large body of writing that Nisbet had contributed to intellectual history and sociology during the previous forty years. If as an academic sociologist Nisbet shared with the American neoconservatives the grounding of his ideas in the empirical discipline of the social sciences, then as a historian of ideas, he shared with many of the Old Right the Burkean veneration of antiquity, history, and tradition, a sense of the mystical charm of things that gave to otherwise mundane and quotidian commonalities of experience a special place in the imagination. Burke's "unbought grace of life" supplied Nisbet with a persistent concern with how societies conducted their activities and what larger meaning and value they gave to them.

But this concern also led Nisbet repeatedly to those various organizations in any society that attach individuals to their natural communities, to the several local, tribal, and kinship organizations that were for Nisbet the crucial basis of a healthy pluralism and the essential protection of any citizen against the aggrandizing power of the state. For Leviathan, ever since the French Revolution, constituted for him if not a reality, then a menacing potential in modern political life even among the democracies. Nisbet believed whole-heartedly that only the historical norms and values of conservatism could preserve these essential communities. For liberalism, as we shall see in examining his ideas, meant for Nisbet an ideology that begins with the priority of the autonomous individual and ends by surrendering him to the supremacy of the state.

Of all the conservative thinkers studied in this book, Nisbet is the one most directly situated in European conservatism. Much of his career was an effort to outline an identifiable core of conservative values articulated by European conservatives and to relate these values in turn to the conditions of contemporary American society. In an essay he wrote in the late 1970s, Nisbet summarized these conservative values, citing first the indispensability of religion and a sensitivity to the sacred, and adding the need for family, the importance of social rank, the imperative right of property, the necessity of intermediate social bodies, the significance of local community and region, the value of tradition, and the decentralization and diffusion of political power.[2]

All these listed priorities could be found elaborated in the greater part of Nisbet's writings. But one was left with the unshakable impression that the value he listed fifth—the necessity of intermediate social bodies—was the dominating, cardinal principle in Nisbet's conservatism. When he wrote his book *Prejudices* in 1982 and filled in the entry for "conservatism," Nisbet summarized its core value. "The essence of this body of ideas," he wrote, "is the protection of the social order—family, neighborhood, local community, and region foremost—from the ravishments of the centralized political state."[3] In his *Twilight of Authority,* published in 1975, Nisbet warned that "the gradual disappearance of all the intermediate institutions" that derived from the predemocratic past of Western society now threatened to make democracy itself "a new science of despotism."[4]

Robert Nisbet by Shelly Fischman

Dualities prevailed in Nisbet's conservatism. In his view, Western civilization had been a struggle between forces that sustained intermediate societies
and those that eroded them. Conspiring against the intermediate societies were,
on the one hand, ideologies of individualism and movements to "liberate"
the individual into an autonomous freedom and, on the other hand, the power-

ful state that made itself the alleged protector of such interests. In his extended analysis, the intellectual historian in Nisbet outplayed the sociologist, for the struggle he described centered essentially on ideology. It began in the universalist and cosmopolitan prejudices of the eighteenth-century philosophes and their culminating influence in the disastrous French Revolution. Conservatism, Nisbet argued, was born as a reaction to the social, intellectual, and political legacy of the French Revolution. Burke inspired that reaction, but of even greater importance than Burke to Nisbet were Alexis de Tocqueville and Émile Durkheim, to whom Nisbet turned time and again for appropriate quotations. Thus, though Nisbet's conservatism was rooted in European thought, it had a distinctly French accent. In Nisbet, it is by the French that we are damned and by the French that we are saved.

Another dialectic recurred in Nisbet's writings, but this one was less satisfactorily resolved in his conservative philosophy. Nisbet placed his own career as a sociologist in the original mold of that discipline in the nineteenth century. What the founding thinkers bequeathed, he asserted, was not only a conservatism that gave Nisbet a permanent model: they also created what Nisbet called "sociology as an art form." One sees in the characteristics of the pioneering sociologists, Nisbet believed, a revolt from the rationalist rigor of the Enlightenment, a felicity of imaginative insight, a poetic sensibility. If Max Weber once likened his own concept of rationalization to the poet Schiller's sense of the "disenchantment of the world," so might Tocqueville, Auguste Comte, Georg Simmel, and Durkheim have acknowledged in their perspectives an artistic sense of society that underscored their great achievements in understanding it. But rationalism, Nisbet believed, gained an ascendant and restrictive influence in sociology, a reliance on logico-empirical analysis and problem-solving that deprived it of insight and sympathy. Nisbet said of the early sociologists: "Plainly, these men were not working with finite and ordered problems in front of them. They were not problem-solving at all. Each was, with deep intuition, with profound imaginative grasp, reacting to the world around him, even as does the artist, and also like the artist, objectifying internal and only partly conscious states of mind."[5]

But Nisbet, on the other hand, was compelled on many occasions to criticize the retreat from reason that he saw as a stylistic attribute of modern culture. This phenomenon, he perceived, had become endemic in the social upheavals of the 1960s. For Nisbet, society needed always to tap its resources of tradition, memory, and folk wisdom, which indeed were irrational in their essential functions. The liberal mind, in fact, usually found these modes of cognizance and judgment inauthentic and restrictive. But these stabilizing uses of imagination and insight had been corrupted, Nisbet believed, by a deliberate cult of the subrational, a retreat to the subjective and autonomous self as the singular vindication of all experience. What had been a quirk of the counterculture of the 1960s, Nisbet feared, had become a commonplace of the general population afterward. That development signified for Nisbet one of the manifest signs of the deterioration of authority in the United States.[6]

Nisbet's complaints pointed to a difficult problem for conservatives. They have almost always upheld a mythical or religious sense of life to pose against the chilling effects of intellectualism, rationalism, and scientific empiricism. But conservatives also sounded their fears of the anarchist and solipsistic revolt against technology, bureaucracy, and the functionalist society that spurred the countercultural movement. There were, to be sure, ways of reconciling these plausible prejudices. Nisbet accepted the irrational and emotional priorities in human behavior as long as he could connect them to the rooted and safe confinements of intermediate and traditional societies. When they became the means of sanctioning personal whim and arbitrary behavior or when they attached themselves to the mass worship of the collective society, the state, he perceived in them the menacing influences of modern life.

Robert Nisbet was born in Los Angeles in 1913, and until he became Albert Schweitzer Professor of Humanities at Columbia University in 1974 his career had been associated mostly with California. He received his bachelor's and doctoral degrees from the University of California, remained to teach at Berkeley from 1939 to 1942, and was professor of sociology at the University of California–Riverside from 1953 to 1972, a tenure that included a deanship as well. Nisbet held many visiting appointments, including ones at Princeton, Smith College, and the University of Bologna. He was a resident scholar at the American Enterprise Institute from 1978 to 1980 and then returned to California as a fellow at the Hoover Institution at Stanford. Nisbet had studied with the famous sociologist Frederick J. Teggart at Berkeley and, incidentally, wrote an interesting account of Teggart with reminiscences of academic life there in the 1930s.[7]

Nisbet's recollection of this period of his life mentioned another great influence on his scholarly development. "I am not likely myself to forget soon the thrill . . . when I first read *Democracy in America,*" he wrote. "Of a sudden, a great deal about modern Western history and society took on new meaning for me." What he learned first from Tocqueville, Nisbet said, was the capacity of democratic governments, extolling their people in whose name they rule, to become themselves tyrannous. Nisbet always emphasized in his political essays that totalitarianism was not a reversion to a dark predemocratic past. It was a product, however corrupted, of democracy itself.[8]

Nisbet's first book was *The Quest for Community,* published in 1953. This work, and indeed the whole corpus of Nisbet's works, recalls the career of another Californian, Josiah Royce. That famous product of the frontier individualism of a rugged and feverish society in its gold-mining years formulated a philosophy, defended with the vigor of a powerful mind, that derived all meaning from the social basis of human life. His philosophy recoiled from subjectivism, from the individualism of his great philosophical rival at Harvard, William James. Royce posited loyalty as the ultimate human ethic and the moral basis of life, an ethic that brought the evolutionary directions of human life under the brooding and laboring will of the Absolute. So also for Nisbet, individualism would mean anomie, subjectivism would always threaten to become solipsism, inwardness would yield to narcissism, and the loosening of the social bonds in the name of individual freedom would weave the familiar and horrifying patterns of tyranny in the totalitarian systems that aspired to consolidate society's sundered parts.

But community was a two-edged sword. *The Quest for Community* influenced young American radicals in the 1960s, and Nisbet could appreciate why. Community was indispensable to revolution, Nisbet asserted. Revolution, he said, does not arise spontaneously from the masses but relies instead on the organizational efforts of leaders and strategists, the shaping forces of community.[9] Nisbet himself, however, became more and more fearful of the revolutionary community that self-consciously sought to reconstruct the world. That community knew only the tradition of its own antitraditionalism, and what it did in the name of liberation it defended with the tools of oppression.

But any community, traditional or revolutionary, justifies itself in part by its ability to sustain interest, provide meaning, and even evoke excitements. Nisbet understood this situation. He himself thrived in a rich sensual milieu. He confessed in an interview with *Psychology Today* that he was committed to watching all major sports events on television. At home and at work he played music constantly, and musical strains from classical to modern jazz accompanied the sounds of his typewriter.[10] In 1982 his book *Prejudices* appeared, a sparkling volume that addressed a great array of subjects and showed the versatility of Nisbet's conservatism as it discussed with insight such unlikely subjects as effrontery, fatalism, reification, metaphor, and nostalgia. But on one subject, war, Nisbet spoke autobiographically and in a manner that illustrated his appreciation of the emotions and the imagination as the critical components of the human personality. Nisbet in 1941 had but recently settled into a promising academic career, was situated with wife and family, and was enjoying the "good life" when the United States declared war on Japan. Nisbet remembered:

When, as became true in 1942, I saw all around me the fevered activity of Americans as we became overnight a nation in arms, became caught up in whatever ideology governed American entry into World War II, began to see the uniform, female as well as male, everywhere and read daily of Allied operations in distant parts of the world, even the comforts and normal stimulation of career became more and more disquieting. An occupation that only a year or two earlier had seemed inexhaustible in its psychological benefits now seemed routine, exasperating at times, and produced a sense of ennui that no amount of service on war-related academic committees, no amount of patrolling of blocks at night as an air-raid warden, could lighten.[11]

Nisbet proceeded to volunteer as an enlisted man and found that his service in the war fulfilled a need for new experience, for participation in a noble cause, and for enrichment of community.

Nisbet's conservatism was rooted in his academic career in sociology. Going back to 1952, we find a suggestive essay that Nisbet wrote in the *American Journal of Sociology,* titled "Conservatism and Sociology," and reprinted later in Nisbet's collection of essays *Tradition and Revolt.* Nisbet knew that his essay was taking him into a mined field. "To the contemporary sociologist," he wrote, "to be labeled a conservative is more often to be damned than praised."[12] Nisbet wished to hold up to his academic colleagues the achievements of the late nineteenth-century sociologists, who in turn drew on the insights of conservative writers from the early part of that century. Indeed, said Nisbet, the frightful trends of recent history made reading the works of all these early writers imperative for an intellectual grasp of the modern crisis. For too long, he argued, academic sociology had been enraptured by liberal notions of individualism and progress. It was time to recover the perceptions of the conservatives, specifically their preoccupation with the phenomena of mass society, alienation, and power, the monolithic power that arises from and is nurtured by the existence of masses of rootless individuals.

These masses, Nisbet urged, have turned with desperation to the centralized state to supply the want created by social dislocation and the erosion of traditional social bonds and mores. The conservatives, Nisbet explained, had usefully corrected the Enlightenment political theory of Hobbes, Locke, and the English Whigs who, he said, saw society as a mechanical aggregate of individuals subject to whatever contractual arrangements were made for the collective organization of the whole citizenry. The conservatives, by contrast, said Nisbet, substituted the idea of society as an organic unity held together by an infinitely subtle arrangement of institutional balances and personal relationships.[13]

Among the conservative sociologists, Émile Durkheim most effectively formulated for Nisbet these sociological values. Durkheim, who lived from 1858 to 1917, authored books on the division of labor, suicide, and religion, and his general perspectives on society and the individual, as expressed throughout his many writings, provided Nisbet with his own angle of vision on the modern world. When Nisbet published *Émile Durkheim* in 1965, he began his book by noting that Durkheim had been slow to make an impact on American sociology. "Between American sociological thought and the acceptance of Durkheimian perspectives," Nisbet wrote, "lay the wilderness of homespun individualism, pragmatism, and general suspicion of theory that Europeans, starting with Tocqueville, were so struck by."[14] But the writings of A. R. Radcliffe-Brown, Talcott Parsons, Robert Merton, and Harry Alpert, Nisbet believed, had helped to bridge the gap. American sociology had begun to move away from what Nisbet called its "empirical atomism, [its] aimless individualism." Indeed the prevailing conditions of American life, wherein the specter of anomie loomed so threateningly and wherein the attending problems of suicide, crime, family instability, and social strife were becoming more troublesome, gave Durkheim special relevance. "For Durkheim is par excellence the sociologist of anomie," Nisbet wrote, "and few societies have offered more abundant and diversified examples of this than America in the twentieth century."[15]

But Durkheim also enjoyed a special recommendation to Nisbet because he stood estranged from a progressive, individualist, rationalist, and ameliorative view of history that joined the Enlightenment thinkers of the eighteenth century to the voices of liberalism in the nineteenth and twentieth. Against a liberal prejudice that hailed the movement away from traditional society and the liberation of the individual from the confinement of narrow and prescriptive communities and institutions, Durkheim opposed a profound skepticism. He saw in industrialism, urbanism, and secularism the seeds of insecurity and anomic withdrawal, even suicide. Tradition, convention, and the various corporate unities of society Durkheim judged to be essential preservatives against these social derangements. Herein lay Durkheim's essential conservatism, said Nisbet. He believed that Durkheim was simply echoing the sacred canons of the earlier conservatives—Burke, Joseph de Maistre, Louis de Bonald, Karl Ludwig Haller, and others who opposed rationalism, reform, and revolution.[16]

Durkheim, said Nisbet, also derived and further developed from the earliest conservatives a concept of the reality of the social. Nisbet was always ready to grant to society its own being, its own life and essence. This life, he insisted, represented the accumulated cooperative efforts of generations and constituted the roots of individual identity itself. The collective representations and symbols that transmit meaning and shape consciousness are the essence of personal identity. Nisbet delighted to quote from Durkheim, with respect to collective representations, that a "special intellectual activity is . . . concentrated in them which is infinitely richer and complexer than that of the individual."[17] Robert Nisbet, as we shall observe, incorporated into his conservatism an anti-individualist prejudice that until recently stood against the grain of most American conservative thinking.

But we need to stay with the eighteenth century for awhile. For Nisbet, the original sin of Western civilization came late in its history. It was the French Revolution, and it left a three-part legacy of tragic proportion. Indeed conservatism has found its raison d'être, Nisbet believed, in combating this legacy. All the distinguishing features of liberalism and its revolutionary offshoots and everything set against these manifestations have their roots, in Nisbet's analysis, in the French Revolution.

First, the Revolution of 1789 set a pattern for later revolutions. In heroic language its celebrants idealized personal liberty, the freeing of the individual from the confinements and authority of traditional institutions through the systematic dismantling of their authority. At the same time the revolutionaries made the state the vehicle for the creation of a new, centralized authority that filled the vacuum created by the destruction of the older intermediate societies. The French Revolution always suggested to Nisbet the pattern by which movements celebrating "liberation" invariably became oppressive. Thus, through the efforts of the National Assembly, the National Conventions, and the Committee on Public Safety, the Revolution in France proceeded along a double path of the individualization of society on the one hand and the rationalization of society on the other. This process occurred, Nisbet explained, through laws directed against the patriarchal family, the guilds, and the church. Through the reorganization of education, which now became the monopoly of the state, and through laws affecting private property, coinage, and weights and measures, the Revolution completed a thorough rationalization of French society. The new revolutionary state in France, Nisbet maintained, acquired an authority far more extensive and more deeply implanted than that of any of the "despotic" French kings.[18]

Both Marx and Lenin, Nisbet believed, were the true heirs of the Jacobins. Indeed, he maintained, there has persisted in the modern revolutionary mind a consistent animosity against all authorities positioned between the individual and the state. Nisbet quoted Marx's references to the family, the state, law, morality, and culture as "only particular forms of production." The elimination of private property, Marx avowed, would destroy these sources of alienation and enhance the individual's true self-realization. From this process of liberation would emerge a society fully remade. What did emerge, of course, was not Marx's classless society, dissolving the state, but the wholly rationalized political systems that have characterized Communist governments everywhere.[19]

In still another way, the French Revolution presaged others. It was a revolution born of intellectuals' dreams and given to the realization of certain powerful abstractions, Nisbet averred. He quoted Tocqueville, who virtually paraphrased Burke on this aspect of the Revolution. Tocqueville saw in the revolutionaries "a fondness for broad generalizations, cut-and-dried legislative systems, and a pedantic symmetry . . . [the] desire to reconstruct the entire constitution according to the rules of logic and a preconceived system."[20] Nisbet as a conservative registered a dread of dogma and ideology. Ideology, he said, tends inevitably to invest more and more of the components of society with political importance, compelling their incorporation into the larger formulations of the new rational social system. This objective particularly characterized revolutionary movements of the Left, Nisbet believed. The result, he warned, is a terrible legacy of tyranny. "The human capacity to bend ideals into dogmas is inexhaustible," Nisbet wrote, "and there is no comfort in reflecting on the record of the twentieth century in this respect." He recounted the consequences: "More lives have been tortured, terrorized, shot, hanged, poisoned, imprisoned, and exiled in the name of one or another of the modern political dogmas of freedom, equality, fraternity, and justice than in all other centuries combined." What has been done in the name of "the people," said Nisbet, has wrought far more human destruction than any tyranny exercised under the divine right of kings.[21]

Nisbet's conservatism registered a cautious and skeptical attitude toward liberal democracy. Historically it has been the guardian of freedom, and this tradition at its best, he believed, has been a cherished element of Western civilization. But liberal democracy has a totalitarian potential that must ever be guarded. What has arisen, even in the twentieth-century United States, Nisbet asserted, is a society perilously transformed by the incidence of its democratic ideals. More even than modern dictatorships, Nisbet wrote, "democracy has done the most to widen and deepen the state's supremacy over other social allegiances." In his *Twilight of Authority,* Nisbet recounted the many facets of the "invisible power" by which a modern democratic state like the United States exercises an ominous and omnipresent control. This invisible power, Nisbet said, is "a function of the vast infragovernment composed of bureaucracies, commissions, agencies, and departments in a myriad of areas." The evolution of power to this condition also illustrated for Nisbet the capacity of democratic government to become the modernizing enemy of traditional society. This new situation, Nisbet wrote, reflects "the result of the general disappearance of all the intermediate institutions, which, coming from the pre-democratic past, served for a long time to check the kind of authority that almost from the beginning sprang from the new legislative bodies and executives in the modern democracies." In this transformation Nisbet located the major change in liberalism from John Stuart Mill to the Great Society. Liberalism has become, wrote Nisbet, "a vast celebration of bureaucracy."[22]

But there was another lesson here, of which Tocqueville forewarned. Everything that the democratic state takes from intermediate societies, wrote Nisbet, it does so in the name of a large humanitarian program that appears utterly benign in its intentions and that does not in fact immediately abridge our greater freedoms. Tocqueville's lesson went to the point: the state enslaves not through its assault on our larger liberties but through its control of the mundane details of life. Nisbet put his own prejudices on display in describing these details as matters pertaining to welfare, taxation, education, and health and environment. The particularities of these concerns generate commissions and regulatory agencies "of every kind." They enter into the daily routine of citizens, and consequently "the new despotism confronts us at every turn." The benevolent exterior of this invading Leviathan was for Nisbet one of the most disconcerting facts of modern democratic statecraft. And curiously, perhaps ingeniously, Nisbet, in describing the functions of this state, gave a new rendering of what the New Left liked to call "friendly fascism," or what Herbert Marcuse referred to as "the smooth, comfortable, democratic unfreedom" that prevailed in Western societies.[23]

Nisbet blamed modern liberalism for this late state of democracy. Though liberalism had shifted significantly from Mill to its contemporary practitioners, Nisbet found in it a critical and decisive element of continuity, and he contrasted it with conservatism. Nisbet wrote: "Whereas liberalism, classical and collectivist alike, tends to focus on *individuals* and their direct relationships with governments, conservatism begins with the *social contexts* of human beings—family, religion, and so forth—seeing in these contexts the necessary protections from government power."[24] Even the American Constitution, Nisbet believed, reflected the deficiencies of classical liberalism and its myopic sense of society as simply an aggregate of individuals.

Nisbet did not deny that the state, in many historical instances, had been an agency in the advancement of individual freedom and collective welfare. From Pericles to Caesar, Napoleon, Andrew Jackson, and Lyndon Johnson, political leaders had used government to advance these gains. The danger lay in the fact that the state can make itself the author of these liberties and protections, and what the state can author it can also unwrite. The state can also affect the meaning of rights. The constitution of the Soviet Union, Nisbet pointed out, recognizes no rights that are anterior to the state's creation of them. That document elaborates a list of material rights—to housing, jobs, even vacations—but omits rights of the mind and spirit—of thought, dissent, worship. Nisbet, however, greatly worried that the proliferation of governmental programs that a zealous liberalism had inspired over a half-century or so was acculturating Americans to a view of the state as their benevolent protector. The Soviet model was a great temptation, Nisbet believed. In the Third World it had gained ascendancy. He was not at all certain that programs such as Social Security, Medicare, Medicaid, and Aid to Families with Dependent Children, programs that change the language of "rights" into the enactment of entitlements, would not produce in the United States, too, a fundamental change in the traditional understanding of citizenship and state power. Should such a change occur, wrote Nisbet, "it will mean that the essential prerequisites of liberal democracy have eroded away."[25]

For Nisbet, modern liberalism had not only moved in the direction of a materialist paternalism, but it had done so while advancing an ideology of personal freedom. Liberal society had become marked by its enhancement of personal discretion in an unlimited area of activities. In this country, Nisbet said, First Amendment freedoms had brought subject matter to the stage, to the movies, and to public speech that would have been unthinkable only a quarter-century before. And while indulging in a libertarian rash of manners and morals, Americans had at the same time acquiesced in restrictions on business, on schools and universities, and on local units of government, restrictions that made centralized political authority arbitrary and undemocratic. Nisbet could not be indifferent to this trend. It had for him too much of an ominous historical pattern about it. From the time of the Caesars through Napoleon and beyond, he warned, the powerful state had grown and flourished simultaneously as indulgence and permissiveness beset the populace. The United States, he believed, had succumbed to such a condition itself. The situation, he said, softens the impact of political power, for it gives the illusion of individual freedom while the leviathan state extends its reach into every corner of society.[26]

This unhappy course of recent history, Nisbet asserted, could happen only because of a serious misunderstanding, by liberals and conservatives alike, of such terms as individualism, freedom, and liberty. For both liberalism and conservatism, he believed, had been too often based on the notion of the autonomous individual. The idea was mythological. From Durkheim, Nisbet had become persuaded that all human behavior above the strictly physiological must be understood as emanating from or conditioned by society.

Furthermore, Durkheim had written that "the individual gets from society the best part of himself, all that gives him a distinct character and a special place among other beings, his intellectual and moral culture."[27]

Such an assumption, of course, is not exclusively, or even mostly, a conservative one. John Dewey had made the social nature of human beings the basis of a comprehensive liberal philosophy and reformist political program. But Nisbet wanted to stress another point, that any meaningful freedom is possible only when the individual is rooted in a system of social and moral authority. One who is liberated from all restraint, Durkheim had written, yields to a despotism of his wants that enslaves him wholly. This argument is familiar to any who have read the major writings of the American Puritans, who made obedience to God the essential exemption to the otherwise tyrannous rule of our sinful human nature. Durkheim, in turn, with Nisbet's endorsement, described individual self-realization as a process by which society's norms and incentives become internalized in the individual, providing the basis of self-awareness and self-discipline.[28]

Such practical and moderate notions of individualism and autonomy, Nisbet admitted, had suffered from later misuse, such as in fascist ideologies that taught that the realization of self coincided with the identification of the self with the purposes of the state. Nisbet stressed that societies are rendered totalitarian in form only when an absolute authority replaces the pluralist structure of the *corps intermediares* that form the multiple substance of that society.[29]

Anyone decrying the growth of government and the rise of the servile state would almost certainly these days be classified as conservative. While a liberal libertarian is more likely to dissent from the tribal morality and public mores that constrict personal freedom — free speech or sexual practice, for example — the conservative libertarian more often makes government, and its interference with business and property rights, the special target of his wrath. Occasionally one finds consistent libertarians — H. L. Mencken, Albert Jay Nock, Robert Nozick — who are temperamentally or intellectually averse to all constraints. But Nisbet thought that Nock, and others who made the individual the main victim of the state's power, had misconstrued the real nature of the state's threat to freedom. For, said Nisbet, "the chief prey of political power is not the individual but society."[30]

The argument was pure Nisbet. By "society" Nisbet meant the ordinary relationships that bind human beings together. The state, he said, always grows in power at the expense of groups thus formed. It does so, furthermore, because the political ideologies from which the state acquires its legitimacy invariably begin by proclaiming the autonomy of the individual, his liberation from these intermediate structures. A tradition in political science that ran from Bodin through Hobbes to Rousseau, Nisbet said, makes this pattern understandable. "All that was vested by theorists and rulers in the state," he wrote, "was taken from such competing groups as the church, the guild, the commune, and the family."[31] For Nisbet, a fatal course in conservatism's legitimate revolt against the leviathan state would be the lapse of its political principles into the pieties of individualism and libertarian dogma.

We might look briefly at yet another intriguing ingredient in Nisbet's conservatism. As a historical antidote to the French Revolution, he invoked the Middle Ages. From the German romantics of the early nineteenth century to the Americans Henry Adams, Ralph Adams Cram, and Russell Kirk, medievalism has long held a special mystique for a certain conservative way of thinking. It evokes a kind of pre-modernism that accents the anti-modernism of many conservative writers. It provides natural law and Thomist certitudes that are invoked to fortify the modern intellect against the corruptions of relativism and secularism. The appeal of the Roman Catholic Church, furthermore, has provided a powerful ingredient of medievalism to intellectual and social conservatism. The Church appears to offer to any soul adrift in the confusion of modernism a sanctuary of authority, tradition, continuity, and permanence, to say nothing of a visual splendor and Gothic magnificence. The Middle Ages have commended themselves to conservatives not only for their religious forms but also for the power of pageantry in worldly expressions — the rites of royalty, the traditions of the nobility, the heroism of soldiers, the virtues of the fair sex, and the rich vernacular and folk culture of medieval life. The loss of these qualities in the era of secular democracies, this kind of conservative knows, has deprived the human imagination of a daily nourishment.

Nisbet too invoked the Middle Ages throughout his writings. But he extracted from that period a significantly different conservative application, one that was sociological and political more than cultural or intellectual in substance. The medieval social structure, Nisbet said, realized a special combination of freedom and order, of liberty and authority. Individuals were assumed to be members of social groups, not arithmetically equal and autonomous units. The notion of freedom connoted not exemption from authority but the right of a corporate group to its special and exclusive functions. Nisbet spoke of the medieval social ethos: "Both liberty and authority were inescapable aspects of a chain of groups and associations rising from the individual to the family, church, state, and ultimately God."[32] Quite appropriately, Nisbet said, feudalism, in all its manifestations in the Middle Ages, was "rich in the symbolism and nomenclature of the family."[33] The erosion of this social order, accelerating as it did in the twentieth century, was for Nisbet the essence of modern social history. Capitalism, he allowed, was partly responsible, but not nearly as much as the unprecedented aggrandizement of the state. When individuals, with the blessings of all modern liberal thought, became liberated from the structures of guild, clan, family, and church, the state filled the resulting vacuum of authority. The democratic state especially offered the illusion of compensation for lost community, and it easily grew to totalitarian proportions in its efforts to amend the loss.[34]

The retreat from medievalism has been a recurring historical theme from the Enlightenment and the French Revolution to the modern liberal state, Nisbet believed. The most insidious aspect of this conceit was the flattery with which liberal intellectuals in America have interpreted the significance of their own country. Certain historians had sanctioned the idea that the special significance of the United States was its wholesale exemption from a feudal past. That "liberal myth," Nisbet said, had allowed the United States to claim for itself a special democratic heritage and an exclusively liberal tradition. The notion underscored a mythology Nisbet wanted to correct. From the early manorial estates of the colonial period and the several established religions of that era through the rise of the colleges and universities, the urban political machines, and the Cosa Nostra and its familial loyalties and blood rituals, the medieval influence, Nisbet asserted, has assumed various and persistent forms in American life.[35]

In the meantime, Nisbet warned, another threat loomed. He was convinced that in Western society, and in the United States especially, a culture of subjectivism had become ascendant. While trivial in its manifestation, it was serious in its possible consequences. Nisbet believed that subjectiveness denoted every era marked by the erosion of social institutions. That erosion produced a turning inward by individuals, a pronounced interest in the self and its reflexive preoccupations. To Nisbet, a decade like the 1960s, characterized in part by an interest in the occult and a fascination with the demonological, indicated this phenomenon.[36]

Tocqueville had earlier and correctly observed, Nisbet said, that such phenomena have a special likelihood in open, materialist societies like the United States, in which mobility and rising expectations create a loosening of the social bond. The idea of "society" loses force and reality. There may follow a turning inward to the family, but that turn may further devolve onto the individual alone, who now becomes the singular locus of authority and reference. The various subjectivist phenomena describe a society in which individualism has become anomie and in which community is makeshift and merely narcissistic. Confidence in science and reason, in empirical knowledge

and formal learning, suffers. Here again for Nisbet the counterculture of
the 1960s had proved to be contagious.[37] Nisbet found the turn to Eastern
religions and new expressions of ethnic and racial identity, with their mystique
of separateness and uniqueness, to be facile and escapist, and ultimately unhealthy. "I agree with Goethe," he said in an interview, "that progressive
ages are objectivist; subjectivism goes with decadence."[38] And he laid the
latter phenomenon again at the feet of a corrupting cult of individualism,
the American sickness. "From Emerson's self-reliant individual needing nothing but his own inner resources to the desocialized, hedonistic, narcissistic
free spirit of the late twentieth century," Nisbet wrote, "is really not a long
journey."[39]

Nisbet found subjectivism a highly infectious force, and he was not surprised
to see it joined to the New Left movement of the 1960s and afterward. But
he observed a significant departure here. The historic modern Left, born
with the French Revolution and attaining its dominant form in Marxism, had
been objective in its reform program, Nisbet wrote, devoted to the annihilation
of such external obstacles to progress as guilds, monasteries, the patriarchal
family, monarchy, church, and ultimately private property. Nisbet found the
New Left, with its obsession with states of consciousness, its neo-Freudianism,
a radical departure. Even the early humanist writings of Marx, with their
theme of alienation, had located their source in the objective institution of
property, the elimination of which thereby became the corrective of the defect.[40] The New Left, by contrast, seemed essentially subrationalist in character. From the Frankfurt school to Theodore Roszak and Charles Reich, the
Left, Nisbet observed, had been pursuing a new state of consciousness that
would liberate the true self that had been buried beneath the layers of a socially
created superego. A new vogue for encounter sessions, drugs, and other forms
of self-therapy thus conjoined the New Left and the counterculture with older
patterns of the destructive individualism that Nisbet always found so menacing.[41]

In 1975 Nisbet published *Twilight of Authority,* a book that focused on contemporary America. It had many things to say about the direction of American
life, and it covered topics from sports to heroes and villains. Nisbet's points
reinforced with impressive consistency his main themes of community, individualism, and power. At times that consistent framework became excessive, stretched too far to contain so much of recent American history within
a dominant construct. But the book's theoretical ambition did make it thought-
provoking, and it made Nisbet the American conservative intellectual with
the most concise and inclusive perspective on the Western experience over
the last two centuries. Two subjects from *Twilight of Authority* and related
writings merit a brief examination here.

By the 1970s Nisbet had become persuaded that American politics was suffering from a dangerous symbolism of power, one that was already creating abuses of authority. This phenomenon, he wrote, had its beginning in the presidential years of Franklin Roosevelt, when expensive budgets for entertainment gave the presidency a veneer of royalism that successors soon rendered immodest. In fact, presidential politics under John F. Kennedy, Nisbet believed, attained a new pinnacle of royalism, as "of a sudden the White House became a palace in every sense of the word, and the actual life of the occupant from day to day was regarded and written about in terms which had previously been reserved for European monarchs."[42] Since then, he added, we have seen the personal retinue of staff officers and special assistants proliferate and add invisible ink to the Constitution. We have seen the press follow the president through the details of daily itinerary and dining hall dress, seen every pronouncement on matters cosmic or trivial recorded with holy reverence. We saw President Nixon adorn the White House guards in praetorian splendor. The object of veneration and doting, the president had become insulated and protected from all grossness of reality, Nisbet believed, a transcendent figure of magisterial image in our rough democracy.[43] This is not what a conservative means by social distinctions.

Nisbet's other point of emphasis was the growing military character of public life and discourse in America and the prominence of the military in the public consciousness. Nisbet did not mean war or the attraction of war. In fact his essay on war in *Prejudices* summarized many progressive effects of war in human history. Nisbet was reacting instead to the increasing use of military rhetoric and of the images of war as applied to problems of civic life. We do not simply try to solve the problem of poverty, he wrote, we must have a "war against poverty." Words like "battle," "attack," and "mobilization" had gained currency.[44] But here Nisbet fell into another ambivalence. He was no pacifist: he had described war as a cause of intellectual and scientific advancements and the cross-fertilization of cultures. But his conservative sociological instincts warned him also that by war great power always accrued to the state, accelerating the process of its absorption of authority from other social organizations. "Nothing has proved more destructive of kinship, religion, and local patriotisms than has war and the accompanying military mind," Nisbet said. The military creates its own values, symbols, constraints, and processes of consensus that increasingly demand the loyalty of the nation and the machinery of the social system.[45]

Nisbet's strictures carried another warning, that there has existed historically, and especially in the twentieth century, a clear affinity between the military ideal and the revolutionary cause. For revolution is but war turned against its own social system. The revolutionary state comes to power by means of armed revolt and must garrison itself against a host of enemies, real and imagined. Revolutionary states remain military states for obvious and necessary reasons, and the image of things military dominates the visible culture in those countries of the world today that are socialist and Communist. (Nisbet acknowledged this characteristic also in nations like the several rightist ones in South America but did not believe that these countries imposed the same degree of militarization in all aspects of society as pursued by those on the Left.) In these countries, Nisbet argued, the revolutionary state assumes a military guise in the most mundane ways. "With every reason," wrote Nisbet, "Stalin, Mao, and Castro chose the military tunic as their invariable public dress." Democracies, however, were hardly immune to the lure of the military. In times of insecurity and loss of public confidence, especially when crime and violence threaten to impair public order, the militaristic temptation rises. Nisbet, in any case, was not at all assured that the time might not arrive when Americans would happily trade some of their liberties for the prospects of personal safety and domestic tranquility.[46]

Despite the general thematic cohesiveness of Nisbet's writings, we have seen already that they were not without tensions. Nisbet seemed to be aware of ambivalences in his judgments without trying to reconcile all of them. He did write on a number of subjects that can be discussed under the general heading "tradition and progress," one that also indicates opposing values. But Nisbet's reconciling efforts in this instance constitute an important consideration for us. They serve usefully to define Nisbet's place in intellectual conservatism.

The story of human civilization for Nisbet was the story of progress. But he had to concede that from the beginning the advancement of learning and the gains of science, which he celebrated, had to overcome the rivalry and resistance of tribal authority. Even at the level of formal learning, the major hindrance to the bold and imaginative breakthroughs of ideas that advanced knowledge met the resistance of conventional scientific wisdom as guarded by dogmatic authorities among the learned. "Ideas, theories, paradigms, and values become as ensconced in the scientific, as in the theological fraternity," Nisbet wrote. That was the lesson of Galileo's troubles. "Rivalry, jealousy, and vindictiveness from other scientists and philosophers were Galileo's lot" but not his alone, Nisbet wrote. The "collective consciousness of tribe" was invariably an enemy of the new. Furthermore, Nisbet the sociologist acknowledged that the great historical challenges to social tradition and tribal ways—trade and commerce, migrations of people, war—were also the nourishing influences of expanded human contacts, new discoveries, and technological innovation. They were agencies of progress.[47]

How then to accommodate a philosophy of progress in a social philosophy that so systematically defended the importance of traditional local communities, tribal and kinship organizations, and church and cultural authorities? The challenge, of course, was to define a correct notion of progress, a conservative one that could deflate the claims of a rival liberal philosophy. Progress was the subject of Nisbet's book of 1980, *History of the Idea of Progress.* Nisbet considered himself a believer in progress even to the point that he despaired of the prevailing apocalyptic imagination that seemed to have become acute in Western society in the late twentieth century. Furthermore, it should be noted that in giving prejudicial sanction to the idea of progress Nisbet upheld a notion that had long been suspect to many conservative thinkers. Their suspicions, Nisbet allowed, were well founded, for the Western intellect had always produced fallacious notions of progress that were indeed the enemies of the conservative mind.

Nisbet first insisted on the communal basis of the individualism and creativity that underlie progress. That idea brought the concept back within the larger sociological perspective of Nisbet and paralleled Hilton Kramer's defense of modernism in art. Nisbet wrote: "Creativeness and innovation cannot be separated from tradition, as every great age in the history of culture witnesses and confirms. The great man of thought and action, however radical, works with materials he has inherited, through ways that are normally given, and towards ends that are firmly planted in his culture. That the great creator rearranges and directs these, applies to them energies and uncommon dedication, does not detract from the role of tradition and community."[48]

This fact, said Nisbet in an essay in *Prejudices,* makes originality an ambiguous and more likely a "treacherous" virtue. "How fatuous," wrote Nisbet, "the writer, painter, or inventor whose overriding aim is that of being original, nothing more."[49] Nisbet insisted, furthermore, that the idea of the past was vital for the idea of progress, that historical consciousness necessarily underscored the most useful and meaningful ideas of progress. The true idea of progress is both retrospective and anticipatory. If the connections of time are not properly made, then progress becomes a merely formal, rationalist idea, or it lapses into a subjectivism in which various forms of the occult, magic, and irrationality deprive the concept of public symbolism.[50]

A rival idea of progress, Nisbet knew, had long flourished in Western thought, but it had not become dominant until the late eighteenth and early nineteenth centuries. Nisbet described Jeremy Bentham's rationalist and utilitarian philosophy as its quintessential expression. In many ways, said Nisbet, Bentham was a greater revolutionary than Rousseau or any of the French Enlightenment thinkers. He opposed concepts of natural rights and reduced all good to the calculation of pleasure and pain. His principle also inspired him to advance a format of legislative reform based on such calculations of the public weal. All social institutions came under the probe of a utilitarian scrutiny. But conservatives from Newman to Disraeli, Nisbet pointed out, recoiled from this "nightmarish world of cold reason, permanent reform, bloodless charity, and total absence of emotion and feeling that Bentham foretold." More acutely offensive to Nisbet was Bentham's contempt for pluralist diversity, for the local and regional—"sordid fingers of the past," Bentham called them—that his "icy rationalism" led him to scorn. It was a contempt, Nisbet believed, that Bentham bequeathed to the whole reform tradition that followed him.[51]

Against this liberal standard of rationalism, Nisbet wanted to pose the conservative value of "prejudice." He borrowed this antirationalist weapon from Burke. Nisbet described prejudice as "a distillation of a whole way of knowing, of understanding, and of feeling." Conservatism recognizes that people require for their nurture and pleasure something more than reason or calculated objectivity. Prejudice is a product of tradition and history and has a reason and a wisdom of its own. For Nisbet it was a crucial complement to the discipline of the empirical mentality.[52]

Nisbet was describing two polar mentalities that had severe consequences for modern history. In Bentham's vision of the world Nisbet saw the secularizing direction of Western society and culture. What Weber described as secularization was precisely this substitution of utility, rationality, and efficiency for traditional norms that had acquired over time a certain sacred connotation: monarchy, social class, marriage, property, and more ethereal norms such as honor, fealty, and virtue.[53] Nisbet saw in the rationalist vision of progress, with its faith that a single mode of intelligence could govern society, the roots of modern totalitarianism.[54]

The prospect of a rational society has been to conservatives a frightening specter, depicted and decried from Burke to Nisbet and other contemporaries, such as Edward Shils. Shils, a University of Chicago sociologist, produced, like Nisbet, an abundant scholarship, much of which supported conservative insights. In his book *Tradition,* Shils analyzed in great depth the historical enmity between rationalism and what he called substantive tradition. The liberal ideal of rationalism, Shils noted, had shifted its focus from the individual to the state over a long history, until it became almost axiomatic among liberal thinkers that the state was the best agent for bringing all components of a society or nation into one unified, rational scheme. The rationalist impulse ultimately reached its extent, he believed, in the various Communist countries of the later twentieth century.[55]

How fared the notion of progress, so essential, Nisbet believed, to civilization's well-being, in contemporary culture? Nisbet described several influences that had conspired to weaken it. One was the prevailing sense of discontinuity in modern life, an American phenomenon especially. For all that had been said about this subject, about the United States as a nation recklessly futuristic in its vision, Nisbet believed that for a long time Americans had done well in keeping alive a sense of their traditions and history. "A respect for the past," he wrote, "no where more dedicated than in the United States, continued into the twentieth century. There were innumerable festivals, holidays, and rituals, the purpose of which was the fusing of a people into a community, and this through a kind of telescoping of past and present." Community must have its festive dimensions, and their function in enhancing patriotism, through celebrations of heroes, leaders, and great events, Nisbet judged entirely legitimate and necessary.[56] But Tocqueville, he added, had earlier warned that people in democratic societies do not readily comprehend the utility of forms. Ritual, Tocqueville wrote, has a special positive influence in democracies because it serves to ameliorate inequalities between the strong and the weak, the ruler and the ruled. Nisbet seemed to endorse this statement, but in disregard of the blatant use of ritual by totalitarian governments to create a monolithic and one-dimensional society that enhanced the power of the state. Nisbet was more concerned about the decay of the sense of the past in general. The demise of this awareness could only encourage the more dangerous and bogus notions of progress that had raised havoc in recent history.[57]

Nisbet was troubled. The West, he believed, had lost faith and confidence in its own civilization. Its citizens lived with a sense of its decline, and what had once been pride in its achievements had become guilt, alienation, and indifference. There had entered into Western life, Nisbet feared, a debilitating sense that its technology, its culture, and the extensions of its forms of government and administration throughout the world had been corrupting influences, injurious to other peoples. That affliction Nisbet traced to the intelligentsia that had begun in the eighteenth century to succeed the clergy as the dominant class shaping the attitudes of others toward the world. By the late twentieth century a mood of negativism and self-flagellation had become endemic, enhanced by a media that served as an effective conduit of an adversary culture. "Clearly," wrote Nisbet, "any idea of progress must be precariously based indeed in such an environment."[58]

The disaffection that troubled Nisbet was especially acute as it applied to ideas about economic progress. He found within increasingly numerous sectors of Western society, and in American society especially, a disenchantment with or open hostility toward economic growth. Against a romantic notion that pre-industrial society was somehow more happy and more humane, Nisbet asked technology's critics not to forget how, in most of human history, sheer drudgery characterized the norm of human experience. Nisbet wished to counter the antitechnology dogma by a different romanticism, one that joined technology and the human imagination. From the Parthenon of Athens to the cathedrals of the Middle Ages and the moon landing in our own time, technology, he said, grew from the human imagination and captivated it in turn. "Just as high technology in its awe-inspiring ways is the present-day cathedral," he wrote, "so the rocketed vehicles in outer space are the modern *Pinta, Santa María,* and *Niña.*" Henry Adams, in his morose and self-pitying disparagement of the dynamo, Nisbet added, was simply wrong.[59]

Nisbet had tried to formulate a philosophy of progress consistent with conservatism, but he had not quite squared the circle. He stated confidently that technology, that critical ingredient of progress, had no disintegrative impact upon traditional societies. "What has such impact," he said, "is the state and a system of power that has usurped the natural authorities of the institutions." One should not blame the automobile for its disruption of family life, he added.[60] But this generality surely passed over too much societal change in modern history. Nisbet's endorsement of technology, however useful a corrective it surely was to the vociferous Cassandras of our day and to many a nostalgic conservative thinker, admitted into his conservative edifice an intruder he otherwise reviled — the rationalist mentality. Technology can evoke drama and excite the imagination, to be sure, but technology, as Veblen hypothesized in 1904, also imposed on society and culture "the mental discipline of the machine process," which threatened to erode every aspect of human thinking not in conformity with the matter-of-fact and cause-and-effect pattern of the industrial process. Neither industrial society nor the emerging postindustrial culture, to be sure, had effected so drastic a change (Marshall McLuhan is the corrective to Veblen), but the habit of rationality has flourished in the modern corporate and bureaucratic social system. Economic progress is unimaginable without it, and Nisbet as much as anyone was familiar with its chilling presence.

Nisbet's conservatism could be at cross-purposes with itself in this and other ways, but he did as much as any conservative intellectual in America to describe enduring conservative values and social arrangements. Though he adhered to a carefully formulated idea of progress, Nisbet was anything but an optimist. His book *Twilight of Authority* showed that when it came to finding solutions to the problems in American society, Nisbet was agnostic.

Nisbet seemed to find conservatism fighting a rear-guard reaction against the liberal state. Conservatives could do much good by resisting the inroads of bureaucracy, "the fourth branch of government" as he called it, but erosion of traditional society had deprived them of the tools by which this fight might be successfully waged. Bureaucracy, he believed, had so stifled society's vitality and so immersed itself with intermediate societies as to render them no longer the historically critical agencies for resisting Leviathan. What we may flatter ourselves is a pluralist society in America, Nisbet believed, is really only a litigated society, in which all distinctions born of history and tradition, of special and valuable cultural differences, are neutered by the rationalist imperialism of the judicial complex and the bureaucratic state. The Benthamite passion to standardize and rationalize every aspect of human life, Nisbet warned, had brought democratic governments, crucial differences notwithstanding, to a likeness with the totalitarian states of this century. "When every relation in society becomes a potentially legal relationship," Nisbet wrote, "the very juices of the social bond dry up, the social impulse atrophies."[61] Nisbet saw little reason for Americans to be sanguine about the future health of their country.

Nisbet intended these animadversions for his fellow conservatives as well as his liberal critics. He wanted conservatives to have a sense of their shared values, and he insisted that conservatives, both the Old Right and the neoconservatives, shared a common ideology going back to Burke.[62] But Nisbet was also warning conservatives in the 1980s that conservatism was in trouble also for reasons of its own making.

First, with specific reference to the Reagan administration, Nisbet warned that conservatives "seemed far more interested in capturing Leviathan for their own purposes than in freeing human beings from it."[63] Conservatism was taking on the aspects of a moral crusade—the fight against abortion, the movement to permit prayer in the schools, the effort to prevent parents from deciding that a severely unhealthy baby should die.[64] All these efforts, if successful, said Nisbet, could only deliver to government new inquisitorial powers. These actions, he admonished, represented the ideology of a "far right, not a true conservatism, a grasp for control of power, not its diminution." For Nisbet the lesson was clear: "From Burke on it has been a conservative precept and a sociological principle since Auguste Comte that the surest way of weakening the family, or any social group, is for the government to assume, and then monopolize, the family's historic function."[65]

Second, Nisbet warned, conservatives would be false to their own tradition should they try to make of it a "progressive" social philosophy. Here, though they were unmentioned, conservatives like Peter Viereck and George Will were surely in Nisbet's mind. Each had proffered that the true concept of a paternalist government, protector as it should be of all its citizens, had its modern origins in such nineteenth-century statesmen as Disraeli and Bismarck. Conservatives like Viereck and Will found a model of the modern welfare state in the reforms of these leaders and used it to confirm a conservative principle of state promotion of the public good. Nisbet tried to meet these contentions by showing that the measures in question were essentially ad hoc and defensive and of peripheral significance in the larger careers and public philosophies of the two leaders. Charitable activity, Nisbet said, is essential to the well-being of society, but the state has the duty only to preserve those groups, beginning with the family, that are "duly constituted to render assistance." For the conservative today, as for every conservative from Newman, Disraeli, and Tocqueville in the nineteenth century to Michael Oakeshott, Eric Voegelin, and Bernard de Jouvenal in the twentieth, Nisbet wrote, only one rule maintains: "the bounded necessity of the political state holding as far back as possible from meddling in economic, social and moral affairs; and conversely, in *doing* all that is possible in strengthening and broadening the functions of family, neighborhood, and voluntary, cooperative association."[66]

Nisbet's search for a consistent conservative tradition took him, as it must every conservative, to the subject of religion. Here Nisbet confronted the essential cultural problem of conservatism, how to derive a prescription for social order, unity, tradition, a sense of belonging, and an arena for the human imagination in an age when religion and the church can no longer supply these needs to a sufficient number of individuals. Nisbet shared with the neoconservatives, and some of the Old Right too, precisely this perspective on religion, making it at once a matter of sociological consideration. He appealed to religious values and institutional authority without invoking theological foundations for them, however useful, of course, personal faith may be to the individual.

Two issues were important here. First, Nisbet, like earlier conservatives such as Irving Babbitt, turned to religion for that measure of the imagination that could offset the rival dominant culture. Thus for Babbitt, the struggle of humanism against romanticism centered in what he called the "ethical imagination" of Burke and the "idyllic imagination" of Rousseau. For Nisbet the contest was slightly different, and he appealed to Durkheim in formulating it: "The greatest of all distinctions the human mind is capable of," Durkheim wrote, "is that between the sacred and the profane or merely utilitarian. Even the distinction between good and evil is small by comparison. . . . To endow anything with sacred significance—human life, birth, marriage, death, the community or nation—is to remove it from the sphere of things which must be justified by expediency or pragmatic consideration."[67] Nisbet believed that the disappearance of the sacred underlay every decay that plagued Western society. "For behind the death of the past, the displacement of Western pride of civilization, the waning faith in economic growth and in the works of reason," wrote Nisbet, "lies the moribundity of religious conviction, of belief and faith in something greater than the life immediately around us."[68]

Second, on the other hand, when Nisbet spoke of religion he emphasized almost exclusively its communal role. Nisbet's religious edifice was really institutional, not inward and personal. In fact, he greatly feared religion's strenuous subjective expression. In his book *Conservatism* Nisbet stressed that the early conservatives—Burke, Disraeli, Coleridge, Robert Southey, even Newman—had one overriding concern about religion. "Religion for them was predominantly public and institutional," Nisbet wrote, "something to which loyalty and a decent regard for form were owing, a valuable pillar to both state and society." Against this view stood a wholly different Christian tradition, the "enthusiast" tradition of the Dissenters, for whom private experience, the personal relation of God to the individual, the unmediated religious moment, was quintessentially important. Ages of religious enthusiasm (though Nisbet did concede that they produce examples of heroic defiance of state authority) are too often ages of political enthusiasm as well, and they combine to generate new and grand schemes for the moral perfection of the world. It was not impossible, he admitted, that out of the heightened religious fervor of our subjectivist culture there might emerge a disillusionment with politics that would be healthy.[69] But otherwise, Nisbet felt it important to say that Christianity had its celebrated beginnings not as a church but as a "congeries of tiny communities, each autonomous, scattered throughout Roman civilization." The early churches, often as burial societies, created community for the alienated, the rootless, and the disinherited of Roman society.[70] Therein was religion's perennial value.

Nisbet's conservatism revolved always around the communal arrangement of intermediate societies that constituted for him the essential safeguard against the usurpations of the state. This chapter has suggested that Nisbet's social philosophy gave him a distinct place among the conservative intellectuals while allowing him to share many themes in common with them. He had endeavored to define a conservative tradition that began with Burke and survived among other thinkers in the late twentieth century. Many times he described how that tradition differed from alternative liberal and revolutionary views of government, authority, and citizenship. But Nisbet's own outline found at least a few points of contact with a forceful liberal critique in the 1970s and 1980s, one that may offer an instructive concluding note.

Modern American liberalism, let us say that beginning with Progressivism and finding fuller expression in the New Deal, judged harshly the consequences of classical liberalism as an economic imperative and turned to the state as a regulatory agent with intercessory powers against the operation of the free market. But another mode of liberalism, liberalism as individual moral discretion, artistic creativity, nonconformist separation from the herd morality or liberation from family, tribal, and communal constraints, retained its high priority in liberal values. Individualism had received extensive treatment in Tocqueville's study of the Americans. A century and a half after Tocqueville expressed his thoughts on the matter, a team of sociologists headed by Robert Bellah examined the subject anew in a 1985 book titled *Habits of the Heart: Individualism and Commitment in American Life.* Their study derived from extensive interviews with white middle-class men and women. The conclusions of these academic liberals were every bit what Nisbet himself might have confirmed.

The book was first and foremost a critique of individualism. The authors stated their conclusion in the preface: "We are concerned that [American] individualism may have grown cancerous—that it may be destroying those social institutions that Tocqueville saw as moderating its more destructive potentialities, that it may be threatening the destruction of freedom itself."[71] The American social ethos, they argued, continued to honor the idea of the autonomous self. It spoke "in the language of radical individualism." For the authors these facts meant that the American value system was directly at odds with an adequate social science and a true philosophy of human nature. Their understanding of the human personality echoed Nisbet's, and through him Durkheim's. Against the normality of individualism they urged this maxim: We find ourselves independent not of other people and institutions but through them. We never get to the bottom of ourselves on our own. We discover who we are face to face and side by side with others in work, love, and learning. All our activity occurs in relationships, groups, associations, and communities ordered by institutional structures and interpreted by cultural patterns of meaning.[72] These truths, the authors feared, had somehow failed to take root in the individualist soil of America, where a different code altogether persisted. Bellah and his associates discovered everywhere the unhappy consequences of the individualist ethic—in careers in which even triumphs proved unfulfilling, in attenuated family life, in incomplete and unsatisfying love relationships.

The American individualist ethos, said these investigators, flourished most significantly in work and business and in what they called "life-style enclaves." Life-style enclaves, in fact, described what had become of community in American life, how insubstantial and amorphous the whole idea had been rendered under the assault of an individualist culture. "Where community attempts to be an exclusive whole," said the authors, "lifestyle is fundamentally segmental and celebrates the narcissism of similarity."[73] Even many old and traditional communities (Suffolk, Massachusetts, was studied) were now on their way to becoming simply life-style communities, places where people chose to live merely to support a social style appropriate to their tastes. Indeed, said the sociologists, the tendencies of American life pulled everyone irresistibly into these looser and more informal communities, and human relationships became increasingly tangential in the process. The authors could not disguise a mood of poignancy as they documented this phenomenon—the superficiality of American life as rendered by the assault of a corrosive individualism. Traditional communities, the authors acknowledged, had often shown themselves to be constricting and suffocating. But they hastened to add, in language familiar to conservatives, that "in our desperate effort to free ourselves from the constrictions of the past, we have jettisoned too much, forgotten a history that we cannot abandon."[74]

Habits of the Heart offered no radical solutions for America. Indeed its recommendations were diverse and cautionary. The book was, in places, quite sympathetic, as we noted, to "communities of memory," and the authors hoped for their recovery. They departed from other liberals who might have looked to government for ultimate social solutions. Nisbet would have concurred in their warning that "in the liberal world, the state . . . has become so overgrown and militarized that it threatens to become a universal policeman."[75] These liberals in fact were more inclined to invoke moral solutions to the problems they had discovered. They wanted the United States to call upon the rich legacy of its biblical and republican culture to fortify the moral guidelines in American life. Nisbet as conservative and Bellah and his group as liberals were citing commonly perceived defects in that life and even recommending similar correctives to them.

Nonetheless, one point of difference is worth noting. *Habits of the Heart* concluded that the United States needed a new public philosophy, that the prescriptions of both neocapitalism and the welfare state were now flawed and outmoded. They urged serious consideration of alternatives such as the "administered society" as outlined by Felix Rohatyn and "economic democracy" as advanced by Michael Harrington. What had prompted these considerations was the authors' fears of a growing inequality in American society. The disparity of wealth and poverty, they believed, threatened the one assumption about society that underscored the religious and republican values of the United States—"that free institutions could survive in a society only if there were a rough equality of condition." Solution of this problem would demand at least an enlargement of the welfare state, toward which Americans, the authors feared, were profoundly ambivalent.[76]

For Nisbet, the modern liberal state was one of the many signs of the social course of Western life by which the arrangements of traditional societies had broken down, leaving centralized government the dominant power broker for the individual citizen. Moreover, Nisbet recoiled from almost any expression of egalitarianism, and that fact especially distinguished his conservative prejudices from the liberal prejudices in *Habits of the Heart*. A spirit of resolute egalitarianism, an intolerance of distinction of rank and condition, he believed, marked the dangerous course of liberalism in the 1960s and afterward. Moreover, egalitarianism had been an arrow in the quiver of the liberal tradition such that it always threatened community, which by its nature, Nisbet said, is hierarchical. Nisbet discussed the subject of the new egalitarians in *Twilight of Authority* and related their program to a disdain for the traditional family. From the prejudices of the counterculture to the somber reasoning of theoreticians such as John Rawls, Nisbet judged the egalitarian ethos to be a divisive and ultimately tyrannous influence. "There is no principle more basic in the conservative philosophy," he wrote, "than that of the inherent and absolute incompatibility between liberty and equality."[77] Again, Tocquevillian distinctions reigned in Nisbet's conservative priorities.

These distinctions again brought Nisbet back to the standard of community, the intermediate society, as the measure of social value, individual identity, and democratic freedom. Nisbet's success was the consistency, the erudition, and the resourcefulness with which he applied that standard. He made of it a conservative philosophy that drew upon a rich body of European intellectual history. Nisbet's conservatism contained the widest scope of that of any of his conservative contemporaries.

So what can one say, finally, of community, that linchpin in Nisbet's system? Must one concur with Nisbet's judgment that community died in the revolutionary dreams of radical theorists? A whole battery of social forces had been working for a century and more to render individuals' lives more distended and variegated. What we once meant by community was in large part a factor of habit, of inheritance, of one's given allotment in life. Community has been attenuated to a considerable extent today, and Nisbet, in a way that liberals and conservatives alike can appreciate, warned of the malaise of an unfulfilling individualism and the resultant disillusionment. But by the same token, is not community today more natural, more the expression of meaningful commitments and intrinsic needs that fortify one against the dreaded anomie that Durkheim acutely perceived in the society of the emerging modern era? And to that extent is it not more authentic than ancient tribalisms? Americans are still a nation of joiners, but one fears also that they are still a lonely crowd. Whether our thinner community life can serve, as Tocqueville believed our intermediate societies did, as barriers to Leviathan, is a compelling question. Nisbet at least raised appropriate fears. His warnings about the unhappy alternatives may prove to be his most enduring contribution.

In the end, the question of community raises for everyone the question of loyalty. None knew that better than Josiah Royce, whose quest for the "beloved community" anticipated that all along the way loyalties lie in conflict with each other. This dilemma would seem to be even more difficult when the proliferation of thinner communities divides and pulls us. Ultimately, Royce told us, we should be loyal to loyalty. There is much to ponder in that maxim, but little practical advice. It does, however, invite a final reflection on Nisbet. As a father of two, I take my children every school morning to meet the bus that drives them far from the immediate neighborhood to a school in the city's desegregated public school system. Around the corner another bus arrives to take the Jewish children to their religious school. Another takes some Catholic children to a parochial school. Soon another bus passes, carrying other boys and girls in the area to a private school fifteen miles to the north. All these children sometimes make brief summer friendships with each other. But the school year and the long winter intervene, and these relations wane. Each of the various families involved pursues an institutional, religious, or community loyalty of its own. Each supports some kind of intermediate society. But what is left of neighborhood? Where is community?

8

R. Emmett Tyrrell, Jr.
H. L. Mencken
à la Mode

HE WAS DUBBED the Bad Boy of Bloomington—by one of his friends.[1] His enemies were not so charitable. By any measure, though, R. Emmett Tyrrell, Jr., was conspicuous as the most caustic and acidic journalist of the American intellectual Right. The "bad boy" earned his laurels for his mischievous sport, his zeal for making the starchiest liberal appear at one with the personnel of a traveling circus. Hyperbole was his mode, caricature his art. And he arrived on the scene with the most awesome vocabulary since William F. Buckley, Jr. Readers of Tyrrell had to adopt to the weighty prose, as in Tyrrell's references to the "oleaginous" activists of the 1960s, the "add-lepated enthusiasts of reform politics," the "quiddities of enlightened policy," the "arpeggios of left-liberal platitudes," the "sclerotic liberalism" of Hubert Humphrey, and the "Laodicean banalities" of Jimmy Carter. Tyrrell's critics were always crying foul. He did not confront issues, they said. His sarcasm shunned rational discourse. But Tyrrell counted as gain every rustled feather on a liberal's wing. In the "establishment" centers of liberal America—the universities, the federal bureaucracy, the courts—there were many, he believed, who deserved only ridicule. With these partisans serious dialogue was a waste of time, Tyrrell thought. All these facts raised the main question on the subject of Tyrrell: Was he to be taken seriously? In certain key respects, yes he was. Tyrrell does indeed represent two important themes for this study— the libertarian tradition in American conservatism and its fate amid the countercultural movement of the 1960s, and conservatism as cultural exorcism. Both topics raise questions about style and substance in American conservatism.

Tyrrell was a native of Chicago, born in 1943. His ancestors were Irish, and he named among his forebears two Irish "thugs" involved in conspiracies to murder English kings. A great-grandfather was a Secret Service agent who broke the plot to steal Lincoln's body from its crypt, and another predecessor was a policeman who survived the famous Haymarket violence of 1886 in Chicago. Tyrrell's paternal grandfather, John Tyrrell, was a lawyer with Clarence Darrow and a Republican in Democratic Chicago. On his mother's side, his grandfather made considerable money from the Crown Gas Range Company and then invested successfully in real estate. Tyrrell's father simply managed the money, and the son described him as one of the most successful men he had ever known—he never wanted to work and never did.[2]

Tyrrell pursued an undergraduate education at Indiana University in Bloomington and stayed to take a master's degree in history. There in the late 1960s, he remembered, the radical winds blew furiously. Tyrrell put his nose to the breezes and caught a bad odor. These conditions furnished the background of a success story in American conservative journalism. With the efforts of colleagues John "Barron" Von Kannon and Ronald Burr, Tyrrell initiated campus counterculture by launching *The Alternative: An American Spectator.* Tyrrell recalled: "I was furiously pasting galleys down in the summer cottage of a friend while he held off his enraged parents and their eviction notice." As Tyrrell pursued his graduate studies, the staff of the journal moved to a farmhouse outside Bloomington and set up shop there. The new publication was getting noticed. Prominent individuals in the conservative movement, William F. Buckley, Jr., most noticeably, took an interest in it, and the *Spectator* became a progenitor of a boom in campus conservative publishing that had become full-fledged by the mid-1980s. One had to wonder how the bon vivant Tyrrell managed through the squalid conditions of the *Spectator's* early years. As Von Kannon recalled: "The bathroom at the Establishment [the group's name for its headquarters] was just a disaster. There were toadstools growing out from around the toilet. And Pat Moynihan and Bill Buckley both had the same reaction when they walked in there: they walked right back out and took a leak off the front porch."[3]

Success brought better if not elegant working conditions. For years the magazine was published in a walk-up office above one of Bloomington's familiar monuments, the Betty Jean candy shop on the courthouse square. Then the *Spectator* opened a New York office, presumably one proximate to handball courts for the editor in chief. When the magazine celebrated its tenth anniversary in 1977, the staff feted itself at the St. Regis Hotel in New York, and every neoconservative under the sun was there. Tyrrell used the occasion

R. Emmett Tyrrell, Jr., by Shelly Fischman

to disavow any great achievement in the *Spectator's* rise from Bloomington to the Big Apple. The job was easy, he said, and he expressed thanks to the Chicago Seven, Students for a Democratic Society, the editors of the *New York Times Book Review,* the Association of American University Professors, and the majority of the United States Senate for making it so. "All the louts were in their places," he said. He and his writers needed only to pin the tails on these "assorted jackasses."[4]

Nineteen eighty-seven was the occasion for another celebration, and that year saw the publication of the *Spectator's* twentieth anniversary issue. The journal still paid homage to its midwestern roots and hailed midwestern values of "common sense, individualism, and cussedness." Reminiscences of Bloomington from former staff of the *Spectator* also usefully reminded readers what this enterprise was about. Writers recalled the two cultural worlds of Bloomington in the 1960s. Some remembered the radical culture and its New Age manifestations: shampoos with honey or wheat germ, rinses with cucumber or egg milk. Others recalled the vogue of radical politics. Indeed a member of Students for a Democratic Society had been elected student president. These unsavory trends sent the *Spectator* group in search of alternatives in Bloomington. Fifteen and twenty years later they remembered hours spent at the Walnut Lounge, where Pabst Blue Ribbon and Busch Bavarian beer flowed freely. They remembered Tom's Fried Pork Rinds and the A&W Root Beer drive-in. Here were earthy sanctuaries from the heady age of Aquarius that seemed to have become ascendant on the campus.[5]

By the time of its twentieth anniversary, the *Spectator* could count several successes. Many of its writers had moved on to careers with major journals, and others had joined the Reagan administration in various capacities.[6] In 1986 the *Spectator* ratified these connections by moving to Arlington, Virginia.

Tyrrell was a self-conscious descendant of H. L. Mencken ("Uncle Henry," as he called him). Nearly every review and discussion of the *Spectator* made the connection. In his day, the Baltimore sage surveyed the American scene and found it populated by Methodists, prohibitionists, Rotarians, and moral enthusiasts of all kinds. He prescribed the horselaugh as an antidote for the attending nausea. America to Mencken was a place recommended mostly because one could so easily laugh oneself to sleep simply by reading the evening paper.[7] But these old nuisances, Tyrrell believed, had long since departed, leaving only a tattered remnant. The "Christian wowser" and the "prehensible husbandman" no longer flourished. William Jennings Bryan was gone. Decent, fun-loving Americans, it seemed, were now safe.[8]

Or so one would have thought. But then came the decade of the 1960s, reminiscent for Tyrrell of nothing so much as the 1920s. "Bogus salvation" plans of all kinds surfaced. "In the late 60s," he wrote, "charlantry was being practiced on the most awesome and enormous scale ever envisioned." We had Jerry Rubin and William Sloane Coffin, "at one with every snake-oil salesman who ever dustied his feet in the ghostly regions of east Tennessee." And "there stood McGovern, the Bryan of his time." They even looked alike: "An issuer of volupt and glorious moonshine, [McGovern] even had the same enormous dome, of a kind by all rights hairless and by all means brainless." We had Paul Goodman, "the Stuart P. Sherman of his time." Madalyn Murray O'Hair was merely "the flip-side" of Aimee Semple McPherson. It was a vast procession—from opponents of the flush-toilet to lesbians and health food addicts. "Surely," wrote Tyrrell, "idiots like this have never been seen on this earth before."[9]

What was happening? Tyrrell looked around and described a dizzying scene. As he reported it, America in the 1960s had become a nation loosed from its moorings. Dreamers and schemers abounded, the air filled with the cries for new world orders, and ideologues of all kinds trumpeted their causes. At the same time, the national mood was self-abasement, which seemed to Tyrrell a form of hypochondria. The American century, it seemed, had gone sour. Racism, sexism, and imperialism now constituted the tricolors of the American flag. And there was weeping and gnashing of teeth everywhere—for the down-and-out, the deprived, the underprivileged, the culturally disadvantaged—all visible signs of the national shame. America, one heard, needed catharsis: it must show the world a new face. The new politicos spewed forth the rhetoric of peace and human rights. The fight against evil quickened. Vigilantes formed everywhere to sniff out the evildoers, those of visible wickedness who chaired the big boards of corporate America and those hapless souls from middle America still entrapped in conventional pieties and outmoded beliefs. The theme now, said Tyrrell, was purify, purify. Feminists saw their opportunity, and they took it. So did the environmentalists. America needed no longer to make the world safe for democracy; it must make it safe for the snail-darter. What was happening? Tyrrell knew. This was the dawning of the New Age.

Amid the whirlwind the *American Spectator* was born. Tyrrell envisioned himself as a cultural exorcist of the New Age, and he invoked the spirit of H. L. Mencken to provide the magic. The journal celebrated its hedonistic roots: it claimed to have been "founded in 1924 by George Nathan and Truman Newberry over a cheap domestic ale in McSorley's Old Ale House." But the genealogical connection was of course only nominal. What began in 1967 as the *Alternative* became in 1976 the *American Spectator*. From the earlier title, apparently, some people got the wrong notion. Tyrrell reported that unsolicited manuscripts began to arrive from "florists, beauticians, and other creative types." The editors concluded that they might not be reaching the right audience.[10]

One needs but a brief tour through the pages of the *Spectator* to glimpse how much it reflected Tyrrell's guiding spirit. Its opening piece is immediately reminiscent of Mencken's *American Mercury.* For one means by which the Great Iconoclast took the measure of American life was to expose all its folly in the "Americana" section of his publication. Mencken received from his enthusiasts around the country newspaper clippings that documented Americans' freakish ways. An evangelist, for example, gives a lecture showing on what planet hell is located. The Ku Klux Klan in Birmingham tries to close the Chinese restaurants in that city. A lecturer theorizes that the first Rotarian was Jesus of Nazareth.[11]

Tyrrell monthly put together a similar section for the *Spectator,* one called "The Continuing Crisis," full of the witless and perverse inanities that mark life in this great republic. Thus in San Francisco, Sister Boom Boom, a transvestite politico who calls himself Nun of the Above, places ninth in a field of twenty-four in the city supervisor elections. The experience has made a philosopher of him: "Going in drag," he reports, "has taught me a lot about the oppression of women."[12] In San Francisco again (whence came a preponderance of newsworthy items) a female bank robber escapes with $578 after presenting a bank teller with a note: "You have thirty seconds before your life isn't worth the paper its [sic] printed on." Commented Tyrrell: "Police investigators are operating on the hypothesis that the culprit is a recent graduate of a University of California creative writing project."[13] And from Orange County, California, comes news that a transsexual seeks to adopt a young woman of twenty-five years of age. Hormone treatment, the report says, has coaxed a slight breastline on the former male, but the decisive surgery remains to complete the transformation. Nonetheless, Tyrrell says, that's not all bad, for though she is no Venus, "she is one of the few United States citizens whose anatomy actually conforms to the gender guidelines of our federal government."[14]

People mark themselves by what they say, and the *Spectator* listened. Its back-section "Current Wisdom" presented an anthology of quotable absurdities culled from the pronouncements of the day's New Age voices. Journals most often contributing the selected samples were *Ms., Mother Jones,* the *Progressive,* and the *New York Review of Books.* "Current Wisdom" purported to demonstrate that America still had as many fools per square mile as it did in Mencken's day. Thus the *Spectator* reported of a vociferous feminist who calls herself a "separatist." "I wouldn't touch a sexual relationship with a man with a ten-foot pole," she says. The *Spectator* wonders whether such a man exists.[15] Feminist historian Gerda Lerner opines that the oppression of women was the model for the invention of Negro slavery.[16] After the 1989 Alaskan oil spill, Rose Odom, Ph.D., locates the root cause of the calamity in the "(mostly white) male patriarchy."[17] In *Ms.* a modern liberated male writes to lament his shame for the many shapely female legs at which he used to whistle.[18] Cornell University feminist Susan Griffin charges that the lack of tenured women professors at that institution is a cause of rape.[19] *New Age* advertises "energy orgone blankets," ninety-nine dollars each, instructions included.[20] Jane Fonda, in responding to the brutal course of Communist Vietnam since American withdrawal, shrugs: "I don't know enough about what's going on there to criticize."[21] For *Harper's*, Dr. Arthur S. Levine warns of an emerging nation of "haves" and "have nots" in the United States: too many people, he says, are deprived of the right to sex.[22] A twenty-four-year-old man says how much he loves TV personality Mr. Rogers and urges that we all learn from his humaneness.[23] Leonard Bernstein allays all fears of a Russian invasion: "What would they do with us?" he asks.[24] Albert Taylor, writing for the *Humanist*, wants to "liberate" vegetables. How, he asks, can we be so cruel as to skin carrots, pull lettuce, and gut apples? These abuses, he decries, constitute "flora chauvinism."[25] And William L. Shirer volunteers that the United States' invasion of Grenada reminded him of the way the Nazis marched into Austria. The *Spectator* reflects: "Intellectual fashions have changed as has the testosterone level in this old mountebank."[26]

For several years the *Spectator* presented the Harold Robbins award for the worst book of the year. This was Tyrrell's doing. Later the name of the award was changed to honor the less familiar J. Gordon Coogler. Winners of the prize included Lillian Hellman for *Scoundrel Time*, Robert Coover for *The Public Burning*, John Irving for *The Hotel New Hampshire*, Betty Friedan for *The Second Stage*, and Nora Ephron for *Heartburn*. Tyrrell pronounced the accolades, and, as was the case for Theodore White's 1975 *Breach of Faith*, a book about Watergate, mild fanfare often accompanied the presentation. Tyrrell called this book "a book that will not shut up." He labeled White "one of the most garrulous writers ever uncorked on these shores. Next to him Hubert Humphrey could be a model librarian." Tyrrell bristled at White's sanctimonious preaching and at the book's verbiage. "When you purchase it you purchase something more than a bestseller," he wrote, "you purchase a mother-in-law." He concluded: "There will come a time when, the First Amendment notwithstanding, White's books will be banned in every hospital zone in the country."[27]

The *Spectator* made other recognitions, and with particular pleasure occasional issues offered "The Great American Saloon Series." And with good reason, wrote Tyrrell: "I have remained inveterate in my view that a carefully selected saloon generally provides an educational experience superior to that of any university. No one ever set out from Tobey's Saloon to shout America into the New Age."[28] Here too the spirit of the *Spectator* was one with that of Mencken. For there were actually aspects of American life that Mencken happily embraced, as his voluminous published letters and autobiographies indicate. He always remembered with fondness the tavern life in the German section of Baltimore where he grew up, thankfully free in those halcyon years from meddling prohibitionists. A good beer and a good smoke—for both Mencken and Tyrrell there could hardly be better ingredients for the good life. (Tyrrell's face often showed up on *Spectator* back pages, stuffed with a stogie and smug, like Mencken's, in its veneer.)

The *Spectator* bore a heavily masculine, heterosexual cast, reflected in its antifeminist and antihomosexual aspersions and fully evident in the saloon series. *Spectator* contributors liked to celebrate what remained of the tavern tradition in America, where free men lived and breathed, and drank. So, praise God, Hoffman's of San Francisco still thrived—a real haven in this "silk-skirted city of panders and meat markets." And also Arnold's of Cincinnati—no neon signs here. At Cunningham's of Louisville, patrons might not know which is the faster of the two breeds—Kentucky's thoroughbreds or Kentucky's women—but they know which is more faithful. For things in the great German tradition, The Turners in Milwaukee is recommended.[29] But such places, the *Spectator* found, were rare sanctuaries in modern times. As one contributor noted: "The proliferation of singles bars and artsy cloying coffeehouses has made finding a good place to drink beer as difficult as getting a summer job."[30] *Spectator* saloon critics longed for the old and venerable country taverns and their hardwood elegance, but they saw these succumbing everywhere to Muzak and disco. Or they yielded to something worse—female bartenders. "It is stretching the limits of toleration," wrote one authority, "to have sweet young things working the taps for brakemen and boilermakers." Besides, he added, only one in ten knows how to make a good Bloody Mary.[31] Bloody Marys, martinis, and Beck's Imported made for good company, but take note: the *Spectator* shunned the Perrier water crowd.

The *Spectator* thus clearly had strong likes and dislikes. Measured restraint was not its style. It delighted to get under its enemies' skins, and it reported with glee the outraged sentiments of those whom it offended. "I am appalled," critics would say, and that refrain was quoted from several different sources on *Spectator* subscription pages. "A piece of trash," said another offended soul. "An exercise in bad taste," reported another. "Viciously biased," "infantile and vulgar," howled still more. One *Spectator* issue had a back-cover photograph of sign-bearing feminists. In large print next to the picture were the words of Susanna Smith: "I sincerely hope that one of the successes of the women's movement will be to rid society of pestilences such as R. Emmett Tyrrell, Jr."[32]

Thus did the *Spectator* promote itself. But it used other devices too. You could order from the magazine a *Spectator* jacket with the emblematic turkey on it. There were *Spectator* beer mugs available for purchase. Readers were also invited to peruse the "Classified Ads." For twenty dollars you could acquire an Adam Smith necktie. There were T-shirts and sweatshirts bearing the likenesses of Edmund Burke, H. L. Mencken, and Milton Friedman. For those as irreverent as the *Spectator*'s editors, there were bumper stickers that read "Nuke the Whales" and "Have You Slugged Your Kids Today?" The alert, or the needy, might also check the personals. In one, a forty-six-year-old woman sought cultural companionship, but of a select order only: "Smokers, swingers, druggies, religious zealots, and left-wing activists need not apply."[33]

For all its foolery the *Spectator* was predominantly a serious journal. Most of any month's contributions were sober thoughts on weighty, mundane issues. Nonetheless, the jocular, outlandish, and hyperbolic style of Tyrrell explains much of the journal's renown and the forty-thousand-member subscription list it boasted in the middle 1980s. For these characteristics had given the *Spectator* its éclat. Tyrrell took immense journalistic license with his subjects. Caricature invited ridicule by giving a facade of reality to situations that might otherwise be only mildly unusual.

The arrival to Washington of the Carter administration in 1977, for example, provided Tyrrell with endless opportunities for this kind of literary exercise. The Wonderboy and The Grinning Dunce, became his repeated epithets for the president. Tyrrell looked on as there arrived into the midst of the Washington sophisticates the fresh refugees from what Mencken once called the Sahara of the Bozart. Wrote Tyrrell:

August 1978 will be remembered by historians as the catastasis of the Wonderboy's Populist Era. It was then that the White House yokels and their antagonists began asking fundamental questions about political conditions. The yokels began their reassessment right after poor Ham [Presidential assistant Hamilton Jordan] was assaulted while at a Georgetown soirée by an unidentified guest wielding a chocolate mousse, that expensive French dessert that had just become all the rage with the Georgia mafia. After being introduced to the delicacy sometime earlier in the year, the boys grew to love it, and no longer were they so distressed when Georgetown hostesses refused to serve them Moon Pies and Dr. Pepper. Yet when Ham got walloped, and the boys saw what the Gallic potion could do to a double-knit leisure suit, a chill went through the White House. The boys began to wonder if life in Washington was really worth it. Henceforth Georgetown was looked upon with fear, and it was a rare Carter aide who would go near a chocolate mousse. (As one unidentified aide remarked, "Ah'd sooner kiss a pig thun tech one of them thengs.") Morale within the White House was at its nadir, and many of the boys began to yearn for the reassuring sounds of home sweet home: of gentle cows lowing in the front yard, of horseflies struggling to free themselves from flypaper strips, of granddaddy hitting the spittoon from a dozen paces.[34]

The largest target of the *Spectator's* slings was liberalism – liberal politics and liberal culture – particularly the liberalism whose advent occurred in the 1960s. Tyrrell was never a liberal, but the "old liberalism," he conceded, was seldom obnoxious and even encouraged a measure of decency. The old liberalism gave little cause for rancor, but the new liberalism, Tyrrell said, invited contempt. The old liberalism, moreover, was often heroic. It saw the Soviet Union for what it was, a totalitarian tyranny, and postwar liberals of the Americans for Democratic Action usefully sounded the alarm. The old liberalism showed courage, too, as it battled for civil rights and racial equality in inhospitable places. But liberalism had lost its fighting spirit, Tyrrell believed, and it had lost its grip on reality. It became soft, sentimental, and self-indulgent. It degenerated, Tyrrell said, into "a riot of enthusiasms." He wrote: "In fevered depravity the last Liberals ran riot through the 1970s gibbering: consciousness-raising! self-realization! group therapy! sexuality! human rights! animal rights! water beds! wheat grass enemas! sanitary napkins shaped from genuine sea sponges! and on and on, and so forth and so on, and let's get the hell out of here. This is light-years removed from the New Deal."[35]

Liberalism, in Tyrrell's judgment, had become dominated by "perpetual malcontents." Increasingly from the time of Franklin Roosevelt it had assumed a "snootier" attitude toward the middle-class American way of life.[36] It showed, he asserted, a smug contempt for the producing classes of the nation and a resolve to afflict the enterprising and creative forces in American economic life with an array of stifling restraints. Liberalism had also become the new highway to hell, a road paved with good intentions. Massive federal funds employed in a well-meaning assault on poverty had only aggravated it, Tyrrell claimed.[37] He was incredulous to find Hubert Humphrey waxing eloquent in his memoir *Education of a Public Man* about the Model Cities program that he helped to create. Tyrrell replied: "That the program became an enormous botch, costing some three billion dollars, causing grave confusion at all levels of government . . . . Hubert never mentions. The whole thing is palmed off as unassailable, and herein lies another example of the corruption of decency."[38]

The new liberalism abounded with many crusades and crusaders, but withal one cause in particular agitated Tyrrell. It was "women's liberation." "The Continuing Crisis" seldom failed to spot some incident within this movement that documented its follies, and "Current Wisdom" eagerly seized every pronouncement that illuminated feminist extremism. The subject of course was fodder for Tyrrell's 1979 book, the collection of essays he entitled *Public Nuisances*. This volume, which one horrified reviewer labeled "a silly repellent book," made certain that the feminists, the "women of the fevered brow," caught the spotlight.[39] Tyrrell described the origins of women's liberation:

The movement was born amid the sounds of the morning wash being automatically battered and dried in the laundry rooms of suburbia. The last crumbs of breakfast had been lugged away, the coffee was poured, and a scowling Miss Betty Friedan sat with the most awesome circle of women ever gathered under the roof of a modern ranch-type house. Together they deliberated, as rage feathered the linings of their bowels. The whole day yawned before them. Soon it would be back and forth, back and forth to the powder room. Coffee and housework can have that effect. These brave women were trapped with a vast expanse of desolate hours stretching out to that remote time when the kids returned from school and the idiot traipsed in with his evening paper. It was insanity, and still the infernal washing machine kept vibrating in the background. Soon the maid would be emptying it and feeding it, emptying it and feeding it. There would be telephones and shopping and God knows what all. . . . . It was time to hoist the black flag. Penis envy, ha![40]

For Tyrrell the women's movement embodied the menacing liberal puritanism of the day's dominant culture. Women, he believed, had always been the governing spirits behind the secular puritanism that Mencken had found among the prohibitionists, public censors, and PTAs of his time. For the feminist charge that American culture has been dominated by males, was, Tyrrell insisted, mendacious. Every free spirit in America, he claimed, had at one time cause to lament female control of the public morality—from the scribbling women writers of the nineteenth century to the purists who kept blue laws on the statute books and bold literature out of the public libraries, and on to the rabble-rousers who brought the misery that was prohibition.[41] But contemporary feminists, Tyrrell believed, surpassed their earlier counterparts in one regard, for they had learned to appreciate Freud. The sex act was now dubbed political expression. Male aggressor plunders female virgin land, colonizes it, and denies it self-determination. It was the tyranny of "phallic imperialism." *"Mein Gott!"* exclaimed Tyrrell. "It makes you want to burn every bed in America."[42]

Tyrrell preferred the hyperbole of wit, or ridicule, to rational discourse. His manner of using these devices recalls the remarks of Henri Bergson on the subject. "Laughter," said the French philosopher, "cannot be absolutely just. Nor should it be kind-hearted either. Its function is to intimidate by humiliating. Now, it would not succeed in doing this, had not nature implanted for that purpose, even in the best of men, a spark of spitefulness or, at all events, of mischief. Perhaps we had better not investigate this point too closely, for we should not find anything flattering to ourselves."[43]

On the issue of feminism, as in fact on all issues, Tyrrell preferred to deal with personalities rather than facts. Records that indicate discrimination against women in employment or in salaries did not concern him. Rather, he found most causes condemned by the people who led them—by their words, their behavior, or even their looks. In *Public Nuisances,* Tyrrell stared feminist Bella Abzug in the face, and recoiled. The New York City politician had gained notoriety in the late 1960s as an outspoken feminist. "She was a born shouter," wrote Tyrrell. "Her ample jowls were made for scowling." He looked closer, at the "constantly shifting eyes lurking beneath a forehead of concrete, the iron jaw, the thick arms bashing at the air. . . . And her style of dress? *Ugly!* Some laughed, but they missed the mark. She was a woman who really knew how to dress. Her dress harmonized exquisitely with the ugliness of her message."[44]

For Tyrrell women's liberation was pure New Age stuff. The movement exhibited the quintessential characteristic of the New Age—excess. However much the partisans of the age were given to self-indulgence and personal whim, their aspirations were first and foremost totalitarian. Feminism, thus, could not be merely a matter of sexual equality before the law. It had to take on the whole course of Western civilization. From new journals and from universities and the strange amalgam "women's studies," said Tyrrell, there took shape a whole new "genital metaphysics" that would give the modern world yet another orthodoxy. Demands issued to rewrite conventional English, and around the country even the poor old Bible became red-lined with deletions and marginalia that put an end forever to God the Father. Children were to be indoctrinated into unisex. A passion for statistical equality, a cardinal tenet of New Age dogma, according to Tyrrell, meant that none dare rest content until every firehouse station had altered its hiring standards and its plumbing arrangements.[45]

The *Spectator* clearly liked the traditional masculine accent, but for males, not, obviously, for women. It was apparent that a kind of coarse bravado affected its opinions on other matters as well. Liberalism, it found, had fashioned a foreign policy for America that was timid, naive, and idealistic—in a word, unmanly. Tyrrell argued that in confronting world problems the United States had come to place too much faith in talk and too little in action. Americans habitually looked out at the world, Tyrrell said, and saw only people like themselves—benevolent and peace-loving. In fact, Tyrrell warned, there is a bunch of thugs out there. Tyrrell's foreign policy advocacies were vintage Cold Warrior. Soviet leader Leonid "Papa" Brezhnev, he found, was not much distinguishable from Stalin, a bully among the nations of the world and a tyrant at home. His successors will invariably reflect the same mold from which all Soviet leaders have been cut, Tyrrell warned, and speeches and flowers will effect little in America's dealing with them—or with any other of the world's bad guys. In 1978, when Israeli pilots bombed an Iraqi nuclear manufacturing plant, Tyrrell applauded. Even Iran, he reminded, had tried to do the same thing. Why not admit that the Israelis did the world a favor? Pacifists protested, of course, but Tyrrell was unmoved.[46]

No *Spectator* contributor who wrote about the peace movement of the 1970s and 1980s failed to judge it naïve, treacherous, and dangerous. Today's pacifists, Tyrrell wrote, are "struthious pols earnestly inserting their heads into the sand." The peace movement, he believed, was a hangover from the 1960s. "Every peace activist was directed by a brain whose every nook and cranny had been fully stocked by the New Age Zeitgeist," wrote Tyrrell. These were the same zealots who confronted such weighty international crises as infant formula in Ouagadougou, Upper Volta, he added.[47] Only folly inhered in our unilaterally turning our swords into plowshares, Tyrrell insisted. The nuclear age will not be so easily undone. The West, in fact, was remiss, he believed, in not vigorously promoting its interests and its ideals around the world, and democratic aspirations elsewhere had suffered from the neglect. To this extent, Tyrrell thought that the American decision to develop the neutron bomb—which kills people but leaves buildings standing—was good policy. "My kind of Bomb" he called it—a superb device for stopping Soviet tanks if the occasion demanded it. If that fact did not clinch the case, then other recommendations surely would. "It is also good news for those who admire European architecture and for those who deal in the used tank market."[48]

The "no-nukers" truly baffled Tyrrell. They were campaigning single-mindedly, he believed, not only to banish the bomb as a vehicle of international politics, a sympathetic wish however naïve it might be in its application, but to destroy the domestic nuclear energy industry as well. Tyrrell assembled a fistful of statistics to deflate the alarmist visions conjured up by the industry's detractors. These critics were, by Tyrrell's measure, the most reactionary voices in the land. But they had seized the high ground of morality by their rhetoric, however hypocritical it was. For here, Tyrrell pointed out, was the great antinuclear bard Allen Ginsberg, "a literary prankster whose body has been a test tube for every imaginable narcotic." Yet he mounts the stage and lectures to all on matters of health and safety. Tyrrell delighted to point out that on the weekend in 1982 when thousands gathered in Central Park to chant for a nuclear freeze, eleven members of a peace group in Moscow were arrested while trying to meet in a private apartment.[49]

Tyrrell's irreverent journalism, however, centered mostly on the domestic scene. In his capacious menagerie of "public nuisances," politicians formed the largest category. Tyrrell wrote chapter essays on Hubert Humphrey, Jimmy Carter, Walter Mondale ("The Goody Goody Ethos"), Andrew Young ("The Black Man's Burden"), Joseph Califano, Ralph Nader ("The Return of the Shakers"), Ted Kennedy, and the "hellish" Richard Nixon. All were exemplars of some kind of roguery or buffoonery, or a combination thereof. His political essays furnished Tyrrell the opportunity further to ridicule liberalism more through caricatural portrait than through intellectual analysis. For politics was to Tyrrell mostly a matter of style, of personal idiosyncrasy. Among the day's wayward liberals, what one saw rather consistently, he believed, was some residue of New Age reformation. Herein lay Tyrrell's recurring lament: all the esoteric wackiness that was 1960s counterculture rubbed off in heavy portions on the public life and the public culture of the larger society. It did so just enough to become fashionable and chic. While it encroached on Peoria, it emerged full-blown in the California governorship.

Governor Jerry Brown was a natural subject for Tyrrell's satire. Sometimes dubbed a "flake" for his unorthodoxy (he deigned not to live in his father's house, the governor's mansion, and drove around in an old car), he nonetheless convinced many people that he was in touch with the emerging Zeitgeist and held the key to a new redemptive politics. A book title even labeled Brown a "philosopher-prince." Tyrrell was unawed. He quoted Brown: "I see the world in very fluid, contradictory, emerging, interconnected terms, and with that kind of circuitry I just don't feel the need to say what is going to happen. . . . It's the circuitry of semi-conductors and computers and electronic interconnectedness, that's what's happening today." Philosopher-prince indeed! proclaimed Tyrrell. Why was nobody laughing? Have we lost all sense of difference between the realistic and the ridiculous? he asked. To Tyrrell, this New Age politics was just high-toned pretentiousness. "The Mullah Brown," he wrote, disgorges "cryptic flummeries with the effortlessness of some fat swami ensconced in the Waldorf and surrounded by PR hacks. . . . Alas, he is mostly empty space."[50]

The intellectual constituted another category of Tyrrell's public nuisances, equal to the politician in the implausible character of his mind. Both types, it seemed to Tyrrell, had seized on a common purpose to test the gullibility of the citizenry and to see just how much outlandishness they could get away with. Tyrrell's prime example in this instance was "Harvard's Tallest Tale," economist John Kenneth Galbraith. He "is one of the most obvious and entertaining mountebanks since Aimee Semple McPherson or Gerald L. K. Smith," wrote Tyrrell. Some saw the patrician Galbraith as a kind of Tory radical, Tyrrell noted, so current and stylish did his views become among America's privileged leftist elite. After all, "practically anyone ever thrown into a Kennedy swimming pool has at one time or another come under Galbraith's spell." But in fact, said Tyrrell, Galbraith's masterly wizardry made him as American as apple pie. He stood in the tradition of Cotton Ed Smith and his like, who once stalked dusty country crossroads and peddled their fables of slick moneymen on Wall Street and their nefarious doings. Galbraith, said Tyrrell, had simply refashioned this earlier jerkwater populism into a slick intellectual one. Tyrrell found it a measure of our changed times that the rural simpleton of yore, who happily passed hard-earned money into the hands of the snake-oil salesman, had been replaced by the demieducated sophisticate.[51]

Tyrrell found liberal America locked into a corrupted conventional wisdom. It prevailed in big city newspapers and on the national television networks, and it thrived among the "Gucci Bolsheviks" of Georgetown.[52] No assistant professor of sociology went far without paying respects to its homilies. Thus, said Tyrrell, official opinion in America accepted as unchallengeable certain axioms: that the Vietnam War was a moral atrocity, that housewives are the oppressed class of today, that business enterprise is a seedy affair, that blacks fail solely because of white prejudice, and that homosexuality is merely "sexual preference." It furthermore galled Tyrrell that so many of the voices for the oppressed in America belonged to well-off and well-connected individuals who suffered little when their expensive reform measures assaulted the paychecks of the rest of the country. "We need desperately in this country to redistribute more wealth," says Joseph Califano, wealthy Washington attorney turned Cabinet member.[53] On the other hand, radical chic was also big business for its propagators. Handsome are the rewards that come, for example, to Guggenheim fellows and Rockefeller grantees who trade on the "easy nihilism" of the trendy Left.[54] These prejudicial attitudes helped define Tyrrell's brand of 1970s and 1980s conservatism. In his excoriation of the intellectual classes and his assault on the "official" counterculture that enhanced bottom-line profits for morally neutral businessmen, Tyrrell embodied neoconservatism without the sociology.

But the hucksters knew what they were doing, Tyrrell conceded. One has

only to invoke a righteous cause or the name of an oppressed group or sect
to gain a kind of respectability for even the most unsavory of deeds. Thus
Tyrrell could hardly believe the story of one Robert Preston who, in 1974,
took a UH-1 (Huey) helicopter and tried to fly it right into the White House.
What followed left Tyrrell dumbfounded:

> What this poor fish did was, in this glorious era, well-nigh unthinkable. He
> committed a mischievous and indeed felonious act and did not make the faintest
> gesture to embroider it with noble purpose or high-toned symbolism. He merely
> stepped from his wounded helicopter and confessed to the assembled reporters
> and secret servicemen: "There wasn't anything else to do"—not a word about
> political repression, ecological suicide, or alienation and the search for one's
> sexuality. Preston could have mentioned the cruel condition of our women, the
> political castration of our homosexuals, the impending demise of the black-
> footed ferret, or the heartbreak of psoriasis. Rather, he grinned. . . . Had he
> possessed the astuteness to boom for any of the aforementioned causes he
> would be a free man today with a gorgeous publishing contract, a decade's
> lecturing engagements on the college Chautauqua circuit, and an office in
> Washington paid for by some occult rivulet of the Department of Health,
> Education, and Welfare.[55]

Tyrrell took pity on the hapless Preston and wished him well: "*Au revoir,* oaf."[56]

This improbable case elaborated a larger point for Tyrrell. Our liberal culture, he believed, thrived on a trite and trivial sentimentality. It seemed desperate, amid all the cruel and harsh facts of modern life, to distract individuals
with facile deceptions. Thus, said Tyrrell, our public culture has taken the
most boorish or commonplace individuals and bestowed on them a phosphores-
cent glitter. They acquire a stature, even a heroism, he said, that is but skin-
deep and essentially substanceless. An occasion that brought such reflections
from Tyrrell was the much-touted retirement in 1981 of newscaster Walter
Cronkite. Columnist Mary McGrory led the public bathos surrounding the
national tragedy: "I just don't know how we can face the '80s without him."[57]
Why all the hullabaloo? Tyrrell asked. "Here is a man who in all of his
public years never passed on more than a hint of intellectual substance. He
just sat there in front of that infernal microphone! Yet he is esteemed as
an authority and a moral paragon. He leaves behind him no books, no essays,
no memorable epigrams." But ours is the age of celebrity, said Tyrrell, and
visibility supersedes wisdom. The same culture of glitter that gives credence
to offhand opinions of "vacuous mannequins" like Bianca Jagger or Brooke
Shields also makes Delphic oracles of newscasters.[58]

G. K. Chesterton once said that when religion fades the problem is not that
people believe nothing; the problem is that they believe anything. Tyrrell's

writings centered on that theme. He invited readers to be witnesses to the New Age's preponderance of faiths and cures. But he was also sensitive to a related ailment, to wit, a compulsion to distort reality, to take the dross off commonplace rogues and rascals and make fairy-tale characters of them. Puffery and embellishment had become cultural norms, assisted by an eager media. The habit, Tyrrell believed, can be downright mischievous.

Consider, he said, the strange mystique of the Kennedy family, the "Camelot" mystique. It was, exclaimed Tyrrell, a remarkable myth: "The myth that a wheeler-dealer vulgarian [Joseph Kennedy], as rich as he was brutal, sired a family of archangels, fairy godmothers, and three genius sons who, despite private lives of sham and shallowness beyond belief, would somehow pull America—then the richest and freest nation on earth—out of a mysterious torpor into an Augustan age."[59] To Tyrrell, the efforts of H. L. Mencken and others to rid American intellectual and cultural life of its dominant strain of piety, idealism, and sentimentalism were obviously for naught. Because the most arresting fact of the Kennedy myth, Tyrrell found, was its hold on the "intellectualoids." Nowhere, observed Tyrrell, was the saccharin thicker than in the scholarship of Arthur M. Schlesinger, Jr., and James MacGregor Burns, "sitting at their typewriters, devotedly pecking out their lamentations to fallen banners, 'shining moments,' and tribunes for the dispossessed"—with immense profits to themselves, of course.[60] "Camelot," Tyrrell wrote, "is the pornography of American politics, always promising the unattainable and rendering those who participate inflamed, infantile, and ludicrous."[61]

Tyrrell once read a *New York Times* report that described UN ambassador Andrew Young's rather favorable assessment of Third World dictators. Tyrrell wondered why the national press doted on such ruminations, when "every washroom attendant in New York" knew they were preposterous.[62] The reference to "every washroom attendant" indicates a revealing democratic strain in Tyrrell's conservatism and his single important departure from Mencken. For when Mencken observed all the human folly in this broad land, he readily became the scourge of democracy. He found no redeeming vision or even common sense in the masses of America, only the timidity of the peasant mind, characterized by fear of the new and the daring and a sinister compulsion to render low the few superior persons among the populace.

To counteract democratic norms, Mencken espoused an unabashed elitism, celebrating such rare aristocratic breeds in American history as the colonial Virginians who helped secure the constitutional blessings of liberty. In fact, Mencken's writing on the subject of aristocracy makes a telling comparison with Tyrrell's uneasy conservative anti-elitism. Mencken saluted "a civilized aristocracy, secure in its position, animated by an intelligent curiosity, skeptical of all facile generalizations, superior to the sentimentality of the mob, and delighting in the battle of ideas for its own sake." But Tyrrell saw these standards run amuck. The open forum of ideas had prepared the way for New Age inanities. "All progress goes on at the higher levels," Mencken had written.[63] At the higher levels of American authority, Tyrrell saw only the corruption of wisdom and common sense.

Tyrrell, for all his inspired arrogance and belittling sarcasm, did not embrace an elitist conservatism. He was constrained in part because the governing elites in America, as he saw them, were the entrenched guardians of liberal culture. They had contrived successfully to foist on the nation an agenda that won little sympathy from the people at large but thrived as the conventional wisdom of isolated and immune policy-makers and bureaucratic assistants. (Tyrrell never labeled himself a democrat. He told me that he admired the character of the common people but not necessarily their habits. Of America's elites he said that the only thing he admired was their taste in cuisine.)[64] The agenda thrived too among the intellectuals. When Tyrrell penned an essay on Charles Reich, author of a superficial but immensely popular book in 1970 titled *The Greening of America,* he took pause to reflect. Professors across the land were making this volume required reading for their students. Reich was mounting the national lecture circuit and reaping handsome honoraria. Commented Tyrrell: "Perhaps in another time it was the average Americano who was a poltroon and a sap for any fabulist intent on working him over, but times have changed. Today one has a better chance of finding good sense and generous sentiment in the corner barbershop than at practically any cultural redoubt."[65] Mencken was never enamored of America's cultural redoubts, but never, on the other hand, would he have so complimented the democratic mind.

Tyrrell saw the issue in large outline. "New Age Liberalism," he wrote, "was in essence nothing more complicated or noble than a running argument with life as it was led by normal Americans." There was no doubt which side Tyrrell supported, and insofar as this theme recurs in the writings of most of the conservatives in this book, it indicates the extent to which conservatives had appropriated the language of liberalism in its deference to the injured majority of Americans. Tyrrell, on the same grounds, could celebrate the defeat of the Equal Rights Amendment as a "truly grass roots movement" that prevailed without benefit of the national media, the academic establishment, Congress, or the presidents' wives.[66]

Tyrrell went further. Democracy in America today, he avowed, needed renewal. Americans have suffered a loss of their liberties without ever once having voted on the matter. "Legal atrocities" like affirmative action found their way into operation without public referenda. So too did busing, abortion, hiring quotas, and the fifty-five-mile-per-hour speed limit. "No democracy in the West," Tyrrell wrote, "has lost more of its freedoms in recent years than the land of the free, home of the brave. And the confiscation of liberty was accomplished without this great democracy even putting the matter to a vote."[67]

The "democracy" in fact was betrayed, Tyrrell believed. He lamented, with a populist refrain, that "it was not the plainfolk who were corrupted or hood-winked. They jeered and hooted at every asinine notion."[68] Indeed Tyrrell had to wonder, given the basic commonsense conservatism of the American electorate, why had advocates on the Left so loudly trumpeted the ideal of a "people's democracy"? Barry Commoner ("The Great White Ph.D.") headed the ticket of the Citizens party in 1980, a party that championed itself as the new voice of the suffering average American. Tyrrell asked: "Would Dr. Commoner really like to live under a government whose policies reflected the average American's views on busing, capital punishment, prayer in public schools and Proposition 13 fever?"[69]

Tyrrell thus accommodated the democrat that Mencken abhorred, but he had as much contempt nonetheless for the democrat's brother-under-the-skin, the puritan. In fact, it was the separation of these two that Tyrrell saw as a distinguishing mark of America's recent history. For elitist liberalism, he believed, had become a species of puritanism, as meddlesome, as fun-denying, and as cranky as any before it. It rose triumphant on the shoulders of such self-appointed and self-righteous guardians of the public good as "Citizen" Ralph Nader, the noted consumer advocate, whom Tyrrell labeled "the latest edition of American puritanism." It thrived among the legions of officious bureaucratic regulators in the various levels of government and among the partisans of uplift in Washington's countless lobbyists, "the most humorless hinds of all."[70] Like Mencken's farmer, who, bored and work-weary on his Kansas plot, would have shut down the gambling houses at Reno and locked up the city saloons, Tyrrell's puritan was motivated by similar envy. He was "a stern prig howling at the voluptuaries of this world and intent on putting them under his thumb."[71] If he is not agitated by the fear that someone, some-where, is having a good time, it is a simple holier-than-thou personality that sets him into action. Tyrrell basically did not understand this liberal puritan, and he took refuge in sidewalk psychology to explain the phenomenon. Self-hatred, he asserted, explains the puritan's yen to save someone else or to redeem the world whole. "My guess," Tyrrell offered, "is that today hardly a goody-goody Liberal exists who does not hear a voice in the back of his skull whispering 'You are a little creep.' . . . . The voice does not lie."[72]

Nor does the "little creep" go away. Everywhere he looked Tyrrell saw
the "moral imperialism" of liberalism. It "disrupts every human relationship
and every human value," he wrote. The legislative program of Walter Mondale, exemplar of the "goody-goody ethos," was a nightmare for Tyrrell.
Mondale's liberalism, he believed, threatened havoc with human affairs, from
education to marriage. On this subject, Tyrrell referred to Mondale's 1973
Senate bill, the Full Opportunity and National Goals and Priorities Act. Tyrrell
considered the bill a piece of legislative arrogance that "would leave us with
a bureaucracy empowered to keep society in an incessant pother and to snoop
into every area of a citizen's life."[73] Mencken once belittled the American
Puritan's determination to "ram [salvation] down reluctant throats, to make
it free, universal and compulsory."[74] Tyrrell described the "postindustrial Puritanism" of Mondale in parallel terms: "a working relationship with God for the
expiration of other people's sinfulness, personal salvation through good intentions, good public relations, good government, and the taxing power."[75] For
Tyrrell there could be only one response: it was time for the resurrection
of the healthy libertarian spirit in America.

Libertarianism means a preference for the discretionary rights of individuals
against the authority of the state and the priorities of the public. Tyrrell became
a leading voice of conservative libertarianism in the United States. He wrote
in the manner not only of Mencken but also of Albert Jay Nock—elitist,
aristocrat, denigrator of democracy, and a man of pronounced taste for classical literature.[76] Nock believed that he stood in the tradition of Thomas Jefferson in articulating the merits of a responsible and aristocratic hedonism. Tyrrell
believed that he himself did too. He was a devotee both of classical music
and of expensive automobiles. But his libertarianism, attended by its many
compromises, revealed all the difficulty and confusion of that tradition in
American conservatism.

When anyone committed to the libertarian ideology opens wider the door
of freedom, he must be prepared for what walks in. Paul Elmer More once
observed that Emerson's "divine light" was an inspiration to most earnest
seekers, but it attracted many bats and insects of the night.[77] In the New
Age culture of the 1960s, that widening door made room for a diversifying
fringe that expanded exponentially, to an accompanying chorus of "new freedoms." To Tyrrell this culture was nothing short of the corruption of libertarianism, and that corruption was for him the most unfortunate truism of
contemporary American life. The ideological libertarian who wants defense
against the moral imperialist, working to inflict his will through the arm of
the state, has no intellectual defense against the pornographer, the drug user,

or the abortionist. The only plausible alternative is to make distinctions within the libertarian ideology, to make an effort at purification, really. This Tyrrell tried diligently to do, scoring some useful points but yielding to expediency as well.

He took up the question of pornography. The pornographer is a public nuisance. In an essay on Larry Flynt, publisher of the sexually graphic magazine *Hustler,* whom Tyrrell dubbed "a hopelessly pathetic slob," Tyrrell tried to distinguish between an authentic libertarianism and a vicarious libertarianism. Political, economic, and intellectual liberty, Tyrrell said, is a matter of gravest importance and of highest priority to any authentic libertarian (and Tyrrell called himself "a strict civil libertarian"). But the vicarious libertarians would add pornographic license, in the name of "sexual freedom," to the libertarian repertoire, equating it with political freedom. Tyrrell quoted author Gay Talese: "Sexuality is not divorced from the politics of government. Its suppression is entwined with attempts to regulate human behavior through control of imagery." Tyrrell was almost nonplussed at the analogy. "Think of it," he wrote, "the freedom to vote, to assemble, to form political parties, and to speak out on political issues is all of a piece with the freedom to sell marital aids."[78]

Any good thing can be ruined by cheapening it. That would seem to be Tyrrell's conclusion on the matter of libertarianism. Other libertarians argue that any distinctions are illegitimate in a genuinely libertarian philosophy. They also often add that once infringement on any liberty occurs, all liberties are in jeopardy. Once ban *Hustler* in the bookstores, and *Huckleberry Finn* is in trouble in the school library. This hypothesis Tyrrell called the "slippery slope" argument, and he found it unpersuasive. "Intelligent people can distinguish between pornography and art," he wrote. There are ways to mediate between the pornographer's license to sell and the community's interest in limiting accessibility to what he sells. Tyrrell thus would make the libertarian ideal more a matter of discretion and less a matter of *a priori* truth. Furthermore, he pointed out, liberals themselves treat American freedoms quite oblivious to the "slippery slope" phenomenon. In having income tax laws, Tyrrell asks, are we in danger of appropriating all income? Do prescribed speed limits threaten all mobility? "The absurdity of the slippery slope argument," Tyrrell added, "stands up and roars for attention when one considers that those who use it to preserve and protect pornography are the very statists who so often demand strict regulation of commerce, affirmative action, busing, and other such tyrannies."[79] But the illogic, of course, was two-sided and applied equally to the "libertarian" Tyrrell.

Discussion of libertarianism leads sooner or later to the marketplace. Some

conservatives make the rights of property and free competition the essence
of a free society, and many have been critics of liberal America from the
New Deal to the present on these grounds. Dogmatism in this defense has
not served the conservative cause well, enabling critics to associate conservatism with a base and materialist philosophy of life. To the conservative
Tyrrell that criticism irked, indicative as it was of what he considered the
sham morality of the Left. "Though the New Age Liberal still scowls at materialism," Tyrrell wrote, "material terms are all that he has for measuring the
good society. He has fallen into the absurd condition of frothing alternately
over America's high consumption of the earth's resources and over the inadequate number of color television sets in Bedford-Stuyvesant."[80]

For Tyrrell, furthermore, capitalism was without peer, the world's only
successful economic system, certainly the only one compatible with personal
freedom and the reasonably restricted power of the state. No, it was not
the hope of the world, he said, and no economic system can be. The average
businessman, he believed, was probably something of a philistine, but he
was hardly the scoundrel and villain that television in the New Age had irrever-
ently and viciously made him out to be. The New Age needs villains. How
else to explain, when the record of modern history discredits it completely,
the continuing appeal of socialism in some exclusive quarters? Socialism thrives
today, said Tyrrell, only as soap opera, moral drama in which the malefactors
of great wealth meet their fate at the hands of their righteous conquerors.[81]

Tyrrell despaired of ever solving the libertarian argument, or any other for
that matter, by sophistry. Besides, he said, it was simply a waste of time
so to engage the modern Neanderthals on the public podium. Today's public
nuisances, from women's liberationists to homosexual advocates, from black
nationalists to antismokers, do not merit intellectual response, he insisted.
They merit the horselaugh. Or as Tyrrell wrote of consumer advocate Ralph
Nader: "Why waste wind on such a lout? Ridicule him and spare the courtesies."[82]

Of the reforming groups in general, Tyrrell was also preemptive: "No amount
of careful argumentation is going to disabuse these fools of their moonshine."[83]
Tyrrell alleged that he became aware of this fact in the early 1970s. At that
time, he said, he and presidential candidate George McGovern had one thing
in common. They both agreed that what America needed was a good laugh.
"My opportunities for comedy were limited," Tyrrell wrote, "but McGoo
was better placed. He spent most of 1972 criss-crossing the country, selflessly
restoring the horselaugh to its former eminence. The campaign elicited many
ho-ho-hos and almost as many votes."[84]

Tyrrell and the *American Spectator* articulated a kind of gut-level conservatism. They touched exposed nerves and gave verbal expression to the ingrained prejudices of their readers. A series of issues in 1989 illustrated how the *Spectator* delivered its punches.

P. J. O'Rourke, another conservative renegade from the Left (he was long associated with the *Village Voice* and authored a book titled *Republican Party Reptile*), issued a call in the July issue of that year for a "New McCarthyism." His essay was rhetorically heavy-handed. "There are more fuzzy-minded one-worlders, pasty-faced peace creeps, and bleeding-heart bed-wetters in America now than there were in 1954," he wrote. O'Rourke himself presented a formidable list of individuals and groups marked for persecution and then invited the *Spectator* readership to supplement it. Enlistments to the cause came from all over the country. More than their earlier anti-Communist patron saint ever did, the respondents named names. The names were familiar to any contemporary: Amy Carter, Joan Baez, Mitch Snyder, Alice Walker, "Anyone whose name is Fonda," Ronald McDonald, Dennis Miller ("the geek who does the 'SNL News' on 'Saturday Night Live' "), and the liberal arts faculty at Stanford University. They also named organizations, such as the Ford Foundation, the ACLU, Greenpeace, and the Order of Maryknoll nuns. They listed broad categories of individuals: people who pronounce Chile "Cheelay," people who hyphenate their last names upon being married, people who go "Humph!" and roll their eyes when the name Nixon is mentioned, and people who say "Oh, God! You read *that*?" when someone refers to the *American Spectator*. They also compiled a tableau of generic items: "Anyone belonging to any group that has 'Coalition,' 'Community,' 'Solidarity,' 'Citizen,' 'People,' or 'Popular,' in its name," "Any union of concerned anybodies," and "Anything 'Quaker' which ain't oats."[85]

Ultimately, then, the conservatism proffered by Tyrrell and the *American Spectator* was a kind of exorcism. Tyrrell saw America infected by a malignancy, an invasion of demon spirits that must by rite be driven from the corpus. The treatment should be harsh and should be applied in heavy doses. Tyrrell's elixir was the guffaw. He believed that it was the only medicine that worked. Of course, he warned, the cure induces violent reaction from the assaulted parts. The doctor is called names—a quack, a mountebank—and he stands accursed. But many stood by the "bad boy," and not only the loyal coterie of *Spectator* fans. Now and then a voice from journals of more sober tones than the *Spectator's* came to Tyrrell's defense. Elliott Abrams wrote in *Commentary:* "Though Tyrrell is often rough, he is usually fair, and he is right to propose ridicule as an appropriate response to solemn incantations that are, quite simply, ridiculous. No respect should be paid to the claptrap that passes for political speech today."[86]

By the middle 1980s R. Emmett Tyrrell, Jr., was occupying a visible position in the conservative intellectual movement. He was appearing frequently on the national television medium that he disparaged, and his syndicated column issued from the *Washington Post*. Clearly, something about the brash and acerbic Tyrrell had caught on, and American political journalism was freshened by his presence. Tyrrell struck many as an eccentric, a devilish if not nefarious individual who used gilded prose to shortcut intellectual engagement. But in substance, what Tyrrell ultimately stood for was the ethic of normality. He represented more than any other the cultural aftershock of the 1960s, from its heady idealism on the one hand to its debilitating nihilism on the other. Tyrrell tapped a growing yen for normalcy. He was a Warren G. Harding of the intellectual set. He looked back to a saner and simpler America, of saloon fellowship and barbershop pieties. On the relations between the sexes, he was traditionalist to the core. But much of his achievement was to give expression to those unarticulated prejudices that had in fact emerged battered but still alive through the decade or more of cultural strife, prejudices that could often find outlet only by casting a vote for Ronald Reagan at the ballot box. Tyrrell more than once, as we have seen, took a cue from the New Left. There was a hardy element of "people's democracy" in his repertoire and a refined voice of the inarticulate millions in his crusty rhetorical assaults on the new liberal America.

American journalism has had recurring voices of this kind. Mencken has furnished us one comparison with Tyrrell, but he was much less the voice of a democratic conservatism than was Tyrrell. Tyrrell in fact was in some ways more reminiscent of the nineteenth-century publicist James Gordon Bennett. Bennett, a Scottish immigrant and originally a southerner in the United States, became the founder and editor of the first modern newspaper, the *New York Herald*. Bennett waged editorial war against many types in his day—dreamy radicals, evangelical moralists, "white-coated philosophers"—and championed the case of the southern slave-owning aristocracy amid the abolitionist fervor of his time. Bennett registered a robust interest in the commonfolk of America, while being at the same time a great respecter of tradition and social hierarchies. If we seek continuities in America's past that provide historical context for Tyrrell, then historian Bertram Wyatt-Brown's description of Bennett is certainly suggestive:

Like many of the *Herald*'s subscribers, Bennett feared that middle-class pieties would feminize the nation. They would snatch the convivial tankard from the honest toiler, close down dance halls and theaters, shut up the Post Offices and railroad depots on Sundays, encourage blacks "to seek white mates," and bring on a return to the theocratic tyrannies of puritan New England. Ancient social and gender rankings would disappear along with "the purity of Anglo-Saxon blood." All these policies threatened the traditional image of the male as master of his destiny, arbiter of his own morals and sexual habits, protector of his own dependents, whether inside the family or outside it on the plantation.[87]

Bennett's world was one in which, as he said, antislavery women wore breeches and their male compatriots wore petticoats.[88] Tyrrell saw himself as not so far removed from such a world.

About Tyrrell's long-term mark on the conservative intellectual movement it is difficult to speculate. By the time his manifesto *The Liberal Crack-Up* hit the bookstores in 1984, much of the New Age was history, even a species of nostalgia, like some frivolous part of one's youthful past that is recollected in chagrin but which one would probably not choose now to have been without. But as America moved to the last decade of the twentieth century, it was uncertain whether or not Tyrrell would be left merely to tilt with the shadows and ghosts of a vanishing past. One might have surmised that this was to be the case, but the 1984 presidential election gave pause. The landslide victory of conservative Ronald Reagan set committed liberals and Democratic party stalwarts to wonder whether liberalism itself carried too much of the 1960s into the succeeding decades. Liberalism in that twenty-year period had taken on a lot of new weight, and many worried that it had seriously and perhaps permanently changed its character in the process. If the Democratic platform of 1984 was indeed the New Age on paper, then Tyrrell's relevance was assured.

Granting his relevance, what then of his achievement? One could not deny his skills. He was an artist, a cartoonist, a Jackson Pollock of the word. Whether received in muffled laughter or outraged indignation, Tyrrell was memorable and effective. He stood to gain more, however, by improving in intellectual precision. He struck with effect at the outer fringes of American culture, but his hyperbole often missed the substantive center of American life. There were, also, too many loose ends in his thought. The New Age that he excoriated was at once for him both too permissive and too puritanical. It was both totalitarian in its reach and anarchic in its cult of whim and idiosyncrasy. New Age America in Tyrrell's description of it was a curious animal, a mongrel of diverse components somehow living under one shaggy skin.

Furthermore, one might have wished from Tyrrell a clearer vision of a United States remade by conservatism. Once we have seen the New Age for all its frivolity and nonsense, its narcissism, its solipsism, and its ideological fever, what remains? Tyrrell was attuned to the problem. He knew that a meaningful culture and system of values had been threatened by the Right and the Left in America. The New Age, he believed, had, in its nihilistic fury, left a world stripped of meaningful distinctions. "Having depreciated all social hierarchy, tradition, kinship, and every other sort of distinction," he wrote, "the New Age Liberals were left believing only in an egalitarian tomorrow while today was made uncomfortable with alienation, anomie, identity crises, and other modern horrors." On the other hand, Tyrrell admitted, spokesmen for the Right should not be sanguine about the ability of any economic system to sustain our social values. Mischief and mayhem attend the operations of free-market capitalism, and its ethic of freedom is no substitute for "higher cultural and moral commitment."[89]

Tyrrell thus paid his respects to a traditionalist conservatism, but he rarely did more than tip his hat. A conservative vision of the good life failed to emerge from his polemics, and such a vision, at least, would certainly have enhanced his contribution. In one part of *The Liberal Crack-Up,* for example, Tyrrell went after the environmentalists: "Alarmed in the 1960s by civilization's advances against the last strongholds of indiginae," he wrote, "the environmentalist was moved to fulminate and to rage, and the range of his ire has been stupendous: DDT, aerosol cans, research into recombinant DNA, the flush toilet, the Concord supersonic passenger plane."[90] But since when have the aerosol can and the flush toilet been the cherished symbols of "civilization's advances," such that it behooves the conservative to revere and preserve them? What has happened, in the conservative scheme of things, to what Russell Kirk liked to call "the unbought grace of life"?

On matters ranging from the environment to smokers' rights, against which ridicule was his only weapon, Tyrrell often sounded terribly obtuse. The causes seemed to weigh less with him in their substance than the laugh he might enjoy at the expense of their partisans, the vigilantes, for example, who strove to save the lowly *Staphylococcus aureus.* John Jay Chapman once said that "denunciation is well enough, but laughter is the ratsbane for hypocrites."[91] "Serious things," said Plato, "cannot be understood without laughable things." But laughter has another recommendation: Life is too serious to take seriously. That might be the motto for Tyrrell and the *American Spectator.* It is a healthy thing to remember at a time when all issues become political ones and solemnity is the prevailing mood in all camps. For Tyrrell it was enough that he who laughs last laughs loudest.

9
Michael Novak
Capitalism
and Catholicism

In 1972 Michael Novak produced what was perhaps the most perversely brilliant book in the body of American conservative literature in the 1970s and 1980s. *The Rise of the Unmeltable Ethnics* was one man's attempt to sound the depths of his alienation from American life, to articulate for a whole group of Americans their sense of displacement, their feelings of exclusion and powerlessness. The rhetoric of *Unmeltable Ethnics* carried the passion of a New Leftist position that had but recently made Novak's the voice of radical protest, but it reflected also the author's growing disenchantment with that mood. *Unmeltable Ethnics,* in fact, was a landmark in Novak's pilgrimage from the Left to the Right, but the book accepted no easy labels. To the already confusing terminology of American political culture *Unmeltable Ethnics* added a new dimension of unorthodoxy.

Prophetic visions usually overreach reality, and so did those of *Unmeltable Ethnics.* Novak subtitled his book *Politics and Culture in the Seventies.* He believed he saw in the United States a new self-consciousness and a pride going public among the millions of ethnic Americans – Poles, Slavs, Italians, and Greeks specifically – who had long viewed the world with an angle of vision markedly different from that of the dominant Anglo-Saxon groups in the country. Novak saw a country beset by an oppressive political and moral culture, a rationalist strait-jacket that threatened to suffocate every genuine human passion and spontaneity. He saw an individualism in American history and life that had grown hollow and meaningless, depriving Americans of the bonds of fellowship, family, and tribal affiliations. Only the great potential of an ethnic revival, Novak believed, could correct this course of history and breathe a new humanity into American life.

Novak wrote *Unmeltable Ethnics* at a time when Americans had been experiencing a decade and a half of the civil rights movement. The fight against racism had made familiar references to "two Americas," the world of whites and the world of blacks. In the early seventies, too, feminists employed the language of dualism and castigated the privileged life of males and the exclusion of women from all the opportunities of American life. Novak's book completely circumvented these patterns to describe a nation more profoundly divided. Privilege to him denoted Anglo-Saxons; oppression meant discrimination against white ethnics. Dual America for Novak was very real. Everywhere he looked Novak observed how the ethnic American lived and thought differently from the Anglo-Saxon. His descriptions, in this book but even more emphatically in his later writings, marked Novak's special place in the conservative intellectual pattern of the late twentieth century.

The southern and eastern European immigrants brought to the United States, Novak believed, a worldly sense that left them wholly outside the Lockean universe of the English and northern European groups that had so emphatically stamped their thoughts and values on American life. Ethnic culture was blood-rich, full of the enduring bonds of family and kinship ties. It sought permanence in these relationships, and it located life's meaningfulness in them. Ethnic consciousness did not project onto the world the imagination of a new order. It pursued no new moral universes, no politics of purity, no revolutions of holiness. What Novak saw in his ethnics was a culture of earthiness, a naturalism accepting of the world and its evils, even of its dirt, a naturalism embodied in its religious understanding.[1]

Novak described the Anglo-Saxon world, the world of the WASP, quite differently. The WASP's dominant trait, he said, was individualism, enhanced all the more in the United States by the boundlessness of the American continent, the historical mobility of the American people, the loosening of human ties in a culture obsessed with material success, progress, and the reshaping of the land for greater human control. But the Anglo-Saxon flourished also with the passion for order, the drive to control through reason, the will to impose on the terrors of an unrestrained and frightful inner freedom the discipline and control of public order. Indeed the Anglo-Saxon, Novak argued, levied restraints on both his inner and outer life that he at times found intolerable but which he could not help believe were the prerequisites for his ideal of freedom. Novak wrote: "More than most societies, therefore, America can have public mobility and freedom; more than most, it must have extremely high restraint in every private soul."[2]

Michael Novak by Shelly Fischman

Hence too those universalist Anglo-Saxon obsessions: cleanliness, purity, organization for reform and improvement, optimism, inspiration, and moral exhortation. For Novak these traits of character were not simply cultural curiosities. For their essential manifestation was political, and not in any narrow sense of that word. To adjust to America, the immigrant had to learn to repress everything his culture had taught him, Novak said, and from the minute he stepped into a public school or left the confines of his neighborhood enclave, his life had to be a process of reeducation. "Immigrants from southern and eastern Europe," Novak wrote, "had to learn order, discipline, neatness, cleanliness, reserve. They had to learn to modulate emotion, to control passion, to hold their hands still, to hold the muscles of their face placid, to find food and body odors offensive, to quieten their voices, to present themselves as cooly reasonable."[3]

The moral passion of the Anglo-Saxon, the essence of his political life, derived, Novak believed, from his view that human nature is benign, or at least malleable, and that the order imposed within can be imposed without, imposed on the wild, primitive, and passionate world. The immaculate white and pristine functionality of Yankee churches and the speckless cleanliness of Yankee domiciles must be reincarnated in the social and political spheres. Evil, sin, and vice, like dirt on kitchen floors, must be driven from the scene. The Anglo-Saxons, Novak wrote, "are the soap-and-water experts of the world."[4]

Unquestionably, Novak's heavy invective led to harsh stereotyping, for in his effort to describe the dominance of Anglo-Saxon norms in the United States, Novak ranged widely. It was not just "corporate America," the business elite of well-connected executives, that constituted for him the institutions of privilege. These elites, to be sure, thrived in their own highly distinctive mannerisms, language, and personal demeanor. "In all God's world," Novak asked, "is there anything as cool as a Yale lawyer across the carpeted office of a major philanthropic fund? How could any other race ever fashion its psyche to that style?"[5]

Anglo-Saxonism had its grip well set elsewhere too, even in locations where ideology often opposed the capitalist establishment. Novak titled one of his chapters "The Intellectuals of the Northeast" and discussed in one of its sections the "bigotry" of that group. In the universities, especially in the elite eastern universities, Novak located the ethic of the Enlightenment, the cult of reason, the norm of modernism, a skepticism toward traditional values and disdain for traditional institutions. He perceived too the fashion of alienation that reflected the intellectual classes' own sense of separateness. In the angry, heated aspersions of Vice-President Agnew (Spiro Theodore Anagnostopoulos, son of a Greek immigrant), Novak perceived the authentic hostility of the southern European to this quintessential expression of Anglo-Saxon elitism.[6]

For the ethnic American, Novak could find no haven in this heartless land. He even looked to the nuances of language to show how remote these excluded aliens were from American norms. American political language, especially the words of liberal reform activity, utilized mechanistic analogies. Experts spoke a language of function and program, of input and process, as if society were a mechanism and not a living organism. Functional imagery, said Novak, coexisted with bureaucratic government and its rationalist sense of life. Novak found something calculatingly inhuman even in the most progressive and democratic notions of American political life. Anglo-Saxon culture, he believed, had created a democracy of "the masses." Ethnic culture clung to a democracy of "the people." From the former came the tyranny of public opinion polls, a "soulless" norm that could tap only the most shallow and superficial commonality of American life.[7] Novak, in the early 1970s and indeed throughout his career, searched desperately for pluralism. As we shall see, what he once believed the Left could truly promise, only conservatism could preserve.

From both perspectives, however, liberalism conspired against pluralism. By liberalism Novak meant the course of the political and moral reform tradition in the United States. For when the political organism is mechanically conceived, he wrote, one inevitably thinks of persons as units subject to rational schemes. The "masses" represent such a transformation of people whose organic, habitual connections have been severed. Broken into discrete units, the people are assigned to a formless unity from outside, "by those experts whose task is to rationalize and to manipulate social relationships." Novak could not but be amused that the label "machine politics" had been foisted onto the political institution that immigrants had of necessity forged to protect themselves from the monolithic control of Anglo-America. For "if anything in America is a 'machine,' " Novak wrote, "it is reform politics: impersonal, procedural, moralistic, abstract, constructed by rules." Liberal reformism was the antithesis of the blood-thick, personal politics perfected by the Irish and other Catholic immigrant groups.[8]

One might surmise, then, that Novak's tract spoke for a Catholic ethic against a Protestant norm in the United States. To a large extent that division prevailed in the book, and Novak discussed with great insight, albeit with excessive generalization, fine points of religious/cultural differentiation among American Protestants, Catholics, and Jews. But Novak made no case for a Catholic solidarity and indeed largely wrote the Irish Catholic experience out of the ethnic mode in America. The Irish, he insisted, had absorbed too much of American moral piety and individualism. The early Irish stamp on the Catholic Church in the United States gave it too much, for Novak's taste, the temper of Calvinism and its ethic of work, decency, and moral righteousness. The Irish, in short, suffered from an excess of Americanization.[9]

Ethnic politics, Novak believed, had become the key to America's changing society and culture. Indeed it had already created a crisis of impasse in the civil rights movement, an issue that Novak now confronted from a position of unapologetic defensiveness. The great success of Martin Luther King, Jr., he believed, had been his ability to tap the idealistic, abstract moralism of Protestant America. Even in Alabama, and even among the staunchest of white churchgoing segregationists, Novak said, King was able to turn against them the "honeyed, moralistic rhetoric with which they constantly anoint themselves." But moralistic politics would not play in Cicero, Illinois. This was the blue-collar, second-generation, white ethnic community that was at the heart of King's drive for open housing in the northern United States. Elsewhere King might tap with great effect the moral guilt feelings of Americans, but west of Chicago he confronted a culture quite removed from that political strain. Wrote Novak: "White ethnics refuse to feel guilty. Guilt is not their style. They react to guilt feelings with anger. They do not imagine life as an effort to live up to abstract ideals like justice, equality, fairness, reasonableness, etc.; but as a struggle to survive." White ethnicity, Novak insisted, had a different kind of idealism, a group ethic of self-help, of outreach to a brother or sister in trouble or in need.[10]

One could read Novak's *Unmeltable Ethnics* from several political angles. Its aloofness from the liberal sense of a progressive history, its disdain for abstract moral values invoked in the name of justice and humanitarianism, and its often-manifest anti-intellectualism gave to the book a conservative mood. But behind the writing of *Unmeltable Ethnics* lay Novak's years of service in the radical Left and his already extensive writing in the theology and politics of leftist causes. In fact much of that perspective persisted in Novak's view at the opening of a new decade.

At this time Novak read the whole "Americanization process" as an education in loneliness, from the uprooting of the immigrant family and the separation of their children to the modern suburban home, each room with its own television set. But this procedure constituted for him, as it did for many radical thinkers, the prerequisites of the capitalist system. The increasing anomie of American life accustomed Americans to think of themselves as appendages of machines, such that the atomizing of traditional social groups into their separate components reflected symbolically the whole Lockean base, the individualism, of Anglo-Saxon thought.[11]

This process was also one of pacification. America required for its capitalist purposes, Novak argued, a culture that might somehow quiet the inner rage of human beings forced into so unnatural and repressive a discipline as the machine process. In Marcusean language he decried the ascendancy of the superculture in the television media, a discriminatory media of the highest order. For television, said Novak, confirmed the hegemony of the WASP's personality – cool, controlled, placid, unruffled. Television in American culture, wrote Novak, had become a "metaphysical instrument," as cruelly repressive to all outside its universalist norms as any regime inflicted by the laborer's boss in the old coal mines of Pennsylvania.[12]

Finally, in his eagerness to connect with almost everything in revolt against corporate, liberal America, Novak seized on the youth rebellion of the 1960s and made it a compatriot of the white ethnic consciousness that had for three generations suffered under the standards of Waspish America. In a striking paragraph Novak wrote:

> We may also see in the youth culture a profound starvation for a denser family life, a richer life of the senses, the instincts, the memory. No other group of young people in history was ever brought up under a more intensive dose of value-free discourse, quantification, analytic rationality, meritocratic competition, universal standards (IQ, College Boards). What was almost wholly neglected in their upbringing was the concrete, emotive, even tribal, side of human nature. To that they were drawn in a desperate way, like air sucked into a vacuum. Music, dress, sound, sight, and feeling ran to the farthest extreme from industrial, suburban rationality.[13]

Many reviewers did not like *Unmeltable Ethnics*. Nearly all detected in it too many stereotypes and generalizations of ethnic groups and religious traditions. Those most averse, like Kenneth Clark, thought the book had a polarizing effect, a dangerous polemical quality.[14] Garry Wills wrote that "Novak teaches [Archie Bunker] new hates."[15] These criticisms might have had some merit, but no one seemed to have caught Michael Novak's little secret. For although the book was well draped with ethnic, Jewish, Catholic, and other personality types and although none can doubt that Novak's impassioned prose bespoke authentically his real feelings of ethnic pride and oneness, Novak also used these masks to make an oblique but nonetheless devastating critique of liberalism. The little secret of this book was that one did not need to be a white ethnic to share, wholeheartedly or sympathetically, in Novak's assault on the political and social norms of that liberalism. Essentially Novak had simply given new dress to some traditional conservative sentiments.

Novak's Slavic identity pressed itself on him early and easily. He was born in Johnstown, Pennsylvania, in 1933. His grandparents had lived in the Tatra Mountains of Slovakia, within sight of the southern border of Poland. They had emigrated to Pennsylvania from Eastern Europe, settling in a part of the United States that history had made the geographical symbol of the most bitter labor struggles in the annals of working-class life in America. Years later Novak would dramatize part of the bloody record in his book *The Guns of Lattimere.*

Novak would also recall, however, that his parents were the first Slovaks in their community to move out of their ethnic neighborhood in Johnstown into the "American and Protestant" sections above the town. Novak's father worked with an insurance company and, Novak recalled, loved to read and to write poetry. His first purchase, before he had a home or a shelf to put it in, was a set of the famous red Harvard Classics.[16] Michael attended a good public school, but as a Slav, and Catholic too, he was very much in a minority. A teacher who spelled Pope Pius XII's name by inserting an "o" between the "i" and the "u" reinforced in Novak's memory his special status in the largely Protestant new community.[17]

Novak graduated from Stonehill College in North Easton, Massachusetts, and then studied at Gregorian University in Rome, where he prepared for the priesthood for two years beginning in 1956. Although Novak did not enter the Church, his interests always focused on religious, specifically Catholic, understandings of political and social questions. The sense of a separate Catholic status in the United States marked his thinking in the early years. Novak even added his own piece to the literature of "growing up Catholic" in America. "We had a special language all our own," he wrote, "our own pronunciation for words we shared in common with others (Augústine, contémplative), sights and sounds and smells in which few others participated (incense at Benediction of the Most Blessed Sacrament, Forty Hours, wakes, and altar bells at the silent consecration of the Host)."[18]

The Catholic inheritance also carried with it for Novak a certain political bias. After completing studies in Rome, Novak attended Harvard University, where he finished a program in religion in 1965. Catholic ideas remained his dominant interest and informed his political views. He later described those views as a traditional medieval bias against the capitalist order. Novak identified, as he put it, with ideals of the old village community that recalled his Slovakian background. His sympathies lay with "labor" as opposed to "capital." The business people he remembered from central Pennsylvania seemed always to be Protestants, "either Calvinist or Episcopalian."[19] Novak's formal education and his extensive reading in Catholic literature considerably reinforced these prejudices. From Lamennais and de Maistre to Chesterton, Belloc, Scheler, and Marcel, Novak derived a Catholic ethic of personalism and community against "Protestant" ideals of individualism, utilitarianism, and pragmatism. These latter, Novak then believed, underscored the loneliness, alienation, and machinelike existence of the modern secular individual.

Was there some way, Novak wondered, to define a modern Catholic alternative to the dominant Western order thus described?[20]

Novak took up that cause while he pursued a varied academic career. Even before he left Rome, Novak had decided that his passion was for politics and culture, and he even contemplated running for political office. He enrolled at Harvard University in 1960, still studying religion, but all the time he was involved at Cambridge with several political campaigns. He met his future wife, Karen, there, and they moved to Palo Alto, where Novak joined a new program of religious studies as an assistant professor at Stanford University. Other appointments followed, including ones at the State University of New York at Old Westbury and at Syracuse University, where Novak was Distinguished Professor of Religion from 1977 to 1979. By this time Novak had authored several books and had written widely on Catholic issues. He had become an associate editor of *Commonweal,* the Catholic magazine of religion and politics, in 1966 and a contributing editor to *Christian Century* in the same year. More than any other individual studied in this book, perhaps, Novak's career demands a fairly strict chronological account. We leave the formal highlights of his career at this point to consider the background of *Unmeltable Ethnics* and its key transitional place in Novak's movement from the ramparts of the Left into neoconservative prominence by the end of the 1970s.

Throughout his career Novak had a lovers' quarrel with the Roman Catholic Church. The church of his ancestors and family, it was seldom the church of his intellect. But his quarrel with the Church provides the one mark of continuity in Novak's otherwise not easily fathomable transition from the political Left to the political Right. In the 1960s Novak found reason aplenty to be dissatisfied with the Church. Pope John XXIII too was dissatisfied, and Novak soon counted himself among a generation of American Catholics who viewed the events of Vatican II as the exciting opening of the Church to the world. The idea suited Novak and furnished the title of his book of 1964, *The Open Church.* What he wrote about Catholicism in this work soon launched Novak, as it would many newly defined American Catholics, into radical politics. But twenty years later, when Novak was making an elaborate case for democratic capitalism, he brought against the Church the same charge of an inability to be instructed by the real world and by the facts of modern history.

The Open Church narrated the work of Vatican II and page by page pleaded for the acceptance of its reforms. In introducing his book Novak described a Catholic Church that had grown complacent and immobile, a Church that had become sadly irrelevant to modern life, a Church "out of touch." "The great weakness of the Church," he added, "is its limited intellectual horizon." For this encumbrance Novak blamed the influence of Spain and Italy, which had not experienced like other Western nations the fullest impact of modernism—industrialism, social pluralism, and democracy.[21] In chapter essays that dealt with liturgical reform, language, and Church authority, Novak sided with the reconstructionists.

But the book was surely also an affectionate chastisement. Novak's love for the institution showed through forcefully and demonstrated his great hope that the Catholic Church might once again be a respected worldly authority. In concluding the work, Novak rehearsed a late issue in Catholic Church history by importuning an Old World institution to learn from the New. What the Church needed—the lessons of nonideological democracy, pluralism, widespread education, and the advantages of technology and material well-being—constituted for Novak the ascendant concerns in humanity's future. The experience of the United States would soon be the experience of the world, he believed. And those issues should constitute a new Catholic agenda. Novak was very much an "Americanist" in Church politics.[22]

But if liberal Catholicism in the Church made Novak an Americanist, then his Catholicism in America made him a dissenter. For it was the liberalism of American life, by which he meant a materialist faith in progress, a philosophical tradition of pragmatism, and an anomic individualism—every human the center of his own universe—that Novak found so chilling. The United States, he would say repeatedly, was too much a product of the Enlightenment, especially in its Lockean mode. The cult of reason, not the least in the Christian churches, had deprived modern life of the experience of mystery, had severed reason and faith, and had made impersonality the dominant metaphoric vehicle in the interpretation of the universe. Novak advanced the case for belief and faith in this attack on the Enlightenment and in his book of 1965, *Belief and Unbelief.*[23]

Among the many phenomena of the turbulent 1960s, one of surprising prominence was the emergence of the new worldly Catholics. For the opening of the Catholic Church could be no halfway measure for many in its ranks. When an eager and enthusiastic generation of young Catholics hit the world, they hit it hard. Garry Wills narrated with telling effect, in his book *Bare Ruined Choirs,* how cloistered seminarians, such as those at rural Woodstock in Maryland, left their isolated retreats and encamped in New York City, plunging into missionary work in the urban ghettos and affixing their new habitats every symbol of modernity available, even the fleshy iconography of *Playboy* centerfolds. From the earliest draft-resisters to the demonstrative protests and street campaigns of priestly activists, a visible Catholic Left loaned its voice to the growing chorus of radical politics.

Novak never embraced all dimensions of Catholic worldliness. Nonetheless, the last years of the 1960s found him in an intellectual mood that echoed

New Left ideologies in philosophy and politics. He tried to summarize his new state in a curiously unfocused book, *The Experience of Nothingness,* published in 1970. Forsaking a specific Catholic position, Novak expressed views pronounced by many Americans in the New Left, emphasizing especially that new states of consciousness, more than formal Marxist programs of social reconstruction, must underscore any program of liberation from the oppressive cultural mold of rationalist industrial capitalism. The experience of nothingness became for Novak a manner of self-renewal and rebirth, an eradicating process that was in effect liberating, an escape from false consciousness. The book, however ambiguous and vague its program, clearly joined Novak to the existential radical Left.[24]

In *A Theology for Radical Politics* Novak most clearly cast his lot with the New Left. The book was a montage of "new consciousness" radicalism, secular theology, new sexuality (albeit only briefly mentioned), and other leftist notions then in currency. Novak quoted radical voices such as Mario Savio, Stokely Carmichael, and Jack Newfield (author of *A Prophetic Minority*). He invoked the Port Huron Statement and ranged in his cultural reformism from Death of God theology to Buddhism.

Radical Politics took up nearly every issue in the New Left agenda and bestowed on it the author's blessing. It described the United States as the exemplar of liberal fascism, thriving through the conditions of totalitarian freedom: "It is not necessary to use a Gestapo to attain conformity; one may just as easily attain it by paying good rewards. In place of bread and circuses, modern technology pacifies our people with cars and color television." It attacked the pretenses of value-free discourse. It rejected the pragmatic tradition of American politics: "A pragmatic view of life operates *within* a system of values; it seeks to bring about reconciliation and adjustment; it cannot call the system into question." It denounced American militarism: "The wealthiest civilization in history gives top priority to making war and making ready for war." It denounced American universities as bastions of the Establishment. It celebrated the promises of the younger generation: "They will, if they keep up their courage, lead us to a new sense of personal identity, a new sense of community." It justified the use of violence in a one-dimensional society in which all rational discourse was useless: "Against armed ranks of policemen, a grenade is more serious and effective than calling names." And it dismissed with disgust the American working class—corpulent, complacent, chauvinist in its patriotism, racist, and self-indulgent, in short, purged of every radical aspect of its once promising history. In the middle of *Radical Politics* Novak lapsed into despair. "One could cry out in anguish that the suffering and sacrifices of past generations have come to this. A grown man with a can of beer finds his chief fulfillment in a televised game, watched by thirty million others, and believes our land free, brave, and just."[25] *A Theology for Radical Politics* was much more politics than theology. It expressed honest sentiments and conveyed a measure of clichéd truths. But it was pop New Left and withal a rather banal book.

Novak could not express his radical political sentiments through writing alone. The war in Vietnam brought him into the protest movement. By 1967 he was attending mobilization meetings in Washington, D.C., sponsored by the organization Clergy and Laymen Concerned about Vietnam. The next year he and other religious critics of the war collected draft cards at large church rallies protesting the war.[26] What Novak wrote about Vietnam, however, was far more restrained than most of the antiwar literature of the time. Novak was prepared to concede, at least, that the war constituted one of the most complicated issues faced by the United States, both morally and politically. But he could not view the war as a Cold War issue simply, and thus he rejected standard apologetics of American involvement. The problem in Vietnam, he argued, was merely symptomatic of the economic plight of the Third World — poverty, hunger, and the attending political oppression that so many in the world faced. And the influence of these circumstances made Novak fatalistically resigned to a long series of revolutions, a future course of violence throughout the world that he himself legitimated.[27]

It should be noted, finally, that even at this, the most radical period of Novak's career, his position on the Left remained less than a full participation in its political agenda. Novak in particular remained aloof from the Freudian dimension of the New Left, and even his celebration of new consciousness was existentialist in mood and never libidinal in emphasis. Novak made only a few, essentially rhetorical, concessions to the Left's program of erotic liberation, and one finds no evidence that he ever gave much credence to them. When Novak wrote in the 1960s on such a subject as chastity, for example, he reflected quite strongly a natural law, Catholic perspective and a traditional institutional framework.[28]

Novak's voyage leftward actually proved to be rather short-lived. Beginning about 1970 Novak went through a half-decade or so of transition, fascinating to observe and characterized by a withdrawal from leftist positions that nonetheless only vaguely anticipated the emphatic neoconservatism that would follow. *Unmeltable Ethnics,* we have seen, was marked by an ambivalence that expressed both conservative and radical critiques of mainstream America. Books such as *Choosing Our King* and *The Joy of Sports* do reflect Novak's greater accommodation to American life while standing firm in an ethnic-Catholic perspective.

By the early 1970s Novak could cite several reasons for being dissatisfied with the radical movement and the youth rebellion especially. Part of his disenchantment came from his own intellectual Catholicism. Novak always attributed to Jacques Maritain, the French Catholic theologian, a lifelong influence on his thinking, and he accepted especially Maritain's appreciative, albeit critical, understanding of liberal and democratic values. Maritain represented to Novak a rare and intelligent voice of modernism in Catholic literature, and he called Maritain "the true architect of the modern Catholic tradition of human rights and democracy" and "the great genius of modern Catholic thought, at least in the political order." Maritain, Novak believed, had formulated in Aristotelian language the basic tenets of liberal democracy, even more securely grounding them in the Thomist authority of natural law.[29]

Strangely enough, however, a Protestant influence helped Novak articulate his intensifying dissatisfaction with the Left. One of Novak's most important essays in the early 1970s appeared in *Commentary* with the title "Needing Niebuhr Again." In fact, Novak wrote many times thereafter on the ideas of Reinhold Niebuhr, for they proved crucial to a growing rapprochement in Novak's thought between Christian theology and democratic capitalism. For now, however, a Niebuhrian understanding of the radical Left enabled Novak to identify the New Left as essentially an extension of liberal optimism and innocence. Novak by this time could no longer believe that New Left ideology, the youth counterculture, or New Class liberalism had made any substantial changes in the spurious individualism that long characterized the dominant cultural norms in the United States. From the "old moralism" to the new, Novak said, was an easy transition. For the new morality simply coined "Do your own thing" as its own translation of the individualist ethic of America. In place of the old liberal faith in a progressive history through science and technology, the new morality, Novak wrote, offered its own vacuous idealisms ("When the world shall live as one!" at the George McGovern rally at Madison Square Garden in 1972; "If only we have love!"). What Novak had begun to perceive in the leftist movement were assumptions of a superior morality, an innocence, a failed sense of ambiguity, irony, and tragedy in human life. Novak had learned from Niebuhr to distrust all such claims for superior moral vision.[30] All this understanding had always been a part of Catholic teaching, of course, but it required a Protestant theologian to put it into sharpest focus.

Novak's discontents were also growing more specifically political. For the flip side of innocence was the burden of guilt, worn conspicuously on the exposed sleeves of Anglo-Saxon garments. Novak now saw in the profuse moral idealism of the Left a style of self-chastisement, of moral self-flagellation, that wholly escaped the understanding of white ethnics. Novak even charged that "white racism" had become for the Left the smear that communism had earlier been for the Right. A stark dualism had set into the Left's moral assessments of white and black America that Novak found pernicious and specious. This dualism was all the more damning by its manifest self-righteousness. "Left politics," Novak wrote in *Unmeltable Ethnics,* "is the last refuge of those wonderful people who brought us Prohibition." Novak had become thoroughly sickened and distrustful of the "politics of conscience" in the United States. And Catholics, he urged, had special reasons for suspicion. From abolitionism to anti-immigration and the attacks on the city political machines, "reform" and "morality," he warned, were pretty close to being code words for anti-Catholicism.[31]

Novak was now judging much of the political life of the 1970s by the measure of his own white ethnic consciousness and prejudices. *Unmeltable Ethnics* was only the most complete synthesis of a worldview that he applied through articles and essays to American politics and which informed his book of 1974, *Choosing Our King.* Thus, as the liberal political program went in new directions, taking up the cause of "affirmative action" as a means of assuring representative inclusion of minorities and females in government, schools and universities, and businesses, Novak angrily dissented. He opposed affirmative action in principle, and he also asked who gets let in and who gets kept out when these programs are put into operation. Affirmative action, he believed, promised nothing to that element of the population that faced the most discrimination—the white ethnics. To make his case Novak listed figures for the number of Poles in university teaching, journalism and television, banking, and large corporations. "Slavic-Americans," he concluded, "are virtually invisible" in these centers of power and influence in the United States.[32]

This judgment accompanied a more profound change in Novak's view of liberalism, which he now described as a manifestation of a class elitism in America. Novak seemed to have first perceived this transformed character of American liberalism in the Kennedy brothers. What he had first seen in the ascendancy of John F. Kennedy was a step away from the heavy moralism, as represented for example by John Foster Dulles, in the Republican party. The New Frontier promised professionalism, the politics of technique, a celebration of the secular city, a respect for the profane and pragmatic that defied the high religious self-righteousness of Anglo-Saxon Republicanism. But the new Democratic party gradually succumbed. The language of moralism slowly crept into its political rhetoric. The civil rights movement, Novak said, became a "moral crusade" in the politicians' descriptions. Democratic party politics,

Novak said, was becoming the politics of guilt, fully writ by the time of the Great Society.[33]

Novak's reference in this paragraph to the New Class was significant as another measure of his changed perspective on liberalism. He began to see, he wrote a few years later, the "profound class interests" behind the new politics. He saw a new generation, born of affluent parents and products of elite universities, young professionals in law, education, and the media, all armed with a resolve that America must be recharged with new progressive programs. It was the familiar politics of uplift, moral improvement, New World destiny. And it was leaving Novak rather cold. It was certainly changing his perspective on the broad democracy of American politics. Compared to the airy moralism and self-serving elitism of the New Class, the commonfolk majority seemed to Novak to embody a higher political realism. Novak wrote, in a manner that recalled his own earlier words: "I found that there were sources of health in American political traditions, and in the democratic majority. . . . I became more hopeful about the democratic majority – those millions with beer cans watching football on television."[34]

Novak's Democratic party loyalties persisted. In 1972 he worked "extremely hard" for George McGovern, and then after the debacle of that year he joined with other dissatisfied Democrats who were opposed to the party's position on affirmative action and its conciliatory foreign policy to form the Coalition for a Democratic Majority. Four years later Novak campaigned for Senator Henry "Scoop" Jackson, almost an ideal politician in Novak's judgment, but after Jackson's failure Novak remained neutral in 1976 while "privately" rooting for Gerald Ford against Jimmy Carter.[35]

Nonetheless, Novak's own transition to conservatism was not quite as ordinary and familiar as these quarrels might indicate. For its more subtle and special aspects we need to look at Novak's book of 1976, *The Joy of Sports*. Here was a work that any sports fan could read with pleasure, but there was enough reflection and special pleading in this volume to make it irresistibly a document on which one could hazard speculations about Novak and the making of a modern conservative.

At least in one respect *Joy of Sports* struck a sympathetic response. Reviewers loved to quote a paragraph from Novak's introduction to the book: "So, in 1973, in my fortieth year, I am riding on the 5:29 from my job in Manhattan to my home in Long Island, one of 90 million workers weary with the Monday blues. It is early September, my birthday is half a week away. The Scotch is swaying restlessly in my paper cup. Suddenly, I remember. Monday night: television. The Dodgers are at Montreal. My spirits lift. Tonight there is a treat."[36]

Joy of Sports, as one might gather, is a book of celebrations. For Novak it was a kind of homecoming, as indeed was *Unmeltable Ethnics.* But this homecoming brought Novak back to a larger community. Indeed it carried him successfully to a discovered national ethic, the world of sports. *Joy of Sports* was the Americanization of Michael Novak.

Nonetheless, this book was not quite as innocent a matter as it might seem. The radical counterculture of the late 1960s and early 1970s had taken the institution of sports head-on. Books and essays by Jack Scott, Chip Oliver, Dave Meggyesy, Bernie Parrish, Leonard Schecter, Robert Lipsyte, and Paul Hoch had collectively placed sport into a capitalist culture in which money brutally exploited the human body. Sport had become a violent mechanization of life under this regime and had created a managerial class and a labor class as adversarial and as piratical in the power structure that resulted as any that had prevailed in the early years of the industrial revolution.

But for Novak such political renderings of sport wholly misconstrued its special qualities. Nor were the radicals alone in their misinterpretations. The whole legacy of American Puritanism, Novak believed, had caused an undervaluing of sport, and Novak thought that a true understanding of the subject might assist the country in "a post-Protestant understanding of itself." For the Protestant norms had raised to suffocating heights the values of seriousness, moral striving, and spiritual preparation for work, and they had transposed these to sport itself. Novak in turn called for a Catholic view of sport as fun, recreation, and escape from seriousness. Only two years before in *Choosing Our King* Novak had written that Americans really did not know how to be happy: "Joy is not our nation's style." Moral Protestants and Marxists had at least this much in common—a confusion of work with reality. Novak enjoyed being perverse. "Play, not work, is the end of life," he wrote. "Play is reality. Work is diversion and escape."[37]

For Novak sport was above all, then, a humanist enterprise. He wanted his readers to see beyond the violence and vain worship that attended a sport like football. These standard disparagements, he said, overreached their mark; they discarded too much. "Football makes conscious to me part of what I am," Novak wrote. And it became for him also a measure of others. "I have never met a person who disliked sports, or who absented himself or herself entirely from them, who did not at the same time seem to me deficient in humanity," he wrote. What Novak missed in such persons was a certain quality of sensitivity, a certain perspective of life that reflected realism, tragedy, and irony. "Such persons seem to me a danger to civilization," Novak added. "I do not on the whole like to work with them. . . . I expect from them a certain softness of mind, from their not having known a certain number of defeats." Sport instructs one that life is as much a matter of chance and fate as of will and rational scheming, Novak argued.[38] Here and there in *Joy of Sports* one found a clear continuity from the Novak of *Unmeltable Ethnics*.

The best sections of *Joy of Sports* were Novak's descriptions of the major sports. Here was Novak as cultural analyst, bringing many suggestive insights to the social and intellectual aspects of baseball, football, and basketball. This was the Novak, too, who relished the variety and pluralism of American life, the Novak of *Unmeltable Ethnics* who had railed against the numbing uniformity of the dominant rationalist forces of American culture. Throwing himself enthusiastically into a box seat, a seat on the first row, or one on the fifty-yard line, Novak became the spectator as student. He described basketball as a jazzlike improvisational movement, a sport that emphasizes feint and deception, suggestive of its ghetto roots.[39] Football, in turn, represented the immigrant myth. Novak described it as the most nonindividualist of the major sports, the most remote from the capitalist virtues as celebrated by the *Wall Street Journal*. In its roughness, its organizational precision and demands for submission to the team function, football, Novak wrote, reflected the ethos of the early labor organizations. Brotherhood was this game's essence.[40]

But in a strangely significant way baseball emerged in *Joy of Sports* as Novak's favorite. What Novak wrote about baseball invites conjecture about *Joy of Sports* in Novak's odyssey from the political Left to the political Right, even about the defense of capitalism that acutely marked that transition.

Novak was a lifelong Dodger fan, and the year that he moved with his family to Stanford he discovered that his car radio could catch the Dodger broadcasts from Los Angeles. So he sneaked out to his garage and was lost to family life during many nights of the baseball season. But Novak knew that he was indulging in an institution that was quintessentially Anglo-American in its attributes. For baseball was first of all the most cerebral and rational of sports—a games of lines, a legalistic game, a perfectly balanced universe of distances and weights. It was furthermore "a game of magnificent self-control, of cool, of passion transmuted into unruffled instinctual perfection." It was even a "Lockean game," a kind of contract theory in which a set of atomic individuals assent to a discipline of limited cooperation in their mutual interest. More than other sports, baseball was a game of fair play, especially with its constraints on body contact.[41]

Baseball was the Anglo-Saxon sport in another way too. It was the sport of individualism. It had little of the organic qualities of football and basketball, their total, fluid integration of individual components, improvisationally or mechanically brought into coordination. Baseball action proceeded from individual to individual as the direction of the ball dictated. Especially in the encounter of pitcher and batter, baseball, Novak maintained, highlighted "the mythic world of the solitary, lone individual." (Somehow Novak overlooked in his book the existential anguish of a singles tennis match!) Baseball was the American folklore as shaped by its Anglo-Saxon imperatives. It celebrated the individual, who is solitary and alone but ultimately a part of a rational social order whose dictates he has internalized by rules, by a litany of procedural and legalistic mandates. The features of Anglo-American life, Novak wrote, "are almost perfectly dramatized in the rules, distribution of positions, and actions of baseball."[42]

Baseball was Novak's access to the larger world of the Anglo-Saxon. From this point on in his writings he was never as harsh on Anglo-American life, its discipline, its rationalized structures, its morality, as he had been in *Unmeltable Ethnics*. The quotation above, in fact, led Novak directly into this paragraph: "*Anyone* can learn to operate within the Anglo-Saxon mythic world; humans everywhere can, and do, imitate and assimilate a mythos not entirely their own. While the spiritual world of baseball, acted out in a public arena, exhibits almost perfectly the myths of the white Anglo-Saxon population that settled the towns, prairies, and southlands of America, all Americans can share in this 'national pastime.' It is a form of Americanization."[43]

Joy of Sports, finally, was both a book of celebration and a book of excesses. Too often it equated the moral and human qualities of the athlete with sport's larger cultural influence, thus giving a special recommendation to the sports fan, the spectator. The overstatement can be explained in part by the fact that *Joy of Sports* was in quest of a larger meaning. Novak meant to establish sport as the national religion—nothing as superficial as a secular religion but the American ethos itself. He looked not only to the symbols of sports but also to the ritualistic aspects of the games themselves, even as they were aspects of a public that made them parts of their everyday awareness and enthusiasm. "Even in our own secular age," Novak wrote, "and for quite sophisticated and agnostic persons, the rituals of sport really work. They do serve a religious function: they meet a deep human hunger, place humans in touch with certain dimly perceived features of human life within the cosmos, and provide an experience of at least a pagan sense of godliness."[44]

One might have expected from a serious Catholic thinker like Novak a more acute demarcation of even the higher spiritual qualities of sport from more authentic religious sentiments. The easy analogies he used between sport and religion deprived religion of its essential qualities of faith, personal redemption, and supernatural dependence. One might concede to Novak a certain authentic Catholic perspective on sport and American life. Novak felt painfully the thinness of symbol and ritual in democratic and Protestant America, a deficiency that, he believed, rendered the social order fragile and vulnerable.

To locate in sport, "the chief communal ritual" of this secular society, the staying and cohesive ceremonial power of the nation Novak believed entirely legitimate.[45]

This consideration even gave to *Joy of Sports* a certain Burkean flavor. Perhaps it reflected Novak's recoil from the divisiveness of sectarian radical politics. Perhaps it tapped a deeply felt need for a theme of continuity, a basis of a public philosophy in American life, a location for an organic society. All these would be legitimate and traditional conservative habits. But they are also conservatism's great temptation. Novak was positing an easy and low road to conservatism. Do we indeed descend to meet, as Irving Babbitt feared? Was the United States to find its commonality as a nation of spectators, worshiping high-paid gladiators? The Burkean ideal in Novak too quickly became a meretricious conservatism.

A reconciliation of far greater import, however, was taking place in Novak in the late 1970s, one that passed beyond mere accommodation to become a sustained defense – in books and essays – of American capitalism. Moving from Left to Right, Novak spent little time in the center. His defense of capitalism would make Novak very much a thinker in the neoconservative mode and a standout among those conservative intellectuals who spoke from a Catholic podium. In this way Novak's later writings became something more than reflections on contemporary history. Centuries of experience and tradition had to be addressed. Once again Novak set out to confront the legacy of antiquity.

Here again was another element of continuity in Novak's transition. When he wrote *The Spirit of Democratic Capitalism,* published in 1982, Novak recalled the years he spent studying for the priesthood. He had become convinced, he said, that the historical clash of Catholicism and modernity had been overblown and mostly unnecessary. Like Catholic liberals before him, Novak believed that ideals of democracy and respect for human rights were rooted in Catholic teachings and that they justified a social and political progressivism on the part of the Church and lay Catholics.[46] *The Open Church,* we have seen, elaborated Novak's extensive plea for Catholicism's opening to the world. Vatican II seemed to be a harbinger of great promises imminently to be fulfilled.

Catholic traditionalism, Novak said, had meant a hostility to the spirit of capitalism, which it dismissed as materialist, secular, and dangerous to religion. For a long time Novak reflected the influence of Catholic writers like Charles Péguy who stressed in socialism a morality superior to that of capitalism, "a kind of political religion," as Novak called it, that preserved a Christian ethic in conformity with the Church's judgments against capitalism's materialist individualism. Insofar as it clung to these perspectives, Novak believed, Catholic teaching on economics became increasingly unmodern and irrelevant. He concluded sadly in 1982 that the Church "has little to say about markets and incentives, the ethics of production, and their habits, disciplines, and organization necessary for the creation of wealth." The "open Church" now took on for Novak an urgent meaning, distinctively different from its message of two decades previously.[47]

Novak specifically disavowed in *Democratic Capitalism* that he intended to defend capitalism in strictly theological terms. Christian teaching, he averred, sanctioned no specific form of worldly political or economic arrangement. But he had become convinced that human behavior in the marketplace always raised questions of ethics, intellect, and human aspirations that cried out for consideration under theological teachings. The point he stressed especially was that capitalism had been neglected by religious thinkers, particularly in relation to its historical connection to democratic institutions and their spiritual significance.[48]

Novak wished above all to strip capitalism of Catholic prejudices that lay so heavily upon it. Economics, he insisted, must be considered for the spiritual qualities that attend it. And the creation of wealth was above all a spiritual enterprise. For the work that feeds the world and facilitates life, leisure, and art, Novak wrote, is a factor of insight and imagination, healthy mental discipline, capacity for organization and cooperation with others, and a general ideal of human improvement. In *Freedom with Justice,* a book of 1984 in which he exclusively addressed Catholic teachings on social issues, Novak wrote that "the *cause* of the wealth of nations is chiefly the human spirit, focused in a creative and productive way."[49] Nor is the moral ethos of democratic capitalism a materialist one, he believed. Novak had become enamored of the bourgeois ethic that nourished democratic capitalism. He located in it the source of the self-discipline that makes intelligence and its application possible. It resisted hedonism in its cautious and calculating concerns for future enjoyments. For Novak these qualities approximated authentic religious ones and must be incorporated into any useful anthology of Christian teachings about modern life.[50]

Novak meant to make his case for democratic capitalism comprehensive, and he did so. *The Spirit of Democratic Capitalism* offered readers three hundred fifty pages of statistical data and intellectual analysis, moral reflections and historical examples. Even a brief summary of its multifaceted defense would take us into a very extended analysis. What does command our attention briefly, at least, are certain themes that mark important changes in Novak's perspective.

The book above all made a labored effort to associate capitalism with democratic political institutions. "Political democracy," Novak wrote, "is compatible in practice only with a market economy." History, he said, so far provided no instances of dictatorial socialist states becoming democratic. (Novak conceded that authoritarian countries like Brazil could coexist with free markets, but the situation of this and other South American countries raised special questions that he dealt with in other works, as we will observe.)[51] The recourse to capitalist standards was also removing from Novak some of the social prejudices that animated his earlier writings. He was no longer looking at the wealthy classes of the United States as a privileged ethnic group, the dominant Anglo-Saxons who exercised a social control derived from an impersonal rationalist culture. *The Spirit of Democratic Capitalism* now praised wealth and its wielders for their inestimable social contribution, above all in the manner by which their habits promoted a vital, pluralist culture in America.[52]

The old mood of *Unmeltable Ethnics* was fading considerably in Novak, and the pull of democratic capitalism explains why. The Novak of the early 1970s denounced the economic order in America for its impersonal character and cast his lot with the rich emotional culture of the white ethnics for surcease from the chilling effects of Anglo-Saxon and corporate America. But the later Novak was attempting to meet the charges of capitalism's critics, those among them who likewise recoiled from the horrors of a money culture. Novak conceded the obvious abuse that money brings, but he now hailed it for its moral neutrality. It is the unbiased medium, he said, indifferent to the privileges of rank, inheritance, class, or national identity. The dominance of a money economy, Novak wrote, "opens the political economy to men of every class, race, and creed." Here was incarnation of the spirit of Alexander Hamilton in his revolt against the provincial bastions of local privilege in the years of the new republic. But now the capitalist ethic of money and its moral neutrality seemed to be voicing over the once-powerful tongue that had earlier spoken for America's provincial enclaves.[53]

By this time Novak was embroiled in debate with a visible Catholic Left, one that he now understood to be the by-product of Vatican II. He still believed that much good had come of the church reforms, but Vatican II, it was now clear to him, had initiated a process that could not wind down. Vatican II produced new religious leaders, he said, who aspired to be the avant-garde of the Church. They wanted a new "dialogue" in the Church. They sanctioned their causes by invoking the new postures of "dissent," "witness," and "prophetic" outcry. But the little window by which Pope John XXIII had let fresh air into the Church blew in more than the Holy Spirit, Novak feared. When Novak wrote *Confession of a Catholic* in 1983, he had cause to question the "ideology of openness" and the "new libertinism" it had fashioned. Novak attacked the speciousness and trendiness of radical Catholics, and he would not allot them any measure of moral courage. He recalled comments once made by G. K. Chesterton as suitable to the present occasion: "We often read nowadays of the valor of audacity with which some rebel attacks a hoary tyranny or an antiquated superstition. There is not really any courage at all in attacking hoary or antiquated things, any more than in offering to fight one's grandmother." Added Novak: "Pity the defender of orthodoxy."[54]

What was actually emerging in Novak's recoil from leftist politics and Catholic reformism was an ethic of normality. The term seems to fit as a general description of Novak's views on a number of issues, both religious and social. His style became familiarly neoconservative: it embraced a bourgeois moral standard, it renounced all utopian idealism, and it celebrated the merits of capitalism while seeking to solve the problem of its cultural contradictions.

Joy of Sports augured a drift in Novak toward middle-class norms in America, and one focus of his new priority became the family. This concern had earlier made Novak a celebrant of white ethnicity and the familial and kinship ties that constituted its richer humanity. But now he assumed a fortress mentality in his defense of the family. Novak imagined an institution besieged by the new morality, the new openness, and the militancy that accompanied the movements for changed sexual relationships in the United States. There were large symbolic issues, for the Church and public life, in the issue of "gay liberation," Novak warned. Novak said that he welcomed greater tolerance of homosexuals without their being granted any moral sanction. Homosexuals, he wrote, exempt themselves from life's necessary and enriching relationships, those with the opposite sex, and the kind of human communication that those relationships involve. Human fulfillment does not necessarily depend on being heterosexual, or on being married, Novak insisted. "But the marital ideal nourishes every other ideal we have."[55] As for the Catholic Church, it should welcome homosexuals as it welcomes all sinners, but it has no obligation to acknowledge the demands of gay groups or to accept their way of life. Nor, for that matter, must the state, Novak wrote, obligate itself to accept these demands through civil rights legislation. The issue was above all symbolic, he wrote, affecting our whole understanding of sexuality. Novak adhered to the Church position that sexuality had validity for human life only in the context of the family and the "harmony" of the two sexes. What Novak perceived in all libertarian sexual ethics—homosexual or otherwise—was a dangerously experimental attitude. "Sexuality," he wrote, "ought not to be 'open,' unconfined, manipulable by individual human will."[56]

As we have seen, Novak had never conjoined his radical politics with the leftist program of sexual liberation, and his strictures against homosexuals were evident well before his political conservatism. But his changing political views did give Novak a wider perspective on this subject. Novak believed he was viewing a society progressively loosed from all meaningful constraints, and he located this dissolution, as did other neoconservatives, in the ascendancy of a radical, utopian imagination that had charged American thought and heated American emotions in the late 1960s. The utopian imagination, Novak believed, had unsettled every stable and traditional aspect of American life, but now, as always, its first victim was the family. For the constraints of matrimony and child-rearing, he believed, run up against every scheme of moral perfection or individual self-fulfillment that motivates the utopian mind. The radical mood, as Novak saw it, had succumbed to an experimentalism that defined no limits and was denoted by a manifest air of unreality. For Novak the ethic of normality had become the principle of realism, and the principle of realism helped make of Novak a vociferous exponent of democratic capitalism.[57]

"The seminal thinkers who set democratic capitalism upon its historical course," Novak wrote, "were exceedingly practical men, thoroughly absorbed by the human capacity for sin and illusion." The juxtaposition of this pragmatic realism with the life of democratic capitalism was for Novak absolutely critical. Of all systems, democratic capitalism, producing as it does a highly successful commercial life, demands a realist and not a utopian view of human nature. But that judgment inspired another conclusion. "A commercial system," Novak wrote, "needs taming and correction by a moral-cultural system independent of commerce."[58] Here was an interesting situation. Novak had witnessed a historical period of excess and was now looking for principles of order and stability, the ethic of normality that would supply the necessary corrective. But while he was clearly convinced of the economic superiority of capitalism and had come to realize its spiritual qualities too, he recognized in capitalism its own dangerous excesses, its own inherent tendency to yield a population accustomed to affluence and little able to prevent that affluence from becoming a species of self-indulgence or hedonism.

Novak's remarks speak to the dominant theme in neoconservatism. "The success of democratic capitalism in producing prosperity and liberty," Novak wrote, "is its own greatest danger. The virtues required to 'increase the wealth of nations' are less easily observed once wealth is obtained. Parents brought up under poverty do not know how to bring their children up under affluence." For other neoconservatives like Irving Kristol, the capitalist ethic had once included the bourgeois ethic as a part of its identity. Novak differed in his view to the extent that he saw capitalism as always needing, and usually having, a religious and moral code imposed on it from without. In any case, he wrote, the commercial virtues were not sufficient to their own defense.[59]

When Novak came, then, to describe a theology of democratic capitalism, he wanted a viable medium between the excesses of utopian reformism and the excesses of an unrestrained individualism. A chapter in *The Spirit of Democratic Capitalism* was titled "From Marxism to Democratic Capitalism," and it dealt with the intellectual career of Reinhold Niebuhr, who continued to define for Novak the safest route through both of the extremes he feared. The Niebuhrian perspective also informed Novak's concluding effort to suggest what a theology of capitalism would entail. He listed six points of that description, and one, his understanding of the Incarnation, is especially germane to this discussion, since it indicates Novak's concern for a metaphysics of realism against the destructive course of the utopian imagination.

Christians who know and accept the true meaning of the Incarnation, Novak said, must disavow the whole tradition of utopian socialism. For the Incarnation informs us first that God entered the world as flesh and walked among human beings as man. "He accepted for Himself the human condition, including the world it might offer." God did not send legions of angels with Christ to save the world. Christ brought a message of hope, not of utopia. However persistently some Christians have tried to derive a larger promise from the Incarnation and to make it the means of deliverance from all constraints of human evil, they have really misread its meaning, said Novak. "The point of the Incarnation," Novak declared, "is to respect the world as it is, to acknowledge its limits, to recognize its weaknesses, irrationalities, and evil forces, and to disbelieve any promises that the world is now or ever will be transformed into the 'City of God.' " In the Christian conceit that the salvation brought by Christ had somehow changed human nature, Novak perceived the rationale of reformers and the destruction wrought by their zeal. Novak felt compelled to add: "The pure fury of reformers can kill. Those who claim enlightened virtue often carry unexamined viciousness in their hearts."[60] There always lingered in Novak a residual spirit of *Unmeltable Ethnics.*

But there lingered less of it—unquestionably. When Peter Steinfels reviewed Novak's book, he wrote that "it is not too much to say that *The Spirit of Democratic Capitalism* marks the intellectual, if not the social, assimilation of Michael Novak into the world and the worldview he had previously identified with the WASP establishment and the corporate, professional, and intellectual managers of both right and left." For were not capitalism, liberalism, and democracy the achievements of the Protestant and northern European races, and did not Americans once fear the corrupt despotisms of Catholic southern and eastern Europe? Steinfels took no stock in these old myths but believed that Novak had fallen unknowingly into them.[61]

In 1978 Novak became a resident scholar at the American Enterprise Institute in Washington and religion editor at *National Review*. He was nationally visible as a prominent conservative thinker whose views on a great number of issues appeared in a rapid succession of books and essays, many of them published under the auspices of AEI. Novak described himself in 1982 as "a life-long Democrat."[62] But like many other "lifelong Democrats," Novak came out strongly for Ronald Reagan in the presidential campaign of 1980. Concurrently, his views on foreign policy were becoming militantly anti-Soviet. Communism assumed in his mind a monolithic character. Novak's writings helped to elaborate the neoconservative differentiation between totalitarian and authoritarian governments, although their author continued to embrace human rights priorities. In an essay for *Commonweal* in October 1980, Novak defended his "switch" to Reagan. Most of the reasons he gave were related to one issue—foreign policy of the United States.

In the 1980s nearly every public issue that Novak confronted proved in turn to be a Catholic issue. This situation was unavoidably so in the matter of foreign policy.[63] In 1983, in the first of two documents that marked the controversial involvement of the American Catholic bishops in public policy considerations, a pastoral letter on war and peace emerged from prolonged discussion by the bishops on the subject of nuclear weapons. Titled *The Challenge of Peace: God's Promise and Our Response,* the document was actually the third and final formulation by the bishops on this subject. The prior two drafts, on which the bishops had invited open discussion and criticism, were clearly more pacifist in expression.

Nonetheless, there was plenty to invite further reaction. The bishops declared their support for "immediate, bilateral, verifiable agreements to halt the testing of nuclear weapons."[64] With extensive biblical citations, the bishops emphasized the primacy of forgiveness and love in the teachings of Christ and stressed that Jesus "refused to defend himself with force or violence."[65] The document committed the bishops to the support of human rights throughout the world, calling American adherence to these rights the "acid test" of "our democratic values." But the pastoral letter was not a one-sided statement for pacifism, nor was it morally neutral in its view of the world powers. Americans, the bishops said, need "have no illusions" about the true despotic character of the Soviet Union and its Warsaw Pact allies. They granted to the democratic nations of NATO a moral superiority over totalitarian and tyrannical regimes

that suppressed human rights.[66] Also, the bishops disavowed any utopianism
in their views of world affairs and conceded that national defense is a legitimate
consideration and that "force, even deadly force, is sometimes justified."[67]
Nonetheless, peace, as message and policy, dominated the pastoral letter as
the preeminent concern of the bishops.

The Challenge of Peace made headline news. It added to a host of other
issues, from abortion to the role of women in the Church, that were making
Catholicism an embattled institution. To many, this document seemed to place
the Catholic Church in the United States decidedly on the political Left. It
made only passing judgments against the evils of totalitarian communism
and staked out an ultimately conciliatory position toward the enemies of the
United States. From the beginning of the bishops' discussions, a group of
lay Catholics organized to present an alternative view on peace and nuclear
weapons and to press the bishops for revisions of the original text. The outcome
of their efforts was a lengthy essay, published as a small book, written by
Michael Novak. The piece contained an appended list of 114 cosigners, including William J. Bennett (later secretary of education in the Reagan administration), William F. Buckley, Jr., Michael Joyce (then of the John M. Olin
Foundation), Clare Boothe Luce, Henry Regnery, Stephen Tonsor, and William Simon. The essay, *Moral Clarity in the Nuclear Age* (1983), first appeared
in Novak's new journal, *Catholicism in Crisis,* and then became the subject
of an entire issue of *National Review.* Two Republican senators placed the
text in the *Congressional Record.*

Moral Clarity rested on the dominant theme that there is really only one
threat to peace in the world—communism. Part of the essay was a statistical
demonstration of the dramatic acceleration of the Soviet Union's military program over the past fifteen years, to the point that "the nuclear initiative has
passed into Soviet hands." Novak repeated arguments that had become visible
in his recent writings. He stated that the West did not depend for the success
of its ideology on the destruction of socialism, whereas by contrast the Soviets
were propelled by their Marxist-Leninist view of history to secure the destruction of capitalism.[68]

Novak also pleaded for the legitimacy of nuclear weapons. The depicted
horrors of a nuclear nightmare, Novak believed, had obscured the "pacific"
effects of nuclear weapons, which in fact had probably forestalled war by
conventional weaponry that might otherwise have occurred in the absence
of this overriding threat. In fact, "deterrence," a principle that the bishops
had not discredited, became the main burden of Novak's essay.[69]

Novak was defining a kind of neoconservative Christianity. His essay on
pacifism and the Church, in fact, remarkably parallels Irving Kristol's essay

on the rabbinic and gnostic tendencies in Judaism and Christianity.[70] Novak identified two strands in Christianity. One he called the sectarian, denoted by the aspiration to live apart from the world in order to realize as fully as possible the transforming power of the Gospels, a state of holiness and purity. The incarnationist strand of Christianity, by contrast, places the religious in the world, amid its historical structures, to act as leaven in dough for the gradual moral improvement of the world. The pacifist, Novak wrote, invariably falls to the contradictory ways of the sectarian. To the extent that the world fails to make itself a corresponding model of his own moral purity, the pacifist reacts violently against it, in judgment or in action. "Beginning by renouncing arms," wrote Novak, "such perfectionists end up brandishing arms with fierce righteousness, forgiving neither self nor others."[71]

One has to ask whether neoconservatives like Novak made their assessments too categorically. Could one not have said of pacifists, for example, that instead of shrouding the world in a veil of innocence they in fact judged it as entirely evil? Pessimism as much as sentimentalism described their perceptions. They maintained a despairing cynicism so deep that it forsook any hope of managing, by politics, reasoning and compromise, or pragmatism and expediency, the awesome challenge of coping with the fact of contemporary history's great menacing evil, nuclear weaponry.

Novak's writings on Catholic issues in the 1980s remained highly diverse, and he continued to be a conservative of eclectic interests. He also became a conservative of emphatic neoconservative views. But this duality of characteristics gave Novak his special place in the conservative intellectual movement. Almost everything he was now writing strained to demonstrate the necessary alliance of Catholic thought and teaching with the values of democratic capitalism. Novak's achievement was a significant reconciliation, but even conservatives might judge that there were some losses along the way.[72]

None knew better than Novak that his attempted rapprochement of the modernity of democratic capitalism with the antiquity of the Catholic Church was an imposing task. How strangely uncomfortable a challenge for a conservative! Everywhere he looked Novak saw the imposition of history and tradition on Catholicism. Novak now would endeavor to show, in a variety of ways, that the Church's traditions were paradoxically the foundations of its increasingly leftward drift in the 1980s, especially in the phenomenon that he confronted in several essays and a substantial book – the phenomenon of liberation theology.

The problem, however, was a stubbornly Catholic one. "The fondest memories of the Catholic church," Novak wrote, "seem to reside in the humble charity of rural life, recalling the days when even major cities were small in scale, and run by guilds. Still today such images haunt the Catholic imagination." When the Church considers the conditions of the laborer, he said, it sees an artisan or peasant and fails to observe that most of the world's workers are in some aspect of commerce.[73] But the virtues of commerce, which Novak by now had come to associate specifically with democratic capitalism, were precisely those virtues that the Catholic Church had never in its history given a proper theological examination. They seemed always to have a prejudicial place in the religious language of the Church, even to the extent that Catholicism had made itself irrelevant to much of the shaping forces of modern history.[74] In the United States of the 1980s Novak was observing the legacy of that unfortunate fact.

Novak had never been in march step with the Catholic Church in the United States, but only in 1975 did he make a break that showed his opposition from the conservative side. In that year he wrote a "Farewell" editorial and resigned from *Commonweal*. Even in 1975, though, Novak's conservatism expressed itself mostly as a loyalty to traditional worship forms in Catholicism, and he now measured negatively his own earlier enthusiasm for the "open Church." But by the end of the decade, Novak's opposition was clearly political. The American bishops' pastoral letter changed him into a lay leader working against a perceived pacifist tone among the clerics. And in 1982 Novak assumed another leadership role in launching a new publication, *Catholicism in Crisis: A Journal of Lay Catholic Opinion*.

The opening editorial of *Catholicism in Crisis* expressed indignation at the growing political activity of the Catholic officialdom of the United States and the assumption of political wisdom claimed by the clerics. "More and more often," wrote the editors, "priests and bishops make political, economic, and social pronouncements about the temporal order, to which the laity is expected solely to react." Words like "prophecy" and "witness," that derive from the Church's authentic religious assignments, now have been employed for partisan political views, the editors added, and "are less and less used of authentic faith and practice." By "partisan," of course, the editors meant leftist, and they found in this appropriation of political exercise on the part of the clergy a species of "hubris."[75]

There was more to come from the bishops. In November 1986 the National Conference of Catholic Bishops in the United States approved a lengthy document titled *Economic Justice for All: Catholic Social Teaching and the U.S. Economy*. The central concern of the bishops was the poor, and the poor constituted the exclusive priority of *Economic Justice*. The publication, as one might expect, cited scriptural sources abundantly and supplemented these texts by papal writings and academic studies. The weight of biblical teachings, the bishops said, provided the basis for the "preferential option for the poor," and they added that as a nation "we are called to make a fundamental 'option for the poor.' " Economic policy "should be specifically directed to benefit those who are poor or economically insecure." Under this consideration, they added, it must be concluded that people have a "right" to employment.[76]

Novak had a number of quarrels with the pastoral letter. He faulted it on misuse of papal writings, especially in its claim that John XXIII's *Pacem in Terris* gave a Catholic endorsement to "economic rights" — food, clothing, shelter, and medical care. Rather, said Novak, the pope meant by this term the right to economic initiative and enterprise and the right to humane working conditions. Novak further rejected any notion that such "economic rights" as may be bestowed by the state can have any parallel status with the political and intellectual freedoms assured by the American Bill of Rights and the Constitution.[77] But perhaps most surprising was Novak's attempt to undermine the bishops in their major support, the Bible itself. Wrote Novak: "Another great weakness in the second draft is its treatment of biblical texts. It is not enough to recount what the Bible said in a pre-democratic, pre-growth, pre-capitalist era. It is also necessary to show how the themes of the Bible, reflected on over centuries, have led to the invention of a political economy such as that of the United States."[78]

Now this exhortation shows as much as anything the extent of Novak's effort to merge Christian teaching with American capitalism. A biblical literalism, he believed, yielded little useful wisdom. Novak had become a liberal Christian, if one means by that designation one concerned mostly with the spirit of the Christian message and its evolution in history. Novak sought to enhance his message by giving his Christianity a dynamic and progressive quality, even a modernist one, by making it forward-looking and anticipatory, rather than orthodox and retrospective. On this basis, Novak could argue that the Bible contains ideas "decisive in the invention of the U.S. political economy." The Founding Fathers, he believed, had placed their ideas in useful juxtaposition to these biblical imperatives. The doctrine of original sin led to the political formulation of checks and balances in the political and economic arena; the vocation of human beings to become images of God the Creator sanctioned invention, enterprise, and the betterment of humanity through worldly activity; and the ideal of voluntary and energetic association established the principle of community appropriate for the modern business world.[79]

If there seemed to be something urgent in Novak's forging of the dual kingdom of Christianity and capitalism, then it was partly because a new challenge had emerged, one more potentially serious than the American bishops' interpretation of Catholic social thought. The larger challenge was "liberation theology." The new movement was one of the most potent expressions of anticapitalist ideology in the 1970s and 1980s, embracing a class view of society, denouncing the evils of private property, and above all expressing a Christian and Marxist solidarity with the oppressed of the world, all of whom defined for the liberation theologians the marked victims of the dominant economic powers of the North, the United States most conspicuously.

Exponents of the view, of course, would claim that liberation theology was as ancient as Christianity itself, indeed that it was Christianity's essential message. But its name emerged in the late 1960s. At the Conference of Latin American Bishops meeting in Medellín, Colombia, in 1968, some of the essential sentiments and ideas of liberation theology appeared and drew attention to a rising tide of revolutionary ideology among certain Catholic thinkers. A substantial literature of the new movement appeared in the 1970s: Gustavo Gutiérrez, *A Theology of Liberation;* Juan Luis Segundo, *A Theology for Artisans of a New Humanity* (five volumes); José Míguez Bonino, *Christians and Marxists: The Mutual Challenge to Revolution;* Hugo Assmann, *Theology for a Nomad Church;* and José Miranda, *Communism in the Bible* and *Marx and the Bible,* among others. Despite the preponderance of Latin American writers in the literature of the theology, the liberationists were winning a substantial audience in the United States, the Peruvian Gutiérrez especially. Orbis Press of the Maryknoll Sisters was producing a prodigious amount of liberation tracts, and its publication list indicated a main focus on Latin America.

But liberation theology aside, Latin America was attaining a special focus in the attention of the American public. The dramatic successes of the Sandinista revolutionaries in their 1979 overthrow of a reactionary regime in Nicaragua, one headed by the dictator Anastasio Somoza, had again highlighted the subject of American policy in that region of the world. Furthermore, Nicaragua, with South Africa several years later, provided a regenerating force in the American Left. Cuba had suffered embarrassments, and the horrors of Cambodia and Vietnam after the American departure mocked the once-boastful claims of many in the American Left that all good, and all progress, lay with the heroic fighters against American "imperialism" in the Far East.

Father Miguel d'Escoto, once the director of communications at Maryknoll, became the foreign minister of Nicaragua when the Sandinistas took power. The connection indicated to Novak the special significance of liberation theology to the history and fate of Latin America, the subject that became Novak's overriding interest in the middle 1980s. Novak expressed hostility against the corrupt and oppressive course taken by the Communist regime in Nicaragua.[80] But Novak was especially disturbed that Catholic opinion in America, as witnessed, for example, by the *National Catholic Reporter,* so uncritically accepted the propaganda of the Sandinistas and their interpretations of events in Nicaragua.

For Novak, liberation theology reflected all the traditional shortcomings of Roman Catholic thought. But for that reason, he knew, it had a compelling appeal to the Latin American mind and even superficially to many Catholics generally. Liberation theology, he believed, authentically reflected the characteristics of an institution born of feudalism. Its meaning of "class struggle" was located within the Latin American social context of peasants posed against wealthy landowners, supported in turn by entrenched state power. Liberation theology was to this degree several steps removed from traditional Marxism, which was a product of nineteenth-century capitalism. It situated itself geographically where a strong middle-class social ethic had never flourished, where no traditions of democracy, pragmatism, or consensus politics existed, and where an upper class unredeemed by any spirit of social largess exercised power. Both liberation theology and traditional Catholic teaching, however "conservative" by tradition the latter may have been, held a crucial commonality, Novak believed. Both had been ignorant of the ethos on which a free, capitalist democracy is based, the virtues of the commercial and industrial life. (This fact, said Novak, shows in the extent to which Catholic countries traditionally lag behind others in economic growth.) "Liberation theology, alas," Novak wrote, "intensifies the weakest features of the [Catholic] tradition."[81]

In 1987 Novak published *Will It Liberate? Questions about Liberation Theology.* Novak addressed a vast literature of Christian theology by writing a book heavy with economic statistics. In fact, *Will It Liberate?* directly supplemented *The Spirit of Democratic Capitalism* more than it answered a radical theology by a countervailing religious viewpoint. *Will It Liberate?* was also a book about Latin America—its economic life, its political structures, its culture. It was one of Novak's best books, fortified by a wealth of information in these categories, and it offered one of the strongest pieces in the substantial literature of capitalist apologetics in the neoconservative repertoire.

Novak advanced his main thesis early in the book. "Liberation theology," he wrote, "says that Latin America is capitalist and needs a socialist revolution. Latin America does need a revolution. But its present system is mercantilist and quasi-feudal, not capitalist, and the revolution it needs is both liberal and Catholic." Liberation theologians, Novak believed, had profoundly misconstrued the problems facing Latin America. His book almost delighted to illustrate, in examples drawn from Mexico to Peru, the situations that hindered

economic progress in the South. These were problems of massive state
bureaucracy, interfering with the economic system at every turn, throwing
up impossible hindrances to business initiative, invention, and creative enterprise. The obstacles to progress and social justice, Novak wrote, approximated
in no meaningful way the traditional leftist portrayal of powerful, privately
owned cartels and monopolies. To the contrary, he said, in Latin America
the state owned or directly controlled the major means of production. The
powerful elites that rule in Latin American nations, Novak argued, know
nothing of risk ventures that typify capitalist growth. They hide behind protective privileges of the law, and they preside over an anachronistic system
that prevents any opening to the poor, any possibility of ambition and initiative
preparing the way for improvements for the long-oppressed people of the
continent. When the capitalist revolution that alone can assure progress in
Latin America does arrive, Novak promised, it will be a revolution against
"entrenched privilege and old hereditary elites."[82]

Novak could account for the persistent vagueness of liberation theology – its
lack of empirical analysis, its recourse to abstract language and simple
sentiments – by only a persistent habit of the Catholic mentality. "In my view,"
he wrote, "socialism in its various forms is a type of nostalgia, looking back-
ward toward a medieval sense of community and the organic, cooperative
society of an earlier period of history." Such a condition furthermore created
what Novak called "the Constantinian temptation." A planned society based
on socialist controls offered to radical church leaders the prospects of imposing
their moral systems on the rest of society through a special partnership with
the state. The worst mistake in any approach to understanding liberation theology would be to confuse its humanitarian surface with its inner drive for
power.[83] Ultimately, then, Novak judged liberation ideology by a neoconservative refusal to concede the pretensions of moral superiority to enemies on
the Left.

Where, finally, did Novak belong in the conservative intellectual spectrum
of the 1970s and 1980s? In the earlier decade, as he retreated increasingly
from his once-perfervid radicalism and as the label "neoconservatism" gained
in currency, Novak insisted that his views were best described as "neoliberal."
But in the 1980s some politicians and writers, most of them associated with
the Democratic party, began to use "neoliberalism" to describe a more centrist
ideology for their party. Presidential candidate Gary Hart of Colorado in
particular became identified with neoliberalism in 1984. The term had clearly
diminishing value and meaning for Novak as he was writing that year in

support of Ronald Reagan. Novak therefore accepted the neoconservative identification.[84]

And well he might. Novak was best described as an emphatic neoconservative with a slight Roman Catholic difference. Why was this so? It was so because on four critical assumptions, ideological principles, or modes of understanding history, Novak elaborated ideas that describe a neoconservative position.

First, Novak shared and extended the neoconservative belief that the menacing forces of modern history derive from the aggressive utopian and gnostic movements that seek the total transformation of human society by imposition on it of some overriding, abstract moral ideal or political ideology. Novak, from the time he outlined his view in *Unmeltable Ethnics,* registered a skeptic's distaste and fear of such movements. From the perspective of his Catholic and Slavic identification, Novak easily equated these forces in American history with the cultural tradition of Puritanism, its intolerance, its hegemonic moralism, and its recourse to the state as the vehicle for the exercise of the dominant will of its reforming zealots. Increasingly Novak perceived these imperial tendencies as the driving forces behind various movements on the Left. Not surprisingly, therefore, in studying liberation theology Novak saw a red flag when he came across a passage by Juan Luis Segundo in a 1974 essay. In attempting to identify the common core of the various expressions of liberation theology, Segundo wrote: "There is something common and basic for all of them—the view that men, on a political as well as an individual basis, construct the Kingdom of God within history now." In this line alone Novak could see the utter estrangement of liberation theology from the language and pragmatic style of democratic capitalism.[85]

Second, Novak shared with neoconservatism its preference for liberty and inequality over egalitarianism. Many neoconservatives had marked liberalism's shift in America from equality of opportunity to equality of results as their own point of departure in the 1970s. Often the tendency of this shift as much as the actual consequences, dangerous as these indeed were perceived to be, disturbed neoconservatives. For Novak, when liberalism moved in that direction it began to take on the essential character of socialism. Socialism, he wrote, is moved by its intolerance of the economic liberties that are rooted in individual will and of the differences of economic well-being that will inevitably result from these freedoms. Neoconservatives not only resented the corrective measures that the Left takes to overrule these differences by an agenda of state action, but they also shared with older conservatives a thoroughgoing distaste for the society of programmed equality or uniformity. Novak in this criticism remained true to the spirit, the plea for variety and differentiation, of *Unmeltable Ethnics:* "Since it is not natural for human beings blindly to accept economic uniformity, socialism must contrive by all available means to suppress an innate hunger for individualization. This necessarily accounts for the drabness, grayness, and uniformity in every known socialist regime."[86]

Third, there persisted in neoconservatism, in a manner that some might find curious, paradoxical, or even contradictory, a democratic and populist strand that yet coexisted with its anti-egalitarianism. Novak shared both these prejudices. But the apparent contradiction dissolves somewhat when we recognize that neoconservatives located egalitarianism in an elite of liberal professionals, intellectuals, journalists, and public bureaucrats whose power and influence, they believed, stood square against the democratic will of the majority of Americans. Novak himself was as convinced as any neoconservative that a New Class had come into power in the United States since World War II and that this class had a privileged and interested connection to government and was, particularly in its connection with the media, a major countercultural influence in the United States. However weak in its analysis was the neoconservative depiction of the New Class, the neoconservative expression of a democratic populism was not lacking in merit in an era when bureaucratic decision-making easily and often arrogantly circumvented the popular will and its often-greater measure of common sense. Of all the neoconservatives, Novak came earliest to this kind of populism, and it marks a point of continuity between *Unmeltable Ethnics,* and his endorsement of Ronald Reagan's presidency. Novak's own judgment of Reagan as an individual amplified neoconservative populism: "He is not as sophisticated as some with graduate school training, but on his feet he thinks as quickly as, and with greater common sense, clarity, and humor than, the two pietists [Jimmy Carter and John B. Anderson] with whom he is competing for our votes. He has faced relentless heavy weather from the more sophisticated parts of our population. This, too, endears him to me."[87]

Fourth and finally, Novak took his part in the rehabilitation of bourgeois values by the neoconservatives. He did so out of the standard neoconservative concern that the economic success of the capitalist system, so ardently defended by neoconservatives, had greatly jeopardized itself by fostering a hedonism and self-indulgence, materialist and emotional, that undermined the morals and virtues, the bourgeois ethic, in short, that made capitalism legitimate. To this extent, Novak's essay of 1981 "In Praise of Bourgeois Virtues" is one of his most significant.[88]

Although these four identities conjoined Novak to neoconservatism, I have nonetheless stressed that his was a neoconservatism with a difference—a Catholic difference. Of course, the Catholic presence had been a visible, even an essential, component of the Old Right intellectual conservatism, in both its Roman and Anglican expressions.[89] But Novak's Catholicism was not pictured with high Gothic forms and ritualistic church worship. It did not offer itself effectively as the rock of tradition and stability in a world loosed from its cultural moorings. Nor in fact did it place itself in the tradition of such Catholic thinkers as Orestes Brownson and Jacques Maritain, who would fortify democracy, its liberties and rights, by invoking a Catholic tradition of natural law. The democratic capitalism of Michael Novak, which he endeavored so strenuously to bring the Catholic Church to acknowledge and appreciate, grew from a different intellectual tradition altogether. Its values were pragmatic ones: it shunned intellectual absolutes and ideologies; it honored compromise, adjustment, and adaptation and focused its attention on the contemporary. But for all these habits and ideals, democratic capitalism, Novak believed, needed something else if it aspired to be more than merely mundane, merely individualist, and merely functional. Thus, Novak had ultimately to conclude, the alienation of democratic liberalism and Roman Catholicism was a historical tragedy for the West. "Liberalism," Novak wrote, "needed the Catholic sense of community, of transcendence, of realism, of irony, of evil. And Catholicism needed the institutions of liberalism for the incarnation in society of its own vision of the dignity of the human person, of the indispensable role of free associations, and of the limited state respectful of the rights of conscience."[90]

Novak's Catholic voice persisted in another way. In his years on the Left Novak had resented, in the more strident voices of radical politics, the disparagement expressed toward the "pigs" and the "hard hats," those patriotic and law-abiding loyalists of the working classes.[91] Later, as a conservative, Novak was pained that the conservative writers of the 1970s and 1980s, with the significant exception of some Jewish and Catholic conservatives, had neglected the working classes, or, specifically, the labor unions. It was a dangerous oversight, Novak warned. "Laboring people," he wrote, tend to be "family people, oriented toward 'conservative' social and moral values, and profoundly realistic both about power politics in the world and about the deceptive illusions of totalitarian ideologies." The Republican party especially had unexploited advantages here, Novak urged, and he set the social ethic of the unions against that of the New Class and its affinities for the Democratic party. Here Novak articulated a historical voice of alienation and underprivilege that had familiar Catholic intonations in American culture.[92]

All things considered, it must be said that in Novak's forged alliance of democratic capitalism and Catholicism, democratic capitalism was the stronger partner. The Novak who had raged in *Unmeltable Ethnics* against the dreadful impersonalism of the corporate life of Anglo-America, its cool and passionless personality, was writing in the 1980s such tracts as *Toward a Theology of the Corporation,* published by the American Enterprise Institute. Yet what was emerging, in a way that Novak strangely did not press hard in his analysis, was a kind of Catholic understanding and appreciation of capitalism and business enterprise. Again, this understanding did mark a significant continuity with *Unmeltable Ethnics.* What this amounted to, more precisely, was Novak's description of capitalism and its attending cultural values as modes of experience conformable to a Catholic ethic.

First, Novak presented business enterprise as "inherently social," divorcing it thereby from a Protestant, Lockean, and Anglo-American individualism, the norms he had so severely castigated in his earlier book. Novak was bestowing on business and the corporation itself the organic social ethic of the medieval Church. "Economic activities are inherently social," wrote Novak. "No one can be an economic activist in total isolation. Economic activism is necessarily expressed through activities in association with others. Thus, liberty for the individual is consistent with powerful social virtues of teamwork, cooperation, and civic responsibility."[93]

Second, Novak conceded quite rightly that it is "absurd" to call capitalism a "conservative" idea, and he went on to argue that the institutional effects of this economic system have marked the changes in modern life. But they have done so, he believed, in a way quite understandable to a religious tradition that has always viewed life, and not Church life only, in its institutional rather than its individualist perspective. Thus the corporation, the elaborate techniques of budgeting and accounting, the rise of credit and insurance institutions, and the legal protections of inventions, discoveries, and trademarks constitute advances that are both institutional and social. They express the social ethos of democratic capitalism. Only hardened Catholic reactionism, Novak claimed, prevented the Church from perceiving its essential compatibility with the Roman tradition of Christianity.[94]

Thus Novak had built a huge bridge and walked across it. He constructed this edifice of Catholic planks, drawn first from the thick, blood-rich, and passionate world of the white ethnics, that Catholic world rich in symbol, color, and folk tradition. But the last parts of the structure took Novak into the rational world of accounting books, business efficiency, industry and enterprise, self-discipline, prudent planning, and delayed gratifications. Novak could never admit that he had crossed from a Catholic place to a Protestant one, for he had taken every bit of Catholic baggage he could carry in his traversing. A certain kind of conservative, another Catholic, a traditionalist perhaps, might say that Novak left behind, regrettably, the feeling for antiquity, the lament for all that was endearing in the pre-modern, pre-industrial life that separated the prelude to the capitalist era from its unsavory aftermath. Another Catholic might say that Novak deprived the Church of its historical, indispensable role as critic of the acquisitive life and its materialist culture. Well into the twentieth century, indeed, the moral and aesthetic judgment against the bourgeois mode of life had been a special contribution of the Catholic Church and Catholic intellectuals. (The impassioned prose of Christopher Dawson comes to mind.)[95] Novak's journey to the dynamic world of bourgeois capitalism passed over too much of what these Catholic intellectuals could legitimately lament. His bridge too easily soared above the unsavory aspects of capitalist America in the 1980s – the mentality of the "bottom line," the leveraged buy-outs, junk bonds, Wall Street duplicity, and the fulsome corporate salaries of executives who presided over a sick American automobile industry, the shortsighted philosophy of dollars over environment.[96] But Novak had succeeded in bringing into the Catholic mind an appreciation for the small virtues of the economic life – the ambitions, inventiveness, and the spirit of improvement that everywhere has marked capitalism's spiritual superiority to other economic systems. In this way above all, Novak helped to define and broaden the intellectual outline of neoconservatism.

Afterword

WHERE DID American intellectual conservatism stand in the late decades of the twentieth century? The eight individuals studied in this book and the many references to other writers and thinkers who embraced or acquired the label "conservative" should discourage any effort to codify the word. These conservatives differed significantly in their ideas and styles, even as they shared in common a conservative mistrust of all ideologies and all efforts to contain or refashion the world by intellectual scheme or rational formulation. But that commonality suggests a point of continuity between the conservatives of the 1970s and 1980s and their intellectual predecessors in Europe and the United States. Let this possibility be a beginning point for some final reflections on American conservatism in the later period. Had conservative thought in the United States, as some averred, taken a new departure? What remained alive and useful in its own tradition? What new conditions in American society and in American political life most challenged conservative assumptions, and how had they altered conservative opinion? This concluding afterword will not be an extended essay, but a series of reflections on successes and failures, needs and opportunities.

It will help in addressing these questions to recognize three historical roots of modern conservatism, each of which was a reaction against a watershed in modern history. One kind of conservatism derives from the intellectual changes that have characterized Western thought for a half-millennium. We observed this strand earlier in discussing Richard Weaver and others of the Old Right who variously opposed those tendencies in Western ideas leading toward nominalism, empiricism, pragmatism and utilitarianism, and, in general, any legitimation of relativistic truth. Religious and metaphysical conservatives, as a rule, have traced the consequences of this intellectual movement to the menacing aspects of modern civilization—from subjectivity and individualism in the arts to totalitarianism in politics, each in turn the result of a loss of cohesive and sustaining values in the common core of Western civilization. We have seen the continuation of this protest even among the later conservatives, as the Old Right dissented from neoconservatism in the 1980s.

Second, modern conservatism derives from the opposition to the French Revolution. It is most famously expressed in Edmund Burke's defense of the traditional order of society against the revolutionary temperament that would destroy it. As further expounded by such Burkean disciples as Irving Babbitt, Peter Viereck, and Russell Kirk, this conservatism invokes tradition and the past as moral and emotional restraints on the prevailing whim of the moment, and it would translate conservative thought into a certain quality of imagination that is responsive to this appeal.

But the French Revolution is important in another way. Conservatives from Burke to Robert Nisbet have identified it as a revolution by intellectuals, one in which abstract theory envisioned a new order for human society. This inspiration, born of a rationalist reconstruction of the world, these conservatives believe, set the modern pattern of revolutionary change, one characterized by extraordinary powers allotted to the state and by the militancy of those entrusted to fulfill new blueprints for the redemption of the world. Herein was the conservative mistrust of all secular ideologies and its normative skepticism toward human nature as well. Conservatives have generally warned against the human capacity for evil—above all in those most vociferous in their proclaimed intentions to do good—and have looked to the influence of traditional authorities and institutions, rather than to schemes of amelioration through political reform, to contain or temper that capacity. Conservatives describe human life and history as intractable and stubbornly unyielding to the designs of individuals and groups to alter their essential character.

Third, modern conservatism is born of the reaction against the industrial revolution and the attending phenomenon of mass society in the West. From Carlyle to Kirk to M. E. Bradford, this reaction has, from time to time, given conservatism some peculiar qualities—a romantic medievalism, agrarian sympathies, certain forms of aestheticism, a general recoil from the mechanization of life, and even some clear aversions to the capitalist system associated with the industrial revolution.   •

With this background in mind, we can see that American conservative thought in the late twentieth century stands clearly and usually comfortably within a tradition but that it has also made some refinements and modifications of that tradition. It has also succumbed to what I shall call conservative temptations that are not compatible with the best of this tradition. Several factors and issues are especially important to a concluding summary of the conservatism discussed in this book.

A dominant theme of conservative thought in the period considered was the critique of what conservative intellectuals described as the New Class. Our study began with a discussion of the roots and sociological forces behind this phenomenon and reviewed in the work of several individuals the conservative analysis of the new power of the professional elites of the media, academe, the professions, and assorted governmental bureaucracies. This theme raises important questions. To some, it seemed that this preoccupation defined a new conservatism that took on an uncharacteristically anti-elitist and even populist character. It suggested to others an unbecoming, ill-serving anti-intellectualism. It conveyed to these observers something, if not new, at least untypical of intellectual conservatism.

The origins of modern conservatism in the French Revolution suggest a certain point of continuity in this matter. Conservative intellectuals have always feared the theorizing class. Burke warned emphatically against the linking of intellect and power. In the "metaphysick rights" proclaimed by the reformers of his day, Burke saw chaos and social upheaval, the realigning by abstract theory of the complex and historical fabric that constituted the social bond. "The pretended rights of these theorists," Burke wrote in his letter to the sheriffs of Bristol, "are all extremes: and in proportion as they are metaphysically true, they are morally and politically false."[1]

We have seen in this study other examples of a certain kind of intellectual anti-intellectualism among conservatives. It is a point on which the Old Right had no quarrel with the neoconservatives. It was Russell Kirk, indeed, who vilified the intellectual, the thinker who "presumes to meddle with the great complexities of the workaday world." Combine the intellectual with the ideologue, Kirk said, and the world is soon turned upside down. "When a man is both a professor and an intellectual," Kirk wrote, "he is loathsome; when he is professor and intellectual and ideologist rolled into one, he is unbearable."[2]

As such sentiments were pronounced with equal fervor among American conservative intellectuals in the 1970s and 1980s, they suggested to some, perhaps quite reasonably, that an anti-intellectualist populism had superseded conservatism's traditional respect for high culture, for wisdom, for rule by a natural aristocracy, and, even, for reason as the needed stabilizing forces in a tempestuous world. This clearly was not the case, but conservatives themselves were often responsible for these appearances. Their attacks on the New Class were too categorical, and their rhetoric was excessive. More seriously, they had failed to define a conservative philosophy of knowledge.

One who made the effort was the remarkable black sociologist Thomas

Sowell. Author of such empirical studies as *Ethnic America, Civil Rights: Rhetoric or Reality?* and *The Economics and Politics of Race,* Sowell in 1987 wrote *A Conflict of Visions.* This book was one of the most successful efforts to outline the differences between the liberal and conservative mentalities. Sowell, to be sure, used the terms *constrained vision* and *unconstrained vision* to describe what nevertheless usually corresponded to conservative and liberal habits of thought and imagination. Sowell was especially deft in describing a conservative understanding of knowledge. One view of knowledge, said Sowell, sees it as the unlimited application of reason, as formulated by a privileged core of intellectuals entrusted with its formulation, to the solution of social problems. Such was the unconstrained view of knowledge. In the constrained vision, he wrote, "knowledge is . . . the social experience of the many, as embodied in behavior, sentiments, and habits, rather than the specifically articulated *reason* of the few, however talented or gifted those few might be." Interestingly, Sowell quoted Friedrich von Hayek, the influential Austrian economist, on this subject. Wrote Hayek:

The growth of knowledge and the growth of civilization are the same only if we interpret knowledge to include all the human adaptations to environment in which past experience has been incorporated. Not all knowledge in this sense is part of our intellect, nor is our intellect the whole of our knowledge. Our habits and skills, our emotional attitudes, our tools, and our institutions—all are in this sense adaptations to past experience which have grown up by selective elimination of less suitable conduct. They are as much an indispensable foundation of successful action as is our conscious knowledge.[3]

Such renderings as these stress not the visionary and reformist aspects of knowledge that focus on social change but the evolutionary and functional qualities of knowledge that link past, present, and future in the organic manner of traditionalist conservatism.

At a time when American universities, and often the "best" universities, were the sources of teaching and scholarship that were servants of leftist ideology and were often the proponents of ideas and sentiments that held much of ordinary, "bourgeois" America in contempt, conservatives might be forgiven their tendency to dichotomize learned elites, even all of the New Class, and the rest of American society. And when conservative prejudices of this kind seemed to have a vindication by the American voters in the presidential elections of the 1980s, the temptation to wear a populist guise was sometimes irresistible.[4]

But it was a temptation to be avoided. The most astute conservatives have always been skeptical of democracy and mass society without being at the same time antidemocratic or contemptuous of ordinary people. Conservatism is most useful to democratic society in seeking not to emulate it but to improve it. It has sought to guard democracy from its worst tendencies—excessive flattery of the people (and conservative politicians had certainly perfected that art), emotional excess, and national chauvinism. Conservatism has best served democracy by its effort to locate and encourage within it aristocratic qualities—by urging self-improvement and by inspiring higher standards of conduct and taste, by endeavoring to elevate the middling habits of its citizens by invoking the selective achievements and wisdom of the past. When conservatism becomes populist, anti-elitist, anti-intellectual, and narrowly nationalistic, it becomes fascism.

Another conservative temptation is libertarianism. Like populism, libertarianism thrives on the extremes of the political spectrum. As American history has many times witnessed a populism of the Left—William Jennings Bryan, Robert La Follette, Huey Long—so has it seen forms of populism on the Right—Joseph McCarthy, George Wallace, Lyndon LaRouche. Libertarianism is often divided by a leftist ideology that wants complete individual freedom in matters of thought, culture, and morality, and by a rightist ideology that espouses total economic freedom in the marketplace. But frequently too one finds the purest of libertarian ideologues standing for the priorities of individual freedom against the state in all matters.

At least from the time of the industrial revolution conservatives have recoiled from the social consequences of libertarianism. They protested the erosion of their ideal of an organic society by the inroads of a capitalist revolution that they associated with the Manchester school of economics. Well into the twentieth century, traditionalist conservatives like Irving Babbitt lashed out against the cruelty of that system.[5] Conservatives such as Irving Kristol have often registered a moral disgust with the abuses of privilege in corporate headquarters and boardrooms that an indulgent libertarian capitalism has permitted. On the other hand, cultural libertarianism was also a problem for conservatives. The decade of the 1960s virtually assured that fact as the rhetoric of individual choice and personal freedom came to suggest the hedonism of a sexual revolution, the defiance of parental and institutional authority, the recklessness of a drug culture, and the opting for a counterculture defiant of bourgeois constraints.

The problem of freedom for conservatives is a difficult one. Consistently in the 1970s and 1980s they were describing a liberalism to which the word "totalitarian" was often affixed, however exaggerated that application was. From governmental regulations in the marketplace to the bureaucratic edicts that elaborated requirements for sexual quotas in high school pom-pom squads, liberalism, conservatives charged, was programming a society on the ideological caprice of power-craving reformers. So the libertarian temptation, despite what conservatives could see as its obvious corruptions, remained a temptation, especially in the public realm. In fact, the more conservatives appealed to individual freedom in social and economic considerations, the more they appealed to restraints in morals and culture. They reinvoked the Protestant ethic and traditional bourgeois virtues, and they looked urgently to a revitalized role for religion and the institutional churches in American society.

Conservatives might note that etymologically libertarianism derives from its rival, liberalism. Twentieth-century free-market economists are heirs of the Manchester school and nineteenth-century liberalism. Libertarianism will always be a double-edged sword for conservatives. It is always potentially a threat to their ideals of the organic society, tradition, and the appeal to standards in all issues, from the arts to education. But human freedom and personal liberty cannot be superseded in even the most traditionalist conservatism. They are too much bound up with the ethos of American history, too important to those distinctions by which American conservatives for a half-century and more have made their case against the socialist and totalitarian Left and most recently against the aggressive, contrived egalitarianism that liberalism embraced in the 1960s and afterward.

Furthermore, from the Whig Burke in the eighteenth century to the free-market economist Hayek in the twentieth, conservatives and libertarians have often been able to define compatible grounds. In his book *The Constitution of Liberty* (1960) Hayek declared inherited moral rules to be a condition of liberty and legitimated the efforts of any society to define its cultural norms and stabilizing traditions. His words deserve quotation: "There probably never has existed a genuine belief in freedom, and there has certainly been no successful attempt to operate a free society, without a genuine reverence for grown institutions, for customs and habits and 'all those securities of liberty which arise from regulation of long prescription and ancient ways.' Paradoxical as it may appear, it is probably true that a successful free society will always in a large measure be a tradition-bound society."[6]

If we return to the historical sources of intellectual conservatism, we encounter another problem. The moral and aesthetic recoil from the industrial revolution, we have noted, gave conservatism its long-standing aversion to the materialism, hedonism, and dehumanization of bourgeois and industrial society and often carried its criticism into an attack on capitalism itself. There have always been American voices of such recoil.[7] Russell Kirk again illustrates this theme. Kirk's intellectual biography essentially began with his disgust for what he called the "assembly-line" civilization that Henry Ford was spreading around the Michigan of Kirk's youth.[8] Kirk ever afterward expressed an antimodern alienation from certain aspects of bourgeois America, especially in the triumph of its utilitarian standards over the relics of traditional ways and their continuity with the past.[9] He pressed a conservative judgment against the barren spiritual landscape and hollow inner life of modern America, "the neat tedium of American middle class life," as he called it, that leaves "no reason for existence except flirtation with paltry amusements."[10]

Among American conservative writers of the late twentieth century, much of what Kirk said had become axiomatic. From George Will to Irving Kristol there was an understanding that capitalism, with its heavy toll in social change, its creating of a population in perpetual motion, its mentality of newness and change, and its amoral standard of the bottom line, was inherently incompatible with certain conservative values and with a certain conservative temperament. We have noted, however, that the pragmatism of the neoconservatives especially permitted them no alternative to capitalism's record of economic growth. They were led all the more, then, to embrace traditional moral and religious values as the needed restraints on an economic system that readily produces a vulgar and all-consuming materialism.

But in some respects the conservatives have thrown the baby out with the bathwater. They have often exhibited with the intellectuals they disdained a deep aversion to the bourgeois life of their own country. Irving Kristol could celebrate bourgeois morality while dismissing as "vulgar" or "prosaic" the bourgeois life in which these values grew. In the late twentieth-century United States one did not need to be an intellectual of any political or moral persuasion to locate what was vulgar, rude, trivial, and ugly in American life. On the other hand, one could search conservative literature far and wide and find in it little appreciation for the cultural achievements of bourgeois life in Western civilization. Conservatives complained that radical reformers on the Left had only contempt for ordinary people, but they in turn were usually uninterested in locating what measure of idealism, cultural interest, and even amenities of grace and charm middle-class life utilized, has always utilized, to humanize and soften the coarse and often brutalizing effects of its economic system. In 1988 the director of the National Endowment for the Humanities issued a study that purported to show that public interest in art museums and cultural institutions of all kinds was flourishing, that purchases of books in classical literature and history had increased significantly over a thirty-year period, and that the appreciation of the Western cultural heritage thrived among ordinary people more than it did in American universities.[11]

The alienation of some conservatives from bourgeois life has given rise to another conservative temptation. They have sought to superimpose on centuries of social and cultural change some abstract intellectual formulation or some ideal historical edifice. This is the temptation of orthodoxy. It makes of conservatism a metaphysical or religious system or attaches it to a transcendent or supernatural basis of authority. It is one of the most difficult and challenging problems for intellectual conservatism, for certainly religion will always be conservatism's alter ego. It will supply for conservatives their need for intellectual authority or, institutionally, will answer their felt want of a principle of unity and cohesiveness in a socially fragmented modern world. From the discussions and debates between Irving Babbitt, Paul Elmer More, T. S. Eliot, and Allen Tate in the 1930s to the later warfare between the Old Right and neoconservatism, this issue has divided individuals who shared common conservative sentiments. But orthodoxy dangerously becomes a test of membership, or it otherwise locks conservatism into an inflexible temporal framework—a Straussian quest for a Greek moment in the nation's beginnings, or Russell Kirk's high medievalism, or M. E. Bradford's paeans to the Old South.[12]

The point is simply this. For conservatives who claim a heritage from Burke and who look to tradition as the link to the present, as its source of order and direction, it would seem imperative that they find a usable past in the dominant bourgeois tradition of their country.

The history of American conservatism entered a new era with the election of Ronald Reagan to the presidency in 1980. One could look forward to an expansive scholarship of Reagan's tenure in office, its significance for American politics and life, and its relation to conservative intellectual history. I wish to deal but briefly with one aspect of the relationship between the Reagan presidency and conservative intellectual history and the addenda it provides for this study.

The career of Ronald Reagan contained many themes, but one point that Reagan stressed repeatedly in his path to the presidency was that a new order in Washington would liberate the nation from the constraints and interference of government and inaugurate an era of economic fulfillment. Reagan, as Harvard political scientist Hugh Heclo wrote, celebrated an American faith in an unimpeded future of economic and technological progress. Whatever conservative ideas of human limitations there were in Reagan's rhetoric seemed to be reserved for the public sector. But the Reagan message also embraced a traditional morality—of family, community, and religion. What Reagan conveyed, Heclo said, was "a kind of space-age, high technology version of Norman Rockwell's America."[13] Likewise Garry Wills, in his biography of Reagan, found this coupling of economic dynamism with moral nostalgia the essence of Reagan's career, from his sportscasting days in Iowa through his Hollywood sojourn and his salesmanship with General Electric and into his political ventures. To Wills, Reagan embodied quintessential Hollywood, and thus he was an authentic expression of a certain strain in American culture. "Hollywood," Wills wrote, "works at sustaining the illusion that a world totally altered in its technology need not touch or challenge basic beliefs. . . . We are whisked off by Technicolor to Oz, only to make us end up claiming there is no place like the black-and-white farm in Kansas."[14]

There may indeed be a certain parallel here between these Reagan sentiments and the neoconservatives' endorsement of dynamic capitalism when undergirded by traditional morality and bourgeois constraints. But in certain ways the language of Reagan was not the language of traditional conservatism. George Will, for one, was vexed at Reagan's fondness for quoting the words of Thomas Paine: "We have it in our power to begin the world over again." Paine's statement, said Will, is the "most unconservative statement that ever issued from human lips," defiant of what the true conservative knows to be the stubborn givenness of life and the inertia of history.[15] Irving Kristol, in turn, wrote that great expectations are the property of those on the Left, the management of disappointment the expertise of conservatives.[16] Conservative intellectuals, who had written so much against the utopianism of radicals and reformers on the Left and who had become rigidly mistrustful of the gnostic faith, sat uncomfortably with like manifestations of these hopes when they issued from the Right.

When conservatives Paul Gottfried and Thomas Fleming authored their book *The Conservative Movement* (1988), they began with this summary statement: "A distinctive feature of the contemporary American Right is its emphasis on progress: moving beyond the past toward a future of unlimited material opportunity and social improvement." The authors were so taken by this new turn that they felt compelled to conclude that "significantly, what have been described as conservative attitudes may no longer be relevant to what are now the dominant tendencies in American conservatism."[17]

Granted that examples of this theme could be cited, and certainly books such as George Gilder's *Wealth and Poverty* abounded with prose that befit this mood, nonetheless the statements in question seriously misconstrue intellectual conservatism and its message. This book has sought to locate points of continuity between American conservatives of the late twentieth century and their intellectual predecessors. From Edmund Burke's dissent from the ends and aspirations of the French Revolution to conservative criticism of the Great Society and its visions of an America transformed by government, the conservative mind has always been an appropriately skeptical one – toward human nature itself and toward the pretensions of human beings, by whatever means, to remake the world. When conservatives have embraced a philosophy of material progress, as many have, in reaction to the shopworn prophecies by Marxists and others of capitalism's demise, they have invariably espoused a traditional moral or religious philosophy with it. The relevance of that traditionalism, in fact, was the critical link between the Old Right and the neoconservatives. While it accommodated conservatism to free-market philosophies and programs, it also helped to sustain conservatism's historically chastened expectations about the world's capacity to save itself.

If, then, a certain doctrine of progress is compatible with conservatism and if tradition and a sense of history are invariable parts of its mental outlook, then it ought not to be overlooked that conservatism nevertheless has an overriding interest in the present and in the daily and ordinary aspects of life. Conservatism is what makes one at home in one's world. It is that quality of imagination and insight, of historical memory, of awe, of sympathy, that makes of the empirical data of life something more – a habitable world, an inner environment that is personal and familiar. Writing in *Intercollegiate Review,* Donald Atwell Zoll urged that conservatism's historical priorities are understanding and admiration for "the basic simplicities of human life, the joys that should fall within the gambit of all men and women." Conservatism, he added, seeks for each individual a niche in the order of things, "some elemental fulfillment, however varied in character."[18]

When Joseph Sobran formulated a conservative manifesto for the thirtieth anniversary issue of *National Review* in 1985, he located in this quality of conservatism its essential difference from the Left. Commenting on the writings of the British conservative Michael Oakeshott, Sobran noted the recurrence of words like "affection," "familiarity," "happiness," and "attachment." These were the prose music of the conservative, said Sobran. Oakeshott, he wrote, "knows what normal life is, what normal activities are, and his first thought is that politics should not disturb them." On the other hand, Sobran believed, liberalism thrives on the sense of alienation. "Liberalism cultivates alienation," Sobran wrote. "It has a heavy investment in estrangement. It is primarily interested in emergencies and social pathologies." Indulging in an excess of generalization, perhaps, Sobran nonetheless identified critical differences between authentic conservatism and its several rivals on the Left. The course of liberalism in American politics in the 1970s and 1980s emphatically reinforced the distinctions.[19]

These points of emphasis were illustrated in a striking way in the late 1980s as various intellectuals who had been involved in radical protest and leftist causes in the 1960s reflected in the 1980s on their changed views over two decades. The neoconservative literary scholar Joseph Epstein, contributor to the *New Criterion* and editor of *American Scholar,* remembered himself as at one time "a down-the-line, pull-the-lever man of the left." Experience and reflection gave him an emphatic impression of the Left: "There is [in it]," he wrote, "not so very deep down, an element of serious and perhaps immitigable discontent with life, of discomfiture with the world as it is." Epstein added: "For myself, once the blinders of liberalism came off, the present became much more enticing than the future—the way the world *is* became a subject of greater fascination than the way it *ought* to be."[20] Looking for literary depiction of these changed sentiments, Epstein went back to Henry James's young hero Hyacinth Robinson in *The Princess Casamassima.* Epstein quoted James: "What was supreme in his mind today was not the idea of how the society that surrounded him should be destroyed; it was much more the sense of the wonderful precious things it had produced, of the fabric of beauty and power it had raised."[21]

There were other testimonials. David Horowitz, who immersed himself in radical politics for a decade and a half before 1974 and edited *Ramparts* magazine, later described the change that accompanied his abandonment of the Left. "The biggest change in me," he wrote, "is not in any new political convictions I may have. It is in a new way of looking at things. It is in gaining respect for the ordinary experience of others and of myself."[22] Martha Bayles, who became television critic for the *American Spectator* and the *Wall Street Journal,* reflected back on a summer's experience with the civil rights movement in rural Georgia. Leaving behind the discontents of family and school, she had departed New England for a larger fulfillment in a moral cause. Two decades later she reflected that what she then wanted most radicalism could not provide. "Along with authority," she wrote, "the thing I craved most that summer was a thing neither valued nor provided by the late sixties: normality." She enumerated what she most fondly remembered in a community of poor black people: "children's day camp, Mrs. Roundtree's corn pone, softball tournaments, barbecues and picnics—even church."[23]

The danger here is that conservatism will become synonymous with indifference, with a too-easy acceptance of the world as it is. But that will happen only if conservatism forgets the moral and spiritual substance on which it has always drawn, the substance that still provided a basis of unity among the Old Right and the neoconservatives into the 1980s. As Thomas Sowell has shown, from Burke to Adam Smith and Alexander Hamilton, on issues from antislavery to anticolonialism, the constrained vision of life was not a camouflage for acceptance of the status quo.[24]

American conservative thinkers of the late twentieth century had been schooled in skepticism. They had developed a Pavlovian mistrust of the pretensions of reformers, an ingrained suspicion toward utopian idealism or any radical schemes for change. Their position provided a needed corrective to the heady emotionalism and crusading egalitarianism of many on the Left. But whereas this conservatism countervailed the fringes of the Left and exposed the tendencies even of rationalist liberalism to take on, as Charles Frankel once noted, secular millennial hopes, it too frequently parodied liberalism in this way and in turn deprived itself of any idealism of its own. Quite plausibly, therefore, in his book *The Closing of the American Mind,* Allan Bloom could warn against a numbing realism among American conservative intellectuals. "These conservatives," he wrote, "want young people to know that this tawdry old world cannot respond to their demands for perfection." But, he added, "man is a being who must take his orientation by his possible perfection. . . . We need to criticize false understandings of Utopia, but the easy way out provided by realism is deadly."[25]

Another danger is that an enervating skepticism, or "realism," will deprive conservatism of its greater purposes. Conservatism properly facilitates life, as a program of material improvement to be sure but, more important, in the manner suggested above, by making people at home in their world. By the late 1980s as indeed recurrently over several decades, some conservative spokesmen were warning that conservatism had let other concerns stand in the way of this consideration. Donald Atwell Zoll, insisting that "defense of the natural environment" was an inherently conservative priority, faulted the record of conservative spokesmen on this issue. "How much current 'conservative' literature," he asked, "denigrates, condemns, and ridicules the so-called environmentalists?"[26] And in 1988 the Institute for Cultural Conservatism published a noteworthy manifesto, *Cultural Conservatism: Toward a New National Agenda.* It took up a number of issues and formulated conservative responses to them. It declared that "we are also environmentalists," and it called for establishment of a Wilderness Trust. An environmentalism shorn of its zealous antitechnology prejudices, the manifesto argued, was a proper conservative concern.[27]

Altogether these concerns reflected a Burkean corrective to certain strands of conservatism itself. They are reminiscent of Burke's maxim, To make us love our country, our country ought to be lovely. Burke, let us remember, urged this consideration within the context of his attending plea for "all the

decent drapery of life" that makes for a livable world. His concern was ultimately for that which draws toward a society's institutions "love, veneration,
admiration, or attachment."[28] To the conservative, the familiar is not the mundane; the commonplace is not the trivial. As conservatives from Burke to
Babbitt and Will have recognized, there is a certain quality of imagination
that makes such a recognition possible. That habit of mind ought to be conservatism's enduring relevance.

NOTES

INDEX

Notes

CHAPTER 1. THE LAY OF THE LAND

1 Daniel Bell, *The Coming of Post-Industrial Society: A Venture in Social Forecasting* (New York, 1973), 37, 15–17.
2 Ibid., 26, 44.
3 Ibid., 159–60.
4 Kevin P. Phillips, *Mediacracy: American Parties and Politics in the Communications Age* (Garden City, N.Y., 1975), 15.
5 Bell, *Coming of Post-Industrial Society,* 214.
6 Phillips, *Mediacracy,* 17.
7 Ibid., 32–33.
8 Ibid., 41.
9 Ibid., 123.
10 Patrick Buchanan, *The New Majority: President Nixon at Mid-Passage* (N.p., 1973), 18, 29.
11 William A. Rusher, *The Rise of the Right* (New York, 1984), 249.
12 William A. Rusher, *The Making of the New Majority Party* (New York, 1975), 208–9, 221 (quotation).
13 Richard A. Viguerie, *The Establishment vs. the People: Is a New Populist Revolt on the Way?* (Chicago, 1983), 4, 19, 31–33, 51, 76, 87, 91, 95, 97–127.
14 Ibid., 7.
15 Norman Podhoretz, *Making It* (New York, 1967), 5, 8–9, 13–14, 26–27.
16 Ibid., 28–30, 32–33, 44–45, 49–51. Quotation is on 28–29.
17 Norman Podhoretz, *Breaking Ranks: A Political Memoir* (New York, 1979), 91.
18 Ibid., 150 (quotation), 284–85.
19 Ibid., 155, 165–66.
20 Norman Podhoretz, *The Bloody Crossroads: Where Literature and Politics Meet* (New York, 1986), 115–35.
21 For example, see the following Podhoretz essays: "J'Accuse," *Commentary* (September 1982): 21–31; "The State of World Jewry," *Commentary* (December

1983): 37–45; "The Hate that Dare Not Speak Its Name," *Commentary* (November 1986): 21–32.

22 Nathan Glazer, "On Being Deradicalized," *Commentary* (October 1970): 74.

23 Ibid., 74–75.

24 Nathan Glazer, "What Happened at Berkeley," *Commentary* (February 1965): 47; Glazer, "On Being Deradicalized," 76.

25 Glazer, "On Being Deradicalized," 75.

26 Nathan Glazer, "The New Left and Its Limits," *Commentary* (July 1968): 32–35; Glazer, "On Being Deradicalized," 76.

27 Nathan Glazer, *Affirmative Discrimination: Ethnic Inequality and Public Policy* (1975; New York, 1978), 41.

28 Ibid., 200, 219, 110, 202–3. Of considerable additional importance in Glazer's writings were those works that dealt with race, including the relations of blacks and Jews, an issue that gained much attention in the late 1960s and afterward. They significantly elaborate neoconservative views and the neoconservatives' retreat from liberalism. See especially "Negroes and Jews: The New Challenge to Pluralism," *Commentary* (December 1964): 29–34, and "A New Look at the Melting Pot," *The Public Interest,* no. 16 (Summer 1969): 180–87.

29 Nathan Glazer, "Interests and Passions," *The Public Interest,* no. 81 (Fall 1985): 21–22.

30 Glazer, *Affirmative Discrimination,* 77.

31 Richard M. Weaver, *Ideas Have Consequences* (Chicago, 1948), 3.

32 Ibid., 7, 38 (quotation), 55, 75–77.

33 Ibid., 28, 31, 32.

34 Ibid., 51.

35 Eric Voegelin, "The Origins of Totalitarianism," *Review of Politics* 15 (1953): 75; see also Ellis Sandoz, *The Voegelinian Revolution: A Biographical Introduction* (Baton Rouge, 1981), 22.

36 Quoted in John P. East, "Leo Strauss and American Conservatism," *Modern Age* 21 (Winter 1977): 3.

37 Allan Bloom, "Leo Strauss," *Political Theory* 2 (November 1974): 378.

38 Gordon S. Wood, "The Fundamentalists and the Constitution," *New York Review of Books,* February 18, 1988, p. 34; East, "Leo Strauss," 3. The quotation by Strauss is in East, "Leo Strauss," 3.

39 East, "Leo Strauss," 16–17; Wood, "Fundamentalists," 34.

40 Harry V. Jaffa, "In Defense of Political Philosophy: A Letter to Walter Berns," *National Review,* January 22, 1982, p. 42.

41 Charles R. Kesler, "Is Conservatism Un-American?" *National Review,* March 22, 1985, p. 30.

42 Harvey C. Mansfield, "Democracy and the Great Books," *New Republic,* April 4, 1988, pp. 34–36. In this way too the Straussians added to an important and long-standing discussion about democracy and its intellectual foundations in the twentieth century. For a full treatment of this subject, see Edward A. Purcell, Jr., *The Crisis of Democratic Theory: Scientific Naturalism and the Problem*

of Value (Lexington, Ky., 1973). For two useful essays on Strauss and his followers, see Charles R. Kesler, "All Against All," *National Review,* August 18, 1989, pp. 39–43; and Charles Larmore, "The Secrets of Philosophy," *New Republic,* July 3, 1989, pp. 30–35.

43 Allan Bloom, *The Closing of the American Mind* (New York, 1987), 256. As he was for Strauss, Heidegger was the culminating figure for Bloom in modernity's reach into the university. His *Rektoratsede* accommodated the German university to German history and to Nazism (311).

CHAPTER 2. WILLIAM F. BUCKLEY, JR.

1 William F. Buckley, Jr., *Inveighing We Will Go* (New York, 1972), 42–43, 50–51.

2 William F. Buckley, Jr., *The Jeweler's Eye: A Book of Irresistible Political Reflections* (New York, 1968), 143–73.

3 Buckley, *Inveighing,* 40–41, 50–51.

4 Mark Royden Winchell, *William F. Buckley, Jr.* (Boston, 1984), 16. Mitchell S. Ross has written: "Much as he might wish it otherwise, [Buckley] is not at his best in expounding conservative thought." See Ross, *The Literary Politicians* (Garden City, N.Y., 1978), 52.

5 John B. Judis, *William F. Buckley, Jr.: Patron Saint of the Conservatives* (New York, 1988), 202.

6 George H. Nash, *The Conservative Intellectual Movement in America, Since 1945* (New York, 1976), 148–53; Winchell, *Buckley,* 1.

7 Winchell, *Buckley,* 2–9 (quotation on 2). For more details on the Buckley family, see Priscilla L. Buckley and William F. Buckley, Jr., eds., *W. F. B.: An Appreciation by His Family and Friends* (New York, 1979), and a disparaging account, Charles Lam Markmann, *The Buckleys: A Family Examined* (New York, 1973). Also, useful material may be found in Judis, *Buckley,* 23, and chapter 1.

8 Judis, *Buckley,* 23, 26–27.

9 Ibid., 29; William F. Buckley, Jr., interview with the author, August 8, 1988, New York City.

10 Ronald Lora, *Conservative Minds in America* (Chicago, 1971), 196.

11 Buckley, *Jeweler's Eye,* 232–34.

12 William F. Buckley, Jr., *Overdrive: A Personal Documentary* (Boston, 1981), 111–12.

13 William F. Buckley, Jr., *Right Reason* (New York, 1985), 368.

14 John B. Judis suggests that the proclivity of the Buckley children for tricks and subterfuge indicates the outsider mentality of this family. For varying reasons— their Irish background, their Catholicism, their southern roots—the Buckleys met suspicion or hostility in their different places of residence. In response, says Judis quite plausibly, "the Buckley children developed a defensive clannishness." Judis, *Buckley,* 32.

15 Whittaker Chambers, *Witness* (New York, 1952), 9.

16 Ibid., 5, 7, 8 (quotations).

17 Ibid., 9.
18 Whittaker Chambers, "The Direct Glance" [from *Cold Friday*], in William F. Buckley, Jr., ed., *Have You Ever Seen a Dream Walking?: American Conservative Thought in the Twentieth Century* (Indianapolis, 1970), 494; Chambers, *Witness*, 4.
19 Quoted in Judis, *Buckley*, 124.
20 Quoted in Jeffrey Hart, *The American Dissent: A Decade of Modern Conservatism* (New York, 1966), 203, 204-5.
21 William F. Buckley, Jr., *A Hymnal: The Controversial Arts* (New York, 1975), 424-25. Garry Wills has described Kendall as "a walking sign of contradictions, who lost no time, on a first meeting, in contradicting you; everybody's enemy at some time, and always his own." Wills, *Confession of a Conservative* (Garden City, N.Y., 1979), 17.
22 For an extensive analysis of Kendall in the conservative intellectual movement, see Nash, *Conservative Intellectual Movement*, 227-52. Kendall presented the first full synthesis and most important summary of his ideas in *The Conservative Affirmation* (Chicago, 1963).
23 Allan Bloom made the point with a special reference to Rousseau's critique of Locke on this subject. See Bloom, *The Closing of the American Mind* (New York, 1987), 168.
24 William F. Buckley, Jr., *God and Man at Yale: The Superstitions of Academic Freedom* (Chicago, 1951), xiii, 46-55.
25 Ibid., 22-23.
26 Buckley, *Up from Liberalism*, xxiv, 55, 136-37.
27 Ibid., 89, 90-91. Richard Hofstadter had earlier borrowed heavily from Adorno in his essay "The Pseudo-Conservative Revolt," published in *The New American Right*, ed. Daniel Bell (New York, 1955).
28 Buckley, *Jeweler's Eye*, 28-29.
29 Buckley, *Up from Liberalism*, 125.
30 *National Review*, January 14, 1961, p. 8.
31 Buckley, *Up from Liberalism*, 144-45.
32 Buckley, *Jeweler's Eye*, 53. Such dire summaries have always coexisted with Buckley's faith that we are on the side of right and of God and cannot lose despite our foolishness. For all his despair, Buckley saw himself as essentially an optimist. He wrote in 1962, on the visit of Soviet leader Nikita Khrushchev: "Khrushchev is *not* aware that the gates of hell shall not prevail against us. Even out of the depth of despair, we take heart in the knowledge that it cannot matter how deep we fall, for there is always hope. In the end, we will bury him." *The Best of Bill Buckley* (N.p.: *National Review*, n.d.), 43.
33 Arthur M. Schlesinger, Jr., *The Vital Center: The Politics of Freedom* (Boston, 1949), 243-56.
34 Herbert Marcuse, *One-Dimensional Man: Studies in the Ideology of Advanced Industrial Society* (Boston, 1964), 170-99.
35 Buckley, *God and Man at Yale*, 157.

36 William F. Buckley, Jr., "The Pope I Want," *New Republic,* August 26 and September 2, 1978, pp. 15-17. For a larger discussion of Buckley and religion, see Winchell, *Buckley,* 82-90.

37 Buckley, *Jeweler's Eye,* 22-23, 14-15; and Wills, *Confession of a Conservative,* 60-70.

38 Robert Kelley, *The Cultural Pattern in American Politics: The First Century* (New York, 1979), 167.

39 See the suggestive insights on this subject in Wilson Carey McWilliams, *The Idea of Fraternity in America* (Berkeley, 1973), 246-47. Another work that is provocative in this regard is Lawrence Frederick Kohl, *The Politics of Individualism: Parties and the American Character in the Jacksonian Era* (New York, 1989).

40 This phenomenon, which can be discerned in nearly all phases of American history, has many variations and nuances, observable in individual biographies and in political history. The best summary of the literature on the topic that I have seen is John D. Buenker, "Sovereign Individuals and Organic Networks: Political Cultures during the Progressive Era," *American Quarterly* 40 (June 1988): 187-204.

41 Quoted in Buckley, *Overdrive,* xxvii.

42 Buckley, *Jeweler's Eye,* 316-30; *National Review,* April 19, 1985, pp. 20-21 (on his mother).

43 William F. Buckley, Jr., and L. Brent Bozell, *McCarthy and His Enemies: The Record and Its Meaning* (Chicago, 1954), 317, 323, 330.

44 Judis, *Buckley,* 38.

45 Buckley, *Jeweler's Eye,* 188.

46 Buckley, *Right Reason,* 215.

47 Buckley, *Hymnal,* 24-25, 50.

48 William F. Buckley, Jr., *The Unmaking of a Mayor* (New York, 1966), 106-7.

49 Buckley, *Jeweler's Eye,* 257-59.

50 Buckley, *National Review,* December 14, 1967, p. 114. But note also his reservations: "The trouble with [*Playboy* editor Hugh] Hefner's law is that his society is composed of nothing more than a great number of individuals, and if each man's morality is defined merely to suit himself, then everyone will endure the consequences of his autonomously defined ethics. Mr. Hefner's philosophy notwithstanding, there *is* such a thing as the public morality, and that morality has throughout civilized history been primarily sustained by religion." Buckley, *Jeweler's Eye,* 252.

51 Buckley, *Inveighing,* 47.

52 Ibid., 285. In an interview with the author, Buckley elaborated by saying that one cannot exclude the role of the state for strictly utilitarian reasons, that ideology is simply not a reliable guide for determining the right role of the state.

53 Buckley, *Jeweler's Eye,* 17.

54 Buckley, *Inveighing,* 52 (Buckley's words).

55 Buckley, *Right Reason,* 35. Sometimes one had difficulty discerning the frivolous and the serious in Buckley. In 1986, at a time when the homosexual-connected disease AIDS was gaining much public attention, Buckley suggested that AIDS

carriers be tattooed on the buttocks as a health warning to any who contemplated relations with such individuals. Buckley insisted that his proposal fell within government's legitimate concern for the health of the public and was analogous to quarantining practices. The suggestion inspired angry reaction and a cartoon showing a man's buttocks with the tattooed inscription, "Abandon All Hope, Ye Who Enter Here." *New York Times,* March 18, 1986; Buckley, "Looking Out for Number Two," *National Review,* April 25, 1986, p. 63.

56 Andrew M. Greeley, *The American Catholic: A Social Portrait* (New York, 1977), 257, 258.
57 Buckley, *Inveighing,* 52.
58 Buckley, *Up from Liberalism,* 155–67; William F. Buckley, Jr., *The Governor Listeth: A Book of Inspired Political Revelations* (New York, 1970), 101–2.
59 Buckley, *Governor Listeth,* 146–47.
60 Ibid., 158–59.
61 Buckley, *Right Reason,* 64.
62 Ibid., 101–2, 147–51.
63 Buckley, *National Review,* June 14, 1984, p. 63.
64 Buckley, *Jeweler's Eye,* 284–85. Even a brief autobiographical reflection could send a reader to the dictionary: "In those days anything attached to democracy was osmotically desirable, democracy having been postulated as the highest civic good. We had, then, not only economic democracy, but its cousin, industrial democracy. Educational democracy enjoyed moganatic privileges and social democracy was tantamount to eudomania." William F. Buckley, Jr., "Capitalism, Socialism, and Democracy: A Symposium," *Commentary* 65 (April 1978): 35.
65 Henry Fairlie, "The Screwtape Columns," *New Republic,* February 10, 1986, pp. 39–42. On Buckley's computers, see *Time,* December 9, 1985, p. 98. For another illustration of his enrapture with technology, see his description of the Trimble Loran–C navigator in his book *Racing through Paradise: A Pacific Passage* (New York, 1987), 24–32.
66 Buckley, *Best of Bill Buckley,* 38. He wrote not only of Harvard University. Later Buckley added for good measure: "The academic community has in it the biggest concentration of alarmists, cranks and extremists this side of the giggle house." Buckley, "On the Right," *National Review,* January 17, 1967, p. 1.
67 Buckley, *Jeweler's Eye,* 241–42.
68 Buckley, *Governor Listeth,* 206.
69 Buckley, *Inveighing,* 15.
70 Buckley, *Jeweler's Eye,* 40.
71 Ibid., 68–70. Buckley later, however, called the 1968 Apollo 8 flight "the nearest thing to total beauty that science ever created." Buckley, *Governor Listeth,* 244.
72 Buckley, *Hymnal,* 234–35.
73 Buckley, *Inveighing,* 121–22.
74 Ibid., 124.
75 Ibid., 90–91, 97–98.
76 Buckley, "On the Right," *National Review,* March 15, 1968; Buckley, *Inveighing,* 134.

77 Hendrik Hertzberg, "Why the War Was Immoral," *New Republic,* April 29, 1985, p. 15.
78 Buckley, *Hymnal,* 45, 47.
79 Buckley, *Governor Listeth,* 226.
80 Buckley, *Inveighing,* 48–49.
81 Buckley, *Best of Bill Buckley,* 13.
82 Buckley, *Inveighing,* 18–19.
83 Buckley, "On the Right," *National Review,* June 18, 1966.
84 Buckley, *Inveighing,* 148–49.
85 Buckley, *National Review,* June 1, 1984, pp. 54–55; Buckley, *National Review,* November 30, 1984, p. 54.
86 Buckley, *Best of Bill Buckley,* 13.
87 Buckley, *Right Reason,* 96, 97.
88 William F. Buckley, Jr., "So Long, Evil Empire," *National Review,* July 8, 1988, pp. 56–57.
89 Buckley, *Right Reason,* 177.
90 Ibid., 36–37.
91 Quoted in Jack Sullivan, "Behind the Best Sellers," *New York Times Book Review,* March 30, 1980, p. 32.
92 William F. Buckley, Jr., "The Clubhouse," *New York Times Magazine,* April 28, 1983, p. 52.

CHAPTER 3. GEORGE WILL

1 George F. Will, *The Pursuit of Virtue and Other Tory Notions* (New York, 1982), 315; George F. Will, *The Pursuit of Happiness and Other Sobering Thoughts* (New York, 1978), 149.
2 Neal Johnston, review of *Pursuit of Virtue,* by George F. Will, in *New York Times Book Review,* March 29, 1979, p. 16.
3 George F. Will, interview with the author, October 10, 1987, Washington, D.C. On the matter of his professional controversies, Will was widely chastised for editorial praise he gave to a Ronald Reagan television debate the contents of which he himself had helped the candidate prepare. Will was further compromised when an assistant described how he had supplied quotations to Will that embellished Will's editorials.
4 Interview with the author.
5 George F. Will, *Statecraft as Soulcraft: What Government Does* (New York, 1983), 146; George F. Will, *Pursuit of Virtue,* 5.
6 Quoted in Will, *Pursuit of Happiness,* 318.
7 Will, *Pursuit of Virtue,* 40.
8 Will, *Pursuit of Happiness,* 113–14.
9 Will, *Pursuit of Virtue,* 343–45.
10 George F. Will, *The Morning After: American Successes and Excesses, 1981–1986* (New York, 1986), 9–11.

11 Will, *Pursuit of Virtue*, 352-54.

12 George F. Will, "La Plata's Cheerfulness Quotient," *Newsweek*, August 4, 1987.

13 Interview with the author.

14 Will, *Pursuit of Happiness*, 46; Will, *Pursuit of Virtue*, 31.

15 Will, *Morning After*, 30.

16 Will, *Pursuit of Happiness*, 20.

17 Will, *Morning After*, 130.

18 George F. Will, "America Gets Condoized," *Newsweek*, February 14, 1987.

19 Will, *Morning After*, 83.

20 Ibid., 78.

21 Will, *Morning After*, 380-81.

22 Peter Viereck, *Conservatism Revisited* (1949; New York, 1962), 142-44.

23 Will, *Statecraft as Soulcraft*, 142-43.

24 Will, *Pursuit of Happiness*, 7.

25 Will, *Statecraft as Soulcraft*, 129-30; Will, *Pursuit of Happiness*, 105. Will, it should be noted, was by no means sanguine about the likelihood of wholly effective social reforms emerging from these public programs. "The United States," he wrote, "has within its urban population many people who lack the economic ability and character traits for life in a free and lawful society." Will, *Pursuit of Happiness*, 213.

26 Will, *Statecraft as Soulcraft*, 130. Will's "kindly conservatism" found its most moving expression in essays he wrote in defense of retarded children and the right to life of babies born in some ways deformed. The Wills, as some of George Will's family portrait/essays described, had a son, Jonathan, born with Down's syndrome. When he appeared on the "Phil Donahue Show," Will announced that he was going home that evening to teach Jonathan to play chess. Will said, "He can learn." "Phil Donahue Show," August 17, 1987. See also Will, *Morning After*, 187-88, 193-94.

27 Will, *Pursuit of Happiness*, 16.

28 Ibid., 238.

29 Irving Babbitt, *The Masters of Modern French Criticism* (New York, 1912), 23.

30 Will, *Pursuit of Happiness*, xvi-xvii.

31 Ibid., 56-57.

32 Ibid., 192.

33 Ibid., 50-51.

34 See James Nuechterlein, "George Will and American Conservatism," *Commentary* 76 (October 1983): 41.

35 Will, *Pursuit of Virtue*, 124; Will, *Morning After*, 138.

36 Will, *Pursuit of Happiness*, 147.

37 Ibid., 45.

38 Ibid., 99-100. In a 1983 editorial Will defended the so-called Squeal Rule that mandated informing parents when a teenage girl received contraceptive drugs or devices from federally funded birth control clinics. He chastised the ACLU for bringing girls' anonymity in these transactions under the inflated rubric of right to privacy and individual choice. Will, *Morning After*, 49-50.

39 Will, *Pursuit of Virtue,* 103.

40 Will, *Pursuit of Happiness,* 60–61. Will warned, however, that dogmatism on the abortion issue would not suffice in addressing a serious matter. If diagnostic techniques indicate that a child, if born, will die from Tay-Sachs disease by the age of four, having become deaf, blind, and paralyzed by that time, then abortion is not obviously the greater evil (61).

41 Ibid., 70–71.

42 Will, *Morning After,* 52, 101, 150.

43 Ibid., 77; Will, *Statecraft as Soulcraft,* 84–85.

44 Will, *Pursuit of Virtue,* 45.

45 Will, *Statecraft as Soulcraft,* 66.

46 Ibid., 124, 91 (quotation). The words of Burke are: "Society cannot exist unless a controlling power upon will and appetite be placed somewhere, and the less of it there is within, the more there must be without. It is ordained in the eternal constitution of things, that men of intemperate minds cannot be free. Their passions forge their fetters." Quoted in Russell Kirk, ed., *The Portable Conservative Reader* (New York, 1982), 48.

47 Will, *Statecraft as Soulcraft,* 65.

48 Irving Babbitt, *Democracy and Leadership* (Boston, 1924), 16–17.

49 Will, *Pursuit of Happiness,* 21.

50 Will, *Pursuit of Virtue,* 169.

51 Ibid., 168–69.

52 Will, *Pursuit of Happiness,* 191.

53 Will, *Statecraft as Soulcraft,* 159.

54 Will, *Pursuit of Happiness,* 176.

55 Ibid., 4–5.

56 Will, *Statecraft as Soulcraft,* 24, 42–45.

57 Will, *Pursuit of Virtue,* 284–86.

58 Ibid., 94; Will, *Statecraft as Soulcraft,* 35.

59 See Bernard Bailyn, *The Ideological Origins of the American Revolution* (Cambridge, Mass., 1967), and Gordon S. Wood, *The Creation of the American Republic* (Chapel Hill, 1969).

60 Will, *Statecraft as Soulcraft,* 30.

61 Garry Wills, *Inventing America: Jefferson's Declaration of Independence* (Garden City, N.Y., 1978); see especially parts 1 and 2.

62 Kenneth S. Lynn, "Falsifying Jefferson," *Commentary* (October 1978): 66–71.

63 John P. Diggins, *The Lost Soul of American Politics: Virtue, Self-Interest, and the Foundations of Liberalism* (New York, 1984), 58–59.

64 Ibid., 200–201, 243, 322, 325–26.

65 Ibid., 16.

66 James T. Kloppenberg, "The Virtues of Liberalism: Christianity, Republicanism, and Ethics in Early American Political Discourse," *Journal of American History* 74 (June 1987): 9, 28–29, 17–18, 29. I cite Kloppenberg's essay for its many useful suggestions for this chapter and do not mean to implicate him in any way in the extended polemical aspects of this historiography.

67   Will, *Pursuit of Virtue*, 40, 46 (Will's words).
68   Will, *Pursuit of Happiness*, 99, 191–92, 15–16. On this basis Will criticized the mood and rhetoric of Ronald Reagan and described them as "Reaganite conservatism with a smiling face, conservatism singularly lacking in a tragic sense of life, gloomy only about government and cheerfully convinced that everyone else—a.k.a., the 'private sector'—is a realm of harmony and limitlessness." At most, Will wrote, conservatism imbibes a "chastened hopefulness." Will, *Morning After*, 6.
69   Will, *Statecraft as Soulcraft*, 120.
70   Will, *Pursuit of Happiness*, 72.
71   Ibid., 114–15.
72   Will, *Statecraft as Soulcraft*, 20–31, 83–84 (quotation).
73   Ibid., 70–71. On the issue of required school prayer, however, Will stood apart from those who sought to circumvent the United States Supreme Court prohibition by permitting "nondenominational" prayer or simply moments of silence during a part of the school day. Such a device, he said, makes a travesty of religion and prayer, substituting a bland and innocuous formula for the richness of tradition that alone makes religious faith meaningful. See Will, *Morning After*, 175.
74   Will, *Pursuit of Happiness*, 180–81 (quotation), 176–77.
75   Will, *Statecraft as Soulcraft*, 87.
76   Will, *Pursuit of Happiness*, 141.
77   Will, *Pursuit of Virtue*, 16. Will expressed his debt in this essay to Richard John Neuhaus' book *The Naked Public Square*.
78   Ibid., 59–60.
79   Will, *Pursuit of Virtue*, 242–43, 87, 88, 295–97.
80   Babbitt, *Democracy and Leadership*, 61.
81   Viereck, *Conservatism Revisited*, 34–35.
82   Will, *Pursuit of Happiness*, 33. On this matter Will advised against television cameras on the floor of the Senate and the public broadcasting of that body's proceedings. The members of the Senate, he urged, need remoteness from public exposure, "more insulation from the importunings of the immediate." Will wrote, "The healthy working of representative government requires a residuum of detachment, distance, aloofness, even mystery." Television, he feared, would erode the "elevating ambience" that the Senate has been able to maintain even amid the passionate business of American politics. Will, *Morning After*, 220.
83   Forrest McDonald, *Novus Ordo Seclorum: The Intellectual Origins of the Constitution* (Lawrence, Kans., 1985), 90.
84   Robert Kelley, *The Cultural Pattern in American Politics: The First Century* (New York, 1979), 112–13, 142, 167 (quotation).
85   Daniel Walker Howe, *The Political Culture of the American Whigs* (Chicago, 1979), 21.
86   Ibid., 270.
87   Nor should Howe's concluding summary of the Whig political culture be neglected. Although he showed that the cultural forces that had given it birth and sustenance—

classical learning, oratory, academic moral philosophy, New School Calvinist theology – waned and fragmented in later decades, the Whigs' influence could be seen in force thereafter. Howe suggested that the Liberal Republicans of 1872, the urban gentry of the late nineteenth century, and the Progressives of the early twentieth century perpetuated it. Ibid., 303–4.

88 Will, *Morning After,* 408–9.

89 William Manchester, review of *The Pursuit of Happiness and Other Sobering Thoughts,* by George F. Will, in *New York Review of Books,* June 11, 1978, pp. 14–15.

90 Ronald Dworkin, review of *The Pursuit of Happiness and Other Sobering Thoughts,* by George F. Will, in *New York Review of Books,* October 12, 1978, pp. 18–19.

91 Nuechterlein, "Will and American Conservatism," 41–42.

92 Joseph Sobran, "George Will and the Contemporary Political Conversation," *American Spectator* 16 (October 1983): 10–15.

93 Henry Fairlie, "Tory Days," *New Republic,* November 10, 1987, p 34.

94 Will, *Statecraft as Soulcraft,* 119.

95 Will, *Pursuit of Happiness,* 34, 110–11.

96 Will, *Pursuit of Virtue,* 332–33.

97 Ibid., 329–30.

98 Will, *Pursuit of Happiness,* 103.

99 Ibid., 308–9.

CHAPTER 4. IRVING KRISTOL

1 Irving Kristol, interview with the author, July 13, 1986, Washington, D.C.

2 See Irving Howe, *A Margin of Hope: An Intellectual Autobiography* (San Diego, 1982); William Barrett, *The Truants: Adventures among the Intellectuals* (New York, 1982); Lionel Abel, *The Intellectual Follies: A Memoir of the Literary Venture in New York and Paris* (New York, 1984); William Phillips, *A Partisan View: Five Decades of the Literary Life* (New York, 1983); Sidney Hook, *Out of Step: An Unquiet Life in the Twentieth Century* (New York, 1987).

3 Alexander Bloom, *Prodigal Sons: The New York Intellectuals and Their World* (New York, 1986), 51.

4 Howe, *Margin of Hope,* 12.

5 Ibid., 49; Bloom, *Prodigal Sons,* 134.

6 Howe, *Margin of Hope,* 61, 33 (quotation).

7 Ibid., 64.

8 Irving Kristol, *Reflections of a Neoconservative: Looking Back, Looking Ahead* (New York, 1983), 12. The reference is from the essay "Memoirs of a Trotskyist."

9 See, for example, Gertrude Himmelfarb, *Marriage and Morals among the Victorians* (New York, 1986).

10 Walter Goodman, "Irving Kristol: Patron Saint of the New Right," *New York Times Magazine,* December 6, 1981, p. 200; Geoffrey Norman, "The Godfather of Neoconservatism (and His Family)," *Esquire,* February 13, 1979, pp. 37–39.

11 Unbeknownst to Kristol, *Encounter* magazine was supported by the United States Central Intelligence Agency. Kristol reviewed this episode with *Encounter* in the essay "Memoirs of a Cold Warrior" in his *Reflections,* 14–24.

12 Irving Kristol, "From the Land of the Free to the Big PX," *New York Times Magazine,* December 20, 1964, p. 20.

13 Irving Kristol, "Why I Am for Humphrey," *New Republic,* June 8, 1968, p. 22; quoted in Goodman, "Kristol," 202; Norman, "Godfather," 40.

14 Irving Kristol, "Skepticism, Meliorism, and *The Public Interest,*" *The Public Interest,* no. 81 (Fall 1985): 32.

15 Goodman, "Kristol," 40.

16 Josiah Lee Auspitz, "Intellectuals and Power," review of *On the Democratic Idea in America,* by Irving Kristol, *Commentary* 55 (May 1973): 86.

17 Irving Kristol, *Two Cheers for Capitalism* (New York, 1978), 138.

18 From Robert W. Glasgow, interview with Irving Kristol, in *Psychology Today,* February 7, 1974, p. 80.

19 Quoted by Goodman, "Kristol," 90.

20 See the suggestive article by Maarten van Rossem, "The Intellectual Roots of Neo-Conservatism: Its Emergence in the USA and Europe," ed. Rob Kroes (Amsterdam, 1984), 16–25.

21 Irving Howe, "The New York Intellectuals: A Chronicle and a Critique," *Commentary* 46 (October 1968): 29.

22 Irving Kristol, "The New York Intellectuals," *Commentary* 47 (January 1969): 13.

23 Quoted in Bloom, *Prodigal Sons,* 203.

24 Bloom, *Prodigal Sons,* 184; Richard H. Pells, *The Liberal Mind in a Conservative Age: American Intellectuals in the 1940s and 1950s* (New York, 1985), 124–25.

25 Bloom, *Prodigal Sons,* 221–23.

26 Pells, *Liberal Mind,* 276.

27 Bloom, *Prodigal Songs,* 228.

28 Ibid., 232.

29 *Partisan Review* 19 (May–June 1952): 283–326; (July–August 1952): 420–50.

30 Meyer Schapiro, quoted in Bloom, *Prodigal Sons,* 283.

31 *Partisan Review* 19 (January 1952): 494–95.

32 Quoted in Pells, *Liberal Mind,* 296.

33 Mark Krupnick, *Lionel Trilling and the Fate of Cultural Criticism* (Evanston, 1985), 47–50.

34 Barrett made Trilling the major transition to neoconservatism; see Barrett, *Truants,* 168–69. But William Phillips disagreed; see Phillips *Partisan Review,* 75.

35 Lionel Trilling, *The Opposing Self: Nine Essays in Criticism* (New York, 1955), 71, 76–77, 91; Krupnick, *Trilling,* 98.

36 Trilling, *Opposing Self,* 75, 69.

37 Trilling, *Opposing Self,* 74.

38 Quoted in Bloom, *Prodigal Sons,* 201. Howe spoke of the attrition of the American intellect under the extraordinary pressures of the Zeitgeist and warned of a new alliance of wealth and intellect in America, a warning he issued in reference to Trilling. See Irving Howe, "This Age of Conformity," in *America and the*

Intellectuals (New York, 1954), 9-20 (originally published in *Partisan Review,* January-February 1954). Howe went on to establish *Dissent* magazine as a mark of his protest against the conservative shift among the New Yorkers.

39 Lionel Trilling, *Beyond Culture* (New York, 1955), 14-15.

40 Quoted in Krupnick, *Trilling,* 145.

41 Quoted in Bloom, *Prodigal Sons,* 203.

42 Kristol, *Reflections,* 320, 317.

43 Ibid., 320, 318.

44 Ibid., xi, 143-44.

45 Ibid., 150-51, 81-82.

46 What Kristol had also added to Schumpeter was his own analysis of the effects of a dominant urban culture, especially in the United States. See his essay "Urban Civilization and Its Discontents," in *On the Democratic Idea in America* (New York, 1972), 17.

47 Kristol, 138-40; Irving Kristol, "When Virtue Loses All Her Loveliness—Some Reflections on Capitalism and the 'Free Society,' " *The Public Interest,* no. 21 (Fall 1970): 11 (reprinted in *Recollections*); Kristol, "Big PX," 32.

48 Kristol, *Two Cheers,* 166.

49 Ibid., 166-69. Many readers will recognize in Kristol's views the larger outline of the "cultural contradictions of capitalism" as analyzed at great length by Kristol's colleague and former college mate at City University, Daniel Bell, in a book of that title. Bell was a great influence among the conservative intellectuals and has often been included in that group. Bell described himself as a socialist in economics, a liberal in politics, and a conservative in culture. We will refer to Bell again in the chapter on Hilton Kramer. Suffice it to say here simply that any review of *The Cultural Contradictions of Capitalism* (New York, 1976), would help locate Kristol in the larger spectrum of American intellectual life in the 1970s. For now we cite only this observation from Bell's book: "When the Protestant ethic was sundered from bourgeois society, only the hedonism remained" (21).

50 Kristol, "Big PX," 32; Kristol, "Virtue," 10.

51 Kristol, "Capitalism, Socialism, and Nihilism," *The Public Interest,* no. 31 (Spring 1973): 13.

52 Kristol, "Virtue," 43; Kristol, *Two Cheers,* 28-29, 87-89.

53 Kristol, *Reflections,* 28-29.

54 Kristol, *Reflections,* 38. Schumpeter had written: "And we have finally seen that capitalism creates a critical frame of mind which, after having destroyed the moral authority of so many other institutions, in the end turns against its own; the bourgeois finds to his amazement that the rationalist attitude does not stop at the credentials of kings and popes but goes on to attack private property and the whole scheme of bourgeois values." Joseph Schumpeter, *Capitalism, Socialism, and Democracy* (1942; New York, 1976), 143.

55 Kristol, *Two Cheers,* 147.

56 Ibid., 67-68; Kristol, "Capitalism, Socialism, and Nihilism," 12-13.

57 Kristol, "Big PX," 33; Kristol, "Virtue," 8-9, 12.

58 Irving Babbitt, *Literature and the American College: Essays in Defense of the Humanities* (Boston, 1908), 71.

59 Kristol, *Two Cheers,* 117, 114, 76, 79.

60 Irving Kristol, in "Capitalism, Socialism, and Democracy: A Symposium," *Commentary* 65 (April 1978): 53–54. Kristol also made a plea for the large corporation as an essential ingredient of a pluralist political system which, like the parochial school, was a useful component of the critical checks and balances that guard a free society against government's usurpation of all power. Kristol, "On Corporate Capitalism in America," *The Public Interest,* no. 41 (Fall 1975): 139.

61 Kristol, *Reflections,* 114. Kristol did not refer to nations such as Sweden in this essay.

62 Sidney Blumenthal, *The Rise of the Counter-Establishment: From Conservative Ideology to Political Power* (New York, 1986), 167–68; George Gilder, *Wealth and Poverty* (New York, 1981), 47–51.

63 Blumenthal, *Counter-Establishment,* 166–209; see also Gilder, *Wealth and Poverty,* 43–63.

64 Quoted in Blumenthal, *Counter-Establishment,* 195.

65 Irving Kristol, "Pumping Air into a Balloon," *Wall Street Journal,* January 13, 1976; Irving Kristol, "A New Look at Capitalism," in "George Gilder's *Wealth and Poverty:* A Symposium," *National Review,* April 17, 1981. Critics of supply-side economics have faulted it for having a behaviorist view of human nature, saying that its portrayal of a market economy of simple incentives and rewards to which individuals react is but a new-fashioned version of the "economic man" assumptions in classical economics.

66 Kristol, "Pumping Air," 12; Irving Kristol, "Ideology and Supply-Side Economics," *Commentary* 71 (April 1981): 48, 50.

67 See *Harper's Magazine,* May 1963, and *Atlantic Monthly,* May 1967.

68 Kristol, "Capitalism, Socialism, and Democracy," 54.

69 Irving Kristol, "A Foolish Americanism – Utopianism," *New York Times Magazine,* November 14, 1971, p. 99.

70 Kristol, *Two Cheers,* 48–49, 46 (quotation).

71 Ibid., 128–29, 133–34; Kristol, "Big PX," 30.

72 Kristol, *Two Cheers,* 63.

73 Irving Kristol, "The Old Politics, the New Politics, and the New New Politics," *New York Times Magazine,* November 24, 1968, p. 177.

74 Kristol, in Glasgow interview; Kristol, *Reflections,* 30–31; Irving Kristol, *On the Democratic Idea in America* (New York, 1972), 32–33.

75 Irving Kristol, "Equality," *Commentary* 54 (November 1972): 47 (quotation); Kristol, *Two Cheers,* 63.

76 George H. Nash, *The Conservative Intellectual Movement in America, Since 1945* (New York, 1976), 57–84; J. David Hoeveler, Jr., *The New Humanism: A Critique of Modern America, 1900–1940* (Charlottesville, 1977), 153–78; Peter Viereck, *Conservatism Revisited* (1949; New York, 1962), 47–48.

77 Kristol, *Two Cheers,* 65–66.

78 Ibid., 70.

79 Abel, *Intellectual Follies,* 262.

80 Phillips, *Partisan View,* 74.

81 Howe, *Margin of Hope,* 137; Howe, "New York Intellectuals," 43 (quotation).

82 Quoted in Bloom, *Prodigal Sons,* 145.

83 Goodman, "Kristol," 202. Kristol said: "I am all for religion but I am for institutionalized religions. I don't like religious passions running amuck in society. There is no telling which way they will go." Kristol, in Glasgow interview, 80, and Kristol, *Two Cheers,* 253–54.

84 Howe, *Margin of Hope,* 351.

85 Paul Hollander, *Political Pilgrims: Travels of Western Intellectuals to the Soviet Union, China, and Cuba, 1928–1978* (New York, 1981), 24.

86 Kristol, *Reflections,* 27.

87 Kristol, "American Universities in Exile," *Wall Street Journal,* June 17, 1986.

88 Kristol, in Glasgow interview, 76.

89 Irving Kristol, "The Common Sense of 'Human Rights,' " *Wall Street Journal,* April 8, 1982.

90 Kristol, *Reflections,* 178.

91 Irving Kristol, "What Business Is a University In?" *New York Times Magazine,* November 23, 1969, p. 106.

92 Quoted in Hollander, *Political Pilgrims,* 90.

93 Alfred Kazin, *Starting Out in the Thirties* (1962; New York, 1980), 4–5.

94 Howe, *Margin of Hope,* 73.

95 Quoted in Pells, *Liberal Mind,* 273.

96 Both Trilling and Phillips quoted in Bloom, *Prodigal Sons,* 254–55.

97 Kristol, "Skepticism," 33.

98 Kristol, *Reflections,* 29.

99 Robert M. Crunden, "Cheering Is Not Enough," review of *Two Cheers for Capitalism,* by Irving Kristol, in *Modern Age* 22 (Fall 1978): 422–32.

100 Hollander, *Political Pilgrims,* 434–35, 435n.

101 Gilder, *Wealth and Poverty,* 3, 36–37.

102 As reported by Joseph Sobran, "Capitalism and Ecstasy," *National Review,* July 10, 1981.

103 Irving Kristol, "A New Look at Capitalism," in "George Gilder's *Wealth and Poverty:* A Symposium," *National Review,* April 17, 1981, pp. 414–15.

CHAPTER 5. HILTON KRAMER

1 Hilton Kramer, *The Revenge of the Philistines: Art and Culture, 1972–1984* (New York, 1984), 230–31.

2 Ibid., 242. For a dissenting view on Kramer's writing, see Milton Esterow, "Ethics, Journalism, and Art Criticism, or Watch Out for the Syntax," *Art News* 77 (April 1978): 77. An intemperate, almost hateful, essay on Kramer, motivated mostly, it is clear by Kramer's anticommunism, is Thomas Lawson, "Hilton Kramer: An Appreciation," *Artforum* 23 (November 1984): 90–91. Richard Woll-

heim, on the other hand, said of Kramer that "he restores to art criticism a humanism that constant inroads upon the subject in the past thirty or forty years have tried to eradicate. The artist breathes again with his art." "Modernism: Smothered By Its Enemies" *New York Times,* November 12, 1985.

3 Hilton Kramer, *The Age of Avant-Garde: An Art Chronicle of 1956–1972* (New York, 1973), 294–95.

4 Hilton Kramer, "Interface: Hilton Kramer" (interview), *Performing Arts Journal* 10, no. 1 (1976): 68.

5 Peter Berger, "Our Conservatism and Theirs," *Commentary* 82 (October 1986): 65–66.

6 Kramer, *Avant-Garde,* 395.

7 George F. Will, *The Pursuit of Virtue and Other Tory Notions* (New York, 1982), 319.

8 Hilton Kramer, interview with the author, July 12, 1988, New York City.

9 Ibid.

10 Ibid.; Kramer, "Interface," 67.

11 Kramer, *Philistines,* 18, 324–25; Kramer, *Avant-Garde,* 526.

12 Editors, "A Note on *The New Criterion," The New Criterion* 1 (September 1982): 1, 4. The name of the journal thus had a more literal origin than might have been surmised, even though it did have an intellectual ancestry and common surname in T. S. Eliot's *The Criterion.*

13 Editors, "Problems and Perspectives in Revolutionary Literature," *Partisan Review* 1 (June–July 1934): 3–9. See also Philip Rahv, "A Season in Heaven," *Partisan Review* 3 (June 1936): 11–14, 18; William Phillips, "The Esthetic of the Founding Fathers," *Partisan Review* 4 (March 1938): 11–21; Harold Rosenberg, "Poets of the People," *Partisan Review* 3 (October 1936): 22–26; Philip Rahv, "Proletarian Literature: A Political Autopsy," *Southern Review* 3 (1928–1929): 617–21; Clement Greenberg, "Avant-Garde and Kitsch," *Partisan Review* 6 (Fall 1939): 36. And for a full report, see Terry A. Cooney, *The Rise of the New York Intellectuals: "Partisan Review" and Its Circle, 1934–1945* (Madison, 1986).

14 Irving Howe, *The Decline of the New* (New York, 1963), 5–9. Howe's views would seem to be more descriptive of modernism in art than in architecture, where it was more rational and less subjective.

15 Hilton Kramer, *"Partisan Review:* Down the Memory Hole," *The New Criterion* 2 (September 1983): 7.

16 Kramer, *Avant-Garde,* 502, 511–13; Kramer, *Philistines,* 301–3. See also Harold Rosenberg, *The Tradition of the New* (New York, 1965), 25, 32, and Harold Rosenberg, *Discovering the Present: Three Decades in Art, Culture, and Politics* (Chicago, 1973), 75, 79.

17 Kramer, *Avant-Garde,* 4–5.

18 Ibid., 6.

19 Ibid., 11.

20 Ibid., 12–13.

21 Ibid., 13.

22 Ibid., 2–3, 15–16.

23 Quoted in Sam Hunter and John Jacobus, *American Art of the Twentieth Century* (Englewood Cliffs, N.J.), 372.

24 Ibid., 312.

25 Denis Donoghue, "The Promiscuous Cool of Post-Modernism," *New York Times Book Review*, June 22, 1986, p. 37.

26 Ibid., 37.

27 Hunter and Jacobus, *American Art*, 325–26.

28 Kramer, *Philistines*, 5–6.

29 Kramer, *Avant-Garde*, 18.

30 Kramer, *Philistines*, 3.

31 Ibid., 10 (quotation), 3.

32 Kramer, *Avant-Garde*, 539–40.

33 Kramer, *Philistines*, 30.

34 Kramer, *"Partisan Review,"* 6–7.

35 Ibid., 8–9.

36 Kramer, *Philistines*, 287–88.

37 Hilton Kramer, "Muddled Marxism Replaces Criticism in *Art Forum*," *New York Times*, December 21, 1975, sec. 2.

38 Kramer, *Avant-Garde*, 524, 522–23.

39 Kramer, *Philistines*, 340.

40 Kramer, *Avant-Garde*, 527.

41 Ibid., 525.

42 Serge Guilbaut, *How New York Stole the Idea of Modern Art: Abstract Expressionism, Freedom, and the Cold War* (Chicago, 1983), 2–3, 51, 85, 170–72, 118.

43 Ibid., 188–89, 191–92.

44 Ibid., 200.

45 Dore Ashton, *The New York School: A Cultural Reckoning* (New York, 1972), 57.

46 Hilton Kramer, "American Art since 1945: Who Will Write Its History?" *The New Criterion* (Summer 1985): 1, 4.

47 Andreas Huyssen, "Mapping the Postmodern," *New German Critique,* no. 33 (Fall 1984): 21–22, 18.

48 Ibid., 27, 23, 12, 13.

49 Hal Foster, "Postmodernism: A Preface," in *The Anti-Aesthetic: Essays on Postmodern Culture,* ed. Hal Foster (Port Townsend, Wash., 1983), xii.

50 Fredric Jameson, "Postmodernism and Consumer Society," in *Anti-Aesthetic,* ed. Foster, 113–15, 124–25. Quotation is on 125.

51 Hilton Kramer, "Modernism and Its Enemies," *The New Criterion* 4 (March 1986): 3. Bell's book presented an extended lament for the impact of individualism in Western culture, an influence born of the Renaissance but transferred into the capitalist ethos as well as into the anarchic spirit of modernism in culture. The post-modernist strain merely extended the rebellious direction of both capitalism and modernism, Bell believed. See Daniel Bell, *The Cultural Contradictions of Capitalism* (New York, 1976), 61–145.

52 Hilton Kramer, "The Idea of Tradition in American Art Criticism," *American Scholar* 56 (Summer 1987): 327.

53 For a useful treatment of this subject, see Art Berman, *From the New Criticism*

to Deconstruction: The Reception of Structuralism and Post-Structuralism (Urbana, 1988).

54 See, for example, Raymond Williams, *Marxism and Literature* (New York, 1987), 13-20; Terry Eagleton, *Literary Theory: An Introduction* (Minneapolis, 1983), 17-53. For a general review, consult Vincent Leith, *American Literary Criticism: From the 30s to the 80s* (New York, 1988), 366-403. In short, Marxist criticism was history-centered. It resented the deconstructionists' dissolution of literature into word problematics and aporias of meaning. There were exceptions and occasional efforts to make a solid leftist front that would conjoin Marxism and deconstruction. Jameson accomplished something of this, and Michael Ryan made a belabored and frustrated effort in his book *Marxism and Deconstruction: A Critical Articulation* (Baltimore, 1982).

55 René Wellek, "Destroying Literary Studies," *The New Criterion* 2 (December 1983): 1-3 (quotations), 7.

56 Norman Cantor, "The Real Crisis in the Humanities Today," *The New Criterion* 3 (June 1985): 37-38.

57 Kramer, *Philistines,* 40; Kramer, *Avant-Garde,* 305-7.

58 Kramer, *Philistines,* 111-12.

59 Ibid., 26.

CHAPTER 6. JEANE KIRKPATRICK

1   Arthur M. Schlesinger, Jr., *The Cycles of American History* (Boston, 1986), 51 (quotation), 52.

2   Zbigniew Brzezinski, *Between Two Ages: America's Role in the Technetronic Era* (New York, 1970), 3, 19, 255, 272, 302.

3   Zbigniew Brzezinski, "America in a Hostile World," *Foreign Policy,* no. 23 (Summer 1976): 73, 76 (quotation), 73-74.

4   See Michael Joseph Smith, *Realist Thought from Weber to Kissinger* (Baton Rouge, 1986), 137, 146-47, 156 (quotation).

5   Ibid., 144-45, 147, 169, 171, 178. Kennan too carried his realist position over a long career. See, for example, his essay "Morality and Foreign Policy," *Foreign Affairs* 64 (Winter 1985-86): 205-18.

6   Smith, *Realist Thought,* 191.

7   Henry Kissinger, *White House Years* (New York, 1979), 58-60. Kissinger did not dismiss the role of ideology altogether. It did not provide the Soviet Union with a global design for the direction of its foreign policy, but it did shape that country's perception and understanding of events. See Larry David Nachman, "The Intellectual in Power: The Case of Henry Kissinger," *Salmagundi,* nos. 70-71 (Spring-Summer 1986): 242.

8   Kissinger, *White House Years,* 60.

9   Ibid., 119.

10 Norman Podhoretz, "The Future Danger," *Commentary* (April 1981): 40; Norman Podhoretz, "Kissinger Reconsidered," *Commentary* (June 1982): 24.

11 Sidney Hook, in "How Has the United States Met Its Major Challenges Since 1945?: A Symposium," *Commentary* 80 (November 1985): 49.

12 Podhoretz, "Future Danger," 29–30, 45.

13 Midge Decter, in "How Has the United States," 36; Midge Decter, in "Beyond Containment? The Future of U.S.–Soviet Relations: A Symposium," *Policy Review*, no. 31 (Winter 1985): 17.

14 Podhoretz, "Future Danger," 40.

15 Irving Kristol, "We Can't Resign as Policeman of the World," *New York Times Magazine*, May 12, 1968, p. 105.

16 Irving Kristol, in "Beyond Containment," 18.

17 Irving Kristol, "Foreign Policy in an Age of Ideology," *The National Interest*, no. 1 (Fall 1985): 6–7.

18 Ibid., 13–14; Irving Kristol, "Toward a Moral Foreign Policy," *Wall Street Journal*, November 15, 1983, p. 8; Irving Kristol, in "America Now: A Symposium," *Commentary* 59 (July 1975): 54.

19 Mary Schwarz, "Jeane Kirkpatrick: Our Macho UN Ambassador," *National Review*, January 21, 1983, p. 50.

20 "A Very Candid Interview with Jeane J. Kirkpatrick," *Ladies Home Journal* 103 (May 1986): 176.

21 Adam Wolfson, "The World According to Kirkpatrick," *Policy Review*, no. 31 (Winter 1985): 68.

22 Jeane Kirkpatrick, interview with the author, April 8, 1988, Washington, D.C.

23 Schwarz, "Kirkpatrick," 50.

24 Ann Tremblay, "Jeane Kirkpatrick," *Working Woman* 8 (May 1983): 106–9.

25 Jeane J. Kirkpatrick, *Political and Moral Dimensions*, vol. 1 of *Legitimacy and Force* (New Brunswick, N.J., 1988), 468.

26 Jeane J. Kirkpatrick, *Dictatorships and Double Standards: Rationalism and Reason in Politics* (New York, 1982), 148–50.

27 Ibid., 153–54; see also "America's Political System: The Rules of the Game Are Changing" (interview with Jeane Kirkpatrick), *U.S. News and World Report*, September 18, 1987, pp. 55–56.

28 Kirkpatrick, *Dictatorships and Double Standards*, 192, 193–94.

29 Ibid., 198–99, 200; Jeane J. Kirkpatrick, "The Revolt of the Masses," *Commentary* 55 (February 1973): 58–62.

30 Irving Kristol, "Why a Debate over Contra Aid?" *Wall Street Journal*, April 11, 1986, p. 26; Kristol, "Foreign Policy," 12.

31 Henry Kissinger, *Years of Upheaval* (New York, 1982), 238. Kissinger defended the practical results of détente (236–37).

32 Ibid., 240.

33 Schlesinger, *Cycles of American History*, 96–97.

34 Zbigniew Brzezinski, *Power and Principle: Memoirs of the National Security Advisor, 1977–1981* (New York, 1983), 124.

35 Jimmy Carter, *Keeping Faith: Memoirs of a President* (New York, 1982), 143.

36 Robert W. Tucker, "America in Decline: The Foreign Policy of 'Maturity,'" *Foreign Affairs* 58 (1979): 462. Tucker was critical of the Carter program,

which he called "utopian." It assumed, wrongly, that Third World politics would be exempt from traditional conflicts over wealth, status, and power (464–65).

37 Kirkpatrick, *Dictatorships and Double Standards*, 32.

38 Ibid., 49–50.

39 Ibid., 44–45.

40 Maureen Orth, "Jeane Kirkpatrick: A Woman Capable of Reason," *Vogue* 179 (July 1981): 228.

41 Kirkpatrick, *Political and Moral Dimensions*, 5.

42 Samuel Maxwell Finger, "Jeane Kirkpatrick at the United Nations," *Foreign Affairs* 62 (Winter 1983/1984): 446–47.

43 Tremblay, "Kirkpatrick," 108.

44 Schwarz, "Kirkpatrick," 49; "New Troubles for Kirkpatrick," *Time*, June 21, 1982.

45 Kirkpatrick, *Political and Moral Dimensions*, 174.

46 Ibid., 222–23.

47 Daniel Patrick Moynihan, "Politics of Human Rights," *Commentary* 64 (August 1977): 22.

48 Jeane J. Kirkpatrick, *The Reagan Phenomenon—and Other Speeches on Foreign Policy* (Washington, D.C., 1982), 111–12.

49 Kirkpatrick, *Dictatorships and Double Standards*, 37.

50 Smith, *Realist Thought*, 151.

51 Jeane Kirkpatrick, in "Beyond Containment," 17; Kirkpatrick, *Political and Moral Dimensions*, 38.

52 Quoted in Smith, *Realist Thought*, 181.

53 Kirkpatrick, Introduction to *The Strategy of Deception: A Study in World-Wide Communist Tactics*, ed. Jeane J. Kirkpatrick (New York, 1963), xviii; Kirkpatrick, *Political and Moral Dimensions*, 39; Kirkpatrick, *Dictatorships and Double Standards*, 131.

54 Kirkpatrick, *Dictatorships and Double Standards*, 67, 133.

55 Ibid., 69.

56 Norman Podhoretz, "The Reagan Road to Détente," *Foreign Affairs* 63 (1984): 447–64; Podhoretz, "Future Danger," 39.

57 Wrote Draper: "Geopolitics is also no respecter of credibility, prestige, or honor. The geopolitical outlook is peculiarly hard-boiled and cold-blooded. It sweeps aside such vulnerable human sentiments as credibility, prestige, and honor. Its criterion is the conquest of space and power by whatever means may be necessary to achieve the goal." Theodore Draper, *Present History: On Nuclear War, Détente, and Other Controversies* (New York, 1984), 291.

58 Interview with the author; James Watts and Murray Weidenbaum, "Conservatives at Court: A Conversation with Jeane Kirkpatrick," *Public Opinion* 4 (February/March 1981): 11.

59 Kirkpatrick, *Dictatorships and Double Standards*, 241; Kirkpatrick, *Reagan Phenomenon*, 12; Kirkpatrick, *Political and Moral Dimensions*, 26.

60 Kirkpatrick, *Political and Moral Dimensions*, 417.

61 Kirkpatrick, *Reagan Phenomenon*, 12.

62 Ibid., 4–7; Kirkpatrick, *Political and Moral Dimensions*, 39 (quotation).

63 Kirkpatrick, *Dictatorships and Double Standards*, 120-21.

64 Kirkpatrick, *Political and Moral Dimensions*, 104-5. For further elaboration of Kirkpatrick's case against Cuba, see the address "Cuba and the Cubans" in Jeane J. Kirkpatrick, *National and International Dimensions*, vol. 2 of *Legitimacy and Force* (New Brunswick, N.J., 1988), 180-86.

65 Kirkpatrick, *National and International Dimensions*, 141.

66 See Schlesinger, *Cycles of American History*, 66-67, 71, 73-74, 101.

67 Irving Kristol, "A Foolish Americanism — Utopianism," *New York Times Magazine*, November 14, 1971, p. 99.

68 Irving Kristol, *Reflections of a Neoconservative: Looking Back, Looking Ahead* (New York, 1983), 263.

69 Irving Kristol, "The Common Sense of 'Human Rights,' " *Wall Street Journal*, April 8, 1982, p. 28; Irving Kristol, "The Human Rights Muddle," *Wall Street Journal*, March 20, 1978, p. 14.

70 Irving Kristol, "Human Rights: The Hidden Agenda," *The National Interest* (Winter 1986-87): 9.

71 William Barrett, in "Human Rights and American Foreign Policy," (Symposium), *Commentary* 72 (November 1981), 25-26.

72 Nathan Glazer, in "Human Rights," 36-37.

73 Sidney Hook, in "Human Rights," 41.

74 Peter Berger, in "Human Rights," 27.

75 Seymour Martin Lipset, in "Human Rights," 49.

76 Midge Decter, in "Human Rights," 33.

77 Podhoretz, "Future Danger," 42, 38.

78 Kirkpatrick, *Reagan Phenomenon*, 40-41; Kirkpatrick, *Dictatorships and Double Standards*, 90.

79 Jeane J. Kirkpatrick, in "Human Rights," 44.

80 Jeane J. Kirkpatrick, "Overhaul of U.S. Policy on Human Rights? (Interview with Jeane Kirkpatrick)," *U.S. News and World Report*, March 2, 1982, p. 56.

81 Kirkpatrick, in "Human Rights," 42.

82 Kirkpatrick, *Political and Moral Dimensions*, 147.

83 Kirkpatrick, *Reagan Phenomenon*, 44; Kirkpatrick, *Dictatorships and Double Standards*, 63; Jeane J. Kirkpatrick, "Encouraging Democracies Everywhere," *U.S. News and World Report*, March 18, 1986, p. 36; Kirkpatrick, "Overhaul," 56.

84 Kirkpatrick wrote in 1981: "The restoration of the subjective conviction that American power is a necessary precondition for the survival of liberal democracy in the modern world is the most important development in U.S. foreign policy in the past decade." Kirkpatrick, "Human Rights," 44.

85 Kirkpatrick, *Dictatorships and Double Standards*, 25, 32-33.

86 Paul Johnson, *Modern Times: The World from the Twenties to the Eighties* (New York, 1983), 705-8. The quotation is on 707. Kirkpatrick believed that Johnson used the term "totalitarian" too loosely and that especially in the area of cultural change the Shah fell far short of total control in Iran. Interview with the author.

87 Kirkpatrick, *Political and Moral Dimensions*, 26.

88 Irving Babbitt, *Democracy and Leadership* (Boston, 1924), 127-57.

89 Peter Viereck, *Conservatism Revisited* (1949; New York, 1962), 61.
90 Kirkpatrick, *Reagan Phenomenon*, 36.
91 Schlesinger made this point. See his *Cycles of American History*, 61.
92 Smith, *Realist Thought*, 140.
93 Johnson, *Modern Times*, 709, 696.
94 Jean-Francois Revel, *The Totalitarian Temptation* (Garden City, N.Y., 1977), 15.
95 "A New Age of Capitalism," *Time*, July 28, 1986, pp. 28-39.
96 Irving Babbitt, *Literature and the American College* (Boston, 1908), 185-87.
97 Quoted in Schlesinger, *Cycles of American History*, 94.
98 Quoted in Johnson, *Modern Times*, 614. Johnson quoted the statement from William F. Buckley, Jr., who in turn cited George F. Kennan.

CHAPTER 7. ROBERT NISBET

1   Robert Nisbet, *Conservatism: Dream and Reality* (Minneapolis, 1986), 2-3.
2   Robert Nisbet, "The Dilemma of Conservatives in a Populist Society," *Policy Review*, no. 4 (Spring 1978): 92-93.
3   Robert Nisbet, *Prejudices: A Philosophical Dictionary* (Cambridge, Mass., 1982), 55.
4   Robert Nisbet, *Twilight of Authority* (New York, 1975), 195.
5   Robert Nisbet, *Tradition and Revolt: Historical and Sociological Essays* (New York, 1980), 144, 154 (quotation).
6   Robert Nisbet, *History of the Idea of Progress* (New York, 1980), 348.
7   Robert Nisbet, "Teggart of Berkeley," *American Scholar* 48 (Winter 1978/79): 71-80.
8   Robert Nisbet, "Many Tocquevilles," *American Scholar* 46 (Winter 1976/77): 66-77.
9   Robert Nisbet, *The Social Philosophers: Community and Conflict in Western Thought*, concise ed., updated (New York, 1982), 209.
10 Robert W. Glasgow, "In the Twilight of Authority: The Obsessive Concern with Self" (interview with Robert Nisbet), *Psychology Today* 7 (December 1973): 49.
11 Nisbet, *Prejudices*, 308-9.
12 Nisbet, *Tradition and Revolt*, 73.
13 Ibid., 75-79; Nisbet, *Conservatism*, 1-2.
14 Robert Nisbet, *Émile Durkheim: With Selected Essays* (1965; Westport, Conn., 1976), 3-4.
15 Ibid., 4-7. The quotation is on 6.
16 Ibid., 18.
17 Ibid., 33.
18 Nisbet, *Social Philosophers*, 213-14; Nisbet, *Conservatism*, 9-10.
19 Nisbet, *Social Philosophers*, 233.
20 Nisbet, *Conservatism*, 6-7.
21 Nisbet, *Prejudices*, 182-83, 92.

22 Robert Nisbet, "Besieged by the State," *Harper's* 268 (June 1984): 50; Nisbet, *Twilight of Authority*, 196–97.

23 Nisbet, *Prejudices*, 34.

24 Nisbet, "Dilemma," 92–93.

25 Nisbet, *Twilight of Authority*, 205; Nisbet, *Prejudices*, 167, 169–70.

26 Nisbet, *Twilight of Authority*, 228–29; Nisbet, *Prejudices*, 210–13.

27 Nisbet, *Durkheim*, 38–39.

28 Ibid., 64–65, 54.

29 Ibid., 62.

30 Nisbet, "Besiegcd," 49.

31 Nisbet, *Durkheim*, 63.

32 Nisbet, *Conservatism*, 36.

33 Nisbet, *Prejudices*, 126.

34 Ibid., 51–53.

35 Ibid., 128–30.

36 Nisbet, *Twilight of Authority*, 140–41; Nisbet, in Glasgow interview, 44.

37 Nisbet, "Many Tocquevilles," 69.

38 Nisbet, in Glasgow interview, 44 (quotation); Robert Nisbet, "Knowledge Dethroned," *New York Times Magazine*, September 28, 1975, p. 35.

39 Nisbet, *Prejudices*, 187.

40 Robert Nisbet, "Radicalism as Therapy," *Encounter* 38 (March 1972): 53–54; Nisbet, *Twilight of Authority*, 8–9.

41 Nisbet, "Radicalism as Therapy," 54–56; Nisbet, *Prejudices*, 244.

42 Nisbet, *Twilight of Authority*, 29–30.

43 Ibid., 8; Nisbet, in Glasgow interview, 51–52.

44 Nisbet, *Twilight of Authority*, 7; Nisbet, in Glasgow interview, 52.

45 Nisbet, *Twilight of Authority*, 152, 192.

46 Nisbet, *Prejudices*, 225 (quotation), 227–28; Nisbet, *Social Philosophers*, 208.

47 Nisbet, *Prejudices*, 198, 200, 194–97, 310. The quotations are on 195 and 197.

48 Nisbet, *Durkheim*, 53.

49 Nisbet, *Prejudices*, 234.

50 Nisbet, *History of the Idea of Progress*, 323; Nisbet, *Conservatism*, 25.

51 Nisbet, *Conservatism*, 25 (quotation), 43.

52 Ibid., 29–30.

53 Nisbet, *Conservatism*, 33.

54 Nisbet, *Durkheim*, 22.

55 Edward Shils, *Tradition* (Chicago, 1981), 288–90, 303.

56 Nisbet, *History of the Idea of Progress*, 324–27.

57 Nisbet, *Prejudices*, 266–68, 242.

58 Nisbet, *History of the Idea of Progress*, 331–32.

59 Nisbet, *Prejudices*, 335, 101, 296–97.

60 Ibid., 295–96.

61 Ibid., 5; Nisbet, *Twilight of Authority*, 240 (quotation).

62 Nisbet, *Prejudices*, 59; Nisbet, "Dilemma," 95.

63 Nisbet, *Prejudices*, 34.

64 Nisbet included an essay on the abortion issue in *Prejudices*. For individuals

who wearied of the strident moralistic and ideological positions of extremists on both sides of the issue in the United States, Nisbet's essay was a model of clarity and good sense and was especially valuable for showing the kind of conservative thought that abhorred ideology. Remembering Hegel's comment that the greatest crises of history are not those of right versus wrong but of right versus right, Nisbet condemned the sweeping position of the United States Supreme Court (*Roe v. Wade*, 1973) for "wiping out the laws, mores, and customs of fifty states" and lifting the issue from the twilight zone of pluralism and compromise into the authority of national mandate." But Nisbet also warned against the harm done to the social fabric by "aggressive antiabortionists," "soldiers of righteousness" who "strike at the heart of both family and private rights" (5).

65   Nisbet, *Conservatism*, 104–5.
66   Ibid., 57–62, 38 (quotation).
67   Nisbet, *Twilight of Authority*, 87; Nisbet, *History of the Idea of Progress*, 353–54.
68   Nisbet, *History of the Idea of Progress*, 354.
69   Nisbet, *Conservatism*, 68–69; Nisbet, *Prejudices*, 97–98, 100–102; Nisbet, *History of the Idea of Progress*, 356–57; Nisbet, *Twilight of Authority*, 88–89.
70   Nisbet, *Prejudices*, 41–42.
71   Robert Bellah et al., *Habits of the Heart: Individualism and Commitment in American Life* (New York, 1985).
72   Ibid., 84.
73   Ibid., 72–75, 82–83. Quotation is on 72.
74   Ibid., 83.
75   Ibid., 286, 277 (quotation).
76   Ibid., 262–71, 284–85, 295–96. Quotation is on 285.
77   Nisbet, *Twilight of Authority*, 24, 217; Nisbet, *Conservatism*, 47 (quotation). See also Nisbet's suggestive essay "Envy" in *Prejudices*, 107–9.

CHAPTER 8. R. EMMETT TYRRELL, JR.

1   Robert Nisbet, "The Bad Boy of Bloomington," *National Review*, May 25, 1979, p. 687.
2   R. Emmett Tyrrell, Jr., interview with the author, September 21, 1987, Brookfield, Wis.
3   Quoted in Stephen Schiff, "Spectator Sport," *Vanity Fair* (September 1985): 103.
4   R. Emmett Tyrrell, Jr., "On Ten Years of Public Service," *American Spectator* 11 (November 1977): 4; R. Emmett Tyrrell, Jr., "Reflections on a Merry State," *American Spectator* 12 (February 1978): 4.
5   See R. Emmett Tyrrell, Jr., "I Remember Bloomington," *American Spectator* 20 (December 1987): 94–99.
6   Writers with major journals include Martha Bayles, television critic, *Wall Street Journal;* Roger Rosenblatt, senior writer, *Time;* George Will; John O'Sullivan, editorial page editor, *New York Post,* and others. Members of the Reagan administration include Aram Bakshian, Jr., director of speechwriting for the presi-

dent; Christopher Buckley, speechwriter for the vice-president; Jeane Kirkpatrick; Daniel Pipes, special adviser to the counselor, Department of State; Eugene Rostow, director, Arms Control and Disarmament Agency.

7   H. L. Mencken, *A Book of Prefaces* (Garden City, N.Y. 1917), 11.

8   R. Emmett Tyrrell, Jr., *Public Nuisances* (New York, 1979), 3.

9   Tyrrell, "Reflections," 5; R. Emmett Tyrrell, Jr., "The Need for a Public Nuisance Law," *American Spectator* 11 (February 1978): 4.

10 Tyrrell, "On Ten Years," 4.

11 H. L. Mencken, ed., *Americana, 1926* (New York, 1926), 1, 16, 35.

12 *American Spectator* 16 (January 1983): 9.

13 *American Spectator* 11 (December 1977): 2.

14 *American Spectator* 16 (March 1983): 7.

15 *American Spectator* 15 (July 1982): 42.

16 *American Spectator* 14 (October 1981): 42.

17 *American Spectator* 22 (June 1989): 58.

18 *American Spectator* 15 (April 1982): 42.

19 *American Spectator* 15 (May 1982): 42.

20 *American Spectator* 13 (September 1980): 38.

21 *American Spectator* 14 (September 1981): 38.

22 *American Spectator* 16 (February 1983): 38.

23 *American Spectator* 16 (May 1983): 39.

24 *American Spectator* 13 (August 1980): 45.

25 *American Spectator* 11 (May 1978): 38.

26 *American Spectator* 17 (August 1984): 47.

27 *American Spectator* 9 (January 1976): 4.

28 *American Spectator* 10 (October 1976): 16.

29 Douglas Bartholomew, "Hoffman's of San Francisco," *American Spectator* 15 (August 1982): 28; James P. Melling III, "Arnold's of Cincinnati," *American Spectator* 17 (October 1979): 23; James P. Melling III, "Louisville's Cunningham's," *American Spectator* 11 (April 1978): 27; J. David Hoeveler, Jr., "The Milwaukee Turners," *American Spectator* 17 (April 1984): 40.

30 Brian Thomas, "The Taproom of the Schoenling Brewery," *American Spectator* 10 (November 1976): 22.

31 Joe Mysak, "Barmaids," *American Spectator* 14 (April 1981): 34.

32 *American Spectator* 13 (January 1980): back cover.

33 *American Spectator* 16 (May 1983): 38.

34 Tyrrell, *Public Nuisances,* 170.

35 R. Emmett Tyrrell, Jr., *The Liberal Crack-Up* (New York, 1984), 11, 28-30.

36 Tyrrell, *Public Nuisances,* 210-11; R. Emmett Tyrrell, Jr., "Mashed Politics," *American Spectator* 16 (November 1983): 6.

37 Tyrrell, "Mashed Politics," 6.

38 Tyrrell, *Public Nuisances,* 132.

39 Robert K. Landers, review of *Public Nuisances,* by R. Emmett Tyrrell, Jr., *Commonweal* 104 (August 1979): 446.

40 Tyrrell, *Public Nuisances*, 106–7.

41 R. Emmett Tyrrell, Jr., "Hoosier Cantos," *American Spectator* 10 (February 1977): 39.

42 Tyrrell, *Public Nuisances*, 113.

43 Henri Bergson, *Laughter* (New York, 1911), pt. 3, p. 1.

44 Tyrrell, *Public Nuisances*, 124.

45 Tyrrell, *Liberal Crack-Up*, 121, 127.

46 R. Emmett Tyrrell, Jr., "Bouquets for the Israelites," *American Spectator* 14 (August 1981): 4.

47 R. Emmett Tyrrell, Jr., "Prime-Time War," *American Spectator* 16 (April 1983): 6. On the accelerating weapons race between the United States and the Soviet Union, Tyrrell asserted that "actually, American power is what saves us from nuclear holocaust," and he decried the "America Last" mentality that he charged to many liberals. R. Emmett Tyrrell, Jr., "America Last," *American Spectator* 13 (January 1980): 13.

48 R. Emmett Tyrrell, Jr., "My Kind of Bomb," *American Spectator* 14 (October 1981): 4.

49 Tyrrell, *Liberal Crack-Up*, 113, 88, 198.

50 R. Emmett Tyrrell, Jr., "The Mullah Brown," *American Spectator* 12 (May 1979): 4.

51 Tyrrell, *Public Nuisances*, 26.

52 Ibid., 165.

53 Quoted in Tyrrell, *Public Nuisances*, 198.

54 Ibid., 69.

55 Ibid., 100.

56 Ibid.

57 Quoted by Tyrrell in *American Spectator* 14 (May 1981): 42.

58 R. Emmett Tyrrell, Jr., "That Warm Oval-Shaped Vacuum," *American Spectator* 14 (May 1981): 4.

59 Tyrrell, *Public Nuisances*, 218.

60 Ibid., 220.

61 Ibid., 217.

62 R. Emmett Tyrrell, Jr., "The Great Jailer of the Caribbean," *American Spectator* 12 (December 1979): 4–5; Tyrrell, *Public Nuisances*, 193.

63 H. L. Mencken, "The Need for an Aristocracy," in *The Superfluous Men: Conservative Critics of American Culture, 1900–1945,* ed. Robert M. Crunden (Austin, 1977), 73–75.

64 Interview with the author.

65 Tyrrell, *Public Nuisances*, 40.

66 Tyrrell, *Liberal Crack-Up*, 33, 144.

67 R. Emmett Tyrrell, Jr., "New Vistas in Bigotry," *American Spectator* 12 (March 1979): 41.

68 Tyrrell, *Public Nuisances*, 244.

69 R. Emmett Tyrrell, Jr., "The Great White Ph.D.," *American Spectator* 13 (June 1980): 4. Proposition 13 was a California referendum to reduce state taxes.

70 Tyrrell, *Public Nuisances,* 213, 197.

71 Tyrrell, "Mullah Brown," 4.

72 R. Emmett Tyrrell, Jr., "The Voice Grows Louder," *American Spectator* 15 (December 1982): 4–5.

73 Tyrrell, *Public Nuisances,* 182–83.

74 Mencken, *Book of Prefaces,* 237.

75 Tyrrell, *Public Nuisances,* 175.

76 One could pursue this comparison at some length. Mencken, of course, played a significant role as a literary critic in leading a realist revolt against the "Genteel Tradition" in American culture, and he welcomed Theodore Dreiser as the major voice of that revolt. Nock, on the other hand, registered mostly disgust for the new literature and stood on strongly classical standards, the literature of ancient Greece and Rome, as "the longest and fullest continuous record available to us, of what the human mind had been busy about in practically every department of spiritual and social activity." Quoted by Robert M. Crunden in *The Mind and Art of Albert J. Nock* (Chicago, 1964), 129–30. Compare Tyrrell: "America has become a junkyard of fourth-rate fiction." In contrast, he added, "the Western literary tradition is such an enormous vault of treasures – treasures which can be read and reread with pleasure and instruction – that I see no reason for an intelligent reader to loiter amongst the trash of contemporary fiction." R. Emmett Tyrrell, Jr., "The Writer, the Publisher, the Gull," *American Spectator* 9 (December 1975): 4. Also, Tyrrell defended his use of big words by appealing to the standards and high tradition of the English language. If words are not regularly and appropriately used, he said, the language atrophies and becomes limp and ineffective. Interview with the author.

77 Paul Elmer More, *Shelburne Essays: First Series* (1904; New York, 1967), 76–79, 72.

78 Tyrrell, *Public Nuisances,* 87, 92 (quoting Talese), 89.

79 Ibid., 93.

80 Tyrrell, *Liberal Crack-Up,* 129.

81 Ibid., 202–3.

82 Tyrrell, *Public Nuisances,* 241.

83 Ibid., 243.

84 Ibid., 150.

85 See the selections from the *American Spectator* 22 (July 1989): 14–15; (October 1989): 14–16; (November 1989): 17–21.

86 Elliott Abrams, "Poison Pen," *Commentary* 68 (July 1979): 78–80.

87 Bertram Wyatt-Brown, "The Abolitionist Controversy: Men of Blood, Men of God," in *Men, Women, and Issues in American History,* ed. Howard H. Quint and Milton Cantor (Homewood, Ill., 1980), 237.

88 Ibid., 237.

89 Tyrrell, *Liberal Crack-Up,* 220, 213.

90 Ibid., 70.

91 Quoted in Page Smith, *The Rise of Industrial America: A People's History of the Post-Reconstruction Era* (New York, 1984), 713.

CHAPTER 9. MICHAEL NOVAK

1 Michael Novak, *The Rise of the Unmeltable Ethnics: Politics and Culture in the Seventies* (New York, 1972), 47, 86, 245–46. Thus Novak wrote: "The feeling for religion among Slavic and Italian peoples is almost totally different from the feeling of WASPS or Irish Catholics: more pagan, more secular, closer to earth, aesthetic rather than moral, meditative rather than organizational" (86).

2 Ibid., 203 (quotation), 195.

3 Ibid., 126. See also 68–71 for an elaboration of this complaint.

4 Ibid., 123.

5 Ibid., 126.

6 Ibid., 164–80. Agnew had referred to intellectuals, the media, radical professors, and student protestors as "an elite corps of impudent snobs."

7 Ibid., 9, 249.

8 Ibid., 249–50, 253. Already at this point Novak was criticizing what he believed was an obsession with procedural democracy in American liberalism and even more so in the New Left. For democratic procedures teach nothing, inculcate nothing of the values that must come first from family and intimate group life. "It is simply not true," Novak wrote, "that the spreading use of democratic procedures — an increase in participatory democracy — will bring people dignity, or satisfaction, or moral pride, or political potency" (272).

9 Ibid., 11, 107, 155.

10 Ibid., 13, 299.

11 Ibid., 107–9, 323.

12 Ibid., 152–54. Actually, Novak considered television "the most recent and thus leftist, enthusiasm." It favored the newest and most modern commercial artifacts, conveying an ethic of progress and modernization that stood square against ethnic sensibility (154).

13 Ibid., 37.

14 Kenneth Clark, review of *The Rise of the Unmeltable Ethnics*, by Michael Novak, *American Scholar* 42 (Winter 1972/73): 158. Novak would later regret that he had dealt so harshly with the Anglo-Saxon ethnic group. For now, however, the only redeeming trait he could find in that group was its willingness to hear criticism of itself. It was easy to play on the guilt feelings of the Anglo-Saxon. But Novak's later endearment to Anglo-Saxon ways led him to state that he was glad that his parents did not move to an area of a different culture in Johnstown (105; interview with the author, April 7, 1988, Washington, D.C.).

15 Garry Wills, review of *The Rise of the Unmeltable Ethnics*, by Michael Novak, *New York Times Book Review*, April 23, 1972, p. 27.

16 Michael Novak, "Orthodoxy vs. Progressive Bourgeois Christianity," in *Once a Catholic: Prominent Catholics and Ex-Catholics Discuss the Influence of the Church on Their Lives and Works*, ed. Peter Occhiogrosso (Boston, 1987), 121.

17 Novak, *Unmeltable Ethnics*, xxxiv.

18 Ibid., 66.

19 Ibid., 23.

20 Michael Novak, *The Spirit of Democratic Capitalism* (New York, 1982), 23.
    Novak wrote: "When in college I first began to read English writers like Hobbes,
    Locke, and Mill, and American writers like James, Peirce, and Dewey, I ex-
    perienced their underlying images as alien and offensive. Their talk of (as it
    seemed to me) atomic individuals forming 'contracts' and 'compacts,' and their
    way of thinking in a narrowly empirical, pragmatic way, seemed to me not
    only foreign but spiritually *wrong*" (24).

21 Michael Novak, *The Open Church: Vatican II, Act II* (New York, 1964), xi–xiii, 6.

22 Ibid., 337.

23 Michael Novak, *Belief and Unbelief: A Philosophy of Self-Knowledge* (New
    York, 1965), 189–90.

24 Michael Novak, *The Experience of Nothingness* (New York, 1970), 29 (quota-
    tion), 32–34.

25 Michael Novak, *A Theology for Radical Politics* (New York, 1969), 13, 17,
    74, 21, 23, 29, 74, 60.

26 Robert McAfee Brown, Abraham Heschel, and Michael Novak, *Vietnam: Crisis
    of Conscience* (New York, 1967), 7; Robert McAfee Brown, " 'A Symbol is
    a Symbol is a Symbol,' A Reply to Michael Novak," *Christian Century,* May
    22, 1974, p. 563.

27 Novak, *Vietnam,* 12, 17, 21.

28 Michael Novak, *A Time to Build* (New York, 1967), 373–81.

29 Michael Novak, *Freedom with Justice: Catholic Social Thought and Liberal
    Institutions* (San Francisco, 1984), 168–69; Michael Novak, "The Greening of
    a Con-III Man," *Commonweal,* December 4, 1970, p. 246.

30 Michael Novak, "Needing Niebuhr Again," *Commentary* 54 (September 1972):
    52–63, 59, 61. See also Michael Novak, "A Changed View of 'The Movement' "
    Christian Century, September 13, 1978, p. 830.

31 Novak, "Needing Niebuhr," 59; Novak, *Unmeltable Ethnics,* 340; Michael No-
    vak, *Choosing Our King: Powerful Symbols in Presidential Politics* (New York,
    1974), 89–90. Although Novak actively supported George McGovern for the
    presidency in 1972, he harbored a deep distaste for McGovern's pious moralism.
    Novak said in an interview, "Every time I hear McGovern speak I hate it."
    "Conversation with Michael Novak," 1972, file, Instructional Media Lab, University
    of Wisconsin–Milwaukee.

32 Michael Novak, "Against 'Affirmative Action,' " *Commonweal,* April 5, 1974,
    p. 102.

33 Novak, *Choosing Our King,* 70–71.

34 Novak, "A Changed View," 830.

35 Michael Novak, "Switch to Reagan for a Strong America," *Commonweal,* Oc-
    tober 24, 1980, p. 589. For Novak's high estimate of Henry Jackson, see Michael
    Novak, "In Memoriam: Henry M. Jackson," *Commentary* 107 (January 1984):
    48–50. Novak later wrote: "I felt the Democratic Party changing its allegiance,
    away from working people and toward the symbol-making class around the
    universities, the news media, and the industries of culture." Michael Novak,

"Errand into the Wilderness," in *Political Passages: Journeys of Change through Two Decades, 1968-1988,* ed. John H. Bunzel (New York, 1988), 257. This essay is a useful autobiographical account of Novak's political evolution.

36 Michael Novak, *The Joy of Sports: End Zones, Bases, Baskets, Balls, and the Consecration of the American Spirit* (New York, 1976), x.

37 Ibid., 40, 216–19; Novak, *Choosing Our King,* 293.

38 Novak, *Joy of Sports,* xv, 44.

39 Ibid., 101, 107.

40 Ibid., 90.

41 Ibid., 58–59.

42 Ibid., 60.

43 Ibid., 61.

44 Ibid., 19–20.

45 Ibid., 284.

46 Novak, *Democratic Capitalism,* 17–18.

47 Ibid., 248. See also Michael Novak, "The Politics of John Paul II," *Commentary* 106 (December 1979): 60.

48 Novak, *Democratic Capitalism,* 13; Michael Novak and Peter Berger, *Speaking to the Third World: Essays on Democracy and Development* (Washington, D.C. 1985), 33.

49 Novak, *Freedom with Justice,* 174–75.

50 Novak, *Democratic Capitalism,* 101–3.

51 Ibid., 14–15. For a rebuttal to Novak on the issue of capitalism and democracy, see the essay by Novak's in-house rival at *Commonweal,* Peter Steinfels, "Michael Novak and His Ultrasuper Democratic-Capitalism," *Commonweal,* January 14, 1983, p. 15.

52 Novak, *Democratic Capitalism,* 212–13. Wrote Novak:

The rich are useful because their odd tastes prevent our architecture from being monotonously bureaucratic. Their taste in hotels makes it possible for millions to stay, at least one or twice, in something other than middle-period Holiday Inn. Their mushy ideological sentiments lead them, often enough, to endow foundations which sponsor scholars who write in favor of overturning the system. Not a few museums, galleries, symphony halls, and libraries owe their nonbureaucratic liberties and real human beauties to the grand ambitions of the rich for public immortality. [213]

53 Novak, *Democratic Capitalism,* 90. Actually, Novak was now arguing that rationalization was more appropriate to a socialist arrangement than to a capitalist one, that Max Weber, in his famous analysis, had made too much of that factor in explaining capitalist values and culture. Novak's public commitment to capitalism might be dated with his article "A Closet Capitalist Confesses," *Wall Street Journal,* April 20, 1976.

54 Michael Novak, *Confession of a Catholic* (San Francisco, 1983), 8–9, 112–13.

55 Michael Novak, "Men without Women," *American Spectator* 11 (October 1978): 16.

56 Michael Novak, "Gay Is Not Liberation," *Commonweal,* May 31, 1974, p. 304.

57 Michael Novak, "In Praise of Bourgeois Virtues," *Society* 18 (January–February 1981): 120–21.

58 Novak, *Democratic Capitalism,* 88, 121.

59 Ibid., 121. When Novak reviewed Kristol's book *Two Cheers for Capitalism,* he found it "astonishing" that Kristol appealed to the need for religion, both in its private experience and public expression, only to draw back from any elaboration of religious belief. Michael Novak, "A Liberal Critique," *Commentary* 105 (July 1978): 68.

60 Novak, *Democratic Capitalism,* 340–43.

61 Steinfels, "Michael Novak," 13–15.

62 Michael Novak, "The Danger of Egalityranny," *American Spectator* 15 (August 1982): 8.

63 For a sampling of Novak's views on foreign policy, see Novak, *Unmeltable Ethnics,* 308–9; Michael Novak, "Reconcilation and the Russians," *National Review,* July 27, 1984, p. 37; Michael Novak, in "How Has the United States Met Its Major Challenges Since 1945?: A Symposium," *Commentary* 80 (November 1985): 77; Michael Novak, "Better Dead Than the Living Dead: The Totalitarian Difference," *American Spectator* 14 (November 1981): 13–14; Michael Novak, in "Human Rights and American Foreign Policy: A Symposium," *Commentary* 72 (November 1981): 57–58; Michael Novak, "Illusions about Nicaragua," *National Review,* June 29, 1984, p. 38.

64 National Conference of Catholic Bishops, *The Challenge of Peace: God's Promise and Our Response* ([Detroit], 1983), introduction.

65 Ibid., par. 46, 47, 49.

66 Ibid., par. 259, 250, 251.

67 Ibid., par. 78.

68 Michael Novak, *Moral Clarity in the Nuclear Age* (Nashville, 1983), 50, 54, 56.

69 Ibid., 25, 61.

70 Irving Kristol, "Adam Smith and the Spirit of Capitalism," in *Reflections of a Neoconservative: Looking Back, Looking Ahead* (New York, 1983), 139–76.

71 Michael Novak, "Why the Church Is Not Pacifist," *Catholicism in Crisis* 2 (June 1984): 33–34.

72 To be sure, Novak too felt the losses. By 1987 he had come to regret the long influences of Vatican II on Catholic worship. He wrote: "Now we endure the Liturgy of Happy Talk and Forced Cheerfulness. It's worse than television, and as I grow older, it affects me badly. . . . The reformers took out all sense of mystery, all sense of real adoration, and all sense of real humility. They took the solitary and the personal out of religion, making it group-think . . . we've lost that connection with the past history of the Church." Novak "Orthodoxy vs. Progressive Bourgeois Christianity," 127.

73 Novak, *Freedom with Justice,* 24, 179.

74 Novak in his book *Freedom with Justice* gave considerable attention to papal pronunciations, from those of Pius XII to those of John Paul II, on issues of economics and politics (see 124–44).

75 Editors, "The Present Crisis," *Catholicism in Crisis* 1 (November 1982): 1–2.

76 National Conference of Catholic Bishops, *Economic Justice for All: Catholic Social Teaching and the U.S. Economy* (Washington, D.C., 1986), par. 49, 52, 87, 92, 103.

77　Michael Novak, "The Christian View of Economic Life," *Catholicism in Crisis* 3 (December 1985): 29–30. Are these rights equal to basic civil freedoms? "No they are not," Novak replied. "These 'rights' undermine human dignity. No one who is a ward of the state can share the same full dignity as persons of self-reliance. The Catholic ideal is self-reliance" (30).

78　Michael Novak, "The Bishops' Second Draft," *Catholicism in Crisis* 3 (November 1985): 54.

79　Novak, "The Christian View," 26.

80　See, for example, Michael Novak, "On Nicaragua," *Catholicism in Crisis* 2 (July 1983): 1–3. Novak called for American intervention in Nicaragua – or at the very least establishment of a blockade to prevent shipment of arms from Nicaragua.

81　Novak, *Freedom with Justice*, 196; Michael Novak, "The Case against Liberation Theology," *New York Times Magazine*, October 2, 1984, pp. 62–63.

82　Michael Novak, *Will It Liberate? Questions about Liberation Theology* (Mahwah, N.J., 1987), 5, 38, 58.

83　Berger and Novak, *Speaking to the Third World*, 43; Michael Novak, *Toward a Theology of the Corporation* (Washington, D.C., 1981), 11–12.

84　Novak, *Will It Liberate?*, 47–48. To be sure, Novak was disinclined to use the label "neoconservatism" to embrace a comprehensive philosophy. His most explicit reference was the following: "This fear of the state places me on the 'neoconservative' side of the debate – neither libertarian nor democratic socialist, but a person of the left who has grown to be critical of the left because of its excesive reliance on politics and the state, to the neglect of economic activism" (177–78).

85　Ibid., 188–89.

86　Ibid., 163–64.

87　Michael Novak, interview, *U.S. News and World Report*, February 25, 1980, p. 69; Novak, "Switch to Reagan," 591. Novak later elaborated: "Now I understand that there are *two* 'power elites' in this nation: (1) the 'old elite,' whose base lies in the business sector, and whose vision of what makes America great looks to her economic and political freedoms, and (2) the 'new class,' whose base lies in education and the new communications industries, and whose vision of what makes America great is a compassionate (therefore, large) government." Novak, "Errand into the Wilderness," 258.

88　Novak, "In Praise of Bourgeois Virtues," 60–62. See also Michael Novak, "Boredom, Virtue, and Democratic Capitalism," *Commentary* 87 (September 1989): 34–37.

89　See George H. Nash, *The Conservative Intellectual Movement in America, Since 1945* (New York, 1976), 80–81.

90　Novak, *Freedom with Justice*, 33.

91　Novak, "Orthodoxy vs. Progressive Bourgeois Christianity," 128.

92　Michael Novak, "Religion and Labor," *National Review*, April 6, 1984.

93　Novak, *Will It Liberate?* 192–93.

94　Ibid., 205.

95 See Christopher Dawson, "Catholicism and the Bourgeois Mind" (reprint), *Catholicism in Crisis* 4 (December 1986): 17–22. Dawson wrote: "The victory of bourgeois civilization has made England rich and powerful, but at the same time it has destroyed almost everything that made life worth living. It has undermined the natural foundations of our national life, so that the whole social structure is in danger of ruin" (18).

96 In an interview with the author, Novak said about this point that it depends where you enter this argument historically. Novak said that he appreciated the cultural conservatives who reject the hubris of humanism, and he mentioned Henry Adams in this context. But one cannot make history a sanction from the modern world, he added. Pre-modernism can too easily become a fruitless fixation.

AFTERWORD

1 Quoted in Russell Kirk, ed. *The Portable Conservative Reader* (New York, 1982), 18–19.

2 Russell Kirk, *A Program for Conservatives* (Chicago, 1952), 3.

3 Thomas Sowell, *A Conflict of Visions* (New York, 1987), 41–47, quotations on 42 and 41. Sowell also applied these distinctions in a manner that reflected neoconservative views of the New Class. Later in the book, Sowell wrote: "What is at the heart of the difference between [the two views of knowledge] is the question as to whether human capabilities or potential permit social decisions to be made collectively through the articualted rationality of surrogates, so as to produce the specific social results desired" (112).

4 Here too, of course, is another interesting parallel between the conservative intellectuals and the Reagan phenomenon. With reference to what he called the "Social Agenda" of the Reagan administrations, Nathan Glazer described two class and geographical coalitions that stood on either side of it. That is, issues such as busing and neighborhood schools, school prayer, and abortion found a less privileged group of "Bible belt" Protestants and working and middle-class Catholics in opposition to a more privileged group of liberal Protestants and Jews in the cities of the East and West. "These issues," Glazer wrote, "have no impact in Ivy League Schools, whose faculty, students, and law professors are generally mystified by the uproar." Glazer, "The Social Agenda," in *Perspectives on the Reagan Years,* ed. John L. Palmer (Washington, D.C., 1987), 7–8.

5 Irving Babbitt, *Democracy and Leadership* (Boston, 1924), 212.

6 Friedrich von Hayek, *The Constitution of Liberty* (Chicago, 1960), 61. Hayek is quoting Joseph Butler. This discussion by no means exhausts the interesting and difficult question of libertarianism and conservatism. For more thought on this subject see Robert Nisbet, "Conservatives and Libertarians: Uneasy Cousins," Murray Rothbard, "Myth and Truth About Libertarianism," and Tibor R. Machan, "Libertarianism and Conservatism," all in *Modern Age* 24 (Winter 1980): 2–8, 9–15, 21–23, respectively. The case for libertarianism was power-

fully presented in Robert Nozick's prize-winning book of 1974, *Anarchy, State, and Utopia.*

7 One example is the 1930s publication *The American Review.* See J. David Hoeveler, Jr., *"The American Review,"* in *The American Conservative Press,* ed. Ronald Lora and William H. Longton (forthcoming).

8 George H. Nash, *The Conservative Intellectual Movement in America, Since 1945* (New York, 1976), 69.

9 Kirk wrote: "The current American passion for turnpikes, freeways, and gigantic roadways under other labels is an instance of my meaning. Scarcely a voice is raised in protest when such a project destroys hundreds of farms, demolishes interesting old neighborhoods, parts a rural district forever into halves, or dehumanizes a landscape. Here is the pure Utilitarian mind at work, contemptuous of beauty and social roots." Kirk, *Program for Conservatives,* 291.

10 Ibid., 107, 147.

11 Lynne V. Cheney, *Humanities in America: A Report to the President, the Congress, and the American People* (Washington, D.C., 1988).

12 Interestingly, the Straussians suggested to one American historian a particularly American kind of conservatism. "The Straussians are peculiarly American sorts of conservatives, basically scornful of historical experience and the restraints it imposes, and eager to change things. Their conception of the Founding only serves to increase our political and judicial flightiness. What we need instead is real conservatism, which entails less veneration for the Founding Fathers and a deeper sense of the historical process. Understanding our entire political heritage, not just the Founding, will give us about as durable and as truly conservative a standard for groping our way into the future as we are likely to get." Gordon S. Wood, "The Fundamentalists and the Constitution," *New York Review of Books,* February 18, 1988, p. 40. See M. E. Bradford, *Remembering Who We Are: Observations of a Southern Conservative* (Athens, Ga., 1985), especially the essay "The Agrarian Tradition: An Affirmation," 83–90.

13 Hugh Heclo, "Reaganism and the Search for a Public Philosophy," in *Perspectives on the Reagan Years,* ed. Palmer, 46.

14 Garry Wills, *Reagan's America: Innocents at Home* (New York, 1987), 148.

15 George F. Will, *The New Season: A Spectator's Guide to the 1988 Election* (New York, 1987), 80–81.

16 Irving Kristol, "Reviewing Reagan's Reviewers," *Wall Street Journal,* September 11, 1985.

17 Paul Gottfried and Thomas Fleming, *The Conservative Movement* (Boston, 1988), vii, xi.

18 Donald Atwell Zoll, "The Conservative Metamorphosis," *Intercollegiate Review* 23 (Spring 1988): 8.

19 Joseph Sobran, "Pensées: Notes for the Reactionary of Tomorrow," *National Review,* December 31, 1985, pp. 24, 33.

20 Joseph Epstein, "A Virtucrat Remembers," in *Political Passages: Journeys of Change through Two Decades, 1968–1988,* ed. John H. Bunzel (New York, 1988), 57.

21 Ibid., 56.
22 David Horowitz, "Letter to a Political Friend: On Being Totalitarian in America," in *Political Passages,* ed. Bunzel, 194.
23 Marth Bayles, "How I Spent My Summer Vacation," in *Political Passages,* ed. Bunzel, 105.
24 Sowell, *Conflict of Visions,* 43.
25 Allan Bloom, *The Closing of the American Mind* (New York, 1987), 67.
26 Zoll, "Conservative Metamorphosis," 11.
27 Institute for Cultural Conservatism, *Cultural Conservatism: Toward a New National Agenda* (Washington, D.C., 1988), 27, 90, 92-93.
28 Quoted in Kirk, ed., *Portable Conservative Reader,* 22-23.

Index

Abel, Lionel, 82; on Jews, 106
Abortion: Will on, 62, 294; Nisbet on, 309–10n64
Abrams, Elliott, 229
Abstract expressionism, 123. *See also* New York School of Artists
Abzug, Bella, 228
Adams, Henry: Nisbet on, 190, 198; Novak on, 319n96
Adams, John, 69; quoted by Will, 61
Adams, John Quincy, 76, 175
Adorno, T. W., 30
Affirmative action, 15, 275; Glazer on, 14; Novak on, 246
Agnew, Spiro T.: Novak on, 236
AIDS: Buckley on, 291–92n55
Allott, Gordon, 54, 57
Alpert, Harry, 184
American Civil Liberties Union: Will on, 73, 294n38
American Committee for Cultural Freedom, 89
American Enterprise Institute, 85, 181, 257, 268
American Journal of Sociology, 183
American Mercury, 212
American Psychiatric Association: Will on, 61
American Revolution: Kristol on, 94
Americans for Democratic Action, 216
American Spectator, 54, 281; Tyrrell on, 208–9, 211–15, 229, 232
Anderson, John B., 266
Anderson, Sherwood, 122

Anglo-Scottish Enlightenment: Kristol on, 93
Anti-intellectualism: Kristol and, 108, 109
Appleby, Joyce, 70
Arendt, Hannah, 90
Aristotle, 19, 28, 66
Arnold, Matthew, 90
Art Digest, 120
Arts Magazine, 120
Assmann, Hugo, 262
Association of American University Professors, 210

Babbitt, Irving, 15, 20, 60, 71, 79, 106, 140, 173, 272, 275, 278; Will and, 55, 59; and capitalism, 99; on Rousseau, 200; on Burke, 200
Bailyn, Bernard, 67
Bakshian, Aram, Jr., 310n6
Baroody, William, Jr., 101
Barrett, William, 82; and human rights, 169
Bayles, Martha, 281, 310n6
Beal, Jack: Kramer on, 116
Becker, Carl, 68
Bell, Daniel, 106, 111, 119; on post-industrialism, 4; on end of ideology, 5; on modernism, 137; and *Cultural Contradictions of Capitalism,* 299
Bellah, Robert, 202–4
Bellow, Saul, 173
Bennett, James Gordon: Tyrrell compared to, 230–31
Bennett, William J., 258